Furnishing the Eighteenth Century

What Furniture Can Tell Us about the European and American Past

EDITED BY

DENA GOODMAN & KATHRYN NORBERG

Routledge
Taylor & Francis Group

NEW YORK AND LONDON

Paperback edition published in 2011
by Routledge
270 Madison Ave, New York, NY 10016

Simultaneously published in the UK
by Routledge
2 Park Square, Milton Park, Abingdon, Oxon OX14 4RN

Originally published in hardback in 2007 by Routledge

*Routledge is an imprint of the Taylor & Francis Group, an informa
business*

© 2011 by Taylor & Francis

The right of Dena Goodman and Kathryn Norberg to be identified as authors
of this work has been asserted by them in accordance with sections 77 and 78 of
the Copyright, Designs and Patents Act 1988.

Printed and bound in the United States of America on acid-free paper by
Edward Brothers

Library of Congress Cataloging in Publication Data

Furnishing the eighteenth century : what furniture can tell us about
the European and American past / Dena Goodman and
Kathryn Norberg, editors.
p. cm.
Includes bibliographical references and index.
1. Furniture--England--History--18th century. 2. Furniture--United States--
History--18th century. 3. Furniture--France--History--18th century.
I. Goodman, Dena, 1952– II. Norberg, Kathryn, 1948–
GT450.F87 2006
392.3'6094209033--dc22 2006018395

ISBN 13: 978-0-415-94953-8 (hbk)
ISBN 13: 978-0-415-88479-2 (pbk)

Furnishing, although largely women's work in the direction, is really no trivial matter . . . Its study is as important as the study of politics; for the private home is at the foundation of the public state . . .; and the history of furniture itself, indeed, involves the history of nations.

—Harriet Spofford, *Art Decoration Applied to Furniture* **(1877).**

Furnishing the Eighteenth Century

Contents

Acknowledgments

This book began as a conference held in 2002 at the William Andrews Clark Memorial Library in Los Angeles. The UCLA Center for Seventeenth and Eighteenth-Century Studies sponsored the event and provided financial support. We thank the Center Director, Professor Peter Reill, for the opportunity to bring our contributors together and the Center staff for making the conference run smoothly. We are also grateful to the J. Paul Getty Museum, which hosted the opening session of the conference. Decorative arts curator Gillian Wilson graciously opened the Getty galleries to our participants and unlocked — quite literally — one of the world's great collections of eighteenth-century furniture. Charissa Bremer-David, associate curator of sculpture and decorative arts, has been an invaluable intellectual resource from the start and an ongoing inspiration for this project. She shared her considerable expertise in eighteenth-century decorative arts and allowed us access to Getty research materials and photos. During a research trip to Los Angeles in 2004, Shelley Bennett, curator of British art at the Huntington Art Collection, also allowed us to inspect furniture in that collection.

A very special thanks goes to the Chipstone Foundation and its Executive Director Jonathan Prown for providing a grant to fund the color plates in this volume. The Chipstone is an important resource for furniture scholars in the United States, and we are grateful for its help in producing this book. We also thank the Getty Museum, which allowed a number of our authors to reproduce images from its collection free of charge. The other images in this book are reproduced with the gracious permission of many museums, libraries, and other repositories, as noted in the captions accompanying them; we thank these institutions as well.

At Routledge, Kimberly Guinta has been an unusually patient and generous editor. During the years it took to bring this book into being, Kimberly fielded numerous emails and provided crucial advice on dealing with the seventy images that grace these pages. Thanks also to her assistants Daniel Webb and Brendan O'Neill for tending to many details and to Robert Sims for overseeing production. This book was first contracted by Karen Wolny, former editor at Routledge. Were it not for her willingness to take on an unconventional project, we would never have been able bring the chairs, desks, and tables in these pages into print. Our greatest debt however is to our contributors. They have opened our eyes to the complexities of eighteenth-century furniture and made editing *Furnishing the Eighteenth Century* an easy and enlightening process.

Dena Goodman
and Kathryn Norberg

Introduction

DENA GOODMAN AND KATHRYN NORBERG

This book deals with furniture in the eighteenth century. Writing desks, tea tables, sofas, and duchess chairs; green brocades, pink porcelains, and red mahogany—all find a place in these pages. The reader will encounter here an equally rich variety of men and women whose lives in France, England, and their American colonies were shaped by the furniture on which they sat or made love, at which they wrote or ate meals, and in which they tucked away their most private words and valued things. Aristocrats and shopkeepers, painters and cabinetmakers, tea drinkers and letter writers, slaves and courtesans are brought together here by the furniture that gave shape and meaning to their lives. To all these people, furniture mattered. It marked their social status (real or invented), projected their identity, determined how they entertained, and constituted a substantial portion of their property.

Today, this same furniture continues to matter, but in different ways, to visitors who fill the decorative arts galleries and period rooms of European and American museums, and to the small elite who fill their homes with the valuable eighteenth-century pieces they have inherited or collected. Exhibitions of eighteenth-century furniture draw crowds. Tourists may visit the reconstructed homes and shops of Colonial Williamsburg one year and the sumptuously furnished royal palace of Versailles the next. At auction houses, eighteenth-century furniture—be it American, English, or French—continues to fetch higher and higher prices. But even those of us who cannot afford an early American pie crust table or a *louis-seize* cabinet enjoy the legacy of the eighteenth-century revolution in furniture when we purchase a set of dining room chairs or take a seat on the living room sofa.

The historians, art historians, and literary scholars whose work is collected here are what Jules Prown has called "contextualizers": scholars who use the words and images created in the eighteenth century to restore meaning to its furniture.[1] We explore the meaning and meaning-making of European furniture during the century that connoisseurs and collectors consider its golden age. While we appreciate the beauty of eighteenth century furniture, as well as the creativity and craftsmanship that went into making each piece, our apprecia-

1

tion extends beyond aesthetic qualities. Our aim is to contribute to a new way of appreciating these objects in the context of the lives of those who bought, sold, made, and used them. We place furniture in the social and cultural world it inhabited and helped to define because we are interested in the interactions of people and things that made European and colonial interiors meaningful.

The reader looking for a connoisseur's guide to tell him whether his antique sideboard is authentic, or by whom it was built, will not find that information here; nor will she learn how to distinguish a *louis-quinze* chair from a *louis-seize*. The names of famous cabinetmakers do appear in these pages, and taste and style do matter to us, but this is not a history of a craft or a guide to stamp marks or provenance. We do believe, however, that anyone who is attracted to the beauty of an eighteenth-century chair, or is fascinated by the techniques by which it was made, will be interested in how that piece figured in eighteenth-century life, how it shaped sociability and identity, what sort of people may have bought or sold it, or how it was used—in short, what a chair meant in that world rather than ours.

Some readers may be skeptical. Can material objects like desks and chairs signify? To borrow from a famous literary essay: Can the settee speak?[2] In a recent essay, Leora Auslander has argued that material objects are "beyond words," incomprehensible through language.[3] But how else can we make sense of furniture created over three hundred years ago? Eighteenth-century novels, plays, and paintings help us to see objects as those who used them did. Texts and images allow us to understand how eighteenth-century people understood their desks, tables, and chairs, and what meanings they gave them.

Texts and images, especially printed ones, are important to us also because they shaped and mediated the eighteenth-century experience of furniture for those women and men who made, sold, purchased, and used it. The period witnessed the publication of the first books devoted specifically to furniture. In 1737, architect Jean-François Blondel's *De la distribution des maisons de plaisance et de la décoration des édifices en général* presented the French reading public with detailed descriptions and images of furnished rooms.[4] Blondel was eclipsed in 1761, when the first volume of the master joiner, André Jacob Roubo's magnum opus, *L'art du menuisier*, was published. With the support of the French Academy of Sciences, the work would grow to four volumes and tackle every aspect of the woodworker's craft, from the construction of coaches and church pews to designs for every variety of case and seat furniture for the home.[5] In England, cabinetmaker Thomas Chippendale published a compilation of fashionable furniture designs that served simultaneously as a pattern book for craftsmen and a connoisseur's guide for their clients. *The Gentleman and Cabinet-Maker's Director* (1754) was itself the pattern for subsequent publications aimed at the mixed audience of craftsmen, clients, and connoisseurs that shaped English and colonial taste well into the nineteenth century.[6] When George Hepplewhite's widow Alice published his furniture designs as *The Cabinet-maker and Upholsterer's Guide* (1788), she included the declaration: "We have exerted our utmost endeavours to produce a work which shall be usefull to the mechanic, and serviceable to the gentleman."[7] In 1803, Thomas Sheraton followed in this same spirit with his *Cabinet Dictionary*.[8] Rather than protecting the secrets of their trade, architects and cabinetmakers revealed them in print to create a market for their services and their wares. The privileged place of eighteenth-century furniture in today's antique market is as much a result of this modern print culture as it is of traditional craftsmanship. Our own contribution to the print culture of furniture acknowledges the importance of print and markets in part by looking at furniture critically in relation to them.

For all its popularity among collectors and museum-goers, eighteenth-century furniture often gets overlooked by scholars because it falls between and across areas of historical study and critical analysis. Historians of material culture, the decorative arts, and the consumer revolution have concentrated only on particular aspects of furniture history; studies of consumption, luxury, fashion, or space rarely focus on furniture. Related to the disciplines of archaeology and anthropology, studies of eighteenth-century material culture tend to be demotic in style and intent, eschewing the luxury goods associated with powerful elites that are preserved in art museums and palaces in favor of the rough-hewn and simple pieces that make historical sites "authentic."[9] Historians and curators of the decorative arts, by contrast, focus on the "finest examples" of work by "master craftsmen" that can be fit into narratives of stylistic development and individual artistic achievement. By definition, those social and economic historians who are trying to understand the consumer revolution of the eighteenth century, like those who studied the Industrial Revolution before them, look for that combination of innovation and broad diffusion that marks the modern, but at the expense of the unique, the timeless, or the "traditional." The focus in the history of the decorative arts on craftsmanship and luxury production has tended to make fashionable furniture invisible to historians of material culture and consumption before the nineteenth century.[10] Meanwhile, historians and theorists of fashion tend to focus on clothing, while historians and theorists of space present us with façade-lined streets and town squares; if they open the doors of buildings, it is only to reveal room upon empty room.[11]

Nevertheless, those of us who study eighteenth-century furniture and interiors have benefited from groundbreaking work in these fields. They have opened up new ways to think about furniture, even if they have not dwelled much upon the subject themselves. For example, historians of material culture in the American colonies, Britain, and France have unlocked the riches of the archives with studies based primarily on probate inventories and account books that begin to suggest how eighteenth-century people furnished their homes. Although each type of source captures only a particular moment in time when objects pass from one person to another—to heirs on the death of the owner, or to the buyer at the moment of purchase—they do place tables, chairs, and beds within a human context.[12] Recent studies in this tradition by contributors to this volume have provided invaluable information: Natacha Coquery takes a single Parisian *hôtel* as a point of departure to examine the commercial relationships between its aristocratic owners and those who supplied them with everything from food to furniture; Ann Smart Martin finds an entry point in the account books of a single shopkeeper in the Virginia backcountry who sold an equally wide range of goods to his rural clientele.[13]

The publication in 1982 of Neil McKendrick, John Brewer, and J. H. Plumb's *The Birth of a Consumer Society: The Commercialization of Eighteenth-Century England* has been important because it shifted attention from production to consumption.[14] Although McKendrick, Brewer, and Plumb did not discuss furniture, they did emphasize changes in the marketing of goods, which made it possible to think about the new ways in which furniture was sold and consumed, not just in England, but throughout Europe and its colonies. They also opened up new questions about the relationship between consumer goods and luxury goods, the transformation of luxuries into necessities, the importance of fashion and taste in the consumer economy, and the ways in which discourse and representation shaped desire and demand. Taking up some of these questions was the Luxury Project directed by economic historian Maxine Berg at the University of Warwick, which resulted in two important co-edited volumes: *Consumers and Luxury: Consumer Culture in Europe 1650–1850* (1999); and *Luxury in the Eighteenth Century: Debates, Desires and Delectable Goods* (2003).[15]

In France, Daniel Roche emerged from the pack of former *Annales* social historians to become the leader in the study of material culture and consumption in the eighteenth century. In *The Culture of Clothing: Dress and Fashion in the Ancien Regime* (1994), Roche brought fashion and consumption into post-Marxist debates about the transformation of France from a traditional to a modern society, but as his title suggests, he identified fashion exclusively with clothing. By contrast, in *A History of Everyday Things: The Birth of Consumption in France, 1600–1800* (2000), Roche devoted a chapter to furniture, but he also shifted his focus away from fashionable goods in favor of the provincial and the rustic. Nor did Colin Jones consider furniture significant in his influential studies of commerce, consumption, and advertising in eighteenth-century France.[16] To date, the most important study of new practices of marketing furniture in eighteenth-century Paris, the very center of the furniture trade at the time, is by a historian of the decorative arts: Carolyn Sargentson's *Merchants and Luxury Markets: The Marchands Merciers of Eighteenth-Century Paris* (1996) opens the doors and the account books of Parisian fashion merchants to illuminate the role they played in the design and distribution of tables, textiles, and other household furnishings.[17]

Historians of art and architecture have begun to turn their attention to the domestic interior, too, if not always to the furniture in it. They have called attention to the way in which modern notions and practices of privacy developed spatially, as public and private zones were more clearly demarcated within houses, and particular rooms were designed for specific practices of sociability and intimacy.[18] Katie Scott's *The Rococo Interior: Decoration and Social Spaces in Early Eighteenth-Century Paris* (1995) has been particularly influential in suggesting the social meanings of consumption and display in the interior decoration of aristocratic houses.[19] Mimi Hellman has taken a different approach, focusing on the ways in which eighteenth-century furniture choreographed the kind of polite sociability that was characteristic of elite life of the period.[20]

Privacy, domesticity, and polite sociability have long been associated with women, which could help to explain why furniture has long been neglected by scholars. In the last decade or so, feminist scholars have made domesticity and the private serious subjects of scholarly and historical interest, not only as the locus of women's lives, but also in order to challenge assumptions about how public and private have been gendered to the exclusion or marginalization of women in history and public life.[21] While public buildings (theaters, churches, and government offices) do contain furniture, and while men as well as women sit on chairs, sleep in beds, and dine at tables, we tend to think of interior decoration as a feminine art and the purchase of home furnishings as women's work. The study of furniture is thus indebted to feminist scholarship not only for making it possible to take furniture seriously, but also for challenging us to look at furniture as a lens through which to examine how gender operated in the past and how our own gendered understanding of furniture has developed.

Both architecture and dress have been heavily theorized, but furniture has received little of this sort of attention. We might want to think of furniture as falling between clothing, which covers the body, and architecture, which organizes the space in which the body moves. Furniture's relationship with human beings and their bodies is both less intimate than that of clothing and more immediate and flexible than that of architecture, more subject to change and control by those who use it. Furniture can be the most sociable of inanimate agents, as when it brings people together around a tea table; it can also create intimacy by bringing bodies into contact on a sofa or a bed. Furniture such as wingback chairs and writing desks can also create privacy and promote introspection, especially if placed in a nook or corner. Furniture can even keep secrets. Eighteenth-century furniture that is meant to impress visitors with the prestige, power, and wealth of its owner can be massive and imposing; but it can also be surprisingly lithe and mobile—even playful.[22] Unlike architecture, furniture can be moved; it can be bought and sold, appropriated by a member of one social group only to be reappropriated by a member of another the next day. Furniture shifts its meaning as it moves from room to room, from owner to owner, from one generation to the next. As it travels from one decorative environment to another, furniture takes on new uses and therefore new signification. Furniture is matter, but it is still mutable. The essays in this volume have much to say about both the matter and the mutability of eighteenth-century furniture.

We begin by placing European furniture in a global context to suggest a remapping of the terrain of European furniture and its meanings across the globe at the intersections of gender, race, trade, and empire. As David Porter observes in his essay, Europe colonized the world in the eighteenth century, and the world in turn "colonized European homes" with Chinese porcelains, Japanese lacquer ware, and furniture made of Caribbean hardwoods.

In "Orientalism, Colonialism, and Furniture in Eighteenth-Century France," Madeleine Dobie explores the contradiction between the material and cultural constructions of French furniture in the eighteenth century: while chairs and tables were made from wood extracted from France's Caribbean colonies through the use of slave labor, this colonial materiality was hidden under an orientalist cultural construction in the forms of sofas and divans and the styles of *chinoiserie* and *turquoiserie*. "East met West" in French furniture, she writes, but in ways that occluded rather than revealed the implication of the elites who owned it in France's slaveholding empire.

In "Mahogany as Status Symbol: Race and Luxury in Saint Domingue at the End of the Eighteenth Century," Chaela Pastore turns our attention to Saint Domingue, the richest and most lucrative colony in the eighteenth century. Through the unique lens of mahogany furniture, Pastore explores the different meanings of luxury in the colony and the metropole. By following the tracks left by mahogany furniture in newspapers and death inventories, she finds material evidence of a social structure that presented the most serious challenge to the old metropolitan order. Saint Domingue, where even mixed-race women owned mahogany armoires, represented a new world, indeed.

David Porter looks eastward in his essay, "A Wanton Chase in a Foreign Place: Hogarth and the Gendering of Exoticism in the Eighteenth-Century Interior." Porter asks why the "Chinese taste" that was as popular in Britain as Dobie shows it was in France failed to win the endorsement of William Hogarth, the one critic whose theory should have embraced it. Through an analysis of Hogarth's engravings as well as his writings, Porter shows that, despite claims to the disinterestedness of the aesthetic, Hogarth's denunciation of the Chinese taste was based on an unwillingness to extend to women aesthetic judgment and the emancipatory power it entailed.

The second group of essays in this volume takes up the question of taste, but through the lens of the artisan-shopkeepers who made or assembled furniture in the eighteenth century and the clients who bought it. Examining the process of diffusion from markedly different vantage points, all three authors find that fashionable furniture and the taste it represented spread well beyond the urban and courtly elites with whom they have traditionally been associated. In her essay, "Fashion, Business, Diffusion: An Upholsterer's Shop in Eighteenth-Century Paris," Natacha Coquery takes us into the boutique of upholsterer

Mathurin Law on the rue Saint-Honoré, the center of the Parisian luxury trade. Through a close examination of this one shopkeeper's accounts, Coquery uncovers business practices that included repairing, reselling, and renting used furniture as well as selling new pieces. In so doing she shows how luxury goods found their way to a much broader group of individuals than had previously been suspected.

David Jaffee's essay, "Sideboards, Side Chairs, and Globes: Changing Modes of Furnishing Provincial Culture in the Early Republic, 1790–1820," also broadens our understanding of the diffusion of fine eighteenth-century furniture. Jaffee, however, is less interested in social categories than in geographical reach beyond the metropole. He traces the emergence of backwoods North American craftsmen who produced sophisticated goods from their rural outposts in the Connecticut River Valley. Inspired by the London design books of Hepplewhite and Sheraton, these artisans built fashionable sideboards of great elegance and urbanity for the rural clientele whose taste they helped develop. From their very different geographical positions, Jaffee and Coquery both show that metropolitan furniture and style cannot simply be identified with a luxury market and an aristocratic elite.

In "Goddesses of Taste: Courtesans and Their Furniture in Late-Eighteenth-Century Paris," Kathryn Norberg turns from artisan-shopkeepers to a unique group of furniture purchasers: a marginal group of women who nevertheless had the wherewithal to buy expensive furniture and build impressive homes. Parisian courtesans, we learn, were fashion leaders whose homes were celebrated and whose furniture was coveted. The source of courtesan taste, Norberg argues, was not the royal palace or polite society; rather, it was the *little houses* where gentlemen engaged in the arts of seduction, and comfort and delight were emphasized. Norberg concludes with the suggestion that the courtesan was herself an important influence on eighteenth-century taste in furniture.

The next set of essays takes us out of the shop and away from practices of buying and selling to consider more deeply the question of interior decoration and its meaning raised by Norberg's courtesans. In "Color Schemes and Decorative Tastes in the Noble Houses of Old Regime Dauphiné," Donna Bohanan uses death inventories to explore the interior decoration of the homes of provincial nobles who, she argues, sought to shore up their weakened social and political position by a display of domestic magnificence. In practice, this meant elaborate furnishings in chic colors. Finding the decorative schemes in distant Dauphiné uncannily similar to those in Paris and strangely uniform, Bohanon asks: Was the price of distinction strict conformity?

In "The Joy of Sets: The Uses of Seriality in the French Interior," Mimi Hellman takes up this question with a close look at the set—from groupings of upholstered sofas and chairs to pairs of vases and matched candelabra. Why this emphasis on uniformity and repetition, she asks? By calling attention to the technological virtuosity required to produce matched sets before the era of industrial production, Hellman shows how differently the set was valued in the eighteenth century than it is today. She helps us to see sets of furniture as those who made, commissioned, and purchased them did, and then speculates provocatively on what they might have meant to their owners. She concludes with the theory that in a world where social interactions were fraught and dangerous, seriality provided a sense of security, a way of making social life feel predictable and safe.

In her essay, "Decoration and Enlightened Spectatorship," Mary Salzman also emphasizes furniture's social power. She shows that the social meanings encoded in furniture could be complex enough to require the kind of education that polite society and the Enlightenment both promoted. Salzman focuses on a pair of paintings by Jean-François de Troy: *The Garter* (pictured on the cover) and *The Declaration of Love*. As the gentlemen in the paintings are required to "read" the furnishings in order to carry off their planned seduction of the lady, so the viewers of the paintings must read the furniture in order to understand the narratives and their social meanings. Salzman reads the furniture in these paintings not as a display of social power and prestige, but as a handbook for polite behavior and the development of critical judgment. Like Hellman's matched sets of furniture and furnishings, this painted pair taught the viewer how to behave through challenging him or her to see the sometimes slight differences within overall sameness.

The authors of the essays in Part IV ask us to look closely at furniture in a different way, by focusing their attention on particular pieces and forms, from their polished surfaces to their most inner recesses. In "Tea Tables Overturned: Rituals of Power and Place in Colonial America," Ann Smart Martin looks at the tea table as a site of social anxiety and personal pride. Surveying first the visual terrain of social satire, in which tea tables featured prominently, Martin turns the tables to show how meaningful they could be for their colonial and middle-class owners. As the social practice of tea drinking spread, she argues, the tea table emerged as a symbol of prestige to be proudly displayed in homes throughout the North American colonies.

From the sociability of the tea table Dena Goodman turns to the personal space of another new furniture form that was diffused widely in the second half of the eighteenth century: the writing desk or *secrétaire*. In "The *Secrétaire* and the Integration of the Eighteenth-Century Self," she compares this new form with the older *bureau plat* or flat desk traditionally used by a man and his secretarial scribes. Goodman associates the invention of the *secrétaire* with the rise of personal writing in France and argues that it provided material support for a reintegration of mind and body necessary to the production and expression of the modern self.

In the final essay of the volume, Carolyn Sargentson looks inside French case furniture to find technologies and meanings hidden from the average museum-goer. If tea tables facilitated sociability and *secrétaires* made new forms of privacy possible, elaborate locking mechanisms, secret drawers, and false bottoms responded to the need for secrecy and security. In "Looking at Furniture Inside Out: Strategies for Secrecy and Security in Eighteenth-Century French Furniture," Sargentson asks why these new technologies became such a salient design element in much eighteenth-century furniture. Her answer suggests that we need to read eighteenth-century case furniture not only within narratives of innovation in design and technology, but within the more fraught stories of risk and pleasure played out in domestic spaces where persons and property, especially those of women, were always vulnerable to exposure.

Indeed, as the essays collected here show, eighteenth-century furniture has many stories to tell. Scholars have long associated it with the aristocratic display of "distinction" and the middle-class desire for enhanced social status.[23] The essays in these pages broaden and deepen our understanding of what furniture could and did mean in the eighteenth century to a wide range of people whose lives it shaped in different ways. They place European furniture in a global context and in a world that was both traditional and modern. Throughout the volume, gender is a key category of analysis, revealing tensions but also new agency in the production of furniture's meanings. The authors draw on literature and art as well as account books, handbooks, inventories, and treatises to bring out these meanings and to show how they were produced, contested, and subverted. But they also look closely at the furniture itself, to give it voice. This is, after all, a book about furniture.

Notes

1. Jules David Prown, "The Promise and Perils of Context," in *Art as Evidence: Writings on Art and Material Culture* (New Haven: Yale University Press, 2001), 243–54.
2. Gayatri Chakravorty Spivak, "Can the Subaltern Speak? Speculations on Widow-Sacrifice," *Wedge* 7/8 (1985): 120–30; reprinted in *Marxism and the Interpretation of Culture*, ed. Cary Nelson and Larry Grossberg (Urbana: University of Illinois Press, 1988), 271–313. In eighteenth-century fiction, objects, including furniture, did indeed speak. Notable in this regard is *Le Sopha* (1749), by Claude Prosper Jolyot de Crébillon (known as Crébillon fils); more obscure is *The Settee: or Chevalier Commodo's Metamorphosis* (1742), which claims to be translated from the French. On such "it-narratives," see Madeleine Dobie, *Foreign Bodies: Gender, Language, and Culture in French Orientalism* (Stanford: Stanford University Press, 2001); and Jonathan Lamb, "The Crying of Lost Things," *ELH* 71 (winter 2004): 949–67.
3. Leora Auslander, "Beyond Words," *American Historical Review* 110 (October 2005): 1015–45.
4. Jean-François Blondel, *De la distribution des maisons de plaisance, et de la décoration des édifices en général* (Paris : Charles-Antoine Jombert, 1737–1738).
5. André Jacob Roubo, *L'art du menuisier* (Paris: Saillant and Nyon, 1761). Roubo's magnum opus grew out of his contributions on furniture making to Diderot and d'Alembert's *Encyclopédie* (1751–1765) and formed part of the French Academy of Science's series on the trades. With its detailed descriptions and engraved plates, it continues to be used today by amateurs, professionals, and collectors alike as a guide to furniture making.
6. Thomas Chippendale, *The Gentleman and Cabinet-Maker's Director* (London, 1754).
7. A[lice] Hepplewhite and Company, *The Cabinet-maker and Upholsterer's Guide; Or, Repository of Designs for Every Article of Household Furniture in the Newest and Most Approved Taste* (London: I. and J. Taylor, 1788).
8. Thomas Sheraton, *The Cabinet Dictionary, Containing an Explanation of All the Terms Used in the Cabinet, Chair & Upholstery Branches* (London: W. Smith, 1803).
9. See, e.g., Laurel Thatcher Ulrich, *The Age of Homespun: Objects and Stories in the Creation of an American Myth* (New York: Knopf, 2001). In the past decade, *material culture* has come to be used more broadly as an inclusive term (like *visual culture*), but this broadening is itself a democratizing move that sees all objects as equally material and meaningful.
10. In *Taste and Power: Furnishing Modern France* (Berkeley: University of California Press, 1996), Leora Auslander reinforces this distinction by theorizing a shift from aristocratic taste, embodied in the stylistic conventions of artisanal luxury production of the Old Regime, and bourgeois taste, represented by mass-produced imitations that were widely diffused in the nineteenth century.
11. Michel Foucault, "Text/Context of Other Space," *Diacritics* 16 (1986): 22–27; Henri Lefebvre, *The Production of Space*, trans. Donald Nicholson-Smith (London: Blackwell, 1991); Gaston Bachelard, *The Poetics of Space*, trans. Maria Jolas (Boston: Beacon Press, 1969); Pierre Bourdieu, "The Berber House or the World Reversed," *Social Science Information* 9 (1970) 151–170 and *Distinction: A Social Critique of the Judgement of Taste*, trans. Richard Nice (Cambridge, MA: Harvard University Press, 2002); Michel de Certeau, *The Practice of Everyday Life*, trans. Steven Rendall (Berkeley: University of California Press, 1984).
12. Significant studies in this genre include Lorna Weatherill, *Consumer Behaviour and Material Culture in Britain, 1660–1760* (London and New York: Routledge, 1988); Carole Shammas, *The Pre-Industrial Consumer in England and America* (Oxford: Clarendon Press, 1990); Annik Pardailhé-Galabrun, *The Birth of Intimacy: Privacy and Domestic Life in Early Modern Paris*, trans. Jocelyn Phelps (Philadelphia: University of Pennsylvania Press, 1991).
13. Natacha Coquery, *L'hôtel aristocratique: Le marché du luxe à Paris au XVIIIe siècle* (Paris: Publications de la Sorbonne, 1998); Ann Smart Martin, *Buying into the World of Goods: Early Consumers in Backcountry Virginia* (Baltimore, MD: Johns Hopkins University Press, forthcoming).
14. Neil McKendrick, John Brewer, and J. H. Plumb, *The Birth of a Consumer Society: The Commercialization of Eighteenth-Century England* (Bloomington: Indiana University Press, 1982). See also the series "Consumption and Culture in the 17th and 18th Centuries," which stemmed from conferences at the William Andrews Clark Library, University of California at Los Angeles in the early 1990s: John Brewer and Roy Porter, eds., *Consumption and the World of Goods* (London: Routledge, 1993); John Brewer and Susan Staves, eds., *Early Modern Conceptions of Property* (London: Routledge, 1995); John Brewer and Ann Bermingham, eds., *The Consumption of Culture, 1600–1800: Image, Object, Text* (London: Routledge, 1995).

15. See Maxine Berg and Helen Clifford, eds., *Consumers and Luxury: Consumer Culture in Europe 1650–1850* (Manchester: Manchester University Press, 1999); Maxine Berg and Elizabeth Eger, eds., *Luxury in the Eighteenth Century: Debates, Desires and Delectable Goods* (New York: Palgrave 2003); Maxine Berg, *Luxury and Pleasure in Eighteenth-Century Britain* (New York: Oxford University Press, 2005). Also on luxury, see Robert Fox and Anthony Turner, eds., *Luxury Trades and Consumerism in Ancien Régime Paris* (Aldershot: Ashgate, 1998).

16. Colin Jones, "The Bourgeois Revolution Revivified: 1789 and Social Change," in *Rewriting the French Revolution*, ed. Colin Lucas (Oxford: Oxford University Press, 1991): 69–118; and "The Great Chain of Buying: Medical Advertisement, The Bourgeois Public Sphere, and the Origins of the French Revolution," *American Historical Review* 101 (February 1996): 13–40.

17. Carolyn Sargentson, *Merchants and Luxury Markets: The Marchands Merciers of Eighteenth-Century Paris* (London and Malibu: Victoria and Albert Museum in conjunction with the J. Paul Getty Museum, 1996).

18. See Monique Eleb-Vidal and Anne Debarre-Blanchard, *Architectures de la vie privée: maisons et mentalités, XVIIe–XIXe siècles* (Paris: AAM Editions, 1989).

19. Katie Scott, *The Rococo Interior: Decoration and Social Spaces in Early Eighteenth-Century Paris* (New Haven: Yale University Press, 1995). See also Rochelle Ziskin, *The Place Vendôme: Architecture and Social Mobility in Eighteenth-Century Paris* (Cambridge: Cambridge University Press, 1999). Peter Thornton's classic study, *Authentic Decor: The Domestic Interior, 1620–1920* (New York: Viking, 1984), provides a holistic view of historical interiors, marrying architectural and furniture history with lavishly illustrated and deeply researched appreciation of social and individual life across three centuries. Mark Girouard takes a similar approach in *Life in the French Country House* (New York: Knopf, 2000), but pays more attention to the social structures of different periods, which supported and shaped country house life. See also John Whitehead, *The French Interior in the Eighteenth Century* (New York: Dutton Studio Books, 1993).

20. See Mimi Hellman, "Furniture, Sociability, and the Work of Leisure in the Eighteenth Century," *Eighteenth Century Studies* 32 (summer 1999): 415–45; and "Interior Motives: Seduction by Decoration in Eighteenth-Century France," in *Dangerous Liaisons: Fashion and Furniture in the Eighteenth Century*, ed. Harold Koda and Andrew Bolton (New York and New Haven: Metropolitan Museum of Art and Yale University Press, 2006), 15–36.

21. See, e.g., Amanda Vickery, "Golden Age to Separate Spheres: A Review of the Categories and Chronology of English Women's History," *Historical Journal* 36 (June 1993): 383–414; Dena Goodman, "Public Sphere and Private Life: Toward a Synthesis of Current Historiographical Approaches to the Old Regime," *History and Theory*, 31 (February 1992): 1–20; Lawrence E. Klein, "Gender and the Public/Private Distinction in the Eighteenth Century: Some Questions about Evidence and Analytic Procedure," *Eighteenth-Century Studies* 29 (summer 1995): 97–109. On the terrain of polite sociability see, for example, Richard L. Bushman, *The Refinement of America: Persons, Houses, Cities* (New York: Knopf, 1992); Daniel Gordon, *Citizens without Sovereignty: Equality and Sociability in French Thought, 1670–1789* (Princeton, NJ: Princeton University Press, 1994); Lawrence E. Klein, *Shaftesbury and the Culture of Politeness: Moral Discourse and Cultural Politics in Early Eighteenth-Century England* (Cambridge: Cambridge University Press, 1994); David S. Shields, *Polite Tongues and Civil Letters in British America* (Chapel Hill: University of North Carolina Press, 1997).

22. On the distinction between fixed and mobile furniture, see Pierre Verlet, *French Furniture of the Eighteenth Century*, trans. Penelope Hunter-Stiebel (Charlottesville: University Press of Virginia, 1991), 11.

23. In this regard Bourdieu's *Distinction* and the theory of conspicuous consumption developed by Thorstein Veblen in *Theory of the Leisure Class* (1912) have been crucial. For a complex and sophisticated application of these theories to the eighteenth century, see Woodruff D. Smith, *Consumption and the Making of Respectability, 1600–1800* (New York: Routledge, 2002).

PART I

Mapping Meaning Globally

CHAPTER 1

Orientalism, Colonialism, and Furniture in Eighteenth-Century France

MADELEINE DOBIE

In the eighteenth century French material culture was enriched by the growth of commercial networks centering on the new colonies established during the 1600s in the Caribbean and North America. The import on a large scale of aliments such as coffee, sugar, and chocolate; raw materials employed in the textile industry, notably cotton, indigo, and cochineal; and tropical woods used in pharmacology, shipbuilding, and furniture-making, stimulated important shifts in both production and consumption. Yet the profound impact of colonial commerce on the economic and material life of France did not register strongly in cultural representations until the final quarter of the century. Before this juncture neither colonial commerce nor the slave trade that sustained it registered significantly in literary works (including, contrary to widely held impressions, the writings of the *philosophes*), the visual arts, or the sphere of material culture. This reticence seems surprising when we consider, for example, that by 1740 France dominated the world sugar market, producing sugar at less than half the price of the British islands;[1] that by mid-century French colonies also supplied 40 percent of the world's coffee, rising to 60 percent for Saint Domingue alone by 1790; that by some estimations as many as one in eight French subjects earned a living in endeavors connected to colonial commerce;[2] that over the course of the eighteenth century, French ships transported over one million Africans to the New World;[3] and that throughout the century, France and England were engaged in periodic struggle for control of North America and the Caribbean basin.

The low profile of the colonial world, striking in its own right, contrasts sharply with the profusion of allusions to the "Orient"—China, Japan, Persia, and Turkey—that occupies such a prominent place in the literature, visual art, ceramics, textiles, and furniture of the period.[4] In this chapter I propose that the attention lavished on the Orient and the contrasting underrepresentation of the colonial world were not simply disproportionate, but at least in a loose sense, structurally linked. That is to say, in both a general sense and in specific instances we can observe in the cultural productions of the eighteenth century a kind of "continental drift" whereby French economic interests in the Atlantic colonies were transposed into a fascination with things oriental. I explore furnishings as a key medium in which this cultural displacement can be traced. Raw materials harvested in the Caribbean or Indian Ocean colonies, notably tropical hardwoods, were often turned into finished consumer goods decorated with oriental motifs, or styled in a recognizably oriental fashion. This transfer can be viewed as a form of aestheticization by which the harsh commercial realities of colonial trade were rendered invisible, while other, more attractive associations were accentuated. It was not the result of a concerted effort of concealment or misrepresentation, but rather the outcome of a complex play of economic and political forces that, until the final quarter of the eighteenth century, limited recognition of the colonies as an important new arena of French economic and political life.

A few preliminary points are necessary. Orientalization was just one of many ways in which colonial commodities were integrated into the French decorative repertory. Tropical woods were as often associated with pastoral imagery or neoclassical themes as with oriental motifs. The number of pieces of furniture in which "East meets West" in the manner outlined below is, in real terms, small. This substitution, however, appears more significant when furniture is examined alongside other cultural productions in which a similar transfer can be observed, notably textiles, foodstuffs, and literature.[5] Methodologically, this is an instance in which an integrated cultural perspective reveals patterns that do not come into focus in the frame of more specialized work. Cross-disciplinary perspectives, of course, have their limitations, and I would like to emphasize that in this study I approach the decorative arts as a nonspecialist and in a way that reflects my training as a literary scholar, that is to say, as a representational medium that shares properties and themes with other representational media. Furniture obviously signifies in other registers, through formal and material qualities about which this chapter says relatively little.

By drawing attention to the exploitation of raw materials of colonial provenance I do not wish to deny either the significance of oriental exoticism as a complex cultural phenomenon, or the material importance of trade with China, Japan, and Turkey. That goods crafted from commodities produced in the Atlantic colonies were sometimes perceived and marketed as Eastern wares is in fact partially attributable to the fact that many plantation crops, such as sugar, coffee, cotton, and indigo, had previously been cultivated in Africa and Asia. To a degree that is underappreciated, European colonialism in the Americas involved the transfer of resources, people, crops, and techniques from Asia and Africa westward across the Atlantic.[6] Nonetheless, given the profound changes that the growth of plantation agriculture effected in European economies, one would expect to encounter, by the mid-eighteenth century, a more acute geopolitical awareness of the developing colonial world.

French Furniture and the Oriental Exotic

The eighteenth century is generally hailed as the golden age of French furniture. The panoply of forms, styles, and techniques generated between the waning years of Louis XIV and the establishment of the First Empire "stuck," and has been reproduced and recycled ever since. As a result the furniture of the period is closely associated with ideas about French taste, and indeed, French culture. Paradoxically, though, the furnishing fashions of the period cannot be described without reference to the importance of foreign influences, notably the prevalence of oriental designs and techniques.

Although European references to the Orient are frequently grouped together in an undifferentiated mass, in the domain of material culture they fall into two broad categories. In the 1600s, European travelers discovered the sophisticated material culture of China and Japan, and for the next century they busily imported and imitated decorative objects including porcelain ware and lustrous lacquer panels used to adorn cabinets and screens. The European embrace of Chinese and Japanese goods and techniques represented an implicit homage to these cultures and their rich decorative traditions. By contrast, Turkey and Persia were for the most part evoked in furnishings in a different way. These references were predominantly linguistic and reflected a growing association of the Muslim Orient with traits such as sensuality and indolence. They offer, in fact, a good illustration of the circle of fashion and vocabulary that critics viewed as a scourge of the age.[7] Given the nature of these associations, it is not surprising that the objects most often designated with Turkish or Arabic names were beds and chairs.

Between the mid-seventeenth century and the end of the eighteenth century, European beds and seat furniture changed in ways that mirror a broader trend toward lighter, more informal furnishings. Whereas the seating arrangements of Louis XIV's Versailles mirrored the rigid hierarchy of the court—to occupy an armchair (*fauteuil*) was the prerogative of royalty, and only high-ranking nobles could lay claim to a stool (*tabouret*)—by the early eighteenth century a relaxation of decorum at court and the growth of spheres of sociability beyond Versailles created a market for chairs whose comfortable forms followed the contours of the body and promoted conversation. This development coincided with another notable trend in the organization of aristocratic and bourgeois households: the growing specialization of both rooms and furniture, both increasingly tailored to the performance of specific daily activities. One facet of this broad shift was the appearance, beginning in the mid-seventeenth century, of a series of comfortable chairs: *lits de repos, canapés, sofas, ottomanes, turquoises*, and *duchesses*, among others (Figure 1.1).

Ottomanne Ceintrée.

Figure 1.1 *Ottomane ceintrée.* Drawing by Jean-Charles Delafosse, circa 1770. Courtesy of Bibliothèque nationale de France.

These new forms, hybrids between the bed and the chair, responded to the new emphasis on comfort and sociability; benches and church pews aside, they were the first seats designed for several occupants. The oriental, feminine names commonly conferred on them—*sofas*, *ottomanes*, *paphoses*, *turquoises*—evoked a distant impression of the Turkish *divan*, the row of cushions arranged against a wall that European travelers encountered in Constantinople, and fed into a complex chain of associations connecting ideas about the Orient to ideas about femininity, sexuality, and sociability.[8] In her recent book on the invention of luxury in Louis XIV's France, Joan DeJean discusses a 1688 fashion plate in which a woman, dressed in the latest style, shows her impeccable, but for the period, informal, apparel off to best advantage while lounging on the equally stylish new chair of the period—the sofa—a piece of furniture which, like her clothes, was far more informal and much sexier than the furniture that preceded it.[9]

The interweaving of associations to sociability, sex, and fashion is illustrated by the different ways in which furniture is portrayed in literary works of the period. Despite the critical cliché that unlike nineteenth-century novels, eighteenth-century texts do not portray material life, a number of well-known works *do* represent furniture, notably oriental beds and chairs. Unsurprisingly, the most abundant source of these references is libertine fiction. In La Morlière's *Angola* (1746), a tale with philosophical and erotic overtones, the Fairy Lumineuse bans *tabourets* from her court because they reinforce social distinctions. The comfortable oriental furniture of her palace promotes uninhibited conversation and fosters a sense of equality, while also creating an atmosphere of sensuality. In most instances the presence of an oriental chair signals in a less complex way the potential for seduction. Choderlos de Laclos's *Les Liaisons dangereuses* (1787) notes on several occasions the fortuitous presence of an *ottomane* or *chaise longue*, while in Marivaux's *Paysan parvenu (The Fortunate Peasant)* (1735), a well-placed sofa paves the way for the seduction of the ingenu Jacob.[10] Evidently the close resemblance between sofas and beds served as an emblematic reminder of the permeable boundary between social and sexual exchange that is a central preoccupation of libertine writing.

In two mid-century oriental tales with libertine overtones, *Le Canapé couleur de feu* (1741) attributed to Fougeret de Monbrun, and *Le Sopha* (1742) by Claude Crébillon, protagonists unexpectedly find themselves turned into sofas. In Crébillon's novel, the protagonist, transformed into a sofa, is accorded a prime position from which to observe the intimate lives of women. However, the tale he tells is less a titillating description of clandestine encounters than a critical portrait of how true intimacy has degenerated into the social performance of sexual conquest, a moralizing reflection of a kind that abounds in libertine fiction. A related point of view, articulated in a very different register, can be read in Jean-Jacques Rousseau's *Lettre à M. d'Alembert sur les spectacles* (*Letter to d'Alembert on the Theatre*). During the second half of the eighteenth century, Rousseau among others began to urge that the serious business of philosophical and political reflection be divorced from the frivolous modes of social interaction he associated with aristocratic circles and women's influence. Rousseau rails that "every woman in Paris gathers in her apartments a harem of men more womanish than she" and invites the reader to imagine guests pacing up and down in frustration, "while the idol lays stretched out motionless on her chaise-longue, with only her tongue and her eyes active."[11] Exploiting the prevalent trope of the seraglio as a confining prison in which men are emasculated by their excessive contact with women, he portrays the salon hostess as an oriental despot, stretched out languidly on a sofa, exercising unjustified and undemocratic power over a coterie of literary eunuchs.

I have dwelled on these literary references to oriental furniture because I want to emphasize the point that *ottomanes* and *sofas* were visible enough to generate several different, albeit related, representations. This resonance is not surprising, because in their names and designs these objects reflect a much broader cultural preoccupation with the Orient. This fascination has been well documented and interpreted in various ways.[12] What has scarcely been examined, however, is the relationship between oriental exoticism and the cultural reception of another key geopolitical arena, the colonial world.

French Furniture and Colonial Commodities

Before the mid-1760s, French, art, literature, and material culture suggest very little interest in France's thriving colonies: the "sugar islands" of the Antilles, the slave ports of Senegal, the Île Bourbon and Île de France in the Indian Ocean, and the vast territories of Canada and Louisiana.[13] In this regard the case of material culture is particularly striking because a number of commodities widely used in the manufacture of goods such as textiles, furniture, and food, were cultivated or harvested in the colonies. The changes in the form and function of furniture to which I have referred were, to some extent, made possible by the availability of an abundant supply of brightly colored tropical hardwoods transported from Africa, the Indian Ocean, and the Caribbean. Representationally, however, eighteenth-century furniture bears little trace of this colonial trade. It is hard to discover on the chairs, beds, and cabinets of the period any allusion to, for example, tropical landscapes or slave labor. By contrast, many pieces of the period built at least partially from wood imported from colonial sources, are adorned with motifs and designs that draw the imagination eastward to Turkey, Japan, and China.

The quest for wood represents an important chapter in the early history of colonial expansion. By 1600 there was an acute timber shortage in many parts of Europe; faced with this deficit European nations began to look elsewhere. Though no European country fully succeeded in meeting the demands of its shipbuilding industry from colonial sources, travelers did quickly discover wood with other valuable properties, notably a combination of color and resistance that appealed to French cabinetmakers.[14] Until the mid-seventeenth century European furniture was principally crafted from domestic wood, notably, depending on the region, oak, beech, cherry, and walnut. Ebony, prized for its deep, almost black color, was imported from Asia in small quantities from as early as the thirteenth century. In the sixteenth century, however, the volume of these imports increased rapidly as the Portuguese, the Dutch, and later the French shipped it in large quantities from Madagascar and Île de France (today Mauritius).

This abundance created the conditions for a new fashion for solid ebony, and toward the end of the seventeenth century, for sculpted ebony furniture. The distinction drawn in French between a *menuisier* who builds furniture, and an *ébéniste*, a specialist responsible for veneers, marquetry, and sculpture, dates to this period, as does the guild of *maîtres ébénistes-menuisiers*, established in 1638. The first concentrated group of *ébénistes* coalesced in the mid-sixteenth century around the port of Antwerp, a busy commercial hub from which luxury goods were transported throughout Europe. French monarchs invited skilled woodworkers from this region to Paris, establishing a distinguished artisanal tradition whose leading lights were often Protestants of Dutch or German origin. André Boulle, the renowned cabinetmaker of the late seventeenth century was, for example, the son of a woodworker who left the Netherlands for Paris earlier in the century.

As European explorers moved westward, the quest for wood remained such a key preoccupation that several new territories, including Madeira and Brazil, were named for their plentiful reserves of timber, and the enslaved Africans brought to labor there were sometimes called *bois d'ébène* (ebony wood). In the forests of the Caribbean and Central America, Europeans discovered woods such as logwood/campeachy (*campêche*), brazilwood (*bois de Brésil*), and green wood or green ebony (*bois vert* or *bois d'ébène vert*), which became staples of the perfume and dye industries, and which were also used to build furniture. As early as 1604, Jean Mocquet, a traveler, naturalist, and director of the *Cabinet des singularités du roi*, described how, in the course of a voyage to Guyana, the crew of his ship collected brazilwood, and later loaded a cargo of 70,000 pounds of fragrant aloe, as well as red and yellow sandalwood (*citrin*) and tulipwood (*bois de rose*). He later sold the aloe to apothecaries in La Rochelle and Tours.[15] Merchants plying the Atlantic and Indian Oceans also filled their holds with tortoiseshell. By the early eighteenth century, fashionable Parisian cabinets, desks, and armoires featured marquetry juxtaposing the contrasting colors and textures of ebony, copper, and tortoiseshell, a style called *Boulle marquetry* after its leading practitioner, André Boulle (Color Plate 1, see color insert after page 118).[16]

Before the seventeenth century, the color of wood was sometimes altered by fire or by the application of stains and varnishes. In the age of colonial imports, however, woods ranging in color from pale yellow to deep purple became available, and the need for such treatments was reduced. One of the principal results of this shift was the further refinement of veneering techniques. By the 1720s, the leading craftsmen had begun to abandon the copper and tortoiseshell of *Boulle marquetry* and to adopt instead the practice known as "painting in wood," in which natural differences in color are used to execute geometric or figurative compositions.[17] As early as 1685 the parquet of the *petite galerie* of the *grands appartements* of the palace of Versailles was composed from *bois des îles*. Its designer, Alexandre-Jean Oppenordt, contracted not to use dyes or fire to alter the color of the woods employed in the parquet, but rather to use oak, *bois de corail* (coral wood), *bois de lis des Indes*,[18] and green and black ebony.[19] Figure 1.2 shows the contrasting colors of a German parquet floor (c. 1715), veneered in satinwood, tulipwood, and olivewood.

In a description of marquetry techniques, the artisan André Roubo refers to the use of "rare colored woods that come to us from abroad and are known by the names of *bois des Indes*, brazilwood, mahogany of all kinds, satinwood, cedar, olive and aromatic laurel. . . ."[20] As this passage suggests, craftsmen did not always carefully distinguish among the different varieties of wood imported from the Antillean islands, South and Central America, and the Indian Ocean, and often referred to them collectively as *bois des îles* or *bois des Indes*. Nonetheless, it is possible to identify some of the most popular hardwoods of the period.[21] Marquetry often featured rosewood (*palissandre*), a veined grey or purplish wood found mostly in the Antilles. *Amarante* (purplewood) from Central America was also popular, having been made fashionable by Charles Cressent, who made furniture in purplewood for his patron, the Regent Philippe d'Orléans. Lemonwood (*bois de citron*) from the Antilles, which had a pale lemon color and pleasant aroma, and tulipwood (*bois de rose*), usually from Brazil, were also prized. These woods, used almost exclusively as veneers, were imported in small quantities and sold by the pound. Woods from the Antilles imported and sold in larger quantities were logwood (*campêche*) and lignum-vitae (*gaïac*), both used in pharmacology and (on France's west coast) to make furniture, as well as the queen of exotic hardwoods, mahogany (*acajou*).

Figure 1.2 German parquet, c. 1720, veneered in satinwood, tulipwood, and olivewood. Courtesy of J. Paul Getty Museum, Los Angeles.

The story of mahogany is intertwined with the history of European colonialism. Mahogany was purportedly discovered by Columbus in Hispaniola (the island that would later be divided between French Saint Domingue and Spanish Santo Domingo); one of the first mahogany tables manufactured in Europe was offered to Queen Elizabeth I by the celebrated explorer, Walter Raleigh; and mahogany was used to craft some of the paneling of the Escorial Palace in Madrid. In fact, both the English term *mahogany* and the French term *acajou* cover several related species. The two principal varieties are *swietana mahogani*, also known as *acajou de Saint Domingue* or *de Cuba,* as it is indigenous to the greater Antilles, Cuba, Jamaica, and Hispaniola; and *swietana macrophylla*, also known as *acajou de Honduras*, native to the Caribbean rim. In the French colonies of Martinique and Guadeloupe, *acajou de Cuba* was introduced in around 1740, with *acajou de Honduras* following in around 1900. In the present context it seems rather telling that in literary works of the period the word *acajou* was appropriated as an oriental proper name: Charles Simon Favart wrote a popular comic opera entitled *Acajou* (1744), and Charles Duclos wrote an oriental tale called *Acajou et Zirphile* (1744), both loosely set in the Orient.

In Britain the eighteenth century has been dubbed the "age of mahogany." The elegant, highly polished mahogany tables and chairs produced by Thomas Chippendale are among the most admired pieces of the period. In France the taste for gilded and painted furniture endured longer, and solid mahogany furniture did not triumph until the end of the century.[22] However, imported hardwoods were widely used in the colonies and in western ports, such as Bordeaux, Nantes, La Rochelle, and Rouen before they became commonplace elsewhere in France. In these increasingly wealthy and cultured centers the availability of colonial imports gave rise to distinctive furnishing fashions. Looking at this furniture, which as we shall see shares characteristics with both English and colonial or "Creole" styles, requires us to think outside the conventional historical frame of a national culture with its center in Paris, and to focus instead on the Atlantic cultural axis created by colonial trade.

From probate inventories and other documentary sources we know that the *hôtels particuliers* of ship owners and merchants in districts such as Les Chartrons in Bordeaux and the Île Feydeau in Nantes, both born of the wealth generated by the triangle trade, were often decorated with furniture that announced the colonial provenance of their owners' wealth. The concept of "port furniture" is hazy to the extent that furniture built in the provinces often bears no identifying mark, even after 1741 when stamps were legally mandated. Judgments about regional origin are therefore often based on a resemblance with other pieces whose provenance is known.[23] This said, it is possible to identify a handful of forms that were proper to the west coast, and which reflect the Atlantic region's special situation as a hub of colonial commerce.

Among these distinctive forms were the tables built in lignum vitae (*gaïac*) that were particularly characteristic of the region around Rochefort and La Rochelle (Figure 1.3).[24]

Figure 1.3 Gayac-and-oak-top table with turned legs and stretcher. Seventeenth or early eighteenth century. Courtesy of Musée du Nouveau Monde, La Rochelle.

The legs of these tables are typically turned, while the feet are joined by a stretcher, often in the form of a cross-link. This style, prevalent during the reign of Louis XIV, had gone out of fashion, at least in Paris, by the end of the seventeenth century. On the west coast, however, it remained current for a much longer period, in part because *gaïac*, a veined wood of contrasting colors that was among the most frequently imported tropical hardwoods, was difficult to work other than by turning.

Another example of the port style is the solid mahogany armoire, a large storage piece used in a variety of ways, for example, as a linen cupboard or a display case for china. Figures 1.4 and 1.5 show a regency-style *armoire bordelaise* in sculpted dappled mahogany (*acajou moucheté*) and a modest mahogany and yellowwood armoire from La Rochelle. Color Plate 2 shows a later armoire in *acajou de Cuba* with a decorative lock, the *serrure à bascule* typical of Bordeaux (see color insert after page 118). The Musée d'Orbigny-Bernon in La Rochelle owns a massive apothecary's armoire of local origin, the only known piece of its kind, in *acajou de Honduras moucheté* and *acajou de Cuba*.

In his detailed study of the lifestyles of the nobility of the Bordeaux area (roughly today's *département* of Gironde) in the eighteenth century, Michel Figeac finds that between 1680 and 1730 armoires were recorded in over 39 percent of the probate inventories of *châteaux* and *hôtels particuliers*, a figure that rises to over 92 percent (and an average of more than six armoires per inventory) between 1760 and 1794. These numbers are considerably higher than those recorded in probate inventories in the surrounding regions.[25] Not all of these armoires were built of solid mahogany, but as we will see below, a considerable proportion were. Eric Saugera, in a study of the activity of Bordeaux as a slave port, describes an armoire housed in an *hôtel particulier* in Agen, up the Garonne river from Bordeaux, which represents in an unusually direct way, the region's involvement in (one might venture to say the armoire's connection to) colonial commerce and the slave trade. The insides of its doors are painted with scenes featuring black servants, a woman on the left and a man on the right. Although the original owner is unknown, Saugera speculates that this armoire may have belonged to a merchant by the name of Nègre, known to have lived on the same street.[26]

Many of the noble and bourgeois residences of the region also contained commodes of solid mahogany, another characteristic piece of port furniture. Commodes were a relatively late invention, dating to around 1690. They are associated with the expansion of consumers' wardrobes and the growing need to store clothing, as well as the availability of new woods and mastery of decorative techniques such as japanning, gilding, and inlaying. Figeac finds commodes listed in over 73 percent of probate inventories executed in the Bordeaux area between 1760 and 1794.[27] Mahogany commodes were designed in several different styles, each associated with one of the major ports. Figure 1.6 shows a mid-century *commode en tombeau* with three rows of drawers in an inverted pyramid, a style associated with Bordeaux. Figure 1.7 shows a more boxlike Louis XV commode in mahogany and purplewood from La Rochelle. Considered collectively, west coast commodes appear strikingly similar to mahogany commodes made in England from about 1750 (Figure 1.8), and, a little later, in the North American colonies.

Regional styles evolved at a slower pace than fashionable Parisian furniture, and sophisticated and expensive techniques, such as intricate marquetry or extensive bronze moldings, were less common. On the west coast the Regency style (c. 1700 to 1730) remained popular even into the nineteenth century, and in fact much of the furniture of the region presents a hybrid appearance, with some traits suggesting the Regency while others are distinctly Louis XVI.[28] In at least one respect, however, port fashion can be said to have been ahead

Figure 1.4 Regency-style Bordeaux armoire in sculpted dappled mahogany. First half of the eighteenth century. Courtesy of Musée des arts décoratifs, Bordeaux.

Figure 1.5 Armoire from La Rochelle in mahogany and yellowwood. Second half of the eighteenth century. Courtesy of Musée d'Orbigny-Bernon, La Rochelle.

Figure 1.6 Mahagony Bordeaux *commode en tombeau*. Mid-eighteenth century. Courtesy of Musée des Arts Décoratifs, Bordeaux.

Figure 1.7 Mahogany and purplewood commode from La Rochelle. First half of the eighteenth century. Courtesy of Musée d'Orbigny-Bernon, La Rochelle.

Figure 1.8 English commode in mahogany and pine with gilt bronze handles. Circa 1760. Attributed to William Vine and John Cobb. Courtesy of Metropolitan Museum of Art, New York.

of Paris. Although as I have noted, the predilection for furniture in which the beauty of the wood, rather than gilding or sculpting, is the focal point, had caught on in England by the 1750s, in France, with the exception of the west coast, this fashion took off only at the end of the century. In the port cities, by contrast, solid mahogany became prevalent at an earlier stage as a result of the ready supply of imported wood.

In the Bordeaux area in particular, the early appreciation of mahogany also testifies to the region's strong historical relationship with England.[29] Another manifestation of this influence was the early diffusion of furniture, especially chairs and daybeds, made from cane (*rotin*). Mobile and relatively inexpensive, cane chairs became fashionable in the Netherlands and Britain in the late seventeenth century as a result of trade with the Far East. They arrived in Bordeaux shortly thereafter, and by the early eighteenth century, also became popular in Paris.[30]

In many respects, port furniture also resembles the furniture constructed in the French colonies. There is unfortunately very little surviving eighteenth-century "Creole" furniture: the few antiques to be seen today in, for example, Martinique and Guadeloupe, are largely nineteenth-century pieces imported from former English colonies such as Barbados or Dominica, or from the United States. What the few surviving eighteenth-century pieces do indicate, however, is extensive use of solid mahogany, a material particularly valued in the Caribbean because of its resistance to humidity. Standard in the master's house of a French plantation were mahogany armoires, chests (*coffres*), and four-poster beds (*lits à colonnes*). Cane seat furniture was also popular because the prevalence of insects made the use of upholstery inadvisable. Figure 1.9 shows a reconstruction of late-eighteenth and early-nineteenth-century colonial furniture from Martinique.

Written sources uphold the evidence of the few surviving antique pieces. For example, the inventory for a plantation in Les Abricots, Saint Domingue, sold in 1792 to three merchants from La Rochelle, gives the following account of the contents of the master's house:

> . . .mahogany *bergère* with its cushions, in bad condition. Item a mahogany bed with a straw mattress, pillow, cotton mosquito net and printed cotton coverlet, all in bad condition. Item a bad cedar armoire, used as a cupboard. Another armoire in mahogany, with copper bolts and locks. A mahogany table . . .[31]

In his exhaustive *Description topographique, physique, civile, politique et historique de la partie française de l'isle Saint-Domingue* (1797), the Martinican-born writer Moreau de Saint-Méry observed that colonists and free people of color typically furnished their homes with armoires and chairs crafted from locally produced materials such as mahogany and cane.[32]

One of the most pressing, and unfortunately most neglected, questions relating to the production of furniture in France and its colonial outposts is the role of enslaved and free black craftsmen. The first European furniture built in the Caribbean islands was crafted by the carpenters who served on naval vessels and merchant ships. This furniture, which

Figure 1.9 Reconstruction of early-nineteenth-century Creole dining room with mahogany table, armoire, and cane chairs. Courtesy of Musée Ethnographique et Historique, Fort-de-France, Martinique.

served as a model for all subsequent colonial woodworking, was strongly influenced by the traditions of the west coast where many of them had trained. When the production of sugar began in earnest in the late seventeenth century, and both the population and the wealth of the colonies soared, a larger pool of skilled labor was needed. The French government encouraged carpenters to sail for the colonies by promising that after ten years' service they would automatically hold the rank of master and enjoy the right to open a boutique in Paris.[33] These inducements were not particularly successful. Moreover, to avoid paying the high wages commanded by French artisans, masters often trained slaves as woodworkers. It is apparent from inventories compiled at the sale of estates, advertisements for slave auctions, and descriptions of life in Martinique and Guadeloupe, that slaves with special skills (known as *nègres à talent*), including carpenters, were highly valued.[34] These individuals were often loaned out for jobs, and in some cases were permitted to earn money for their own account. Enslaved people with special skills were considerably more likely than field laborers to win or buy their freedom. In his study of free people of color in Fort-Royal (today Fort-de-France), Martinique from the late seventeenth to the early nineteenth century, Émile Hayot finds that a majority of free black men were artisans, and that after masonry, carpentry was one of the most common professions. For 1710 alone he identifies 54 free black or mixed-race *menuisiers* in the records of the parish of Fort-Royal.[35]

In some instances, masters brought their slaves to France to learn special skills, including carpentry. Eric Saugera suggests that most of these apprenticeships occurred before 1738, in other words, during the early years of the colonies when skilled labor was in critically short supply. Later, the vast majority of the slaves brought to France were employed as domestics.[36] It is hard to gauge with precision the numbers of these apprentices. During the eighteenth century a series of laws restricted the presence of slaves in metropolitan France, and because both masters and former slaves had an interest in evading these controls, the figures recorded in police censuses certainly understate the numbers.[37] Nonetheless, the censuses of people of color in the Bordeaux region conducted in 1777 and again in 1807 confirm the presence of a small number of men, designated as "mulattoes," whose profession is given as *menuisier* or *ébéniste*.[38] In sum, it is apparent that a small number of enslaved and free blacks worked as furniture makers in France, and that a larger number of enslaved workers built furniture in the colonies themselves. Needless to say, a far greater number of enslaved workers employed in felling trees or loading timber on ships also participated in the production of the French furniture whose beauty derives from the use of tropical woods.

The landscapist Joseph Vernet's *Vue du Port de La Rochelle prise de la Petite Rive*, exhibited at the Salon of 1763 (Figure 1.10), depicts a common activity at the old port of La Rochelle: the unloading of a cargo of timber onto the busy docks. We know that the Americas were, after Holland, the second largest supplier of this timber, but beyond this basic fact it is hard to measure in quantitative or qualitative terms the significance of wood imported from the colonies to the French furniture industry.[39] Figeac's analysis of probate inventories shows that in statistical terms the use of tropical wood was not of major significance, even in the Bordeaux region. From 1680 to 1730 only 1.97 percent of furniture was crafted from *bois des îles*, a figure that rises to 3.52 percent for mahogany between 1760 and 1794. In neighboring regions, these percentages were of course even lower.[40] Mahogany was, however, employed with greater frequency to build certain pieces of furniture, notably *cabarets* (small serving tables with raised edges), *chiffonnières* (small commodes used for lace and linens), commodes, and desks (*secrétaires*). It is Figeac's finding, for example, that from 1764 to 1797 over 30 percent of the *cabarets* and over 18 percent of the commodes listed in probate invento-

Figure 1.10 Claude-Joseph Vernet, *Vue du port de La Rochelle prise de la petite rive* (1762). Courtesy of Musée national de la Marine, Paris.

ries in Bordeaux were made of mahogany.[41] A parallel analysis of the use of tropical wood veneers in Parisian furniture would be virtually impossible. In this context, the quality of the wood and its impact on the creative process is far more significant than its quantity.

East Meets West

The availability of a range of new woods and the development of the woodworking techniques that resulted from these new resources stimulated changes in both the forms and decorative styles of French furniture. Trends such as the fashion for solid ebony that held sway at the end of the seventeenth century, the vogue for mahogany that triumphed a hundred years later, the refinement of Boulle marquetry, and later the turn to "painting in wood," were all made possible by the consolidation of commercial networks radiating from colonial outposts in the Indian Ocean and Atlantic colonies. Given that the commercial impact of trade with the East—Turkey, Persia, China, Japan—from the outset registered strongly in art, literature, and material culture, we would expect to encounter a similar corpus of references to the thriving new colonies and their principal exports, including tropical wood. *Bois des îles*, which were costly and, beyond the port cities, used primarily as veneers, were certainly perceived throughout the eighteenth and nineteenth centuries as luxury commodities. In Flaubert's *Madame Bovary* (1857), for example, the rosewood (*palissandre*) desk in which Emma keeps her love letters, and which Charles refuses to sell after her death despite his crippling debts, serves as a general symbol for the heroine's taste for luxury goods.[42] However, except on the west coast, they were not recognized or marketed as *colonial* commodities. Rather, tropical woods were fashioned into consumer goods that summoned other associations, notably the exotic world of the Orient.

Alongside porcelain and hand-painted silk, lustrous black lacquer furniture was one of several oriental crazes to hit France in the last decades of the seventeenth century. Fashion-conscious consumers created entire rooms filled with oriental furniture and knickknacks, generating a demand that encouraged French furniture makers to try their hand at imitating oriental techniques. As Joan DeJean notes, in the 1692 edition of Nicolas de Blegny's *Guide de Paris*, the neologism *lachinage* is used to designate both the authentic lacquer ware on sale at Paris's fashionable fairs and cheaper domestic imitations.[43] Because of its dark hue, ebony, imported principally from the Indian Ocean, first through the Dutch East India Company and later from the French colony of Île de France, was often used in conjunction with black lacquer panels imported from China and Japan (Figures 1.11 and 1.12).

Imported panels were painstakingly removed from screens and chests and mounted on the body of a European cabinet or commode. The rarest and most costly lacquer came from Japan and was prized for its elegant, minimalist designs and striking relief. The sheen and dark color of ebony made it possible to disguise the border of the lacquer, in order to create a seamless transition from the transplanted panel to the wood that framed it. Even following the patent (in around 1715) of *vernis Martin*, a varnish used both as a substitute for authentic Asian lacquer and to mask the splintered borders of reassigned Asian panels, ebony veneer remained the most popular coordinate wood for black lacquer.[44] Ebony veneer was also sometimes used in conjunction with red Chinese lacquer or domestically produced *vernis Martin*, its dark hue offsetting the blood-red color of the lacquer. Figure 1.13 shows a mid-century piece by Bernard Van Risenburgh, now in the Metropolitan Museum of Art, in which lacquer from a seventeenth-century Chinese cabinet is mounted on an oak chest veneered in ebony. Whether Asian originals or French imitations, lacquer panels usually featured relief paintings (typically gold on a black background), of oriental landscapes, hunting scenes, and human figures.

In some instances, cabinets with lacquered surfaces opened to reveal shelving or drawers veneered in tropical wood. This luxurious combination achieved a striking contrast

Figure 1.11 Three-drawer commode by Martin Carlin. Japanese Lacquer, ebony veneer, bronze ornaments, and white marble top. Musée du Louvre, Paris. Courtesy of Réunion des Musées Nationaux/Art Resource, New York.

Figure 1.12 Desk attributed to Jean-Henri Riesner, 1780s. Oak and ebony with Japanese lacquer and marble top. Courtesy of J. Paul Getty Museum, Los Angeles.

Figure 1.13 Chest of drawers by Bernard Van Risenburgh, circa 1745. Chinese Coromandel lacquer on oak and ebony veneer. Courtesy of the Metropolitan Museum of Art, New York.

between the black lacquer exterior and the reddish-gold hue of the interior surfaces.[45] A different kind of meeting between Asian lacquer and colonial products can be discerned in the fashion for *cabarets* with lacquered tops. These small tables with raised lips were designed for the purpose of serving the hot beverages, especially chocolate and coffee, which grew in popularity from the mid-seventeenth century on as a result of colonial trade.[46]

When we consider the fashion for oriental lacquer, it is interesting to observe that its oriental origin penetrated even the vocabulary of furnishing. In English, the practice of coating a surface in varnish to obtain a hard, lustrous finish was known as "japanning," while in French lacquer was often called—symptomatically from the present perspective—*bois de la Chine*.[47]

Marquetry also sometimes served as a template for oriental designs. An example of this can be seen on a roll-top desk by David Roentgen, a talented German artisan with a studio in Paris who practiced in the late eighteenth century (Figure 1.14). Roentgen used marquetry in a distinctive way, to compose detailed miniature paintings, rather than to decorate an entire surface.[48] As this example shows, several of his marquetry desks are decorated with oriental landscapes featuring conventional *chinoiserie* imagery of parasols and pagodas.

A later illustration of the conjunction of colonial wood and oriental design is mahogany side- or armchairs, such as those for which Thomas Chippendale won an international reputation in the 1750s. One popular English design featured a seatback sculpted in geometrical designs of Chinese inspiration. Chairs of this type made their way to France due to the taste

Figure 1.14 Cylinder-fall desk by David Roentgen, c. 1776. Oak, cedar, and mahogany, with marquetry of maple, tulipwood, ebony, mother of pearl, and brass, partly stained. Courtesy of the Metropolitan Museum of Art, New York.

of anglophile clients, and by the 1780s French makers were also producing such polished mahogany chairs. The backs of these chairs were sometimes carved in an Egyptian design. This style, usually designated *retour d'Égypte* after the Egyptian Expedition launched by Napoleon Bonaparte in 1798, in reality began to appear about a decade earlier.[49] Figure 1.15 shows a *retour d'Égypte* faux-mahogany chair; Color Plate 3 (see color insert after page 118) shows Egyptian sphinx motifs on a late-eighteenth-century mahogany secretary.

As has long been recognized, the national style of the golden age of French furniture was permeated with ideas, techniques, and linguistic references originating in the exotic worlds of Turkey, China, and Japan. This inspiration was directly registered on decorative objects of all kinds. There was no real incentive to portray these goods in any other light; indeed, their market value was tied to their oriental allure. As we have seen, this exotic appeal traversed media as diverse as furniture and literature, such that the allure of a comfortable and elegant sofa could be translated with remarkable fluidity into a fictional narrative. By

Figure 1.15 *Retour d'Egypte* chair, circa 1800, one of a set of six by the Frères Jacob. Beech stained to resemble mahogany. Courtesy of Musée des Arts Décoratifs, Bordeaux.

contrast, the fashion for colonial hardwoods barely resonated either in furniture itself or in literary works. We find occasional references to wood as a colonial import in empirical literatures including the treatises of craftsmen such as André Roubo,[50] and the narratives of travelers such as Jean Mocquet and Père Labat,[51] but it was not until the 1770s that these materials began to figure to a significant degree in literary or scientific discourse. When this awakening finally happened it was associated with the work of a group of colonial botanists, including Pierre Poivre and Philibert Commerson, who studied the environmental impact of deforestation in the Île de France.[52] The literary voice of this school was the maverick Bernardin de Saint-Pierre, who visited the Île de France between 1768 and 1771, and translated his environmentalist concerns into a popular work of fiction, his best-selling novel *Paul et Virginie* (1788), a narrative which, read closely, has as much to do with trees as with people.

Several explanations can be offered for the low profile of colonial commerce, including the timber trade, before this period. Though a detailed examination of these issues lies beyond the scope of this essay, it is clear on a primary level that there was simply not a figurative tradition or thematic repertory for the representation of the American colonies as there was for Turkey, Persia, Japan, and China. This was perhaps due to the fact that whereas in its fascination with the Orient, at least during the eighteenth century, Europe measured itself against other imperial powers with rival cultural traditions,[53] in the context of the Western Hemisphere, this was less possible.[54] What was available instead was an image of the *tabula rasa*, the unspoiled desert populated, if at all, by noble savages, and even this sparse imagery quickly failed to convey the reality of the colonies because it did not keep pace with the dramatic, and in many respects tragic, human and ecological transformations brought about by the slave trade and plantation agriculture.

Enslaved and free blacks began to emerge as exotic figures in the years surrounding the first abolition of slavery by the National Convention in 1794. This development is most apparent in literature, but it can also be observed to a more limited degree in the decorative arts.[55] Tropical exoticism waned quickly after 1810, following the restoration of slavery and colonial control in the French islands, Haiti excepted. It was not until the second half of the nineteenth century that images of colonial life began to appear widely in product trademarks and on posters for tropical commodities. From these shifts it seems plausible to surmise that the imagery of plantation houses shaded by palm trees, colonials in crisp white clothes, and contented black domestics in straw hats, which circulate to this day in the mode of colonial nostalgia, could only coalesce after the definitive abolition of slavery in 1848.[56] After this transition, life on the Caribbean plantation could be exoticized in a way that would have been impossible under slavery.

France's Caribbean colonies were in many respects precursors of today's offshore production sites. In these islands crops, which in many instances had originally been grown elsewhere, were pushed into mass production by the use of inexpensive labor. These crops often remained identified with the place of origin rather than with the place in which they were principally grown, just as today's Nike sneakers are identified with the United States rather than the developing world locations in which they are manufactured. In the eighteenth century the incentive to overlook the colonial conditions of production was particularly strong, as it meant turning a blind eye to slavery along with other vicissitudes of plantation agriculture, notably lasting ecological evils such as soil erosion, drought, and flooding.

A reflection on the history of luxury furniture at first glance has little to do with this kind of ecological reality, and indeed, with the social and economic concerns of people beyond the (literally gilded) elite world of which it is considered a vestige. However, practices of consumption and aesthetic appreciation represent only a single stage in a cycle of production and consumption that begins with the harvesting of raw materials and involves a broad cross-section of the working population including, in this case, members of the enslaved population of the Caribbean colonies. We typically encounter antique furniture in museums and stately homes, where our attention is almost invariably directed to aesthetic qualities and questions of provenance, and not to the social history of labor or the origins of its constituent materials. An illustration of this curatorial approach that has particular relevance here was the exhibition "Chocolate, Coffee, Tea," held at the Metropolitan Museum of Art in New York City in 2004. This small exhibition presented exquisite objects—ceramics, silverware, and furniture—created for the consumption of the new hot beverages popularized throughout Europe in the seventeenth and eighteenth centuries. In their exhibition notes, the curators accurately noted the eastern origins of both coffee and tea and highlighted the oriental motifs that adorn many of the pieces. They omitted to note, however, that by the mid-eighteenth century the bulk of European coffee and chocolate, to say nothing of the sugar with which they were prepared, was produced in the plantation colonies of the Americas, particularly the French colony of Saint Domingue. Similarly, though they observed several times that the English predilection for tea never really took off in France, the curators did not explain that there were economic reasons for these national preferences, namely that by the mid-eighteenth century the dominant French colonial and trading networks lay to the west, whereas the British were still consolidating their empire in India. Omissions such as these signal, perhaps, a subliminal reluctance to approach delicate porcelain coffee cups or elegant mahogany tea chests as the by-products of plantation agriculture and related industrial processes. I believe, by contrast, that awareness of manufacturing history enhances rather than detracts from our appreciation of the aesthetic qualities of these extraordinary works of art.

Notes

1. This difference was due largely to the fact that there were lower rates of domestic investment, and therefore less debt, and fewer absentee landlords in the French colonies.
2. See Jacques de Cauna, *Au temps des iles à sucre. Histoire d'une plantation de Saint-Domingue au XVIIIe siècle* (Paris: Karthala, 1987), 12.
3. France was the third largest supplier of slaves to the Americas. For estimates of the volume of the French slave trade in the eighteenth century see Philip D. Curtin, *The Atlantic Slave Trade: A Census* (Madison: University of Wisconsin Press, 1969); Hubert Deschamps, *Histoire de la traite des noirs de l'antiquité à nos jours* (Paris: Fayard, 1972); Gabriel Debien, *Les esclaves aux Antilles françaises, XVII-XVIIIe siècles* (Basse-Terre: Société d'Histoire de la Guadeloupe, 1974); Robert Louis Stein, *The French Slave Trade in the Eighteenth Century: An Old Regime Business* (Madison: University of Wisconsin Press, 1979); Herbert S. Klein, *The Middle Passage: Comparative Studies in the Atlantic Slave Trade* (Princeton, NJ: Princeton University Press, 1978); James Pritchard, *In Search of Empire: The French in the Americas, 1670-1730* (Cambridge: Cambridge University Press, 2004).
4. I use the terms *Orient* and *oriental*, which are both unspecific and loaded with political and cultural associations, to designate categories of eighteenth-century European thought, rather than to denote a cultural, geographic, or political reality.
5. I am currently working on a book that examines the translation of colonial themes into other concerns across a range of media including furniture, textiles, and literature.
6. This East–West axis was established at the very beginning of European exploration of the Atlantic. The development of Portuguese navigation eastward around the Cape of Good Hope led to the discovery of Atlantic islands such as Madeira and the Canaries, where plantations were established decades before the European discovery of the Caribbean. The fall of Constantinople in 1453 also played an indirect role to the extent that the Ottoman hold on the eastern Mediterranean limited the access of European ships and encouraged exploration elsewhere.

7. For example, Louis-Sébastien Mercier rails: "I believe that the inventory of our furniture would very much surprise an ancient were he to return to this world. The language of the bailiffs and auctioneers who know the names of this immense mass of superfluities is an idiom that is very detailed, very rich, and utterly unknown to the poor." "Légères observations," in *Tableau de Paris*, ed. Jean-Claude Bonnet, 2 vols. (Paris: Mercure de France, 1994), 1: 852–60.

8. On these associations see my discussion of oriental chairs and their literary avatars in *Foreign Bodies: Gender, Language and Culture in French Orientalism* (Stanford, CA: Stanford University Press, 2001), 147–216.

9. Joan DeJean, *The Essence of Style: How the French Invented High Fashion, Fine Food, Chic Cafés, Style, Sophistication and Glamour* (New York: Free Press, 2005), 69, figure 3.4.

10. Pierre-Ambroise-François Choderlos de Laclos, *Dangerous Liaisons*, trans. Douglas Parmée (New York and Oxford: Oxford University Press, 1995), 146, 278; Pierre Carlet Chamblain de Marivaux, *Le Paysan parvenu* in *Romans de Marivaux* (Paris: Pléïade, 1949), 708.

11. Jean-Jacques Rousseau, *Politics and the Arts: Letter to d'Alembert on the Theatre*, trans. and ed. Allan Bloom (Ithaca, NY: Cornell University Press, 1968), 100–101.

12. For example, it has been interpreted as an expression of European cosmopolitanism, a manifestation of cultural anxiety, and an intimation of imperial ambition. On the French literary fascination with oriental cultures in this period see Edward Said, *Orientalism* (New York: Pantheon Books, 1978); Lisa Lowe, *Critical Terrains: French and British Orientalisms* (Ithaca, NY: Cornell University Press, 1991); Ruth Bernard Yeazell, *Harems of the Mind* (New Haven, CT: Yale University Press, 2000); Dobie, *Foreign Bodies*; Michèle Longino, *Orientalism in French Classical Drama* (Cambridge: Cambridge University Press, 2002). On the influence of eastern craft traditions on French decorative arts see Oliver R. Impey, *Chinoiserie: The Impact of Oriental Styles on Western Art and Decoration* (New York: Scribner's, 1977); Madeleine Jarry, *Chinese Influence on European Decorative Art, 17th and 18th Centuries* (New York: Vendome Books, 1981); Dawn Jacobson, *Chinoiseries* (London: Phaidon Press, 1993); Joyce Burnard, *Chintz and Cotton: India's Textile Gift to the World* (Kenthurst, NSW: Kangaroo Press, 1994).

13. There were of course some representations of colonial expansion and slavery. For examples see my discussion in *Foreign Bodies*, 26–31.

14. As Richard Grove observes of ebony-rich Mauritius, "During the Dutch period the rate of deforestation on the island became closely correlated with the state of the European market for luxury goods." *Green Imperialism: Colonial Expansion, Tropical Edens and the Origins of Environmentalism 1600–1800* (Cambridge: Cambridge University Press, 1995), 132. By the time of the French takeover of Mauritius in 1721 these reserves had been greatly depleted, especially in the coastal areas.

15. Jean Mocquet, *Voyages en Afrique, Asie, Indes orientales et occidentals* (Paris : Jean de Heuqueville, 1617), 120.

16. Over the course of the eighteenth century, tortoiseshell in fact considerably exceeded mahogany and other tropical woods in terms of the total value of imports. See *Les meubles de Port Rochelais*, ed. Dominique Chaussat and Florence Chaussat (La Rochelle: Être et Connaître, 2000), 30.

17. See Pierre Ramond, *Marquetry*, trans. Jacqueline Derenne et al. (Los Angeles: J. Paul Getty Museum, 2002), 79.

18. It is hard to know which wood was designated by this name; see below on the often loose use of names denoting different varieties.

19. Guillaume Janneau, *Le meuble de l'ébénisterie* (Paris: Éditions de l'Amateur, 1989), 39.

20. André Roubo, *L'Art du menuisier*, 4 vols. (Paris: Saillant et Nyon, 1769–1775), 1 : 22–23.

21. On exotic woods, their botanical names, and provenance see *Mobilier créole, Cahiers du Patrimoine* 15–16 (1997): 14–29 and Chaussat and Chaussat, *Les meubles de Port Rochelais*, 141–42.

22. This fashion had begun to take shape by 1753 when Madame de Pompadour, a leader in French fashion, ordered six mahogany commodes for her residence at Crécy from Lazare Duvaux, a prominent Parisian *marchand mercier*. See Jacqueline du Pasquier, *Mobilier bordelais et parisien* (Paris: Réunion des Musées Nationaux, 1997), 62.

23. On port furniture as a category, see Chaussat and Chaussat, *Les meubles de Port Rochelais*, 15–16 and du Pasquier, *Mobilier bordelais et parisien*, 113–15.

24. For a period of time, the use of *gaïac* was restricted to naval construction. The existence of a naval shipyard in Rochefort explains the greeter diffusion of *gaïac* in the region. See Thierry LeFrançois, *Musée du Nouveau Monde, La Rochelle* (La Rochelle: Les Musées d'Art et d'Histoire, 1990), 21, 114.

25. Michel Figeac, *La Douceur des Lumières. Noblesse et art de vivre en Guyenne au XVIIIème siècle* (Paris: Mollat, 2001), 289, 296.
26. Eric Saugera, *Bordeaux, port négrier: chronologie, économie, idéologie, XVIIe–XIXe siècles* (Paris: Karthala, 1995), 288–89, 305.
27. Figeac, *La Douceur des Lumières*, 296. This figure represents a dramatic increase over inventories taken between 1680 and 1730, a rise explained by the growing importance of the commode in the first half of the century.
28. On this time lag, see Chaussat and Chaussat, *Les meubles de Port Rochelais*, 45.
29. The English presence of the Middle Ages left its mark in the ties between families. In the seventeenth and eighteenth centuries these bonds were renewed by the expansion of commercial exchanges that turned cities like Bordeaux and Nantes into cosmopolitan centers communicating on a regular basis with Spain, England, the Netherlands, and northern Europe as well as Africa and the Americas. See du Pasquier, *Mobilier bordelais et parisien*, 41 and 132; and Paul Butel, *Les négociants bordelais: l'Europe et les îles au XVIIIe siècle* (Paris: Aubier-Montaigne, 1974), 1-82.
30. See du Pasquier, *Mobilier bordelais et parisien*, 40, 51.
31. *Inventaire et mise en possession de l'habitation Valette*, 27 September 1792. Archives of the Musée du Nouveau Monde, La Rochelle (87-4-2).
32. Médéric Louis Elie Moreau de Saint-Méry, *Description topographique, physique, civile, politique et historique de la partie française de l'isle Saint-Domingue,* 2 vols. (Philadelphia, 1797), 1: 90.
33. These inducements offered a shortcut for artisans wishing to reduce the lengthy period of apprenticeship and practice required to become a master under the French guild system. See *Mobilier créole*, 60–61.
34. See, e.g., Jean-Baptiste Labat, *Nouveau Voyage aux îles d'Amérique*, 4 vols. (Paris: G. Cavelier, 1742), 4 :186–88.
35. Émile Hayot, "Les Gens de couleur libres de Fort-Royal de 1679 à 1823," *Revue française d'histoire d'Outre-Mer* 202–203 (1969): 31.
36. Saugera, *Bordeaux, port négrier*, 296. According to the 1777 police census for the Bordeaux area, 87 percent of these individuals provided some form of domestic service. See Archives régionales de la Gironde (ARG) C3669.
37. In his doctoral thesis, *Les Problèmes des gens de couleur à Bordeaux sous l'ancien régime (1716–1787)* (Bordeaux, 1955), Léo Elisabeth shows that before 1756, 1098 arrivals and 1049 departures of enslaved blacks were registered with the admiralty of Bordeaux. By contrast, for the period between 1756 and 1786, during which laws controlling the presence of slaves in France were more stringent, the figures change dramatically: only 102 arrivals were recorded against 1186 departures. Cited in Saugera, *Bordeaux, port négrier*, 291.
38. For example, the 1777 census lists an unnamed *menuisier* residing in Bordeaux, while the 1807 census lists the following: Joseph Montreuil, a forty-nine-year-old *menuisier* born in Martinique and resident in Bordeaux; Jean-Baptiste Chadonnier, a twenty-seven-year-old *menuisier* born in Guadeloupe and residing in La Réole; and Florimon, a twenty-two-year-old *ébéniste* living in St. Émilion. The last three men all came or were brought to France in the 1790s when revolution and war disrupted business and daily life in the colonies. ARG 1M 332.
39. The summaries of ships' cargoes printed in the *Journal de Guyenne*, a periodical published in Bordeaux between 1785 and 1791 (ARG 4L 1370), along with ships' registers and other sources, show that logwood, lignum vitae, and mahogany were the most commonly imported tropical woods.
40. Figeac, *La Douceur des Lumières*, 290, 297.
41. This breakdown appears in an annex to the doctoral dissertation on which Figeac's later book is based, *Destins de la noblesse bordelaise (1770–1830)* (Sorbonne, 1995), vol. 5, table XXII.
42. Gustave Flaubert, *Madame Bovary*, part 3, chapter 11.
43. DeJean, *Essence of Style*, 243.
44. On the development and use of *vernis Martin*, see Thibaut Wolvesperges, *Le Meuble français en laque* (Paris: Éditions de l'Amateur, 2000), 8ff, 75ff. As DeJean notes, *vernis Martin* was not a technical breakthrough in its own right, but the refinement of French efforts at imitating lacquer by the most accomplished craftsmen in the field, the Martin family. As such it was a brand name rather than an entirely new product. DeJean, *Essence of Style*, 244.
45. See Wolvesperges, *Le Meuble français en laque*, 176–77.
46. Ibid., 71. Mahogany *cabarets* were common on the west coast.
47. Ibid., 75.

48. See François de Salverte, *Les ébénistes du dix-huitième siècle, leurs oeuvres et leurs marques* (Paris and Brussels: G. Vancrest et Compagnie, 1923), 277.
49. The vogue for Egypt in France in this period was in fact one of the driving forces behind the Expedition. See Guilhem Scherf, "L'égyptomanie et la sculpture à la fin du XVIIIe siècle," *Dossier de l'art* 17 (1994): 14-21. One of Marie-Antoinette's favorite furniture makers, Georges Jacob, often used sphinx motifs in a neo-classical register. See de Salverte, *Les ébénistes du dix-huitième siècle*.
50. Roubo, *L'Art du menuisier*, 22–23.
51. Mocquet, *Voyages en Afrique*, 98. Labat describes the different species that he encountered in Guadeloupe and Martinique, and mentions making furniture and other objects from them. *Nouveau Voyage aux îles d'Amérique*, 1:378–79, 2:109–10, 3:207–19.
52. The pioneering work of Poivre and Commerson is described by Richard Grove in *Green Imperialism*.
53. My own research suggests that European interest in Arabs and North Africans as *subjects* of (the Ottoman) empire was only really aroused in the nineteenth century at a time when Europe was poised to become an imperial power in the region.
54. Incas and Aztecs did become fashionable for a time in the 1730s and 1740s. See, e.g., Voltaire, *Alzire ou les Américains* (1736); Riccoboni le fils and Jean-Antoine Romagnesi, *Les Sauvages, parodie de la tragédie d'Alzire* (1736); Aléxis Piron, *Fernand Cortez ou Montézume* (1744); Françoise de Graffigny, *Lettres d'une péruvienne* (1748); and Boissi, *La Péruvienne* (1748). See Gilbert Chinard, *L'Amérique et le rêve exotique dans la littérature française au XVIIe et au XVIIIe siècle* (Paris: Droz, 1934), 236-42, 442.
55. One example of this vogue was the *pendules au nègre* or blackamoor clocks: gold clocks with contrasting black figures that were produced in Paris and the United States around the turn of the nineteenth century. Versions of these clocks in the Musée du Nouveau Monde (La Rochelle), the Musée des arts décoratifs (Bordeaux), the Louvre (Paris), and the Musée d'histoire et d'ethnographie de la Martinique (Fort-de-France) all date from the period 1800–1820.
56. See Dana Hale, "French Images of Race on Product Trademarks during the Third Republic," in *The Color of Liberty: Histories of Race in France*, ed. Sue Peabody and Tyler Stovall (Durham, NC: Duke University Press, 2003), 137.

CHAPTER 2

Mahogany as Status Symbol: Race and Luxury in Saint Domingue at the End of the Eighteenth Century

CHAELA PASTORE

On the final page of newspapers published in Saint Domingue at the close of the eighteenth century, well after detailed proceedings of various assemblies and pages of amateurish prose, sits the richest and most suggestive portion of these documents. Here, in a section called "Miscellaneous Announcements," one finds evidence of how people lived on the island. Entrepreneurs announced shop openings, recently bankrupt businessmen and women declared their intention to return to France, various artisans and professionals offered their services, slave traders touted the specialties of slaves for sale, and overseers listed descriptions of runaway slaves. Also, and most importantly for the purposes of this investigation, colonists on the way out routinely made public the belongings they wanted to sell before they departed. This colonial version of a moving sale portrays a world rapidly coming to an end. It lists the objects that made up that world and reveals the cultural and political meanings that inhered in such objects.

Saint Domingue was a frontier land dominated by the relationship between money and status. Those who lived there both reaped the benefits of and paid a price for social mobility. A newly moneyed colonist might jump ranks and find his way into a new social class, but he might also fall prey to the notion that his shows of wealth were less than honorable. From the mainland, colonists were associated with a get-rich-quick mentality that deemed their accomplishments suspect. "Luxury was everywhere quite excessive," commented a visitor from France, echoing a prevailing sentiment about consumer habits in the colonies.[1] Indeed, the Swiss officer Baron de Wimpffen, who traveled in Saint Domingue from 1788 to 1790, lamented the way that indispensable objects quickly gave way to the "trifling appendages of luxuries":

> The youthful Creole was easily persuaded that a looking-glass in a gilt frame reflected her pretty features more faithfully than the crystal of a fountain. Thus do ingenuous ignorance, and credulous self-love, purchase objects at a hundred times their value, and superfluities become necessities.[2]

From Baron de Wimpffen's point of view, colonists exhibited an unselfconscious vanity and overindulgence that easily succumbed to the lure of mere frills. Inexperienced and unworldly, they were easily seduced by the reflection of their own charm (in Wimpffen's example, quite literally), which they saw in extravagant possessions.

Baron de Wimpffen's disapproving remarks combined two criticisms aimed at the colony during the eighteenth century: it was a place where luxury spun out of control and dangerous autonomist leanings percolated. As will be seen, Wimpffen's critique was tied to a broader denunciation of luxury, but the complaint took on a particular intensity when aimed at the colony. Wimpffen's sense that colonists were different echoed a Parisian fear that they were separated not only by an ocean, but also by their own set of cultural and political rules.

Officially, Saint Domingue was a valuable and convenient offshoot of France. Governed by the idea that "the colonies are established for the metropole's use,"[3] the island was run from France by the Minister of the Marine and managed locally by two royally appointed officials, an intendant and a governor. Together, the intendant and the governor dictated laws, made court appointments, parceled out government land, and authorized arrests in the colony. But colonists had from the start exhibited an autonomist spirit, a tendency to think and act independently that grew from a number of factors including geographical isolation, exposure to colonial Spanish and British worlds, a tropical climate, and a huge non-European population.[4] Also, between 1689 and 1815, France and Great Britain engaged in seven different conflicts, during which the island was effectively isolated and colonists had to fend for themselves. In response to the immutable fact of distance and the contingencies of war, colonists embraced their new lives without depending on or acquiescing to the power of the metropole. Criticisms of luxury were thus inseparable from a general anxiety about the ways that the colony, and those who peopled it, were different. Objects became one more measure of the widening gap between colonists and true Frenchmen.

Luxurious possessions, then, are one important way to analyze the relationship of politics, identity, and consumption in Saint Domingue. Such objects hint at a number of key themes: the relationship of the colony to the metropole, the debate on luxury, the importance of transatlantic trade networks, and the association between consumption and identity. One kind of object, mahogany furniture, is an excellent prism through which to consider these interwoven threads of meaning. First, as a consumer item, mahogany furniture provides valuable information about the historical meaning of consumption.[5] Who owned mahogany furniture and what social value did this ownership bestow? Mahogany furniture connoted luxury in Saint Domingue, as it did on the mainland, but such furniture was more accessible in the colony and thus relatively common. Second, mahogany's presence in the colony reveals an important aspect of the transatlantic trade network that linked France and the colony. Because mahogany was harvested in the Antilles, artisans in France's coastal cities had easy access to it. They in turn used it to develop new styles of furniture that catered to a more modest clientele than that found in Paris—a growing merchant middle class centered in places like Marseilles and Bordeaux. The abundance of mahogany furniture, then, resulted in part from a burgeoning regional trade that allowed for the rise of an entrepreneurial trade class in France's coastal cities. Third, mahogany furniture laid bare tensions inherent in the colony's relationship to the mainland both before and during the French Revolution. Saint Domingue was caught up in debates about luxury that became ubiquitous during the eighteenth century, but with disastrous results. The colony's association with luxury was both promising and threatening to France, and some of those who owned mahogany furniture made such threats palpable. The apparent pervasiveness of luxury items like mahogany furniture gave critics in France more fodder for their claims that the mainland should tightly control and monitor the colony.

When I speak of colonists' everyday lives, I am speaking mainly of white inhabitants, whether Creole or metropolitan born. In Saint Domingue at the end of the eighteenth century, whites were outnumbered by other inhabitants of the colony: the white population totaled roughly 40,000, compared to 28,000 mixed-race inhabitants and 500,000 slaves.[6] For this small minority of whites, movement and impermanence defined colonial life even before the French Revolution reached the island's shores. Saint Domingue teemed with merchants, itinerant residents who traveled throughout the colony and back and forth between the island and France, providing for the needs of the colonists and returning to the metropole with sugar, coffee, indigo, and cotton. For plantation owners, men and women seemingly tied to the land, absenteeism was the order of the day. Those who might have preferred to stay—small shopkeepers, for example—could not always remain, thanks to the fluctuating economy of the island. While Saint Domingue promised quick wealth and status to those who could not find such things in France, this frontier land left most colonists struggling to stay afloat. Because there was so little currency on the island, colonists routinely found themselves in a debit–credit cycle that yielded little tangible profit. And even inhabitants who may have succeeded financially were susceptible to the colony's climate; some people left because of illness, others succumbed to tropical diseases. Finally, the French and Haitian Revolutions forced scores of people to leave the island.

The period considered here, between 1791 and 1792, was a time of tremendous upheaval in both the mainland and the colony. As news of the French Revolution reached Saint Domingue, it sparked a grab for power between the two main groups of whites: *grands blancs*, typically planters, great merchants, and well-to-do maritime agents; and *petits blancs*, less wealthy inhabitants including retail merchants, plantation managers, lawyers, artisans, and so on. Recognizing the possibility for self-rule in the colony, a faction of planters designated itself the Colonial Committee and wrote up its own *cahiers de doléance*, excluding the interests of the *petits blancs*. But when the National Assembly decreed on May 15, 1791 that all *gens de couleur* (free men of color) who had certain property qualifications and were born of free parents would receive political and civil rights, the two groups overlooked their class differences and forged an alliance. Though the law would affect only a small number of mixed-race men, reaction in Saint Domingue was overwhelming; violence broke out as whites throughout the colony united against the decree and free men of color. After a massive slave insurrection on August 22 and 23, 1791, what began as skirmishes between whites and *gens de couleur* erupted into a three-way civil war between whites, *gens de couleur*, and slaves. Slaves, who had been hearing talk about liberty and equality as well as watching different factions vie for power, asserted their own political voice and launched a revolution that ended in Haitian independence.[7] The dual Revolutions—French and Haitian—literally uncovered much evidence of material life in the colony. The objects advertised in colonial newspapers as people left the island create a virtual museum of the colony's former life, making apparent what would be forever lost in the course of a brutal civil war lasting more than a decade.

When in 1791 inhabitants left the colony, they sought to unload their merchandise and their most cumbersome belongings including, of course, their furniture. In April, for example, Jean-Baptiste Reynaud posted a cheerful message in the *Courrier National de Saint-Domingue*, where he announced that the company he had formed with one Alexis Gilard had "expired."[8] Reynaud planned to continue on his own, but in the meantime he would be auctioning off a number of possessions, including porcelain, china, kitchen things, and mahogany armoires and tables. That same month, one M. Hudicourt posted a notice in the *Gazette de Saint-Domingue*, announcing his plans to leave the colony because of ill health. Among the items he wished to sell: a young Creole slave (good dressmaker and nanny) and her nine-month-old infant, a new cabriolet, made in Paris in the latest fashion, and several pieces of mahogany furniture.[9] In October 1791, M. Goupy advertised his plans to leave for New England or France. In addition to soap, candles, and oil from his store, he offered beds, armoires, buffets, bureaus, and mahogany tables.[10] Several months later, Madame Menot, a businesswoman who sold cloth, publicized her intention to depart. She wanted to sell or barter the merchandise remaining in her store, including varieties of muslin, lace, wool, velvet, and satin. In addition to her stock, she advertised four large mahogany armoires.[11]

Mahogany, then, showed up in diverse advertisements, placed by people with different kinds of businesses and different reasons for abandoning Saint Domingue.[12] Why was mahogany so visible in the colony? The wood's abundance was perhaps a simple matter of convenience, as mahogany was plentiful in the Antilles. By the middle of the eighteenth century, Cuba, Honduras, and Jamaica had substantial mahogany trades. Saint Domingue, too, had a modest mahogany trade, but most resources—that is, slaves—were put to work on plantations.[13] Mahogany was also suited to the colony's climate: this indigenous wood resisted insects and indeed historian Gabriel Debien has argued that colonists adopted the wood for this reason alone.[14]

Such matter-of-fact explanations deserve note, but a number of factors suggest that this view is too narrow. Wood was costly. Mahogany's visibility and relative proximity still did not make it cheap. Labor was expensive in the colony, and the value of mahogany reflected this cost. In the death inventory of M. Dussolier, a prominent plantation owner in Saint Domingue, mahogany furniture was given the highest value among his furnishings. Of Dussolier's four card tables, the two mahogany tables were assessed together at 132 livres, while the other two, whose wood was not specified, were valued at 18 livres. A mahogany armoire, worth 400 livres, was the single most expensive piece in his home, and the notary consistently appraised mahogany furniture at higher amounts than other kinds of furniture.[15] Like Dussolier's inventory, the "Miscellaneous Announcements" section of newspapers only distinguished wood if it was mahogany. When M. Roume, for example, announced an imminent sale in the February 1, 1792 edition of the *Moniteur Général*, he emphasized that the furniture "was made of mahogany and other kinds of wood."[16] In Saint Domingue, mahogany furniture was at once ubiquitous and set apart from other kinds of furnishings. On the continent, mahogany furniture was also valuable, but not quite as common.

Mahogany was considered a luxury wood in France, where it became quite popular in the last third of the eighteenth century.[17] Solid mahogany seat furniture appeared for the first time during this period, and Marie Antoinette had her whole boudoir at Fontaine-bleau made with the wood.[18] But the French at first tended to export whatever mahogany they brought to the mainland, and the wood's vogue in France appears to have begun as a British influence. Aristocrats in England had used mahogany to display sophisticated taste since the 1720s, and when a "wave of Anglomania" swept France after the American

Revolution, the French appropriated a similar fondness for the wood.[19] The colony was no exception. As Baron de Wimpffen, striking a typically ironic note, observed: "Furniture, whether of necessity, of comfort, or of luxury, is imported ready-made from France, into a country which offers, in great abundance . . . different species of mahogany."[20] Wimpffen's incisive comment hints at a number of interconnected issues made manifest in mahogany furniture. He alludes to the ready availability of this luxury wood, suggesting that supply alone might account for its noticeable presence in the colony. Yet he also suggests that even though mahogany originated in the colony, mahogany furniture was not made there. Rather, the wood was part of a complicated transatlantic trade network wherein mahogany was exported as raw material and imported as finished product.

Though colonial furnishing may have reflected the use of local resources, the metropole gave form and meaning to the finished product, as Louis Malfoy has skillfully demonstrated in his book on port town furniture in France. Indeed, the popularity of mahogany, combined with a sophisticated trade system that allowed French port towns to receive wood from the Antilles, generated a new style of furniture during the eighteenth century. Throughout this period, artisans in places like Saint-Malo, Nantes, and Bordeaux catered to provincial tastes and created styles that appealed to a newly moneyed merchant class. Artisans and consumers in these areas were just as likely to look outward, toward Holland and England, as they were to take their cues from the French capital and court.[21] While designs among port towns varied quite a bit (furniture from Nantes tended to be functional and sober, while that from Bordeaux was comparatively rich and made for show) all of the furniture was simplified and streamlined compared to that being produced in the capital. In short, in the abundance and transformation of mahogany furniture, we see one of the consequences of colonialism: a rising middle class, a group whose money came from colonial trade, using the raw materials of the colonies (in this case, a luxury wood), to create their own style. Mahogany furniture thus signaled the rise of two provincial middle classes—one in the mainland port cities and the other in the colony—each of which used style to carve out and display its own distinct identity. At once social climbers and innovators, wealthy provincials and colonists took advantage of the wood's increased availability and broadening fashion; in doing so they attracted much critical attention.

In France, conspicuous consumption became a hotly debated issue as more people gained access to luxury goods. During the eighteenth century, when France moved from an economy of dearth to an economy of abundance, moral and economic debates related to luxury took on virulence. While prior to this time, luxury had its place in an economy based on scarcity and the redistribution of wealth through charity, the eighteenth century began to see luxury associated with superfluity and pretension.[22] Indeed, historian John Shovlin's argument for a complete transformation in the concept of luxury during the eighteenth century helps to explain the particularly hostile response to consumer activity and its association with luxury in Saint Domingue during this time. In the first half of the century, Shovlin contends, the word *luxury* was used disparagingly in reference to people who defied the social hierarchy by mimicking the consumption habits of their "superiors." After mid-century, the rising acquisition of wealth and goods meant that the differences in outer trappings between noble and non-noble became less evident. As a result, the traditional practice of deploying commodities to create political and social authority collapsed, and moralists began to argue against the relationship between consumption and social rank altogether.[23] The democratization of consumption thus spelled its downfall as a measure of social distinction. When consumer habits no longer reflected a preordained and fixed status, consumption became suspect as a signifier altogether.

The movement toward critique was not uniform, however. In fact, thanks to economists including Pierre Le Pesant de Boisguilbert, Richard Cantillon, and Jean-François Melon, luxury gained general acceptance between 1700 and 1730. Bernard Mandeville, whose *Fable of the Bees* was translated into French in 1740 and read widely, promoted luxurious consumption by the few as a benefit to society as a whole. By mid-century, Voltaire and the Abbé de Condillac had joined the pro-luxury ranks, and David Hume, whose *Essay on Luxury* was translated in 1752, was in high demand in salons around Paris. More pertinently, Abbé Raynal praised luxury and its reflection on French character in his history of the East and West Indies. For Raynal, the French desire for luxury goods (specifically those produced and consumed in the colonies) bespoke the French public's incomparable taste and its concomitant power: "The French dominate . . . in all things charming or magnificent; and their art of pleasing is one of the secrets of their fortune and their power."[24] Furthermore, Raynal argued, luxury had moral worth; desire for goods instilled in people the love of work, which was the "principle strength of states."[25] In Raynal's equation, a surfeit of desire had positive effects—the goods that circulated in the colony represented a hard-working and productive group of people whose efforts benefited both themselves and the state. Furthermore, consumer items themselves were invested with power. As an illustration of unparalleled French taste, luxury goods demonstrated the cultural superiority that was both an expression and a source of French dominance.

Despite Raynal's enthusiastic praise for luxury and its reflection on French character, the colony's association with luxury was certainly not a positive one. For example, one administrator who argued against colonial representation in the Estates General transformed Raynal's connection between goods and power into one between goods and excess: "It is necessary to have the colonies, where the surplus of culture, arts, and industry can find an easy outlet to be converted into luxury commodities."[26] By rhetorically conflating the colony with luxury, and associating both with immoderation, the administrator was then able to call for their regulation. Both luxury and the colony from which it emerged were unruly; they needed to be kept offshore and under control. However, the administrator's position was peculiar, given that the colonies produced the raw materials for luxury items consumed primarily in the metropole; the accusation of immoderation could have been directed just as easily at the French on the mainland. Though the French raided the colonies to create goods for France, the administrator displaced responsibility for this "luxurious" consumption onto colonists.

Yet the administrator's perception was not entirely surprising, given that mahogany and other forms of property gave colonists access to the symbols of extravagant lifestyles like those found in France. For some colonists, non-nobles by birth, consumption habits were markers of upward social mobility, providing access to roles and status unattainable in the metropole. Moreau de Saint-Méry, a Creole lawyer born in Martinique, commented on the tendency among colonists to show off their newfound wealth: "In Saint Domingue everything takes on a character of opulence such as to astonish Europeans."[27] As Moreau de Saint-Méry's comment intimates, observers often frowned upon the wealth and attendant status that colonists exhibited, deeming it excessive. Joan Dayan has pointed out that contemporary and historical analyses of the colony such as those written by Moreau de Saint-Méry, Hilliard d'Auberteuil, and Pierre de Vassière, tended to replicate the pervasive critical attitude toward consumption habits in the colony.[28] While perfectly naturalized and at times positively evaluated in the metropolitan context, the attachment to luxury and conspicuous consumption became ludicrous in the colony. "When does luxury become cheap?" Dayan asks rhetorically, "When Paris comes to Saint-Domingue."[29]

Mahogany furniture and those who owned it brought these differences into sharp contrast. While I have argued for mahogany's ubiquity based on newspaper advertisements placed by white colonists, there is anecdotal evidence that less privileged members of colonial society also laid claim to the wood. According to Moreau de Saint-Méry, it was not uncommon for mixed-race women in Saint Domingue to own mahogany furniture. Indeed, he included "one or two closets of the best mahogany" in his description of the humble home of the mixed-race woman.[30] Moreau de Saint-Méry's observation complicates the question of mahogany's significance in the colony by bringing the issues of race and gender into the equation. When mixed-race women obtained mahogany, how was its meaning transformed or the status of the owner reflected?

First, mixed-race women were the object of an extraordinary and prurient fascination on the part of colonists, who fixated on their alleged sensuality and feminine cunning. Thomas Phipps Howard, a British lieutenant who accompanied his regiment to Saint Domingue in 1795, admired the mixed-race women's unparalleled style as well as their affinity for fine linen and gold necklaces, rings, and bracelets.[31] Moreau de Saint-Méry marveled at their attachment to clothing,[32] and Baron de Wimpffen noticed how they set fashion trends: "Their favorite coiffure is an India handkerchief, which is bound around the head . . . they are the envy and despair of the white ladies, who aspire to imitate them."[33] The American Mary Hassal, who journeyed to the colony in 1802, echoed Baron de Wimpffen in her description of mixed-race women as the "hated but successful rivals" of Creole women.[34] Attraction to luxury highlighted the sensuality that was the key to the mixed-race woman's gain, both material and social, in the colony; her consumption created an image of superiority, taste, and "bodily perfections."[35] As other scholars have shown in different contexts, such sexualization could be a mode of domination, a way of manufacturing an image of the exotic that pinpointed women's identity and circumscribed their choices.[36]

There is indeed a thorny link between consumption and eroticization implied by the comments of white observers, both men and women. But mixed-race women could also capitalize on this association and use it as a technique for accumulating status and power in the colony. Moreau de Saint-Méry's casual remark about mahogany closets highlighted the self-fashioning that was central to the lives of mixed-race women. And as shown in an anecdote by Mary Hassal, mixed-race women in Saint Domingue used consumption as a way to differentiate themselves from both slaves and white women, thus creating a distinct identity and garnering authority within the colony. Hassal claimed that Creole women, jealous of their mixed-race rivals, agitated successfully for a law restricting the dress of mixed-race women. As a result of their efforts, mixed-race women were prohibited from wearing silk, a customary fabric, and they could not appear in public without a kerchief around their heads. According to Hassal, mixed-race women responded to the decree by remaining homebound. Hassal failed to explain how this simple act caused such an uproar, but she did mention that the law was injurious to commerce and that merchants in particular felt the sting. In fact, their complaints led to a reversal of the law.[37] Hassal's story reveals that mixed-race women's beauty and attraction to luxury attested not only to their sexualized role in colonial society, but to their status as consumers and to the power they derived from that association. Though her account smacks of hyperbole and is vague in detail, we may draw two conclusions from it. First, objects conferred status on the consumer that in certain contexts might overcome the limits of race. In trying both to imitate and to limit the consumption of mixed-race women, white women pointed to the cultural authority mixed-race women gained through their possessions. Second, mixed-race women's power as consumers had a rippling commercial effect. When they opted not to participate in the commerce of the colonies, their absence registered enough to warrant protest. Outside Saint Domingue, however, the consuming habits of mixed-race women crossed a forbidden yet unidentified boundary. The idea that mixed-race women might gain any social status was ludicrous in France. Part of what cheapened luxury in the colony, then, was its appropriation by racially subordinate groups.[38]

The case of mixed-race women gets to the crux of the problem with mahogany. Colonial opulence was not solely defined by the transmission of metropolitan habits. It was also determined by who copied those habits. Taken out of context, and exploited by the wrong people, the French penchant for luxury goods, and the connection between objects and identity, became an embarrassment rather than an asset. French identity may indeed have been visible in ownership of French objects, but only if one was proper to claim it. In Saint Domingue, concerns about who owned what were paramount. Indeed, the primacy of money and the possessions that reflected wealth suggests that race was not always the most reliable indicator of power, at least as measured along cultural lines.

Colonists were of course acutely aware of variations in skin color. Moreau de Saint-Méry, for example, described an exhaustive classificatory scheme that measured "blackness" through the tiniest of fractions.[39] And Baron de Wimpffen claimed that any degree of blackness was degrading in relationship to whiteness:

> The natural consequence of the order of things which prevails here, is, that all those titles of honour which are elsewhere the pabula of emulation, of rivalry, and of discord; which inspire so much pride, and create so many claims in some, so much ambition and envy in others, shrink to nothing and entirely disappear before the sole title of white.[40]

Baron de Wimpffen's words generally ring true for a society where the vast majority of the population was enslaved and could claim no status. Yet for the small percentage of mixed-race inhabitants, the evidence is contradictory and suggests that race was indicative rather than definitive in measuring social status. Certainly whiteness counted, and being of mixed race severely restricted one's choices and civil freedoms in Saint Domingue. But in a society where money translated into rank, some nonwhites raised the bar. In the southern province especially, free men of color became successful landowners whose income placed them ahead of many *petits blancs* in the colony. Mixed-race ownership of luxury items like mahogany came dangerously close to upsetting the hierarchy of wealth that had been established in Saint Domingue.

Yet race, as alluded to by Baron de Wimpffen above, was definitive in another way. With slavery, colonists pushed the limits of just what categories luxury encompassed and how far this opulence could go. Later in his text, Baron de Wimpffen elaborated on the relationship between slave ownership and status in the colony: "That crowd of slaves who await the orders and even the signals of one man, confers an air of grandeur upon whoever gives the orders."[41] In this comment, Baron de Wimpffen exposed the relationship between status and possession at its most extreme. In Saint Domingue law sanctioned a category of property unavailable to those in the metropole: slaves. Baron de Wimpffen's depiction of colonial life,

where people were literally objectified, implied that slave ownership created a kind of rank unavailable in France.

In Saint Domingue, where money trumped inherited rank, status fell into the hands of the wrong people in a number of ways. Luxury became cheap first because it was given over to the new rich, and second because it slowly became available to free men and women of color. But most egregiously, luxury spun out of control when it became attached to slave ownership. This, finally, was the most unforgivable step. Colonists surpassed the metropole redefining not just the boundaries but the nature of luxury by purchasing not just mahogany furniture, but also members of a mahogany race.

Notes

1. Victor Advielle, *L'Odyssée d'un Normand à Saint-Domingue au dix-huitième siècle* (Paris: Challamel, 1901), 137. Advielle traveled to Saint Domingue twice, the first time in 1767 or 1768, and the second time in 1771. His second visit lasted ten years.
2. Francis Alexander Stanislaus, Baron de Wimpffen, *A Voyage to Saint Domingo, in the Years 1788, 1789, and 1790*, trans. J. Wright (London: T. Cadell, 1797), 83–84. Wimpffen's satiric writing, with its nostalgia for the landed wealth of France, often betrayed physiocratic tendencies. His critique of luxury went hand in hand with his critique of merchants and their threat to the independent, thriving landowner.
3. *Encyclopédie, ou Dictionnaire raisonné des sciences, des arts et des métiers par une societé des gens de lettres*, ed. Denis Diderot and Jean Le Rond d'Alembert (1751—65; reprint ed., New York: Readex Microprint Corp., 1969), 1: 650.
4. Gabriel Debien, *Esprit colon et esprit d'autonomie à Saint-Domingue au XVIIIe siècle*, 2nd ed. (Paris: Larose, 1954), 9.
5. For an excellent overview of the history of consumption in Western Europe, see *Consumption and the World of Goods*, ed. John Brewer and Roy Porter (London: Routledge, 1993). Two books stand out in the French and French colonial context: Daniel Roche's superb study of popular culture in Paris during the eighteenth century, and Gabriel Debien's detailed reconstruction of the social fabric of plantation slavery in the Antilles. See Daniel Roche, *The People of Paris: An Essay in Popular Culture in the 18th Century*, trans. Marie Evans with Gwynne Lewis (Berkeley: University of California Press, 1987); and Gabriel Debien, *Les esclaves aux Antilles françaises, XVIIe-XVIIIe siècles* (Basse-Terre: Société d'Histoire de la Guadeloupe, 1974). Finally, a recent book of essays skillfully treats the relationship between luxury and consumption: *Luxury in the Eighteenth Century: Debates, Desires and Delectable Goods*, ed. Maxine Berg and Elizabeth Eger (Basingstoke: Palgrave MacMillan, 2002).
6. Statistics for the colony are notoriously uneven. The numbers cited here are closest to those quoted by Moreau de Saint-Méry, a Creole lawyer born in Martinique, whose history and description of Saint Domingue remains the most important sourcebook for understanding the geography, politics, and social composition of Saint Domingue up to 1789. He gives the following statistics: 452,000 slaves, 40,000 whites, 28,000 *gens de couleur* (free men and women of color). See Médéric-Louis-Élie Moreau de Saint-Méry, *Déscription topographique, physique, civile, politique et historique de la partie Française de L'isle Saint-Domingue* (1797; Paris: Société Française d'Histoire d'Outre-Mer, 1984), 1: 28. The official government census gives the following figures for 1789: 465,429 slaves, 30,826 whites, and 27,548 *gens de couleur*. Cited in Charles Frostin, *Les révoltes blanches à Saint-Domingue aux XVIIe et XVIIIe siècles* (Poitiers: Aubin, 1975), 28. Thomas Ott gives the 1787 breakdown as follows: 24,000 whites, 20,000 *gens de couleur*, and 408,000 slaves. He draws his evidence from the *Times* (London) January 7, 1792. See *The Haitian Revolution, 1789–1804* (Knoxville: University of Tennessee Press, 1973), 9, 23. Carolyn Fick has specified the range of population statistics: slaves have been numbered from 452,000 to 700,000; whites from 30,000 to 40,000; and *gens de couleur* from 24,000 to 37,800. See *The Making of Haiti: The Saint-Domingue Revolution from Below* (Knoxville: University of Tennessee Press, 1990), 278, n. 14.
7. For an excellent and concise narrative of the Haitian Revolution, see Part 2, "The Revolution from Below," of Lester Langley, *The Americas in the Age of Revolution, 1750–1850* (New Haven, CT: Yale University Press, 1996).
8. *Courrier National de Saint-Domingue*, no. 48, April 24, 1791.

9. *Gazette de Saint-Domingue, Politique, Civile, Économique et Littéraire, et Affiches Américaines*, 1, no. 32, April 20, 1791.

10. Ibid., no. 52, supplement, October 29, 1791.

11. *Moniteur Général de la Partie Française de Saint-Domingue*, 1, no. 88, February 10, 1792.

12. For further evidence, see ibid. v. 1, nos. 65 (January 17, 1792) and 151 (April 13,1792).

13. Between September 26 and October 17, 1791, 23 boats left Port-au-Prince with 400 feet of beams of mahogany, as compared to 100,000 feet of other woods. See *Gazette de Saint-Domingue*, 1, no. 51, October 22, 1791.

14. Gabriel Debien, *Un Colon sur sa plantation* (Dakar: Publications de la Section d'Histoire, 1959), 14.

15. The notary was most likely referring to the currency of the colony, which was worth two-thirds that of the metropole. See Ivor D. Spencer's explanation in his introduction to Médéric-Louis-Élie Moreau de Saint-Méry, *A Civilization that Perished: The Last Years of White Colonial Rule in Haiti*, trans. and ed. Ivor D. Spencer (Lanham, MD: University Press of America, 1985), xii.

16. *Moniteur Général*, 1, no. 90, February 1, 1792.

17. Geneviève Souchal, *French Eighteenth-Century Furniture*, trans. Simon Watson Taylor (New York: G. P. Putnam's Sons, 1961), 14.

18. Jacqueline Viaux, *French Furniture*, trans. Hazel Paget (New York: Putnam, 1964), 120; Roger De Félice, *French Furniture under Louis XVI and the Empire*, trans. F. M. Atkinson (London: William Heinemann, 1920), 49.

19. Paul Langford, *A Polite and Commercial People: England 1727—1783* (Oxford: Clarendon Press, 1989), 69; Souchal, *French Eighteenth-Century Furniture*, 90.

20. Baron de Wimpffen, *Voyage to Saint Domingo*, 173.

21. Louis Malfoy, *Le Meuble de Port* (Paris: Éditions de l'Amateur, 1992).

22. Daniel Roche, *France in the Enlightenment*, trans. Arthur Goldhammer (Cambridge, MA: Harvard University Press, 1998), 562.

23. John Shovlin, "The Cultural Politics of Luxury in Eighteenth-Century France," *French Historical Studies* 23 (Fall 2000): 577–606.

24. Abbé Guillaume-Thomas Raynal, *Histoire philosophique et politique des établissements et du commerce des Européens dans les Deux Indes* (1770; Paris: Amable Costes et Cie, 1820), 10: 228.

25. Ibid.

26. *Réflexions d'un administrateur, sur l'admission des deputés de St. Domingue, aux États Généraux, et sur le régime nouveau qu'ils veulent établir dans cette Colonie* (Paris, s.d. [1787/8]), 4. British Museum, FR 401.

27. Moreau de Saint-Méry, *Déscription topographique*, 1: 28.

28. Joan Dayan, *Haiti, History, and the Gods* (Berkeley: University of California Press, 1995), 172; Michel René Hilliard d'Auberteuil, *Considérations sur l'état présent de la colonie française de Saint-Domingue* (Paris: Grangé, 1776); Pierre de Vaissière, *Saint-Domingue: La société et la vie créole sous L'Ancien Régime (1629–1789)* (Paris: Perrin et Cie, 1909).

29. Dayan, *Haiti, Hisory, and The Gods*, 172.

30. Moreau de Saint-Méry, *Civilization that Perished*, 83.

31. *The Haitian Journal of Lieutenant Howard, York Hussars, 1796–1798*, ed. Roger Norman Buckley (Knoxville: University of Tennessee Press, 1985), 104.

32. Moreau de Saint-Méry, *Civilization that Perished*, 83.

33. Baron de Wimpffen, *Voyage to Saint Domingo*, 114.

34. Mary Hassal [Leonora Sansay], *Secret History, Written by a Lady at Cape François to Colonel Burr* (Freeport, NY: Books for Library Press, 1971), 77.

35. *Haitian Journal of Lieutenant Howard*, 104.

36. On the relation between sexual fantasy, domination, and the creation of the exotic in the Asian context, see Anne Stoler, "Carnal Knowledge and Imperial Power: Gender, Race, and Morality in Colonial Asia," in *Gender at the Crossroads of Knowledge: Feminist Anthropology in the Postmodern Era*, ed. Michaela de Leonardo (Berkeley: University of California Press, 1991). Anne McClintock writes on the British case in *Imperial Leather: Race, Gender and Sexuality in the Colonial Conquest* (New York: Routledge, 1995).

37. Hassal, *Secret History*, 77.

38. Anxieties about proper clothing were widespread in the colony. Sumptuary laws for slaves began around 1720, and the emergence of these laws, along with comments made by travelers in the colony, suggests both that slaves made efforts to embellish their appearance, and that colonists found such efforts threatening. Their fears were well grounded in one sense: as Gabriel Debien has pointed out, a well-dressed maroon (fugitive slave) could, for example, pass as a free black. See *Les esclaves aux Antilles françaises,* 247. Not all blacks were slaves, and not all slaves had the same rank. By insisting that their rank be visibly identifiable, colonists could distinguish among different black inhabitants and treat them accordingly.
39. Moreau de Saint-Méry, *Déscription topographique*, 1: 89–100.
40. Baron de Wimpffen, *Voyage to Saint Domingo*, 63.
41. Ibid, 173.

CHAPTER 3

A Wanton Chase in a Foreign Place: Hogarth and the Gendering of Exoticism in the Eighteenth-Century Interior

DAVID PORTER

Once the exclusive domain of collectors and connoisseurs, the furnishings that adorned the eighteenth-century interior have begun—as the essays in this volume amply attest—to attract the interest and admiration of scholars intrigued by the rich and varied contexts of their production and consumption. The eighteenth century has proven especially fertile ground for a cultural history of domestic objects in part, of course, because there were many more such objects in circulation than there had been in any earlier period, thanks to expanding consumer markets and the ever-increasing allure of novelty and fashion across all social strata. But these card tables and writing desks, candelabras and cellarets also acquired layers of meaning—and hence interest for cultural historians—from the ideas and debates that circulated alongside them. In eighteenth-century Britain, two of the most important of these discursive contexts were a fascination with the foreign and the exotic, on the one hand, and with philosophical questions regarding the nature of taste and beauty on the other. The intersection of these two concerns can be seen nowhere more clearly than in the craze for Chinese furnishings—including lacquerware chests and fire screens, but also wallpapers, porcelain vases and statues, and of course tea wares—that made a "Chinese room" de rigueur among fashionable households of the mid-eighteenth century. The emergence of the Chinese taste in furnishings within the space of these intersecting concerns stamped Chinese objects with a set of profoundly gendered meanings that have persisted, in some degree, to this day. This chapter will examine this gendering of the Chinese taste through the works of one of the most prominent artists and aesthetic theorists of the eighteenth century, William Hogarth.

Popular conceptions of beauty today most clearly betray their eighteenth-century origins in their emphatic insistence on disinterestedness as a precondition of artistic value. Theorists from Shaftesbury to Kant argued that a pure experience of the beautiful required a state of transcendent aloofness from the yearnings of the flesh and the pull of ideological attachments.[1] Aesthetic experience is meant to be a chaste, strictly nonpartisan affair; the depth of pleasure it can afford is owing precisely to the freedom it offers from the merely contingent and material. The fact that for many modern viewers, erotic art always teeters precariously on the edge of pornography, and that patriotic art hovers dangerously close to propagandistic kitsch suggests the lasting power of this conception. We are skeptical of the aesthetic value of images suggestive of sexuality or national pride because the desires and attachments conjured up by such images would seem to preclude the disinterested experience of the formal qualities of the work.

The line from Shaftesbury to Kant, however, is not without its serpentine twists and detours. Edmund Burke struggles mightily, in his *Philosophical Enquiry into the Origin of our Ideas of the Sublime and Beautiful*, to sustain a clear distinction between a pure aesthetic love for beauty and an animal lust for the attractive women in whom he clearly found beauty most frequently incarnate. One reason, however, that we hear so much less about his account of the beautiful in the *Enquiry* than about his theory of the sublime is that he is embarrassingly unsuccessful at sustaining this distinction. Whereas Kant has the good sense to limit his examples of beauty to such unproblematic objects as flowers and arabesque designs, Burke severely compromises his credibility as an impartial arbiter of aesthetic value by basing his catalog of the empirical attributes of beauty on his close observation of sexually attractive young women, invoking their lisps, tottering steps, and even feigned distresses as emblems of a universal aesthetic ideal. In his discussion of the importance of "gradual variation" as a formal quality of beauty, for example, he writes with the air of a seasoned connoisseur,

> Observe that part of a beautiful woman where she is perhaps the most beautiful, about the neck and breasts; the smoothness, the softness; the easy and insensible swell; the variety of the surface, which is never for the smallest space the same; the deceitful maze, through which the unsteady eye slides giddily, without knowing where to fix, or whither it is carried.[2]

To corroborate his argument, Burke cites the opinion of "the very ingenious Mr. Hogarth," pointing to Hogarth's famous line of beauty—an elongated S-shaped curve that was meant to represent the highest aesthetic ideal—as if to vindicate his otherwise perhaps too obvious delectation of the female form.[3] But Burke's more important debt to Hogarth goes conspicuously unacknowledged, and that is precisely the invocation of the beautiful, living woman as the cornerstone of an empiricist aesthetic theory. Hogarth's *Analysis of Beauty* (1753), more than any other aesthetic treatise of the period, rejects the Shaftesburian requirement of disinterestedness as a precondition of the experience of beauty, and indeed revels in the possibilities of sensuality and eroticism as components of aesthetic pleasure. According to Ronald Paulson, "Hogarth is attempting to create an aesthetics that acknowledges that if we place a beautiful woman on a pedestal we will inevitably and appropriately desire her and may discover, moreover, that she is not strictly virtuous." It is an aesthetics of "novelty, variety, intricacy, [and] curiosity" that foregrounds the pleasures of the chase and the tantalizing deferral of discovery, an "aesthetics of seeing under or into" that vindicates the natural wantonness of the wandering gaze.[4]

Not surprisingly, this aspect of Hogarth's theory has troubled not only adherents of the doctrine of disinterestedness, but also students of the artist's famous moral satires—such as *The Harlot's Progress* and *Industry and Idleness*—which often convey a decidedly more somber tone. As Paulson points out, "an aesthetics in which sensation and pleasure replace moral judgment apparently contradicts the tenor of [Hogarth's] major works." Thus Wallace Jackson dismisses the *Analysis of Beauty* as "a strangely eccentric document," while other art historians have attempted to neutralize its radical eccentricity by reading it merely as a "rationalization of observed rococo principles."[5] Joseph Burke, who produced the first scholarly edition of the *Analysis* in 1955, likewise tries to redeem the text from the unsettling charge of voyeuristic licentiousness by proposing a reassuringly chaste reading of one of the most pivotal and suggestive phrases in the work. Formal intricacy, Hogarth famously asserts, gives rise to the pleasurable experience we know as beauty by leading the eye on "a wanton kind of chase." Burke suggests that the word *wanton* here is without moral or sexual connotations, and rather means simply "free and frolicsome."[6] Certainly, such an understanding of visual pleasure would appear to be accurate much of the time in practice, as when the eye wanders over an intricately carved rococo ornament. But it is disingenuous to deny the sexually charged overtones of the phrase itself and of the imagery Hogarth deploys in illustrating and explaining it. The *Oxford English Dictionary* quotes Shakespeare, Arbuthnot, and Samuel Johnson, among others, using the word *wanton* in the sense of lascivious or given to amorous dalliance. And the intricate objects that most frequently catch the eye, in Hogarth's account, are not ornamental carvings, but beautiful women. Nor are these the idealized beauties of classical statuary, held safely aloof from the realm of earthly desire by their transcendence of the particularities of actual bodies, but rather the living women of Southwark Fair and Covent Garden. "Who but a bigot," Hogarth famously asks, "will say that he has not seen faces and necks, hands and arms in living women, that even the Grecian Venus doth but coarsely imitate?" These women, moreover, are consistently presented as the objects of an explicitly eroticized gaze. Like the wanton ringlets adorning the fair head of Milton's Eve, "the many waving and contrasted turns of [their] naturally intermingling locks ravish the eye with the pleasure of pursuit." The fashionable adornments of Eve's postlapsarian progeny serve only to heighten the effect: while a naked body soon satiates the eye, Hogarth says, "when it is artfully cloath'd and decorated, the mind at every turn resumes its imaginary pursuits concerning it."[7]

The unabashed eroticism that informs Hogarth's conception of aesthetic experience poses a problem for those who would preserve the phenomenology of beauty from the tyranny of desire. Within the context of Hogarth's text, however, it also presents a second, less frequently considered conundrum. Not the least of Hogarth's radical departures from the established norms of contemporary aesthetic theory is his insistence on the universal accessibility of the aesthetic experience he describes. Whereas Shaftesbury and later Hume depict a sanctified realm of high art whose full enjoyment is limited to an elite cadre of cultivated men of taste, Hogarth insists "that no one may be deterr'd, by the want of . . . previous knowledge, from entering into this enquiry." This anti-academic, populist gesture is clearly intended primarily to undercut the monopoly on taste held by that wealthy class of connoisseurs that was the consistent object of Hogarth's disdain. But Hogarth appears sensitive to the exclusions of gender as well as class implicit in the received ideal of the man of taste: he holds out the promise of aesthetic edification to all readers of his book, "ladies, as well as gentlemen."[8] Given this conspicuous commitment to inclusiveness, it is striking that women are entirely absent as aesthetic subjects throughout the remainder of the text. When the gaze is gendered in the *Analysis*, it is inevitably gendered male. And when a human body figures as the object of aesthetic contemplation, it is, without exception, female. The hegemony of the male gaze is, obviously, an all-too-familiar dynamic in any number of historical contexts. Within the specific context of an iconoclastic work, however, that claims to present a universally valid theory of beauty to readers of both sexes, an aesthetic so closely modeled on the dynamics of an exclusively heterosexual male desire seems especially problematic. Where, we are left to wonder, do the eyes of Hogarth's women turn in their own pursuit of aesthetic pleasure? And how can one account for Hogarth's silence on this point?

Though the well-documented excesses of male foppery in the eighteenth century suggest that the beaux of the period expected a certain reciprocity in aesthetic desire between the sexes, Hogarth's adjudication of the human physique according to the serpentine line of beauty rules out a strict equivalency of pleasure. A simple comparison of the relative appeal of a series of increasingly curvaceous lines illustrated in one of the two plates accompanying the text proves for Hogarth "how much the form of a woman's body surpasses in beauty that of a man."[9] Should the female reader be disheartened by this revelation, she will find in the same plates no shortage of suitably curvaceous alternatives—including corsets, table legs, candlesticks, fingers, and leg bones—provided for her delectation (Figure 3.1). As captivating as some of these emblems of the line of beauty surely are, one can't escape the conclusion that those readers who don't share Hogarth's lusty delight in the spectacle of a consummately attractive woman are somehow getting the short end of the stick.

If Hogarth is silent on the question of women's aesthetic proclivities in *The Analysis of Beauty*, a review of his visual oeuvre suggests that it is not for a lack of information. Not surprisingly, the attractive woman figures prominently as an aesthetic object in many of his paintings and engravings. What is surprising is the number of women Hogarth depicts as aesthetic agents and the uniformity, in one crucial respect, of their aesthetic preferences. The most important literary source for popular conceptions of female taste in the early eigh-

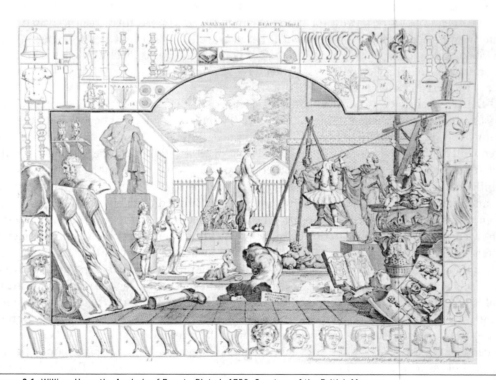

Figure 3.1 William Hogarth, *Analysis of Beauty*, Plate I, 1753. Courtesy of the British Museum.

teenth century is, without a doubt, Alexander Pope's poem, *The Rape of the Lock*. Hogarth's early illustration of the poem, showing a distracted Belinda seated with her companions at tea, reminds us that the taste of wealthy women, at least, tended toward the foreign and the exotic (Figure 3.2). Within the poem, Belinda's tea-drinking habit is associated with vanity, extravagance, and luxury, to be sure, but it is also the mark of a particular aesthetic sensibility privileging rare foreign commodities that tend, according to Pope, to glitter, glow, and shine. The historical context of the reference to tea drinking is the rapidly expanding China trade of the East India Company, a trade that by the 1720s had established the tea party as the preeminent site for the conspicuous display of a woman's taste and social status.[10] Hogarth's early conversation pieces conspicuously illustrate the importance both of tea drinking as a social ritual and of the tea service itself as a marker of wealth and refinement. But imported porcelains and other examples of the fashionable Chinese taste crop up regularly in the satirical works as well, most frequently as a symbol of corrupted taste and, by implication, debauched morality, as in the second plate of *Marriage à la Mode* (which I discuss below), or as an exemplar of the absurd excesses of modern fashion, as in *Taste in High Life*.

So, if Hogarth was clearly aware of a widely held belief in the affinity of female taste for a particular class of exotic commodities, why is there no mention of this taste in *The Analysis of Beauty*? One might have thought that a shapely Chinese vase or teapot would have provided a more visually appealing exemplar of the formal principles he describes than a human leg bone, and that it would have offered the added advantage of being a familiar object that many of his readers would have readily recognized as reflecting their own decorative tastes.

Indeed, Chinese import wares of the period perfectly exemplify many of the aesthetic values Hogarth champions in the *Analysis*. The unique qualities of porcelain itself—purity, smoothness, translucence, delicacy—bespeak the refined elegance and gentility that, as Paulson argues, are at the very center of Hogarth's creed. Many of the shapely objects into which Chinese potters fashioned this magical material likewise demonstrated the truth of Hogarth's claims for the visual power of the serpentine line of beauty. Even the imaginative exercise he advocates as a means of recognizing the lines of beauty in complex three-dimensional objects would seem to be modeled on the visual experience of a thin, translucent

Figure 3.2 William Hogarth, A Scene from *The Rape of the Lock*, engraving for the lid of a snuff box, date unknown. Courtesy of the British Museum.

porcelain vessel: "let every object under our consideration, be imagined to have its inward contents scoop'd out so nicely, as to have nothing of it left but a thin shell, exactly corresponding both in its inner and outer surface, to the shape of the object itself."[11]

One might expect, moreover, that as a champion of the rococo style, Hogarth would have found in chinoiserie more generally a set of decorative principles much in accord with his own. The designers of the Chinese and Chinese-styled silks, fire screens, wall hangings, furniture, and even garden buildings that were colonizing contemporary English sitting rooms and country gardens adhered fastidiously to the rules of intricacy, variety, asymmetry, and nonlinearity he would promote in the *Analysis*. While these compositional attributes guaranteed the formal complexity necessary to engage the eye in its wanton wanderings, Chinese goods in their inescapable exoticism also invited imaginative play on another level entirely. The radical unfamiliarity of their visual language, the obscurity of their local meanings and cultural points of reference would have presented to the Hogarthian viewer an occasion for imaginative pleasure every bit as alluring as its surface design. For Hogarth, after all, it is not only the eye that seeks diversion in art but the mind as well.

> The active mind is ever bent to be employ'd. Pursuing is the business of our lives; and even abstracted from any other view, gives pleasure. Every arising difficulty, that for a while attends and interrupts the pursuit, gives a sort of spring to the mind, enhances the pleasure, and makes what would else be toil and labour, become sport and recreation.[12]

The essence of exoticism as an aesthetic attribute, I would argue, is that it erects precisely such a pleasing barrier to the immediate assimilation of a visual spectacle, a teasing sense of alienation from the familiar every bit as captivating as the wanton ringlets of a lover's flowing hair.

For a whole host of reasons, then, one would reasonably expect Hogarth to recognize and acknowledge the considerable aesthetic appeal of the Chinese goods his readers purchased and admired. And indeed, scholars have established that he owned a number of decidedly chinoiserie pieces himself.[13] Yet in *The Analysis of Beauty*, when the Chinese style is mentioned at all, it is summarily dismissed as an absurd and foolish taste unworthy of the least serious consideration. In a passage about the ubiquity of his line of beauty in depictions of the deities of classical civilizations, Hogarth remarks on the contrast presented by the Chinese case. "How absolutely void of these turns are the pagodas of China, and what a mean taste runs through most of their attempts in painting and sculpture, notwithstanding they finish with such excessive neatness."[14] Hogarth's manuscript notes on academies and the Society of Arts confirm this disparaging view of Chinese artistic production: in a discussion of the appropriate education for young artists, he praises English fabric designers for copying "the objects they introduce from nature; a much surer guide than all the childish and ridiculous absurdities of temples, dragons, pagodas, and other fantastic fripperies, which have been imported from China."[15]

In light both of these seemingly compelling reasons that Hogarth should have looked more kindly on these fantastic fripperies, and the circumstantial evidence that, in fact, he sometimes did, why does he lash out with such uncompromising fury against the popularity of the Chinese taste? A number of possible explanations immediately suggest themselves. To begin with, Hogarth's criticism of Chinese art on the grounds that it did not adhere to conventions of naturalistic representation was a commonplace one at the time. Although Hogarth rejected a classicist conception of nature as idealized form, he believed strongly that nature in its infinite variety was the artist's most trustworthy guide. To the extent, then, that Chinese art seemed to flout any standard of verisimilitude, it was beyond the pale of even Hogarth's postclassicist sensibilities. Furthermore, the popularity of the Chinese style surely grated on Hogarth's keenly developed sense of aesthetic nationalism. While perhaps weakening the claims of the highbrow connoisseurs to being the sole arbiters of fashionable taste, Chinese imports, like old Italian paintings, nonetheless threatened the livelihood of the native-born English artists Hogarth saw it as his mission to promote. To the extent that Chinese art seemed to replicate the rococo stylistics he espoused, there was all the more reason to repudiate it forcefully as a foreign usurper of English artistic glory.

I am more intrigued, however, by a third, less immediately obvious explanation for his disdain— an explanation that returns to the problem in the *Analysis* I raised at the beginning of this essay. Hogarth's repeated insistence on the worthlessness of the Chinese style, I would like to suggest, is intimately bound up with his perplexing silence on the question of female aesthetic agency. A closer look at some of the many contemporary literary and visual representations of Chinese goods and their domestic consumption will help to elaborate this connection. As in *The Rape of the Lock*, Chinese import goods figure prominently in these works as emblems of female vanity and extravagance. More intriguingly, though, their physical qualities are often compared to those of the women who collect them. Both fine ladies and fine porcelain, the familiar simile goes, are prized for their smooth surfaces and radiant splendor, but they are equally fragile as well, and are soon despised for the appearance of a crack or flaw. The analogy could, at times, appear so compelling as to elide any remaining differences between them. In *Royalty, Episcopacy, and Law*, for example, Hogarth imagines a courtly lady as a pastiche of exotic commodities, including a fan for a body and a teapot for a head (Figure 3.3); in a contemporary poem entitled "Tea, or Ladies into China-Cups," the anonymous poet effects a like transmutation of English women into the porcelain vessels of which they are so enamored.[16]

From the perspective of female aesthetic agency, the implications of an imagined identity between female consumers and the objects of their consumption are suggestive, to say the least. If women, in their pursuit of beauty, turn to objects that either resemble or are understood as synecdochical extensions of themselves, the result is an entirely self-contained, self-reflexive economy of female desire. Whether this economy is figured as narcissistic or homoerotic, it inevitably leaves male participants in the drama in the unaccustomed role of passive, powerless spectators. And indeed, those writers who imaginatively pursue the consequences of women's infatuation with Chinese goods invariably figure men as frustrated and jealous rivals, deprived by porcelain vases and teapots of attentions that might otherwise have been theirs. An enigma-solving contest in an issue of the *Woman's Almanack* of 1741 features an intricate, rhymed riddle about a Chinese teapot. "Here the fair Nymphs with each becoming Grace, And studied Art, my varied Charms embrace; Oh! what wou'd Lovers give, cou'd they command So warm a Pressure from their fair one's Hand." John Gay's poem, "To a Lady on her Passion for Old China," similarly laments a lover's displacement by imported exotica: "What ecstasies her bosom fire! How her eyes languish with desire! How blessed, how happy should I be, Were that fond glance bestowed on me! New doubts and fears within me war: What rival's near? A China jar."[17]

This dynamic of displacement is taken to its logical conclusion in a long pornographic poem called *A Chinese Tale* published in 1740. Described as "a tale in the Chinese taste," the mock-heroic fantasy recounts the adventures of the coy and beautiful maid-of-honor Cham-yam as she repels the advances of legions of desperately adoring mandarins. One

Figure 3.3 William Hogarth, *Royalty, Episcopacy, and the Law*, 1724. Courtesy of the Royal Pavilion Art Gallery, Brighton.

of these suitors bribes a maid to conceal him in his tormenter's private chambers, where he watches from inside a large China jar as she masturbates in front of a mirror. The sight sets his soul ablaze, and he bursts from his jar to rape her. What is most interesting to me about the poem, apart from its rather remarkable frontispiece (Figure 3.4), is the setting Cham-yam chooses for her self-pleasuring and the state of mind the decor seems to induce. The room is furnished in the height of the Chinese taste, with motifs of dragons and gilt flowers adorning the ceiling and, as we see here, the furniture. These are juxtaposed with the lavishly described lewd paintings lining the walls, cabinets full of erotic curiosities, and bookshelves lined with novels and romances. Reclining on a sofa amidst all this splendor, Cham-yam's mind wanders over scenes of the triumphs of her sex.

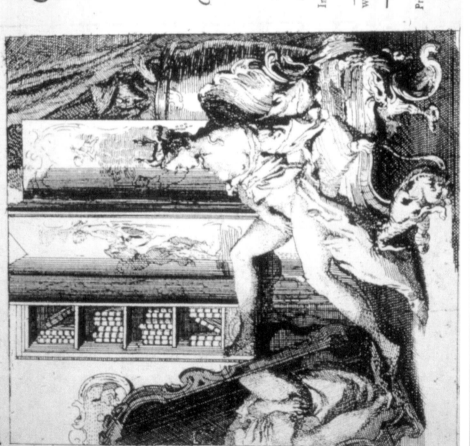

Figure 3.4 Frontispiece and title page to *A Chinese Tale*, 1740. Courtesy of the Institute for Sex Research.

All languishing, supine she lay, Revolving over all that's gay: The Charms of Woman, and her Pow'r, From the Creation to that Hour: What Ravages! what Devastations! What Havoc caus'd among the Nations! What Slaves they made of lordly Man! When sudden thus the Dame began.[18]

While the theme of women's sexual power is a commonplace one, its triangulation here with vivid spectacles of chinoiserie and autoeroticism suggests a powerful and deeply resonant association between the aesthetics of Chinese exoticism and the potentially unsettling specter of female autonomy and self-determination.[19]

A more familiar and genteel locus of male anxiety about the wantonness of women's taste and power was the tea table itself. In an engraving called *The Tea Table* (1710), the social consumption of tea is depicted as a site of viciously malignant female gossip (Figure 3.5). The theme here is homosocial rather than autoerotic self-indulgence, but the iconography is familiar: just as in *The Chinese Tale*, male observers appear only as exiled, marginal figures, while a prominent display of Chinese porcelain suggests the aesthetic context of the women's transgression. The porcelain cabinet also draws our eyes to the devilish figure chasing Justice from the room. Justice appears to have dropped her sword, which lies broken on the floor next to a curiously intact china teacup. This pair of objects conspicuously inverts the iconic cliché of feminine china meeting its ruin at the hands of an impetuously phallic masculinity and provides a striking commentary on the reversal of roles enacted in this scene.

Figure 3.5 *The Tea-Table.* 1710. Courtesy of the British Museum.

Figure 3.6 William Hogarth, *Marriage à la Mode*, Plate II, 1745. Courtesy of the British Museum.

The same pair of icons appears again in the second plate of Hogarth's *Marriage à la Mode* (Figure 3.6). The broken sword on the floor at the husband's feet figures all the more obviously here as a sign of languid, frustrated masculinity; the wife's tea service, elevated and intact, provides a contrasting echo of her own wantonness and excess. It echoes, as well, the debauched taste revealed by the collection of Chinese figures on the mantelpiece above her head. Here Hogarth graphically illustrates his principal charges against the Chinese taste: that it is absurd, inelegant, and unnatural. But this plate, read in the context of the period's rampant associations between Chinese goods and an extravagant, wanton femininity also suggests an answer to the question of female aesthetic agency in the *Analysis* with which we began. Hogarth rejected the Chinese style as an alternative to classicism, I would propose, not so much out of a considered repudiation of its underlying aesthetic values, but rather out of a sobering recognition that to grant the validity of the Chinese taste would be to legitimate a regime not only of female aesthetic self-determination, but also of the autonomy of female desire more generally conceived. As a theorist of art, Hogarth radically asserted the emancipatory power of a spontaneous aesthetic experience unconstrained by classicist pieties. But his gestures of inclusiveness notwithstanding, he stopped short of extending this freedom to women. While beauty could henceforth be safely admired in English as well as Italian paintings, it was still to remain the exclusive preserve of European artists and of a predominantly masculine gaze. To accommodate the errant wanderings of the wanton female eye would have been to invite a wholesale defection from the Western artistic tradition and from the social and sexual order of which it was a well-established part. And this was a travesty that our hero, canon-busting iconoclast and aesthetic libertine though he surely was, finally proved unable to countenance.

ACKNOWLEDGMENTS

This chapter first appeared in *Studies in Eighteenth-Century Culture* 33, ed. Catherine Ingrassia and Jeffrey S. Ravel (Baltimore, MD: Johns Hopkins University Press, 2004). It is reprinted here with the kind permission of the American Society for Eighteenth-Century Studies.

Notes

1. On the history and implications of disinterestedness as a component of the aesthetic attitude, see Jerome Stolnitz, "On the Origin of Aesthetic Disinterestedness," *Journal of Aesthetics and Art Criticism* 20 (1961): 131–43, and Elizabeth Bohls, "Disinterestedness and the Denial of the Particular: Locke, Smith, and the Subject of Aesthetics," in *Eighteenth-Century Aesthetics and the Reconstruction of Art*, ed. Paul Mattick (New York: Cambridge University Press, 1993).
2. Edmund Burke, *A Philosophical Enquiry into the Origin of our Ideas of the Sublime and Beautiful*, ed. James T. Boulton (Notre Dame, IN: University of Notre Dame Press, 1968), 115.
3. Ibid.
4. Ronald Paulson, Introduction to William Hogarth, *The Analysis of Beauty*, ed. Paulson (New Haven, CT: Yale University Press, 1997), xxxiii, xxxvii, xlix.
5. Ibid., xi; Wallace Jackson, "Hogarth's *Analysis*: The Fate of a Late Rococo Document," *SEL* 6 (1966): 543–50; Joseph Burke, Introduction to Hogarth, *The Analysis of Beauty*, ed. Burke (Oxford: Clarendon Press, 1955), xlvi–xlvii.
6. Ibid., li.
7. Hogarth, *Analysis*, ed. Paulson, 59, 34–35, 40.
8. Ibid., 18.
9. Ibid., 49.
10. See the chapters on tea in Elizabeth Kowaleski-Wallace, *Consuming Subjects: Women, Shopping, and Business in the Eighteenth Century* (New York: Columbia University Press, 1997), 19–72; and James Walvin, *The Fruits of Empire: Exotic Produce and British Taste, 1660–1800* (New York: New York University Press, 1997), 9–31.
11. Hogarth, *Analysis*, ed. Paulson, 21.
12. Ibid., 32.
13. Lars Tharp, *Hogarth's China: Hogarth's Paintings and Eighteenth-Century Ceramics* (London: Merrell Hoberton, 1997), 49.
14. Hogarth, *Analysis*, ed. Paulson, 12.
15. William Hogarth, *Anecdotes*, ed. J.B. Nichols (London: Jones and Co., 1833), 37.
16. *Tea, A Poem or Ladies into China-Cups; A Metamorphosis* (London, 1729).
17. "The Prize Aenigma," in *The Woman's Almanack* (London, 1741), 20; John Gay, *To a Lady on Her Passion for Old China* (London, 1725).
18. *A Chinese Tale* (London, 1740), 16.
19. This argument is elaborated at more length in David Porter, *Ideographia: The Chinese Cipher in Early Modern Europe* (Stanford, CA: Stanford University Press, 2001), 181–92.

PART **II**
Diffusing Furniture, Fashion, Taste

CHAPTER 4

Fashion, Business, Diffusion: An Upholsterer's Shop in Eighteenth-Century Paris

NATACHA COQUERY

TRANSLATED BY KATHRYN NORBERG AND DENA GOODMAN

This chapter is part of a larger project dealing with the shop and the city in modern Europe. In that project, my goal is to understand the place of small businesses and small business-men in broader cultural and commercial exchanges. The shop is at the heart of the circuits of redistribution, between production and consumption; it thus provides a good vantage point from which to observe the dissemination of fashion, the circulation of objects, and the inventiveness of merchants—in short, the boom of consumption that so strongly marked Europe and the American colonies in the eighteenth century.

In this chapter, I will focus on certain aspects of the activities of one artisan and shop-keeper involved in the luxury and semiluxury trades in full swing in Paris in the second half of the eighteenth century. I have chosen the shop of upholsterer and mirror-maker Mathurin Law, who was in business on the rue Saint-Honoré from at least the mid-1760s.[1] Because the merchant declared bankruptcy in July 1788, the Archives of Paris have preserved his sales registers as well as his account books; these permit us to follow his operations over the course of the 1780s.[2] Why choose Mathurin Law? This was done for several reasons that constitute his representativeness, despite his uniqueness. First, he belonged to one of the guilds (half artisanal, half retail) upon which Paris's renown for artistry and craftsmanship rested. Here is how the guild was described in the *Almanach du Dauphin* for 1777: "The upholsterers are Merchants who buy, produce, and sell all kinds of tapestries and other furnishings. This community is one of the oldest and most substantial in the Capital."[3]

As an upholsterer, Law exercised a very old trade, but one that, as we shall see, knew how to adapt itself to new modes of consumption and sail with the wind. Alfred Franklin estimates the master upholsterers of Paris to have numbered more than 600 at the end of the Old Regime.[4] They were far from the only retailers of furniture, despite the formal regulations of the guild system: joining them were art dealers, furniture dealers, woodwork-

63

ers, cabinetmakers, makers of game boards (*tabletiers*), secondhand dealers, and others. In this large group, if Law was not famous (like the *mercier* Daguerre or the cabinetmaker Jacob), neither was he unknown. His name was not included in the almanacs of the time, but he had a prosperous business: depending on the year, his transactions amounted to or surpassed 100,000 livres. At the time of his bankruptcy, he had assets of 22,000 livres (of which 13,000 livres was merchandise in stock), and liabilities of 74,383 livres. His shop was located on the rue Saint-Honoré, the most fashionable business street in the city; the one that brought together the shops most visible and appreciated by both Parisian and foreign elites. Law's clientele, which numbered several hundred people, reflected the importance of the two social groups most affected by the new culture of consumption: the nobility and the merchants. Finally, Law maintained his books with care and regularity. For all these reasons—professional, chronological, and geographical—Mathurin Law was at the heart of a system of redistribution of objects and tastes that constituted the new consumer culture of which Paris was one of the beacons.

Since the sixteenth century, Paris had been a producer of luxury goods—silverware, fine furniture, clocks, rare books, and cloth—which the almanacs and guidebooks of the time vied with each other to celebrate. Consider, for example, this entry from an almanac published in 1789:

> The commerce of Paris consists especially in objects that are useful, fashionable, and decorative, like furniture, *bijoux*, clocks, bronzes, gilt bronze, porcelains, and a host of other precious objects of which we shall give the best possible accounting.

> Fine furniture, that is, furniture made with rare woods or veneered . . . which is made in Paris is always greatly appreciated, either for its good construction or for the fine finishes, elegant form, or richness of the decoration, either in bronze, gold, etching, etc. We would add to this appreciation that modern furniture is lighter, better formed, and more striking than the old furniture which, though richer to the eye, lacked the convenience and fine form that results from the good taste and intelligence which guide today's artisans.[5]

Another almanac joined in the chorus of praise:

> As for works of both cabinetmaking and marquetry . . . nowhere else is wood worked as well as in Paris; everything which is produced here has an elegance and beauty which makes them admired by all the nations of Europe; some are so finely wrought that they astonish the connoisseurs.[6]

I would thus like to use this one shopkeeper's sales registers as a starting point to reflect on how the retail fashion trade was exercised. My goal is to make sense of a diverse set of activities across a range of products, clienteles, and professional networks, all linked to the broader economy. These include innovating, inventing new products, and transforming, but at the same time preserving, maintaining, and repairing. They entail offering novelties to a rich and demanding clientele, while at the same time providing a much broader clientele with used and secondhand goods at moderate prices. These were Law's daily activities.

I make use of four account books, which offer only a partial vision of Law's business because they are sales registers: a large register with the title "Extract of Sales on Credit," covers sales to 36 elite clients between the years 1776 and 1786; three other account books chronicle the daily sales on credit and in cash from 1782 through 1787.[7] Without a register of purchases or of objects given to other merchants to be sold on consignment (a very common practice in the eighteenth century) and with no knowledge of Law's purveyors, brokers, or other associates, a major portion of the shopkeeper's activity remains in the dark. Only the list of the creditors who appeared before the bankruptcy court allows us to identify Law's purveyors and professional associates. Of these creditors and suppliers, most (46 out of 50) were merchants and artisans. However, the richness of the available sources lies elsewhere. These registers shed light on the luxury trades' clientele, fashions, consumer practices, and tastes. I am going to focus on three aspects of the upholsterer's trade that were interwoven, but which I will separate for the sake of clarity: clientele, professional networks, and objects sold. I will analyze these three elements in order to demonstrate how a prosperous yet hardly illustrious merchant could, at his modest level, participate in and advance the consumer revolution of the late eighteenth century.

A Mixed Clientele of Aristocrats and Shopkeepers

The variety of his transactions and the importance of credit in his business (which always threatened his economic equilibrium) presented the upholsterer with a major problem: how to control a large and unstable clientele. Law's registers, like those of all shopkeepers, mixed precision, approximation, and confusion. Law noted daily activities conscientiously, but he left many gaps, and the diversity of his business led to confusion due to a lack of overall vision. Still, in order to succeed the upholsterer had to foresee the unforeseeable, because the extension of credit could not be avoided. Law was a typical shopkeeper: although he carefully made entries in his account books (or had it done), vagueness prevailed because he never prepared a balance sheet, a summary, or even an inventory. Take for example the year 1783, a year in which the upholsterer did 108,000 livres' worth of business. In this year, Law noted 800 transactions (65 per month on average), which occurred in a very uneven rhythm. This irregularity was common in eighteenth-century small retail businesses. Some days Law completed no transactions; on other days he completed ten. From 1782 to 1787, his months of maximum activity were rarely the same.[8] The 1783 transactions, which involved over 300 clients, were quite varied. Most (85 percent) involved objects furnished or services rendered by the upholsterer, and thus represent debts. However, a minority (15 percent) involved funds advanced by clients for future purchases: credits, which he used toward future purchases, payments on merchandise already sold, or payments on standing loans. The register of sums due ("Owed by Monsieur . . .") and received ("Received from Monsieur . . .") makes no distinction between these different kinds of transactions. The method of payment and the cancellation of debts, often dated, were noted in the left margin, next to the description of the transaction as, for example, "paid in cash; paid in full October 30, 1784" (for a sale made on July 26, 1783). Other notations include: "paid in kind," "paid with a note," "paid off by compensation and with cash . . . ," "paid with an acknowledgment of debt payable next year," "a payment of what he owes me," and so forth. Calculating a balance was thus impossible. How could a merchant have an overall sense of his financial situation even with such detailed records? Surely the registers were supplemented by other kinds of unwritten knowledge of the accounts and the clients, because Law was able to keep his business going for many years.

Using these registers, it is difficult to analyze Law's clientele. The shopkeeper's registers give detailed descriptions of the objects that were sold but often say nothing about the individuals who purchased them. Nevertheless, Law's registers are much more complete than the norm. More than eight hundred buyers (826) are mentioned in the six years covered by the two account books examined here.[9] The address is mentioned for 70 percent or 587 of the clients, and the profession or title is indicated for 59 percent or 489 clients.[10] Three qualities characterize this clientele: diversity, geographic concentration, and volatility. But a closer look suggests a more nuanced view: some of Law's clients lived far away, a few maintained a special relationship with the upholsterer, and most, but by no means all, clients came from two social groups: aristocrats and merchants.

Well established on the prestigious rue Saint-Honoré, Law counted among his clients employees, clerks and bailiffs, domestics from noble houses, barristers and lawyers, notaries, police commissioners, master surgeons and physicians, architects, quite a few merchants and artisans, *négociants*, contractors and builders, bankers, farmers general and tax collectors, priests and bishops, a few members of the sovereign courts, and many nobles. In short, contrary to what we might have expected in light of his location, Law attracted a varied clientele, from the petite bourgeoisie to the high aristocracy. These buyers, with very different fortunes, constitute an excellent subject for the historian of material culture: the purchases of a merchant, a postal clerk, a dressmaker, a lawyer, a counselor in the Parlement, or a princess will tell us a great deal about the nuances of consumer culture.

Law's location—at the center of a fashionable neighborhood in full swing since the 1770s—attracted clients and explains their diversity. Some of the clients worked in the vicinity (clerks, employees, shopkeepers), while even more resided there (see Table 4.1). The Saint-Honoré quarter contained more moneyed elites (be their origin high nobility, finance, or the merchant elite), than its equivalent on the left bank, the Saint-Germain quarter. At the end of the eighteenth century, the northwest pole of the quarter became a financial and administrative center, while the area surrounding the Palais Royal became the home of the luxury trade. Luxury shops were particularly concentrated on the rue Saint-Honoré, which was several kilometers long and joined the old center of Paris to the village of Le Roule.[11] The ten clerks who were Law's clients all worked very near the rue Saint-Honoré and chose him because of his proximity to their workplace. Pigeau (who lived at the other end of Paris, near the Pont-aux-Choux) was employed at the post office on the rue Platrière. Dizy worked for the Farmers General in the rue de Grenelle Saint-Honoré. Dupon (who lived on the rue d'Anjou in Saint-Germain-des-Prés) was a *greffier* or scribe in the Royal Council, which sat at the Louvre. Erse was a clerk at the Royal Treasury on the rue Saint-Honoré.

However, Law's clientele consisted for the most part of his neighbors, those who resided in the quarter. The two-thirds of his Parisian clients (352) whose address is known lived in this part of Paris; among them, 53 percent (286) lived in the quarters of Saint-Eustache, Palais-Royal, and Louvre, through which the rue Saint-Honoré ran. Not surprisingly, because this was where they tended to live, all of the financiers noted in the register for whom we know the address lived in this area: Tournachou, commercial representative from Lyon; Desverdun, farmer general (rue Neuve-Saint-Augustin); Chacel, receiver general of finances (rue neuve-des-Petits-Champs); Chomat, intendant of trade with China (rue de Richelieu); and so forth. More than 60 percent of the nobles cited in the registers lived in the northwest, an interesting fact because most nobles continued to live in Saint-Germain-des-Prés. As for the merchants, 70 percent of them lodged in the quarter itself, a high proportion considering the dispersion of the merchant class throughout the city. Still, the preponderance of the northwest does not mean concentration: Law's clientele was spread out over 230 different streets. Three-quarters of these streets contained only one or two clients. Only the rue du Faubourg-Saint-Honoré (10), rue Neuve-des-Petits-Champs (11), rue de Richelieu (13), and the rue Saint-Honoré (48) housed a substantial number of clients. Other neighborhoods were left behind: only 9 percent of the clients lived in the northeast, principally workers in

TABLE 4.1 Residence by Neighborhood of the Clients of Upholsterer Law (1782–1787)

Neighborhood	Number of Streets	%	Number of Clients	%
Hôtel-de-Ville	9		9	
Place Royale	12		19	
Marais	8		10	
St-Martin	7		9	
St-Martin/Place Royale	1		2	
Northeastern Paris	37	15	49	9
St-Denis	13		19	
Sts-Innocents	12		21	
Halles	9		24	
Sts-Innocents Halles	1		2	
St-Eustache	33		85	
Palais Royal	30		75	
Palais Royal St-Eustache	3		47	
Louvre	32		79	
Northwestern Paris	133	55	352	65.5
St-Germain-des-Prés	26		49	
Luxembourg	25		46	
St-Germain-des-Prés Luxembourg	1		4	
Sorbonne	3		7	
Southeestern Paris	55	23	106	20
Ste-Geneviève	6		10	
Notre-Dame	3		4	
Southeastern Paris	9	3.5	14	2.5
Cité	9	3.5	17	3
Western Paris	188		458	
Eastern Paris	46		63	
Southern Paris	64		120	
Northern Paris	170		401	
Unknown	3		4	
Total	246	100	542	100

Note: Of the 243 streets in the data, 12 had no name but they could be located within a neighborhood. The rue St-Honoré was counted four times because it crosses three neighborhoods (Louvre/Palais-Royal, St-Eustache/Palais-Royal, St-Eustache). The rue de Richelieu was counted twice because it traverses two neighorhoods (St-Eustache, Palais-Royal/St-Eustache).

the building trades (cabinetmakers, locksmiths) and members of the nobility of the robe (the president of a sovereign court, a counselor of state). Three percent of Law's clients lived in the Cité, which was home to jewelers, gilders, and clockmakers; and 2.5 percent (iron-mongers, engravers) in the working-class districts of the southeast. The southwestern part of the city, a traditional home of the aristocracy, was a bit better represented at 20 percent (106), thus underscoring the significance of Law's noble clientele.

This rapid review of the geographical distribution of Law's clients underscores the impor-tance for clients of the neighborhood and suggests several interpretations. The proximity of Law's shop to his clients' homes, as well as the relative weakness of the southwest among their addresses, indicate that even though Law was well known, he was not among the elite of Parisian shopkeepers. For the aristocracy, proximity to their abode did not play a role in their choice of purveyors.[12] For the artisans and shopkeepers (to whom I will return later) proximity can be explained by professional ties and common specializations.

A large part of Law's clientele was not regular: three-quarters of the buyers appear only once or twice in six years; only 6 percent appear ten times or more. Among this small core of regular customers (about fifty individuals), only two are mentioned from one end of the period to the other; the vicomte de Carvoisin is listed 46 times, but over the course of one year. Almost three-quarters were nobles (25, of whom most were aristocrats) and 17.5 per-cent (6) were shopkeepers: three merchants from the rue Saint-Honoré (Loreau, Sédillot, and Montclar); Guillard, an upholsterer on the rue Sainte-Avoie; and the two famous clock-makers, Ferdinand Berthoud, uncle and nephew (rue du Harlai), who are mentioned 31 and 35 times respectively over the course of the six years in question here. The person most frequently mentioned in the registers (68 times) is a guard of the Royal Treasury, Savalette de Lange.

One finds amplified here the salient trait of the socioprofessional profile of Law's cli-entele: the overwhelming presence of shopkeepers and nobles, who alone represent more than three-quarters of the whole (Table 4.2). Of this group, 149 individuals (30.5 percent) are artisans or shopkeepers and 229 (47 percent) are nobles. This latter group is constituted principally of aristocrats: 53 counts and countesses, 36 marquis and marquises, 12 bar-ons and baronesses, 10 viscounts and viscountesses, 8 dukes and duchesses, 2 princes and princesses; whereas members of the Parlement are a small minority at only 5 percent.[13] As for the shopkeepers, their occupations are more diverse but still linked to Law's business. Leaving aside the twenty-three merchants whose specialty is unknown (15.5 percent), two very unequal clusters emerge: three large groups of equal importance (housing, textiles, and metals) comprise 72.5 percent; followed by three smaller groups involved in the provision-ing of food (12 percent), care of the body or hygiene (2 percent), and music (1 percent).[14]

Law's clientele was, therefore, made up primarily of the two groups most involved in the new consumption patterns; patterns that laid the groundwork for the "commercial revolu-tion" that spread over the course of the century to the middling classes and even the popular classes.[15] For the aristocrats, driven by the need to maintain their rank, to shine was a cat-egorical imperative; they had to be on the cutting edge of fashion. The boundless expenses of the private townhouses, which extended to all domains—food, clothing, architecture and interior decoration, horseracing—demonstrates the courtiers' need for luxury, seconded very quickly by that of the financiers. Let us now return to the analysis of Law's clientele. If we turn from a qualitative, that is socioprofessional, analysis of the clientele to a quantita-tive analysis based on the amount of money spent, the preponderance of the nobles is again evident. Among the thirty-six clients noted in the Extract of Sales on Credit (which

TABLE 4.2 Professions or status of the upholsterer Law's clients (1782–1787)

Profession or status	Number	Percent
High-ranking officials (Directors of the Opera & postal service)	2	0.5
Artistic professions (architects, painters, scupltors)	5	1
Financiers (bankers, brokers, moneychangers)	5	1
Medical professions (doctors, surgeons)	7	1.5
Employees of noble houses	10	2
Lower-level employees (clerks, concierges, messengers, ushers, servants)	10	2
Government financial officers (deputies, tax farmers)	13	2.5
Trade and transport (entrepreneurs, manufacturers, wholesale merchants)	14	3
Clergy (priests, 2 bishops)	20	4
Legal professions (lawyers, judges, barristers, notaries, police)	25	5
Shopkeepers and artisans	149	30.5
Nobles (petty nobility, aristocrats)	229	47
Total	489	100

deals with only 4 percent of the 826 clients in the two account books), only a dozen buyers accounted for purchases of 6,000 livres or more and all were aristocrats.[16] An upholsterer and a goldsmith spent much smaller sums, between 1200 and 1300 livres. The two account books underscore this asymmetry: only the two clockmakers, uncle and nephew Berthoud, together disbursed more than 6,000 livres. This certainly does not mean that all the nobles were big spenders: the marquis of Beauharnais owed Law only 645 livres and the marquis d'Ambray only 578 livres. But the aristocrats' fortunes were in no way comparable to those of the lower and middling bourgeoisie!

Nevertheless, the merchants, who stood at the heart of the circulation of goods, earning large fortunes and aspiring to enter in due course the ranks of the notables, were not left behind. Daniel Defoe had already sensed this well. The author of *A Plan of the English Commerce* (1731) based the growth of domestic consumption above all on that of manufacturers and shopkeepers due to their number and the variety of their demand, much more than on the luxury, vanity, and high living of the gentry and the aristocracy, who aimed only for the high end. "These are the people that carry off the gross of your consumption . . . these are the life of our whole commerce, and all by their multitude," he proclaimed.[17]

A Double Trade Inscribed in a Dense Professional Network

Still, consumer culture is not at all synonymous with consumer society. The upholsterer repaired and rented as much as, if not more than, he sold, indeed a great deal more: the duality of his trade indicated the coexistence of different kinds of ownership. Fashion and novelty are imperious: an object that was no longer rare remained precious, often unique, and not disposable. It was thus maintained, or was then given away, exchanged, abandoned, becoming part of a vast market in secondhand or recycled goods.

A large part of the upholsterer's activity was thus devoted to repairing furniture, maintaining it, or rearranging or renovating interiors, as the frequency of the following expressions reveals: "repaired," "mended," "remade" (curtains), "made solid" (a dressing table), "relined" (a counterpane), "polished" (a dressing table), "re-veneered" (a secretary), "revived" (chimney pans), "cleaned" (a lantern, a porcelain figure, chimney pans), "bleached" (fire grates), "lengthened," "re-sewed," "recovered" (arm chairs, a fire screen), "re-hung" (a bed, a tapestry, an entire salon), "remounted" (mirrors), "re-upholstered" (a chair), "re-stuffed" (a mattress), "re-attached" (shelves), "replaced," "removed upholstery" (from an armchair), "took apart," "removed gilding," and so forth.

The cost of these repairs varied from 1 livre to 50 or 60 livres. To fix wooden furniture was generally fairly cheap, but to repair metal ornamentation was more costly. Most of Law's clients, whatever their social status, asked him to do this kind of work for them. Here are just a few examples: he charged Monsieur Savalette 120 livres to arrange and furnish his salon and dining room for a ball, supplying benches and lighting and relaying two carpets; by contrast, the younger of the Berthoud clockmakers paid only 3 livres to have the canopy on his bed cleaned and rehung. Law repaired a mirror frame for the silk merchant Doucet for 4 livres, a table for the glazier Jerome for 10 livres, and a pair of chandeliers for the chevalier Dourdan for 78 livres. He did a variety of services for the draper Curmer: he replaced a mirror, repaired a couple of games tables, and recovered one with new felt, for a total of 12 livres. Finally, for the marquise de Sabran he repaired and restored three pieces of mahogany furniture, at a total cost of 5 livres.

Renting furnishings was also one of the prerogatives of the upholsterer. Here again, all Law's clients sought out this service: the only difference was the value of the object rented. Renting (by the month) could be a more economical means of remaining in style, no matter what happened, or a way of decorating a temporary apartment (a solution adopted by many aristocrats passing through Paris), or a short-term loan. The bailiff Jaluso rented a bed for a livre a month; Madame de Pellagrue rented a folding bed for her chamber maid for 4 livres; the comte de Vergennes rented four screens for 12 livres; and the marquis de Pezé rented a complete salon for 108 livres a month. On January 24, 1785, Law furnished one of his best clients, a counselor of state named Moreau, with everything he needed for a supper party: "one mahogany table, seven stools upholstered in red Utrecht velvet, two pairs of candle holders, and a pair of gilt girandoles, another pair with three gilt branches; and six crimson curtains for the gallery windows, installed." Law also hung all the curtains (some green and some red) and the lanterns, hung the paintings and prints in the gallery, and furnished the nails and wire, at a total cost (transportation included) of 60 livres.

The upholsterer used an enormous amount of fabric (especially for beds); furnishing apartments, in elaborate forms, was one of his primary occupations. The variety of fabrics is remarkable and corresponds to precise uses: cloth from Flanders, Jouy, Alençon, Lyon; Brussels ticking, Utrecht velvet, Grenada silk; cotton, wool, mohair, felt, serge, striped silk, satin, crepe, damask, taffeta, among many others—not to mention the ribbons, cords, fringes, and feathers used for decoration. He covered furniture (with velvet, *toile de Jouy*, mohair, felt, damask for armchairs, chairs, and bergères, waxed cloth for the buffet, cotton or serge for dust covers, green cloth for the gaming tables, green taffeta for screens); stuffed mattresses and cushions; lined counterpanes, curtains, rugs, and tapestries; and decorated alcove walls. He also made covers for doors and windows and installed all kinds of drapes, curtains, and hangings.

The work of the upholsterer, in the context of great specialization and division of labor, was only possible with the help of numerous artisans and merchants. Most of Law's shop-keeper clients belonged to trades related to his and with which he tended to collaborate. The upholsterers were the most in demand by far, which proves that the trade could not be exercised by an individual alone, but there were also gilders, goldsmiths, jewelers and clockmakers, cabinetmakers, wood merchants and carpenters, silk, cloth, and trim merchants, to name only a few. Lacking a register of purchases, I cannot determine what proportion of these merchants who were Law's clients were also his suppliers. A certain number of them, well known in the Parisian marketplace, must have taken advantage simply of the proximity of the shops, whose density and variety gave such a particular character to the rue Saint-Honoré: the drapers, mercers, and other cloth merchants Rasle, Carmes, Le Mor, Curmer, and Doucet; the goldsmiths Charvet, August, and Tesnières; the famous furniture dealer Daguerre. The majority of the merchants in the second cluster, who were not at all involved in Law's business, lived on the rue Saint-Honoré (such as the apothecary de Londre, the tobacconist Jamais, the violin maker Payant, the pastry maker Rouger) or on neighboring streets.

However, thanks to the list of creditors, as well as the notes concerning barter and exchange of services, I know that several buyers were also suppliers or even associates, for the transactions always went both ways. The following were among those who were both creditor and debtor: the mercer Buisson (to whom Law owed 2,342 livres at the time of his bankruptcy); the silk merchant Lequene (2,081 livres); the sheath maker Mantel (612 livres); the ironmonger Fremin (5,604 livres); the gilder Bulot (278 livres); the jeweler Juliot (399 livres); the furnace maker Kropper (155 livres); the cabinetmaker Topino (150 livres); and the tailor Benoist (155 livres). Law's largest debts were owed to cloth merchants, the Saint-Gobain mirror factory (7,952 livres), the gilders, and the iron monger. Law could not have worked without the help of many artisans, as the numerous notations in his registers reveal: "had a pair of candlesticks gilded," he notes, or "had the marble re-cut for a table," or "had the parquet of a fireplace painted." These notations show how often Law employed the services of his fellow artisans. Ironmongers and locksmiths provided him with a large quantity of hardware necessary to his profession such as nails, tacks, locks, pulleys, keys, and bells. Law often noted the money he owed these artisans as well as the sums destined for those who transported his goods. For example, he owed a locksmith 12 livres for the locks, curtain rods, bolts, and pins "in the Roman style" installed at the home of the marquis de la Salle. To painters he owed 12 livres for painting and varnishing done at the home of the comte de Coucy. To the famous wallpaper merchant, Arthur, he paid 254 livres for the wallpaper hung in the home of the comte d'Aumale. Law required the services of apprentice cabinetmakers, dyers, porcelain makers, painters, and furnace makers, as well as carriers and packers. To a carrier, Law paid 194 livres for the crates and packing of merchandise delivered to the vicomte de Velleurnoy. Charges for crating and transporting goods were very common in Law's business because the nobles had their purchases delivered to their homes—either their Parisian townhouse or their provincial chateau—all arranged by the merchant who supplied the goods.

Another way of ascertaining the links between Law and other merchants is to note the exchanges of goods, bills, and other methods of payment. A few rare notes reveal that Law maintained an ongoing association with other merchants, such as the gilder Delérie and the clockmakers Mera and Berthoud. In September 1782, when he first mentioned Delérie in his register, Law noted that he was the gilder for M. Gigault, a merchant goldsmith. On this occasion, the upholsterer acted as an intermediary between the gilder and the goldsmith. In May 1783, he wrote concerning Delérie: "furnished by his order to sieur Gigault, merchant goldsmith . . . and delivered to Mme Gilbert a commode . . . 120, a similar commode, 120." Again in August, Law noted delivery of a large mirror for a chimneypiece and a secretary to Gigault on Delérie's orders. He sometimes worked in the same way for the clockmaker Mera. For example, on December 1, 1784, he noted that on Mera's orders he delivered a walnut secretary to a customer on the rue Bourg-l'Abbé. Ferdinand Berthoud himself sought to sell one of his armoires through Law: "February 12, 1785, paid 7 livres to two apprentices to dismantle an armoire with glass doors in the niche of (Berthoud's) dining room and bring it to my shop to sell for the same Berthoud."

The registers testify to an important problem, but one that I do not have time to investigate at length here: the broad and varied use of commercial credit (letters of credit, bank notes, receipts, agreements, coupons, installment payments, and accounts paid monthly), and the important role played by barter. Merchants who worked together also frequently "paid" one another by reducing their running debt. In this way, at certain dates Law and the ceramics dealer Bailli retired the debts they had run up to each other for various articles. For example, Law notes in his Extract of Sales on Credit that on April 17, 1783, he received "the reckoning of the articles that (Bailli) provided for me between 20 January 1781 and 30 September 1782, which amounts to 231 livres." He did the same thing with the gilder Delérie, who retired his debt by giving Law a secretary, a commode, and a walnut dressing table. Or take the ironmonger Petit: on February 10, 1783, Law noted that he and Petit exchanged a commode *à la Régence*, a traveling toilette case in walnut, and a writing table, thereby canceling their mutual debts. The cabinetmaker Levasseur purchased a bed and provided Law with 561 livres' worth of merchandise by way of payment. The upholsterer Houdon purchased two old, veneered commodes for 600 livres and provided Law with unspecified merchandise in return.

Barter was a means of payment that was widespread, no matter what the social standing of the buyer. At the end of the eighteenth century, objects served as a means of payment and down payment on loans, just as they had two hundred years before.[18] Several nobles got rid of old or unwanted furniture in this way: Savalette de Lange gave up, for only 36 livres, "five old armchairs covered with worn tapestry." The comtesse de Larbouste bought a secretary, which she paid for with another of lesser value. De Grandmaison did the same with a men's dressing case, which he paid for with an older dressing case and 78 livres. Bartouilh, commandant of the Louvre, paid for a part of his purchases in kind: Law noted that he received an inkstand and sandbox in copper, a rosewood trictrac set, a set of fire irons with their shovel and tongs, a bureau, and two gilded candlesticks. The vicomte de Carvoisin paid in the same way: he provided five mirrors of different sizes and a pair of gilded candelabra. The comte de Coucy offered by way of payment a *chaise percée* in cane with its pot, a marble top for a secretary, a walnut commode, and a veneered sewing table. Payments could be a mixture of several elements: credit, cash, or objects. In 1782, Law took down and rehung the mirrors over the fireplaces in Madame de Poitevin's home. He received in return a down payment of 36 livres cash and an old gaming table. In 1785, the marquis de Gerberviller paid Law 96 livres in cash and threw in a mahogany music stand. Two years before, the marquis de Salle gave Law 2,718 livres in the form of three bank notes payable to the upholsterer, 21 livres in cash, nineteen pieces of tapestry, and eleven scraps of fabric.

Such practices produced a vast secondhand market that allowed less wealthy Parisians to follow changes in taste. Like the secondhand clothes dealer, the upholsterer sold the most fashionable items to the broader public after a short delay.[19] Tables, commodes, chandeliers, and toilet objects thus participated in the celebrated consumer revolution as they passed from hand to hand through the mediation of the merchant. Novelties were thus also diffused by ricocheting outward. Like many merchants at the time, Law was at the heart of a triple market—the new, the used, and items purchased on credit—which brought together different networks. The relations woven between the merchant and his clientele were therefore complex, because they were not limited to a simple relationship between buyers and seller. Barter produced an original kind of redistribution that is essential for explaining the expansion of the market in what historian Maxine Berg has called "semi-luxuries."[20]

Qualities, Prices, and Diffusion

The variety in quality and the divergence of prices confirms the diversity of the clientele and the range of choices offered by a clever shopkeeper like Law. The adjectives Law employed to describe materials (especially the different woods used in furniture) and ornamentation reveal a very rich palette in regards to quality: "bad" (a table, mattress ticking, a tapestry); "old" (a toilet set, bolsters, chairs); "antique" (a dressing table); "common" or "ordinary" (straw for caning chairs, an armoire, silk, a night table); "veneered" (corner cabinets, tables, consoles, bureaus, sewing tables, secretaries, dressing tables, an embroidery frame); "cheap" (commodes, mirrors, armchairs, candlesticks).[21] Furniture was "veneered" in mahogany, satinwood, purplewood, mosaic, or silver. "Fine" materials (gold, wool, straw, cloth, quilting) were opposed to items that were "strong" (a table, a shovel, a lock), "solid" (rosewood, mahogany), "modern" (a trictrac set), or "English" (tables, crystal, paper, leather, varnish, green taffeta, linen, armchairs).

The same differentiation applied to materials and decorations. Among the "ordinary" and the "inexpensive" woods could be found walnut, pine, beech, and cherry. On the side of the rare, exotic, and expensive, veneered or not, were purple or brazilwood, rosewood, mahogany, kingwood, ebony, and lemonwood. The richness of the ornamentation was linked to the value and the craftsmanship of the metal marquetry, be it silver or silver plate, gold or gilding, gilt copper or ormolu, forged in color or gilded.

Law's prices varied enormously from a few sols to several hundred livres, allowing all kinds of clients to purchase something in the shop: 15 sols for an ink pot in copper purchased by a carpenter; 1 livre for a music stand; 4 livres for a hearth bellows; 5 livres for a mirror or a writing table in walnut; 6 livres for a taffeta screen; 7 livres for a folding bed made out of pine; 27 livres for a veneered sewing table; 33 livres for a walnut table or a cabriolet chair covered in Utrecht velvet; 84 for a round table in the English style or a little secretary; 90 for a man's dressing case; 150 for a satinwood commode with gilt bronze mounts and a marble top, a mahogany dining table, or a veneered armoire; 240 for a rosewood secretary-armoire with gilt bronze mounts and a marble top, or a set of fire irons; 400 for an armoire veneered in rosewood; 500 for a mantel clock; 738 for a complete bed; or 1,000 livres for a pair of girandoles on gilded mounts purchased by Prince Xavier of Saxony.

For the same type of item, the prices could vary enormously. Take, for example, a trictrac set.[22] Trictrac was a fashionable game at the time and the trictrac board was sold to a varied clientele (unlike the billiard table, which cost 450 livres and was sold to only two clients). Trictrac boards and tables were purchased from Law by a notary, an upholsterer, a financier, a priest, a countess, and a duke, all of whom shared (apparently) the same passion for the game. According to the size, the fittings, the ornamentation, and the wood—smoked, veneered, walnut, glazed, kingwood, purplewood, ebony, or mahogany—the price of a trictrac set varied between 10 livres and 300 livres. One could buy a board of ordinary wood for 13 livres or a trictrac table in mahogany and black Moroccan leather with ivory and green playing pieces for 264 livres. Between these two extremes there were simple boards veneered in purplewood and accompanied by green and white ivory playing pieces that sold for 84 livres; for 204 livres one could buy a mahogany trictrac table with ivory checkers, whose top reversed to an inlaid chess board, which also contained drawers to hold a gilt bronze ink stand and sandbox.

The variation in prices also applied to less trendy objects, especially to tables, commodes, secretaries, and dressing tables. New or old, more or less ornamented, large or small, secondhand or new, fashionable or unfashionable, the variety seems infinite and responded to the needs of a diverse clientele. The aristocrats did not necessarily choose the most expensive items: everything depended on the use to which the object would be put and where it would be displayed. A pair of candleholders destined to light an antechamber or a commode purchased for a servant could be "common." The price for candleholders varied from 6 livres for a simple silver-plated candlestick to 120 livres for gilt bronze candelabra to be displayed in public rooms. A dressing table could sell for as little as 22 livres, when made from simple walnut, or as much as 430, such as the one purchased by the vicomte de Carvoisin, which was made of solid mahogany, with fluted legs, gilded trim, and multiuse shelves. A table cost between 2 livres, for one of plain cherry wood, and 240 livres, if it was like the Tronchin-style desk purchased by the comtesse de Champagne, which was made of solid mahogany with shelves covered in green leather, gold lacework, two folding candleholders, a baradelle inkwell, a sandbox, and a tray.

Barter, the secondhand market, and recycling were the foundation of an intense circulation and incessant movement of objects and fashions that played as important a role in the consumer culture as the market in new goods. Shopkeepers specializing in luxury and semiluxury goods offered a wide range of prices in the hope of attracting a large number of clients. By doing so, these retailers helped spread the consumer revolution to a broad audience, both urban and rural, and thereby overturned the "social meanings of appearances," despite the always pregnant ideal of an inegalitarian society and the reality of social hierarchies.[23] The success of semiluxuries contributed to the "confusion of symbols" and therefore the confusion of conditions. Daniel Roche and John Styles have shown in regard to clothing that following fashion meant emulating the rich, an activity that must figure in any definition or explanation of popular luxury.[24] For Maxine Berg, who prefers the notion of innovation to emulation, an imitation (such as rhinestones or veneers), which made luxury goods available at a lower price, was a kind of invention, a process of adaptation that created commodities adapted to larger markets, and like luxury goods, provoked desire.[25] Consumers, aristocrats, *grands* and *petits* bourgeois, even poor folk followed fashion, more or less brilliantly, precociously, and permanently, of course. But the spirit of fantasy and elegance touched the whole of society. As the *Magasin des modes nouvelles* stated optimistically in 1788, fashion was "for everyone."

> Forgetting her rank in society, her status, her birth, and even her fortune, every woman can appear at a ball in the richest, most elegant outfit, without fear of incurring a very serious critique.[26]

With the assistance of upholsterers such as Mathurin Law, such a woman could furnish her room or her home just as fashionably and elegantly as she could clothe her body.

Notes

1. Law worked for Princess Kinsky in 1764 and 1765; see Natacha Coquery, *L'hôtel aristocratique. Le marché du luxe à Paris aux XVIIIe siècle* (Paris: Publications de la Sorbonne, 1998), 386; Archives Nationales (AN) T 220/5-7: "Mémoire des ouvrages et fournitures faites pour son Altesse Madame la Princesse Kinsky par Law Marchand Tapissier du 8 février 1764 (2500 l);" and "Mémoire des ouvrages ... pendant l'année 1765 (4600 l)."

2. The account submitted at the time of bankruptcy included both assets and liabilities, with a complete list of the inventory, outstanding credits, and debts. It was accompanied by the depositions of thirty creditors (Archives de Paris, D4 B6 102-7192). The registers are for the years 1782–1787 (Archives de Paris, D5 B6 1024, 3066, 3451, 3209); see also note 7.

3. *Almanach du Dauphin, ou Tablettes royales du vrai mérite des artistes célebres, et d'indication général des principaux Marchands, Banquiers, Négociants, Artistes et Fabricants des Six Corps, Arts et Métiers de la Ville et Fauxbourgs de Paris, et autres Villes commerçantes du Royaume etc.* (Paris: Lacombe, 1777), n.p.

4. Alfred Franklin, *Dictionnaire historique des arts, métiers et professions exercés dans Paris depuis le XIIIe siècle* (Paris, 1905; reprint ed. Marseille: Editions Lafitte, 1977), s.v., "Tapissiers." Franklin counted 150 master mirror makers.

5. Roze de Chantoiseau, *Tablettes royal de correspondance et d'indication général, des principales Fabriques, Manufactures et Maisons de commerce d'épicerie-droguerie, Cirerie, Couleurs et Vernis, Grains, Vins, Fruits, Liqueurs, Eaux-de-Vie et autres Comestibles de Paris et autres Villes du Royaume et des Pays Etrangers* (Paris: Royez, 1789), n. p. On the history of luxury trades in France see *Luxury Trades and Consumerism in Ancien Régime Paris: Studies in the History of the Skilled Workforce*, ed. Robert Fox and Anthony Turner (Aldershot: Ashgate, 1998).

6. *Almanach général des marchands, négociants et armateurs de France, de l'Europe et d'autres Parties du Monde* (Paris: chez l'auteur, 1786), 505.

7. Register D5B6/1024, "Extrait de la vente au crédit. Commencé l'an de Grâce 1782," is an oversized volume in which each client occupies two pages. On the left-hand page (headed "Due") is inscribed what the client owes; on the right-hand page (headed "Received") are the payments or installments on the debt received by Law, the date when the merchandise was delivered, and the price. The register consists of 34 numbered pages, which I have transcribed in their entirety. The three other registers are daily accounts of sales (either on credit or paid in full), which is to say that the notations are in chronological order, regardless of the client or the type of transaction. The credit transactions ("Received") and debit transactions ("Due") are intermingled. Two of these registers are consecutive: D5B6/3066, "Journal de la vente au crédit et au comptant . . .," 379 pages running from January 2, 1782 to November 16, 1784; followed by D5B6/3451, "A la gloire de Dieu et de la très sainte Vierge ce journal soit commencé de 17 novembre 1784 . . .," 254 pages, which begins on November 17, 1784 and ends on April 4, 1787. I took notes on two-thirds of the first register and all of the second register. The third register, D5B6/3209, "Journal de vente au crédit et au comptant . . ." (89 pages), concerns the same time period as the preceding register but was kept in an erratic fashion. It begins on June 16, 1784, continues until the end of April 1786 when there is an interruption, recommences at the end of January 1787, and stops altogether on October 12, 1787. Due to lack of time, and because it covers the same period as the preceding register and is of less interest, I did not take notes on this register.

8. I have observed this same lack of regularity in the business of a jeweler. See Natacha Coquery, "La boutique au quotidien: les rythmes du petit commerce d'après les livres de comptes d'un bijoutier-joaillier parisien à la fin du XVIIIe siècle," *Les Rythmes de la ville (XVe-XIXe siècle)* (Lyon: Presses Universitaires de Lyon, 2002), 33–63.

9. The numbers are very approximate rather than precise. It is nearly impossible to figure out the exact number of clients. In fact, the spelling can vary a great deal for the same name, and certain letters are illegible. For example, a "Payant" is noted 115 times, but most of the time without address or title, which makes it difficult to know when it refers to the same person. Only five people are not named.

10. The upholsterer noted the titles of only 420 purchasers, but with the help of the commercial almanacs of the time, and above all of the high probability that around fifty persons were nobles, I was able to establish the professions of 489 clients.

11. See Natacha Coquery, *L'espace du pouvoir: de la demeure privée à l'édifice public, Paris 1700–1790* (Paris: Seli Arslan, 2000), 85 ff.; see also Coquery, *L'hotel aristocratique*, 194–209.

12. Coquery, *L'hôtel aristocratique*, 35. In this work I studied the spatial relations among five aristocratic families and their purveyors and found that there was no correlation between the location of the townhouse and the addresses of its suppliers because aristocrats took advantage of the entire city to find artisans whom they esteemed the most. Their choices were not based on the location of the merchants, but on their specializations and their fame.

13. The remainder of the nobility consisted of chevaliers (30), several military officers, secretaries in the embassies, and nobles whose titles were not specified.

14. The artisans listed under building trades included 15 upholsterers, 3 cabinetmakers, 3 lumber merchants, 2 locksmiths, 2 china makers, 1 furniture merchant, 1 stationer, 1 carpenter, and 1 *boissellier* or dealer in small wooden items like curtain rods. The textile category includes 7 drapers, 5 silk merchants, 4 tailors, 3 button makers, 3 mercers, 3 canvas merchants, 3 cobblers, 2 seamstresses, 2 boot makers, 1 belt maker, 1 dyer, 1 *dégraisseur* (dry cleaner). The category of metal workers includes 9 gilders, 7 clockmakers, 5 goldsmiths, 4 jewelers, 3 ironmongers, 2 engravers, 2 *fourbisseurs*, 1 silver smith, 1 joaillier, 1 gold picker, and 1 chandelier maker. The artisans from the food trades included 4 grocers, 3 wine merchants, 2 lemonade sellers, 1 pastry cook, 1 butcher, 1 *buraliste* (clerk or tobacconist), 1 candle maker, and 1 flour dealer. The clients who were occupied in various kinds of hygiene included 1 apothecary, 1 perfumer, and 1 wig maker.

15. On the consumer revolution, see (in chronological order) Joan Thirsk, *Economic Policy and Projects: The Development of a Consumer Society in Early Modern England* (Oxford: Oxford University Press, 1978); Daniel Roche, *The People of Paris: An Essay in Popular Culture in the 18th Century*, trans. Marie Evans with Gwynne Lewis (Berkeley: University of California Press, 1987); Neil McKendrick, John Brewer, and J. H. Plumb, *The Birth of a Consumer Society: The Commercialization of Eighteenth-Century England* (Bloomington: Indiana University Press, 1982); Lorna Weatherill, *Consumer Behaviour and Material Culture in Britain, 1660–1760* (London: Routledge, 1988); Carolyn Sargentson, *Merchants and Luxury Markets: The Marchands Merciers of Eighteenth-Century Paris* (London and Malibu: Victoria and Albert Museum in association with the J. Paul Getty Museum, 1996); *Consumption and the World of Goods*, ed. John Brewer and Roy Porter (London: Routledge, 1993); Daniel Roche, *A History of Everyday Things: The Birth of Consumption in France, 1600–1800*, trans. Brian Pearce (Cambridge: Cambridge University Press, 2000); Maxine Berg, "Inventors of the World of Goods," in *From Family Firms to Corporate Capitalism: Essays in Business and Industrial History in Honour of Peter Mathias*, ed. Kristine Bruland and Patrick O'Brien (Oxford: Clarendon Press, 1998), 21–50; *Consumers and Luxury: Consumer Culture in Europe 1650–1850*, ed. Maxine Berg and Helen Clifford (Manchester: Manchester University Press, 1999); John Styles, "Coutume ou consommation? les pauvres et la consommation au dix-huitième siècle en Angleterre," unpublished paper given January 10, 2000, at the Collège de France; Nancy Cox, *The Complete Tradesman: A Study of Retailing, 1550–1820* (Aldershot: Ashgate, 2000).

16. This register is very incomplete for reasons that are unknown. The clients most frequently cited or who spent the most in the other registers tend to be absent. Of the 27 whose profession we know, 20 were nobles and only 4 were merchants. The marquis de Montbrun, Prince Xavier of Saxony, and the vicomte de Carvoisin each spent around 8,000 livres; the marquis de Gerbeviller and the guard of the Treasury Savalette de Langes spent about 12,000 livres apiece; while the *abbé* and the comte de Coucy (1778–1784) noted together, spent 17,000. The governor of the Louvre, Barthouilh (1780–1785) spent almost 20,000 livres, the comte de Vergennes more than 25,000, and the comte de Bouville, 34,000.

17. Daniel Defoe, *A Plan for the English Commerce*, cited in *Consumers and Luxury*, ed. Berg and Clifford, 6.

18. Jean Meuvret, "Circulation monétaire et utilisation économique de la monnaie dans la France du XVIe et du XVIIe siècle," in *Etudes d'histoire économique. Recueil d'articles*, ed. Jean Meuvret (Paris: Armand Colin, 1971), 123–27.

19. Daniel Roche, *La Culture des apparences: une histoire du vêtement XVIIe-XVIIIe siècle*, (Paris: Fayard, 1989), 339ff.

20. On semiluxuries see Maxine Berg, "New Commodities, Luxuries and their Consumers in Eighteenth-Century England," in *Consumers and Luxury*, ed. Berg and Clifford, 63–85.

21. The term Law used here is *hasard*, which today means "used," but at the time could simply mean "cheap" or "a bargain." Note the following definition: "In speaking of a piece of furniture, a painting, a book or some other thing that one has bought at a low price, one says 'C'est un meuble de hasard, un tableau de hasard, un livre de hasard.' In the way one also says *Trouver un bon hasard* (Find a bargain)." *Dictionnaire de l'Académie française*, 4th ed. (Paris: Bernard Brunet, 1762), 1:864.

22. Trictrac resembled modern backgammon. Like backgammon, it was played on a board that was painted or inlaid with ivory, ebony, or other rare woods, and a set included a hinged box or board, playing pieces, cups, and dice. A table might also be inlaid so as to serve as a trictrac board.

23. Roche, *La culture des apparences*, 339 ff.

24. Ibid.; Styles, "Coutume ou consommation," n.p.; George Crossick, "Conclusion," in *La Boutique et la ville: commerces, commerçants, espaces et clientèles : XVIe-XXe siècles*, ed. Natacha Coquery (Tours: Edition de la Maison des Sciences de la Ville, 2000), 400 ff.

25. Berg, "New Commodities, Luxuries and their Consumers."
26. *Le Magasin des modes nouvelles*, cited in Jennifer Jones, "The Taste for Fashion and Frivolity: Gender, Clothing and Commercial Culture in the Old Regime," (Ph. D. dissertation: Princeton University, 1991), 221–22.

CHAPTER 5

Sideboards, Side Chairs, and Globes: Changing Modes of Furnishing Provincial Culture in the Early Republic, 1790–1820

DAVID JAFFEE

After the American Revolution, artisan-entrepreneurs made more and a wider variety of goods than ever before by using new techniques, tapping available sources of power, and experimenting with redesigned objects in the new United States. The British colonial gentry's goods had often been imported or fashioned by urban artisans in a few port cities in North America. Now, middling families and enterprising artisans challenged the pre-Revolutionary elite's monopoly on status-bearing domestic furnishings and loosened the solidity of cultural meaning contained in the goods of colonial households as understood and controlled by their gentry owners. New centers of production in the hinterlands emerged where none had existed before.

Only a few years after connecting through a network of trade and turnpikes to Boston or New York, developing towns saw the arrival (and sometimes success) of cabinetmakers and other artisans who provided the very latest (if not the upper, upper end) of cosmopolitan work. After the Revolution, full-time cabinetmakers and chair makers who limited themselves to furniture production had replaced woodworkers and shop joiners. In the last quarter of the century, young people increasingly trained for craft production, as population mounted and land grew scarce. Indeed, by the middle of the nineteenth century, the region had become the center of chair manufacturing: first Sterling, Massachusetts, then Gardner, where the Heywood-Wakefield Company emerged out of the household economy and its accompanying small shops.[1]

In 1832, Alexis de Tocqueville saw how the destruction of the aristocratic and hierarchical colonial system of goods had created new opportunities for craftsmen (and consumers). He noted that those who were rising as well as those who were falling in society would want goods, dramatically expanding the domestic market. This new market would, in turn, change the way craftsmen produced their wares:

"In an aristocracy," wrote Tocqueville, the artisan would seek to sell his workmanship at a high price to the few; he now conceives that the more expeditious way of getting rich is to sell them at a low price to all. But there are only two ways of lowering the price of commodities. The first is to discover some better, shorter, and more ingenious method of producing them; the second is to manufacture a larger quantity of goods, nearly similar, but of less value.[2]

Postrevolutionary American craftsmen pursued both paths. The remarkable saga of James Wilson, a woodworker, farmer, and blacksmith who created the first commercial globes in North America from his provincial station in Bradford, Vermont, offers a vision of a backwoods craftsmen navigating among the arts and sciences to produce new cultural commodities in the new American nation (Figure 5.1). Wilson was born in Londonderry, New Hampshire, in 1763, and received little formal education. He worked on his father's farm where he received a rural training in woodworking. On a 1795 trip across northern New England, he stopped at Dartmouth College, where according to family accounts, he saw a pair of terrestrial and celestial globes, probably for the first time. This visit only furthered his resolve to manufacture his own globes at a time when all globes were imported from Europe. The next year he made his first globe, a large solid wooden ball covered with paper, with the continents and countries drawn in pen and ink. Wilson overcame his limited knowledge of geography and cartography by purchasing the eighteen volumes of the *Encyclopaedia Britannica*, published in Edinburgh, with its vast repository of information

Figure 5.1 James Wilson, bookcase and globe, ca. 1810. Courtesy of Bennington Museum, Bennington, Vermont. Vermont blacksmith and globe maker James Wilson built this bookcase to house his eighteen-volume *Encyclopaedia Britannica*. He relied on the encyclopedia's ample entries on geography and globes for his globe-making ventures.

about the arts and sciences related to globe making. Encyclopedias, the archetypical arti-facts of the Enlightenment with their compendia of all recognized knowledge, made that information available through print, even in remote northern New England.[3]

Wilson approached New Haven's Amos Doolittle, the engraver of the two maps in Jedidiah Morse's *Geography Made Easy* (1784), the first geography text published in the United States, and Morse himself, of Charlestown, for additional training in projecting a map onto a spherical surface. He worked on all aspects of globe making over the next decade: he built his own tools (lathes and presses), mixed ink, shaped the spheres, and designed and printed all of his own maps. By 1810 he produced his first globes (terrestrial and celestial) out of paper on a paper core suspended in a birch frame with turned legs, fashioned on his shop's lathe (Figure 5.2). Wilson boldly signed his terrestrial globe, "A NEW TERRES-TRIAL GLOBE . . . By J. WILSON, VERMONT," celebrating its homegrown and democ-ratized qualities. He then opened a shop to manufacture and market these prized items on a commercial basis, and another decorative and cosmopolitan object became available for American households.[4]

The story of James Wilson and his globes shows how commerce and culture came together in a process, really a transformation, which I have called elsewhere the "Village Enlighten-ment," where ordinary men and women made a business of providing and using cultural commodities. Artisan entrepreneurs often employed decorative or literary neoclassical motifs that promoted the democratization of knowledge within American society as well as a fascination with the new, the most up to date—all diffused and delivered by means of the commercialization of the countryside. This up-to-date information, acquired through direct contact with metropolitan figures or through the medium of print, was then materialized in a whole range of commodities, from globes to furniture, which made American homes

Figure 5.2 James Wilson, terrestrial globe, ca. 1810. Courtesy of Vermont Historical Society, Montpellier, Vermont. James Wilson began his globe-making business in Bradford, Vermont with this globe some time around 1810, after working for over a decade on all aspects of globe making.

look very different in the decades after the Revolutionary War than they had before. These new goods celebrated the new nation's maturity by making European objects into American ones, as Americans asserted their own political and cultural identity and autonomy.[5]

This essay focuses on a part of that process by examining the two-way transmission of artisans and ideas between Boston and the provincial northern countryside (along the upper Connecticut River valley and central Massachusetts) to show how, through the production and consumption of furniture, provincial artisans and consumers constructed a new cosmopolitan culture in early-nineteenth-century America. These rural regions were no longer isolated, but connected by a growing network of trade and information with urban centers and other commercial villages. Provincial cabinetmakers did not merely mimic urban shops; they combined London designs and sophisticated urban shop practice with traditional rural tastes and modest prices to fashion things that were both distinctive and suitable for the local clientele.

In the colonial era, the few commercial furniture makers in British North America clustered in port cities such as Boston, New York, or Philadelphia, where their clientele of merchants or government officials lived. However, after the Revolution there was a dramatic expansion of both craftsmen and patrons of all sorts. Although the American Revolution caused great disruption and distress in the American economy—per capita income dropped by nearly half by most estimates—opportunities for innovation also appeared. Entrepreneurial merchants broke the hold of established Boston or New York merchants and networks and replaced them. At the same time, patriot households took a new interest in manufacturing. Enterprising artisans, whether rural folk from the backwoods, migrants from across the Atlantic, or urban journeymen seeking niches in growing villages, vastly expanded the manufacturing sector during the war and its immediate aftermath.[6] An entirely new class of men and women, a rising village gentry, embraced the project of refinement—of their persons, homes, and country towns—creating opportunities for cultural entrepreneurs to develop a market for culture in the countryside.

The postrevolutionary career of the painter Ralph Earl (1751–1801) provided a pattern for new men to follow as artisans and as patrons in the changing countryside. Born in central Massachusetts, the loyalist Earl fled to England at the onset of the Revolutionary War. There he attracted a provincial clientele and picked up a freer brushstroke and poses, command of a livelier palette, and an interest in landscape settings (Figure 5.3a). In 1785, Earl returned to the newly independent United States. Landing in Boston, he moved first to New York City with his newly developed expertise. However, Earl soon decided to make his way and his fortune in rural Connecticut, in inland places that had never seen the need for a portraitist. In Connecticut he painted almost one hundred known portraits in the 1790s, mostly in the northwestern corner of the state. While Litchfield might be an understandable destination, with its nationally recognized law school and female academy, a place like New Milford was less so. But that was where in 1789 Earl collaborated with Elijah Boardman on a powerful likeness of the new republic's entrepreneurial man, an aristocrat of the new republican order (Figure 5.3b).

Merchants traditionally had been portrayed as gentlemen, in domestic settings; Earl's more literal portrait of Boardman displays him at work in his store. The portrait stands as an advertisement for its subject—his books and his cloth, his clothes and his imposing stature. The painting displays Boardman's commanding presence in the world of commerce; his fashionable garb was a testament to the quality of his stock in trade. This illusionist portrait,

(a)   (b)

Figure 5.3a and b Portraits by Ralph Earl. (a) Anne Whiteside, 1784. Courtesy of Mead Art Museum, Amherst College, Amherst, Massachusetts, gift of Herbert L. Pratt (Class of 1895). (b) Elijah Boardman, 1789. Courtesy of Metropolitan Museum of Art, New York, gift of Mrs. Russell Sage, 1908. Massachusetts-born Ralph Earl fled North America because of his loyalist beliefs and his desire to improve his portrait-painting skills. His decade of work in England allowed him to become familiar with the world of Sir Joshua Reynolds and other neoclassical painters, as seen in this portrait of his fiancée, Anne Whiteside, with its brushy strokes of paint and cartographic references. Earl found the rising gentry of provincial Connecticut, such as New Milford merchant Elijan Boardman, eager to purchase grand style portraits that made their refined stature clear to their village neighbors.

in which the left foot appears to step off the shop floor and into the viewer's space, must have been quite a revelation to Boardman's neighbors in New Milford.[7]

Earl was kept busy over the next decade painting other new gentry families in portraits and landscapes of newly built mansion houses. While Earl offered traditional but fashionable full-length images based on his English training, he also produced them in a simplified style, with less modeling and stronger colors, for his provincial clientele. By leaving behind the major urban center, where artists had always made their way by painting the likenesses of the leading families, Ralph Earl showed by example the future that lay with the newly genteel of New England and the nation beyond. He advanced tastes in the countryside, bringing his British training in the eighteenth-century grand manner of portraiture, while also incorporating local tastes for direct pose and plain line.[8]

Earl was a pioneer. Soon other artisans, fresh from their training in metropolitan centers, began to seek places in the new towns of the backcountry. In the 1790s, cabinetmakers and clockmakers flocked to the region to meet the demand for their elegant wares. They set

Figure 5.4 Julius Barnard, Sideboard, ca. 1800. Courtesy of Hood Museum of Art, Dartmouth College, Hanover, New Hampshire. Bequest of Philip H. Chase, Class of 1907.

up large rural workshops, sometimes with many workers, retailing a wide range of elegant and sophisticated commodities over a great distance in northern New England and beyond. Julius Barnard, for example, a former native of Northampton who had received a portion of his training in New York City, set up shop in Windsor in 1802, where he produced sideboards for such luminaries as Mills Olcott the treasurer of Dartmouth College and a prominent businessman and lawyer (Figure 5.4).

The sideboard, a dramatic surface for displaying a family's household treasures, was a large and imposing new furniture form.[9] With its elegant outlines and expert craftsmanship, the expensive mahogany sideboard demonstrates Barnard's familiarity with high-style shops of New York City. Its serpentine surfaces and protruding drawers are very similar to perhaps the most elaborately decorated American sideboard made there by Simeon Deming and William Mills for Oliver Wolcott, Connecticut's first governor and one of Ralph Earl's sitters. The particular configuration of the piece—the innovative, indeed exuberant arrangements of inlays, dramatically festooned with bellflowers, some applied upside down—spoke to the eagerness of valley residents to acquire the latest fashionable furnishings and shows that elegance took a different form in the provinces.

While Barnard was working in his Hanover, New Hampshire, shop in 1801, he exchanged several letters with his client, Olcott. Barnard was busy securing cherry wood and awaiting orders, but he warned Olcott that "if there is any Mahogany furniture wanted, will need time to get it from Boston." Barnard had started out in Northampton where he advertised his training "with the most distinguished workmen in New York," but he moved north in 1801 to Hanover before crossing over to Windsor the next year. He purchased land and a share in a new brick building in Windsor from Nathan Hale, a local clockmaker, and advertised more frequently than any other Windsor furniture maker. His workshop, the largest in Vermont at the time, with its six to eight apprentices and journeymen, turned out a wealth of fashionable furniture. One detailed 1805 ad listed twenty-five separate forms of furniture available at his shop, including:

> Sash-corned, commode, & strait front Sideboards—Secretaries and Bookcases—Ladies Writing desks . . . Card and Pembrome [sic] Tables & Clockcases.—Field, High post, Low post, and Cross Bedsteads.—Sofas, Easy and Lolling Chairs, Windsor and Dining Chairs, Bamboo and Cottage Chairs.

Barnard may have fashioned the case for a Massachusetts-style kidney-shaped dial shelf clock, a design pioneered in the 1780s by the Willards, Roxbury clockmakers. But the clock movement featured an engraved brass dial rather than the newer painted one, while its two-part mahogany case with veneered and inlaid panels on French feet clearly indicated affluence and eastern Massachusetts ties.[10]

Boston influence went up the river too: in 1798, Elijah West, the owner of a dry goods store and tavern in Windsor, Vermont, purchased a dramatic sideboard there as a wedding gift for his daughter Sophia and her new husband, West's business partner Allen Hayes (Figure 5.5). The sideboard would take pride of place in the Perez Jones house in Windsor, which Hayes bought soon after the wedding. The Hayes's sideboard illustrates the innovative compromises inland villagers sought when they purchased refined furniture. Its bow front was derived from Boston furniture, but its style of manufacture was similar to eastern Massachusetts work. But not in every way: the secondary wood was very thick cherry and the maker used several drawer divides. The inlays were sophisticated in concept and execution but applied with three of four shells facing left, and one right. Finally, the banding around the top edge continued only two-thirds of the way around the sides, a gesture toward frugality in an otherwise sophisticated piece. Village cabinetmakers like West did not merely mimic urban shops; they combined up-to-date designs and sophisticated urban shop practice with traditional rural tastes and modest prices.[11]

Windsor was not the only upper valley community to attract artisans and produce cosmopolitan commodities. Across the river, Charlestown and Walpole, New Hampshire, attracted fourteen cabinetmakers and chair makers before 1825. Thomas Bliss brought his Boston training to Charlestown. Sometime around December 1797 he set up a partnership

Figure 5.5 Sideboard, 1798. Courtesy of Bennington Museum, Bennington, Vermont. A Windsor, Vermont, cabinetmaker manufactured this bow-front sideboard as a wedding gift for a local couple; not quite as grand an object of display as Olcott's sideboard, but still one with contemporary styling and a few concessions for price.

there with John Horswill, a cabinetmaker who probably had a Rhode Island background. Their labels and ads boasted of being "cabinet and chair makers from Boston," and their furniture displayed a familiarity with metropolitan design and construction, including both older rococo favorites and the newer neoclassical forms. A cherry chest of drawers with a plain front followed eastern Massachusetts practice, with its deeply overhanging top attached directly to the sides of the case. Its façade borrowed from Boston serpentine forms evident, for example, in a chest made between 1770 and 1795 that is now owned by the Society for the Preservation of New England Antiquities. This example is one of four similar chests with an oxbow form and ogee bracket feet or "swelled brackets." An even more pronounced and dramatic model would be the well-known George Best chest of 1770, a rounded Boston blockfront with carved fan glued to the front base.[12]

Bliss and Horswill offered metropolitan fashions to their New Hampshire customers, often inflected with local customs. They found themselves in New Hampshire, so they followed the valley practice of fluted quarter columns, similar to a 1793 Kneeland and Adams chest from Hartford (Figure 5.6). The Hartford entrepreneurs' chest had a serpentine front, a design popular for much of the last half of the eighteenth century. It appears as late as 1794 in a Hepplewhite plate of a plain serpentine chest, but with updated feet flared in the French style. The Connecticut product had not only ogee bracket feet but claw feet, columns, and brasses similar to those of the New Hampshire chest. Its columns were brass and adapted

Figure 5.6 Kneeland and Adams, Chest of Drawers, 1793. Courtesy of Winterthur Museum, Delaware. The Hartford, Connecticut, cabinetmakers Kneeland and Adams produced stylish furniture for their customers, advertising their products in newspapers up and down the Connecticut River valley.

from clock parts—a rare touch. A more austere relative was a cherry and pine Amos Denison Allen chest (belonging to the Tracy family) with a plain front but serpentine top and fluted chamfered corners.[13]

Little upholstered furniture was made in the provinces in the eighteenth century. Bliss and Horswill, who did their own upholstery, advertised from the start, "Easy Chairs, Lolling Chairs, Sofas and stuff the same." Their upholstered easy chair of mahogany with whitewood inlay (Figure 5.7) had a Serpentine crest, high flared wings on horizontally rolled arms (a newer fashion than the rounded cylinders of a Martha Washington style lolling chair), and front legs, and featured double stringing with light wood. A handwritten label reads "price $16" (Figures 5.8). Other attributed pieces include a mahogany inlaid veneered card table and two upholstered armchairs with shaped crest and concave arms. Bliss and Horswill eventually opened a branch in Woodstock, Vermont, with two other partners, and by March 1798 they had extended their wares to include a desk, bookcases, a sideboard, clock cases, and other items. They made sure to add that their "work [was] done with as much neatness as at Philadelphia, New York, Boston or any other Sea port." However, despite the fact that in their ad they requested two apprentices for an expansion of their shop, the partnership dissolved later that spring, and Bliss moved on to western New York.[14]

When Julius Barnard left Windsor to continue his northern perambulations in 1809, Thomas Boynton (1786–1849) took over as the region's leading cabinetmaker. Born in Hartland, Vermont, Boynton had gone to Boston for training but returned home in 1812. Upon

Figure 5.7 Bliss & Horswill, Easy Chair, 1797. Courtesy of New Hampshire Historical Society, Concord, New Hampshire. Upholstered seating furniture was rarely found in provincial cabinetmaking shops, but Thomas Bliss and John Horswill made this expensive easy chair with its fancy inlays and a stylish shape along the Connecticut River in Walpole, New Hampshire.

Figure 5.8 Bliss & Horswill Label. Courtesy of New Hampshire Historical Society, Concord, New Hampshire. Thomas Bliss and John Horswill boasted of their metropolitan experience at every opportunity — in furniture labels such as this one, as well as in advertisements in local newspapers.

his arrival in Vermont, Boynton made full use of the Windsor newspapers to promote himself and his metropolitan designs to his northern New England neighbors. He recorded his feverish activity that spring in obtaining supplies and labor for the opening of his new "Manufactory." By summer he could proudly announce to his neighbors the opening of his "Japanned Furniture Manufactory," located one-half mile from the village of Windsor. There he offered a few hundred chairs in a broad variety of styles, colors, and functions: "Fancy and Single Top, dining or Childrens, Bamboo or Windsor," as well as tables and bureaus and clock cases, all done "in a style superior to any in the state." His accounts list fashionable imitation bamboo work for "gilt fancy bamboo chairs," then all the rage in stylish public houses. In 1815, Frederick Pettes ordered half a dozen chairs from Boynton at a cost of $3 apiece for his Windsor coffee house, "the best Public House in Vermont," one traveler recalled. Boynton kept busy in those years, expanding his workshop and his production, building another lathe and adding more workbenches. By 1815, he likely employed at least a dozen workmen in the allied branches of cabinetwork, chair making, and painting. Painting and ornamenting were significant activities for the ambitious Boynton, who integrated several branches of furniture production. He secured labor for the manufactory from regular employees, from pieceworkers, or through exchange of goods and services. And Boynton did well: he reckoned at the close of his 1816 accounts that his income that year had been $1234 and his expenses $806, leaving him a net gain of $428. When he subtracted clothing, debts, and other expenses, his profit was over $100.[15]

Such obvious success highlighted Windsor's promise. Soon, Thomas Pomroy (1782–1843) and Lemuel Hedge (w. 1811–1826), one a native of Windsor, the other born in Northampton, challenged Boynton's supremacy. Boynton boasted that his Windsor manufactory featured experienced workmen with many years of Boston and New York experience, and that he could "furnish those who like the fashions and taste of the metropolis with the newest patterns—Grecian, card work and tea table." Pomroy and Hedge countered that they could manufacture "any kind of Cabinet Work, either in the French, Grecian, Arabian, Chinese, Italian, English, or American Style, almost as well as those who give their unqualified assurance that they will not permit their work to be equaled in Vermont." Boynton's indignant retort, that his firm was "not in the habit of bungling up their store in the 'Chinese,' 'Arabian,' or any other heathenish or savage 'style,'" only brought forth this extraordinary parody the following week, lampooning the very appeal of metropolitan culture:

MINE ADVARTISMENT

T. BUNGLETON & CO

mak de pest CABINET VORK dat ever vas mak in dis country fore it vas settle . . . Vone "Vorkman experience" jus stop at dair Shop who travel all de vay thro de big town of Bosson, and the city New York, an bring all de fashun an de taste of de Tropolis on de back.

Later that year a disastrous fire totally destroyed the Tontine Building, the town's commercial pride, and Pomroy and Hedge soon dissolved their partnership. Thomas Pomroy faded from sight and Lemuel Hedge manufactured cabinetwork and musical instruments for others. Boynton's ads appeared less frequently, and in 1828 he sold his shop.[16]

In nearby Athol, Massachusetts, Alden Spooner (1784–1877) opened a cabinetmaking business in the first decade of the nineteenth century. Although he was born in nearby Petersham, his up-to-date forms betray Boston or eastern Massachusetts training; his chairs and chests, quite cosmopolitan, are often mistaken for Boston or Portsmouth case furniture. The earliest known piece is an inlaid cherry bow-front bureau with "Alden Spooner/athol/july 1807" written on the underside. The solid construction and sophisticated use of contrasting woods suggest professional training and experience, but its stylish French bracket feet use ash rather than mahogany banding, fans in each corner, and cherry rather than mahogany veneer; it is also structurally overbuilt. However, the facade is quite striking, close to the designs used by George Hepplewhite for dressing drawers (chests of drawers) in his *The Cabinet-Maker and Upholsterer's Guide*, one of the eighteenth-century English pattern books that transmitted London designs across the Atlantic world.[17]

By April 1808 Spooner had partnered with George Fitts. The two men were twenty-three and twenty-four years old, respectively, and worked together for five years. One of Spooner's chests from this period (now in Historic Deerfield) is made of cherry wood with mahogany, birch, and maple veneers (Figure 5.9). The chest has cross-banding along the top, and its elaborate skirt is scrolled and contains an oval panel. The side stiles have reeding for added visual impact, and there is considerable turning to the legs to display the artisan's skill at the lathe. In addition, its brass fittings were high-end products made by Thomas Hands and William Jenkins of Birmingham, England. Collectors and connoisseurs have looked at the oval panels, the birch and bird's-eye maple veneers, and other high-style features and attributed the chest to a center of cosmopolitan neoclassical furniture making such as Portsmouth, New Hampshire. Scholars have also noted that the Historic Deerfield chest is quite similar to a series of chests of drawers with flashy patterns of oval panels, executed in veneers and inlays, made by the shop of Cumiston and Buckminster in Saco, Maine, forty miles northeast of Portsmouth. The design was probably brought north by one of Spooner's

Figure 5.9 Alden Spooner, Chest of Drawers, 1809. Courtesy of Historic Deerfield, Deerfield, Massachusetts. In central Massachusetts, Spooner made bow-front chests of drawers and other furniture so similar to Boston or Portsmouth examples that many collectors and curators have assumed his work had to come from an urban shop. He used fashionable veneers to decorate the front of this chest and added brass fittings imported from England.

workmen (Figure 5.10).[17] However, in this very elegant piece, Spooner is not just replicating metropolitan forms and styles, but playing with shapes in an experimental but organized fashion by compartmentalizing the facade with rectangles of contrasting mahogany.[18]

The Historic Deerfield chest is an ambitious piece, with qualities of sophistication that display all the vocabulary of Boston in its contrasting woods, decorative work, drop panel, and decorative skirt. It represents the complex offerings Spooner created for his Athol neighbors. Similarly ambitious pieces that can be viewed today include a chest of cherry wood with bird's-eye maple veneer, applied cock-bead inlay, and round turned legs now in Old Sturbridge Village. It has a decorative panel with a central oval-banded bird's-eye inlay, a checkerboard inlaid band that goes along all the edges, and another central rose brass fitting. A final elaborate example with ivory escutcheons (marked Spooner and Fitts) visually suggests a Thomas Seymour bow-front bureau of more expensive mahogany and

Figure 5.10 Cumiston and Buckminster, Chest of Drawers, 1809-1816, Sacco, Maine. Courtesy of Winterthur Museum, Delaware. When one of Alden Spooner's workmen moved north from central Massachusetts to Sacco, Maine, he brought along his familiarity with cosmopolitan styles and modes of construction, such as the oval panels of contrasting woods that make this chest of drawers a striking piece of furniture.

mahogany veneer, veneered with rare Australian casuarina wood, outlined with mahogany cross-banded veneers, bands of curly maple, and partial circle inlays that edge the top and bottom.[19]

Spooner also made stylish card tables based on metropolitan models, such as two in the Yale University Art Gallery made of black cherry with mahogany, black cherry, and maple veneers. Both were derived from Thomas Sheraton's designs in his *Cabinet-Maker and Upholsterer's Drawing Book* (1793), another of the neoclassical English pattern books. Spooner also kept up with changing chair fashions. Windsor chairs were a relatively new form of seating furniture that had crossed the Atlantic at the end of the eighteenth century and undergone a succession of changes or fashions thereafter. Spooner followed the fashion, as the square back Windsor with single bows and bent backs moved to a slat-back Windsor, and then to a fancy double-bow back, and finally a shaped tablet-top Windsor side chair (1816–1822). Spooner put together the most fashionable forms, sometimes with spandrels and cartouches coming from specialty inlay shops in Boston and brasses from Birmingham, England. Still, Spooner's story lasted only a generation; eventually he and others like him joined the new business model of ware. Increasingly, Spooner focused on purchasing specialized forms and stocking ready-made furniture in order to compete with mass produced seating. In 1827, he advertised that he "has now on hand, and offers for sale . . . at his FURNITURE WARE ROOM, a large and elegant assortment of ready made Mahogany and Cherry Furniture."[20]

The rise of the neoclassical style in American furniture coincided with the proliferation of rural cabinetmaking shops. Spooner and his contemporaries obtained designs either from plates of European design books, or by examining available objects in local homes and collections, or through their own working out of design problems at the workbench. Neoclassicism, which had gained popularity in England during the 1760s and 1770s, provided an obvious model for those Americans who sought to communicate status and understated style. "Because of the emphasis on plain and planar surfaces, rectilinear forms, and restrained use of carving," historian Kevin Sweeney writes, "neoclassical interiors, furniture and metal wares were invariably described as 'neat and plain.'" Furniture exhibited a striking shift in form, becoming lighter and rectilinear; ornamentation featured clean surfaces embellished with rich veneers and intricate inlays, rather than rococo heavy carving. With a reawakening of interest in antiquity, neoclassicism appealed to republicans looking to establish associations with the great republics of classical Greece and Rome. Sideboards and chests of drawers with undulating surfaces followed the aesthetic statements of Robert Adam, Scottish popularizer of neoclassicism:

> *Movement* is meant to express, the rise and fall, the advance and recess, with other diversity of form, in the different parts of a building, so as to add greatly to the picturesque of the composition. For the rising and falling, advancing and receding, with the convexity and concavity, and other forms of the great parts, have the same effect in architecture, that hill and dale, fore-ground and distance, swelling and sinking have in landscape: That is, they serve to produce an agreeable and diversified contour, that groups and contrasts like a picture, and creates a variety of light and shade, which gives great spirit, beauty, and effect to the Composition.[21]

Material objects like James Wilson's globes and Alden Spooner's cherry wood chest of drawers remind us that we sometimes too readily dismiss the backwoods as a source of innovation. The modern model of an urban monopoly on curiosity and sophistication fails to capture the intellectual world of entrepreneurs like Wilson and Spooner. They made rural peoples' homes look very different in the decades after the Revolutionary War and moved the center of the story of American innovation from its familiar setting of Philadelphia or New York far into inland communities. Bradford, Vermont, a town perched along the upper Connecticut River where James Wilson set up his globe-making shop, was the unlikely setting for such a story. And Alden Spooner's cabinetmaking shop opens up all sorts of possibilities for learning from artifactual evidence.

Neoclassical designs came from local resources and ornaments as well as from imported concepts. Globes and sideboards enabled producers and consumers to participate in processes of integration and creolization, through which they moved toward a vision of dynamic and complex fields of cultural negotiation. Because they worked without a strict grammar, any equation with language fails to capture the innovation of their practice. Rural style did not evolve in a vacuum. We can map provincial design perhaps as a wagon wheel with an urban hub, and vernacular production located deep on the outer rim, but as Philip Zea has reminded us, the spokes are linked—along the rim and often with the presence of separate traditions. "Fashion rode on the back of commerce," he writes, as a hybrid creation in "the back of beyond."[22] Too often, we still cling to the mystique of rural isolation. When we document rural culture, we find cosmopolitan influences and expectations, and other times neat and plain products. But plain did not mean naive or unconscious. Rural craft traditions had links far beyond local boundaries. Late-eighteenth-century provincial culture had deep roots in the commercializing countryside and dynamic access to distant design centers. What we find confounds categories, and indeed, brings into question the very categories themselves. Wilson's globes and Windsor's sideboards formed a marriage of skills, materials, and intent that hybridized all that had gone before to create something new.

Notes

1. Donna K. Baron, "Definition and Diaspora of Regional Style: The Worcester County Model," in *American Furniture 1995,* ed. Luke Beckerdite and William Newell Hosley (Hanover, NH: University Press of New England, 1995), 172–73; David Jaffee, "Artisan Entrepreneurs of Worcester County, Massachusetts, 1790–1850," in *Rural New England Furniture: People, Place, and Production,* ed. Peter Benes and Jane Montague Benes (Boston: Boston University, 2000), 100–19.
2. Alexis De Tocqueville, *Democracy in America*, trans. Henry Reeve, ed. Philip Bradley, 2 vols. (New York: Knopf, 1945), 2: 49–50.
3. Harold W. Haskins, "James Wilson—Globe Maker," *Vermont History* 27 (October 1959): 319–30; Leroy E. Kimball, "James Wilson of Vermont, America's First Globe Maker," *Proceedings of the American Antiquarian Society*, n.s. 48 (April 1938): 29–48; Kenneth Zogry, *The Best the Country Affords: Vermont Furniture, 1765–1850* (Bennington, VT: Bennington Museum, 1995), 139; James Wilson: Collections Records, Bennington Museum, Bennington, Vermont; Wilson Family Papers, University of Vermont, Burlington, Vermont; *Encyclopaedia Britannica, or a Dictionary of Arts, Sciences, Miscellaneous Literature, Constructed on a Plan, by Which the Different Sciences and Arts are Digested into the Form of Distinct Treatises or Systems*, 3rd ed. (Edinburgh: Bell and MacFarquhar, 1788–97).
4. James Wilson: Collections Records, Bennington Museum; Wilson Family Papers, University of Vermont, Zogry, *Best the Country Affords*, 139; Haskins, "James Wilson–Globe Maker;" Kimball, "James Wilson of Vermont;" Matthew Edney, "Reconsidering Enlightenment Geography and Map Making: Reconnaissance, Mapping, Archive," in *Geography and Enlightenment*, ed. David N. Livingstone and Charles W. J. Withers (Chicago: University of Chicago Press, 1999), 165–98.
5. David Jaffee, "The Village Enlightenment in the Rural North, 1760–1860," *William and Mary Quarterly* 47 (July 1990): 327–46; Philip Zea, "The Emergence of Neoclassical Furniture Making in Rural Western Massachusetts," *Antiques* 142 (December 1992): 842–51; Wendy A. Cooper, *Classical Taste in America, 1800–1840* (New York: Abbeville Press, 1993).
6. David Jaffee, "The Ebenezers Devotion: Pre- and Post-Revolutionary Consumption in Rural Connecticut," *New England Quarterly* 76 (June 2003): 239–64; Lance Mayer and Gay Myers, eds., *The Devotion Family: The Lives and Possessions of Three Generations in Eighteenth-Century Connecticut* (New London, CT: Lyman Allyn Art Museum, 1991); Robert D. Mussey, *The Furniture Masterworks of John & Thomas Seymour* (Salem, MA: Peabody Essex Museum, 2003); James A. Henretta, *The Origins of American Capitalism: Collected Essays* (Boston: Northeastern University Press, 1991); Lawrence A. Peskin, *Manufacturing Revolution: The Intellectual Origins of Early American Industry* (Baltimore, MD: Johns Hopkins University Press, 2003).
7. Elizabeth Mankin Kornhauser, *Ralph Earl: The Face of the Young Republic* (New Haven, CT: Yale University Press, 1991); 154–56; Elizabeth Kornhauser, "'By Your Inimitable Hand': Elijah Boardman's Patronage of Ralph Earl," *The American Art Journal* 23 (1991): 8; Samuel Orcutt, *History of the Towns of New Milford and Bridgewater, Connecticut, 1703–1882* (Hartford, CT: Case, Lockwood, and Brainard, 1882); Charlotte Goldthwaite, *Boardman Family Genealogy, 1525-1895* (Hartford, CT: William F. J. Boardman, 1895), 331–32; John F. Schroeder, ed., *Memoir of the Life and Character of Mrs. Mary Anna Boardman* (New Haven, CT: s.n., 1849), 397–99; Elijah Boardman Files, American Wing, Metropolitan Museum of Art (New York).

8. Franklin Bowditch Dexter, *Biographical Sketches of the Graduates of Yale College with Annals of the College History*, 6 vols. (New York: Henry Holt, 1885–1912), 4:52–54; 219–20; Robert Blair St. George, *Conversing by Signs: Poetics of Implication in Colonial New England Culture* (Chapel Hill, NC: University of North Carolina Press, 1998), 336-40; Mrs. Noah Smith Portrait Files, American Wing, Metropolitan Museum of Art; Richard L. Bushman, *The Refinement of America: Persons, Houses, Cities* (New York: Knopf, 1992).

9. James D. Wing, "Mills Olcott and His Papers in the Dartmouth Archives," and Margaret Moody Stier, "Note," *Bulletin of the Dartmouth College Library* 22 (April 1982): 76–86; William N. Hosley Jr., "Vermont Furniture, 1790-1830," in *New England Furniture: Essays in Memory of Benno M. Forman*, ed. Brock Jobe (Boston: Society for the Preservation of New England Antiquities, 1987), 245–86; Margaret J. Moody, *American Decorative Arts at Dartmouth* (Hanover, N.H.: Dartmouth College Museum & Galleries, 1981); Deanne Levison and Harold Sack, "Identifying Regionalism in Sideboards: A Study of Documented Tapered-Leg Examples," *Antiques* (May 1992): 824–33; Philip Zea, *Useful Improvements, Innumerable Temptations: Pursuing Refinement in Rural New England, 1750-1850* (Deerfield, MA: Historic Deerfield, 1998), 56, 77–78; J. Michael Flanigan et al., *American Furniture from the Kaufman Collection* (Washington, DC: National Gallery of Art, 1986), 208.

10. Julius Barnard to Mills Olcott, Letter, February, 28, 1801, Mills Olcott Papers, Dartmouth College Library; (Windsor, Vermont) *Post-Boy*, September 24, 1805; Wing, "Mills Olcott and His Papers," and Stier, "Note," 76-86; Zogry, *Best the Country Affords*, 109-10; Hosley, "Vermont Furniture."

11. Levison and Sack, "Identifying Regionalism in Sideboards;" Zogry, *Best the Country Affords*, 111; Collection Records, Bennington Museum; Edward S. Cooke, *Making Furniture in Preindustrial America: The Social Economy of Newtown and Woodbury, Connecticut* (Baltimore, Md.: Johns Hopkins University Press, 1996); William Hosley, "Architecture and Society of the Urban Frontier: Windsor, Vermont, 1798-1820," (M.A. Thesis, University of Delaware, 1981), 10.

12. The Bliss and Horswill chest of drawers is illustrated in *Plain and Elegant, Rich and Common: Documented New Hampshire Furniture, 1780-1880* (Concord, N.H.: New Hampshire Historical Society, 1979), 124–27, 146; for Boston chests, see Philip Zea, "Rural Craftsmen and Design," *New England Furniture: The Colonial Era*, ed. Brock Jobe and Myrna Kaye (Boston: Houghton Mifflin, 1984), 77, 142–46.

13. Nancy E. Richards et al., *New England Furniture at Winterthur: Queen Anne and Chippendale Periods* (Winterthur, DE: Winterthur Museum, 1997), 379–81; The Amos Denison Allen chest is illustrated in John T. Kirk, *Connecticut Furniture: Seventeenth and Eighteenth Centuries* (Hartford, CT: Wadsworth Atheneum, 1967); Gerald Ward and William N. Hosley, *The Great River: Art & Society of the Connecticut Valley, 1635-1820* (Hartford, CT: Wadsworth Atheneum, 1985), 256–57.

14. *Plain and Elegant, Rich and Common*, 124–27, 146; Collection Records, New Hampshire Historical Society; Decorative Arts Photographic Collection, Winterthur Museum (DAPC); *Farmer's Weekly Museum*, January 2, 1798, April 3, 1798.

15. Thomas Boynton, Account Books, 1811–1847, Baker Library, Dartmouth College, Hanover, New Hampshire; Zogry, *Best the Country Affords*, 97–101; Hosley, "Vermont Furniture," 242, 249–50; Charles A. Robinson, *Vermont Cabinetmakers and Chairmakers before 1855: A Checklist* (Shelburne, VT: Shelburne Museum, 1994); Nancy Goyne Evans, *American Windsor Chairs* (New York: Hudson Hills Press, 1996).

16. *Vermont Republican and Statesman*, March 23, March 30, April 6, 1818; Boynton, Account Books; Zogry, *Best the Country Affords*, 97–101.

17. For Spooner chest, see Baron, "Definition and Diaspora of Regional Style," 172–73; George Hepplewhite, *The Cabinet-maker & Upholsterer's Guide* (1794; reprint, New York: Dover, 1969), Plate 76 for dressing drawers and Plate 77 for a decorative skirt on a commode; Morrison H. Heckscher, "English Furniture Pattern Books in Eighteenth-Century America," in *American Furniture 1994*; Brock Jobe, ed., *Portsmouth Furniture: Masterworks from the New Hampshire Seacoast* (Boston: Society for the Preservation of New England Antiquities, 1993); Jaffee, "Artisan Entrepreneurs;" and Frank White, "Sterling, Massachusetts: An Early Nineteenth Century Seat of Chairmaking," in *Rural New England Furniture*, ed. Benes and Montague, 100–138.

18. Jobe, *Portsmouth Furniture*; Thomas Hardiman Jr., "Veneered Furniture of Cumiston and Buckminster, Saco, Maine," *Magazine Antiques* 159 (May 2001): 754–58; Zea, "Rural Craftsmen and Design," 57–58. Hardiman has hypothesized that David Buckminster, a native of Worcester County, worked with Alden Spooner in Athol, came north, and brought with him the design for the oval panel drawer fronts that were then combined with Cumiston's training in the Portsmouth tradition of an apron with its prominent central panel.

19. For Seymour bureau, see Mussey, *Furniture Masterworks*, 242–43.

20. For Spooner's card tables, see Benjamin Hewitt, Patricia Kane, and Gerald Ward, *The Work of Many Hands: Card Tables in Federal America*, 1790-1820 (New Haven, CT: Yale University Art Gallery, 1982), 179-81; Gerald Ward, *American Case Furniture in the Mabel Brady Garvan and Other Collections at Yale University* (New Haven, CT: Yale University Art Gallery, 1988), 179-82. Thomas Sheraton's designs in his *Cabinet-Maker and Upholsterer's Drawing Book of 1793* (1802; reprint, New York: Dover, 1972). For Spooner's chairs, see Evans, *American Windsor Chairs*, 490-94. On Spooner's later career see 1820 Census of Manufactures, Worcester County, State of Massachusetts; *Athol Freedom's Sentinel*, December 18, 1827.

21. Kevin Sweeney, "High Style Vernacular: Lifestyles of the Colonial Elite," in *Of Consuming Interests: The Style of Life in the Eighteenth Century*, ed. Cary Carson, Ronald Hoffman, and Peter J. Albert (Charlottesville: University Press of Virginia, 1994), 1–58; Robert and James Adam, *The Works in Architecture of Robert and James Adam, Esquire*, no.1 (London, 1773): 3, quoted in Charles F. Montgomery, *American Furniture: The Federal Period, in the Henry Francis DuPont Winterthur Museum* (New York: Viking Press, 1966), 373.

22. Philip Zea, "Diversity and Regionalism in New England Furniture," in *American Furniture 1995*, ed. Beckerdite and Hosley, 61–112.

CHAPTER **6**

Goddesses of Taste: Courtesans and Their Furniture in Late-Eighteenth-Century Paris

KATHRYN NORBERG

The April 1760 entry in Edmond-Jean-François Barbier's journal of his observations of daily life in Paris concerns an auction held on the rue Saint Nicaise. The goods offered for sale belonged to Marie-Anne Deschamps (1730–1764) who, like many other Parisians, had seen her income drop during the long Seven Years War. Rather than endure long and costly legal proceedings, Deschamps put her possessions up for sale to the delight of a large and avid public.

For days before the auction began, "gentlemen and women crowded into the house," drawn by their curiosity to see the collection of fine furniture and porcelains. On April 15, when these same items came up for sale, "carriages blocked the streets in both directions." So tumultuous were the crowds that a Swiss guard was posted at the gate, and tickets were issued to "those who appeared to be of distinction." According to Barbier, "The rooms were so packed with people, lords, decorated officers (*cordons bleus*) and women that the auction had to be moved to the courtyard." Deschamps, dressed in a tasteful spring gown, presided over this bustle with "decency and modesty."[1]

The Parisians did not come to gawk at the home of a great noble or a wealthy courtier; they came to inspect the goods of a prostitute, a dancer at the Paris Opera whose lovers included the Duc d'Orléans and several wealthy tax farmers. Deschamps was, in Barbier's opinion, the "most celebrated courtesan" of the day, one of the "girls of the Opera" who occupied the highest levels of the *demi-monde*. Her fine porcelains, tulipwood commodes, and damask sofas were, as Barbier accurately observed, the fruit "of debauchery and prostitution."[2]

Deschamps was one of about a dozen courtesans whose furniture was displayed, described, and publicly critiqued in the late eighteenth century. Duthé, Laguerre, Guimard, Dervieux, and others all offered their gilded commodes and marquetry desks for public scrutiny at auction, in print, or in their homes. Thanks to the publicity that surrounded them, courtesans provide an unusual vantage point from which to view taste and fashion in the eighteenth century. Their position was ambiguous: a courtesan was an outcast and

97

yet a consort of aristocrats, a stigmatized woman and still the friend of dukes. She circulated in (male) high society but could never join it. She had both elegant commodes and a large police file. Her social ambiguity combined with her high-profile consumption sheds light on how fashion was formed, style adopted, and furniture made meaningful. How did the courtesan purchase furniture? Was her taste unusual and how did she acquire it? How did her sex shape her acquisitions? Did she follow the trend toward privacy, comfort, and domesticity that was emerging in the eighteenth century, or did she develop a more idiosyncratic decorative vocabulary? These are the questions that this essay seeks to answer with the help of three kinds of documents: police records, inventories, and auction catalogs. Of the actual furniture owned by courtesans we have (to my knowledge) only one surviving example, a *secrétaire*. Consequently, this essay will focus on four kinds of objects described in texts but long since vanished—the formal bed, the dining table, the neoclassical chair, and the collectible—before turning to this intriguing *secrétaire*. But first a word about the courtesans themselves.

Eighteenth-century courtesans were performers, actresses, singers, and dancers at the official theaters of Paris, but mainly at the opera. Most came from lower middle-class families, from the ranks of minor officials, domestic servants, and artisans. Many began their careers around fourteen years of age in the opera ballet chorus, the aptly named *magasin* (shop), which many regarded as little more than a brothel.[3] As a debutante in the chorus, a girl quickly became a kept woman. If she had some talent or great beauty she might rise to stardom, find opulent lovers, and become a courtesan. In any case, an actress's wages were insufficient to sustain her. Performers, whether they were famous singers, renowned actresses, or obscure dancers, depended on gifts from wealthy men to make ends meet.[4]

The courtesans placed a great deal of importance on furniture because furniture was what stood between them and sordid prostitution. To have furniture (*être dans ses meubles*) was to be above the miserable streetwalker, to be free of rooming house, brothel, and madam. Both the police and the women themselves used the expression. Owning furniture indicated independence and a small measure of security. For the courtesan, however, it was not enough to possess a bed and a chair. She had to have a silk-draped bed, mahogany chairs, and a collection of porcelain.

Two courtesans who had all these things and luxurious homes to boot were Marie-Madeleine Guimard (1743–1816) and Anne-Victoire Dervieux (1752–1826). Both will concern us here because their possessions are unusually well documented. Guimard was the illegitimate child of a minor official from Dauphiné, and Dervieux was the daughter of a Parisian washerwoman. In 1760, Guimard first appeared as a dancer on the stage of the Comédie Française. Dervieux debuted as a dancer five year later at the opera, but eventually switched to singing. Both women had wealthy protectors. The financier Jean Benjamin de La Borde and the bishop of Orléans supported Guimard, while the duc de Conti and the comtes d'Artois and Provence provided for Dervieux. The duc de Soubise supported both women. Thanks to his generosity, Guimard and Dervieux erected mansions in the new western quarters of Paris and filled them with elegant *secrétaires*, tables, and commodes.[5]

While there were only about a dozen women in Paris like Guimard and Dervieux, they made up for their small numbers with high visibility. All the courtesans performed on the stage and were therefore before the public on a daily basis.[6] Some became so popular that their romances and rivalries, witty remarks, and personal failures, were reported in gazettes and scandal sheets. Their furniture and interior decoration did not escape notice either. The *Correspondance secrète* published descriptions of some courtesan homes, and engravings were struck of others. Financial exigency also put the courtesan's goods before the public eye, for Deschamps was not the only courtesan to seek to avoid bankruptcy by selling her furniture. Those less desperate had recourse to the monthly auctions sponsored by Paris *marchands merciers*. Usually the *marchand mercier* had a printed catalog circulated and then displayed the furniture and curiosities for several days in advance of the sale.

Courtesans frequently sold their furniture, but how did they buy it? Were they different from other consumers? Police records suggest that courtesans bought furniture more often than most Parisians. They changed furniture whenever they changed lovers, so they frequently found themselves in the market for new commodes and tables. "Mlle B," the police records inform us, "has been installed in an apartment by the Duc de V who has spent 4,000 livres on the furnishings." Only two years later, Mlle B had moved on.[7] She then lived in a different apartment provided and furnished by a different lover. Each move involved the acquisition of new wall coverings, curtains, and of course furniture. And each move meant the expenditure of substantial sums of money—much more money than was spent by other Parisians. According to police records, most courtesans spent between 8,000 and 12,000 livres on the decoration and furnishing of a new apartment. Many spent more.[8] When sieur Pajot de Villiers installed his lover, Mlle Labordière, in a large apartment on the rue Poissonnière, he spent 20,000 livres furnishing and decorating the place.[9]

These were very substantial sums of money. In 1784, the century's most famous courtesan, Marie-Madeleine Guimard, possessed furniture estimated at 27,000 livres.[10] When Dervieux sold her little house in Pantin in 1773, the furnishings were purchased for 11,000 livres.[11] By comparison, in 1777 Princess Kinsky ordered a whole houseful (eighty-five pieces) of new furniture for only 6,000 livres.[12]

Given the sums involved and the frequency with which they moved and refurnished, courtesans (or even kept women) were a gold mine for merchants (such as the upholsterers studied by Natacha Coquery in this volume), and the courtesan availed herself of their myriad and varied services.[13] Courtesans rented furniture. For example, at her death the actress Liard owned tulipwood commodes, extensive silver plate, and quite a few diamonds, but the imposing bed *à la polonaise,* which sat in her salon, belonged to a merchant upholsterer who had laid claim to it within hours of her demise.[14] Courtesans also purchased on credit. In December 1730, when seals were affixed to the home of the courtesan and former opera dancer, Mlle Kerkoffen, among the creditors were a cabinetmaker, two upholsterers, and a *marchand mercier*.[15] Sometimes the courtesan (or rather her lover) even paid off the debt. In 1761, the marquis de Royan gave an upholsterer 4,000 livres to forestall the repossession of his lady friend's furniture.[16]

If the upholsterer benefited from the courtesans' business, so too did the *marchand mercier*. Courtesans were avid collectors of curiosities as well as fine furniture, so they probably had frequent dealings, and maybe even close relationships, with these luxury merchants. One *marchand mercier*, Brunet, whose shop was located on the chic rue Saint-Honoré, was a virtual fixture in Mlle Deschamps's vestibule. When in August 1757, Deschamps's husband broke into her house demanding money, who was waiting with his assistant in the dancer's antechamber but Mathieu Brunet. Several months later Brunet testified on Deschamps's behalf in her attempt to acquire a separation from her abusive husband.[17]

Brunet's devotion to Deschamps raises an important question: who actually selected the courtesan's furniture? Was it the *marchand mercier* or (more likely) the lover who paid for it in the first place? Brunet's position vis-à-vis Deschamps appears to have been that of a supplicant, waiting upon, rather than dominating, the buyer. As for the courtesans' lovers, the degree to which a man interfered in the purchase of furniture seems to have varied with his wealth or lack of it. When a gentleman had only modest funds, he would usually keep a close eye on what his girlfriend purchased or even negotiate himself with the upholsterer. Take, for example, Monsieur Delon, who personally doled out lengths of brocade to his mistress depending on how warmly she greeted his advances.[18] Brocade might be the price of love for a minor official, but it is unlikely that the great aristocrats who financed a Deschamps or a Dervieux fretted over a few yards of cloth. Surely, neither the duc de Soubise nor the bishop of Orléans, lovers of Mlle Guimard, gave any thought to their girlfriend's upholstery.

The greater the courtesan, the more likely she was to select her own furniture. Her lover had other worries, and once her attachment to a well-known aristocrat was established, a courtesan could buy whatever she chose on credit.[19] In this regard, the courtesan's notoriety worked in her favor. Known to be supported by not one but two rich aristocrats, Guimard had no trouble borrowing money to build and furnish her own house. Others, such as Mlle Laguerre, bought what they liked and then had their lovers settle their debts, thereby opening the way for yet another round of buying on credit.[20]

In fact, the courtesan was probably freer than the aristocratic wife to choose her furniture and install it as she wished. Just who—husband or wife—planned and purchased the family home in the eighteenth century is not clear. At least among the financiers of the Place Vendôme, men made design decisions single-handedly with little help from or even consultation with their wives.[21] Unlike the financier wives, the courtesan had no husband and no lover resident in her home.[22] She could choose her furniture freely according to her own needs, desires, or even whims.

The Formal Bed

Five kinds of objects were typical or emblematic of the courtesan's preferences and tastes: the formal bed, the dining table, the neoclassical chair, the porcelain collectible, and the *secrétaire* or writing desk. Elaborate beds, draped with costly silks and surmounted by ostrich feathers, appeared in the homes of most courtesans. Those unfamiliar with eighteenth-century decorative conventions might assume that this bed was where the courtesan earned her keep. However, as its formality suggests, such a bed was not an erotic piece of furniture. The consummation of a seduction or extramarital affair was usually reserved (at least in literature) for a more comfortable, less ostentatious piece of furniture: an ottoman or a sofa. Actual sleep occurred in one of the bed chambers located either on the first story or in another part of the apartment. The formal bed was a formal piece of furniture in a formal receiving room: a salon, *salle de compagnie*, or *chambre de parade*. This is how Dufort de Cheverny describes Mlle Deschamps's "bedroom" around 1760:

> A valet in livery was waiting when our carriage arrived, holding in each hand a candelabra with four lighted candles. We went up a staircase that was polished and illuminated like a salon. . . . We passed by a salon magnificently ornamented, then a bedroom with columns and a bed of incomparable beauty hung in the most expensive Persian silk. I'm not exaggerating when I say that fifty candles were lighted. . . . I admit that although I was accustomed to seeing the best and the most beautiful, I was dazzled, even stupefied by such a setting.[23]

The room through which Dufort passed was certainly a *salle de compagnie* or formal receiving room, and the bed almost certainly the single most expensive piece of furniture in the house. Another courtesan, Mlle Rotisset, a singer at the Comédie Italienne, had a similar room and bed. When her house was inventoried in 1752, it included a very elaborate bed *à la reine* draped in yellow brocade. The same fabric covered walls, canapé, and seven armchairs.[24] Thirty years later, Mlle Dervieux included the traditional *salle de compagnie* in her newly built pavilion. The focal point of the room was a bed draped in the Persian style, with blue brocade and topped with ostrich feathers. The ceiling of the bed was covered in mirrors, and a large crystal globe was suspended in the center of the room.[25] Even Mlle Guimard, the most avant-garde of the lot, placed a bed *à la reine* draped in red and white brocade in her salon, which also contained four armchairs, six cabriolet chairs, and two banquettes, all upholstered in identical scarlet and white striped brocade. More money (13,600 livres) was lavished on this room than on any other in the house, much of it, one imagines, on the bed and its draperies.[26]

In each of these cases, a traditional piece of furniture absorbed a great deal of money. The *chambre de parade* derived from the royal apartments at Versailles and sometimes included not just the elaborate bed but a gilded balustrade as well. As early as 1740, the formal chamber began to disappear. Where it still existed it, it was rarely used, being (like many living rooms today) just for show.[27] A more informal space, the *salle de compagnie*, was replacing it and eliminating the formal bed.[28] With its abundant seating and garden views, the courtesan's rooms came closest to the new *salle de compagnie*—but there was that bed. Of all pieces of furniture, the formal bed most embodied the aristocratic provenance of French furniture. What was it doing in the house of a notorious actress?

The formal bed seems doubly out of place because the courtesans were known for their innovative tastes. They employed the most avant-garde architects of the day: Charles-Nicolas Ledoux (1736–1806) drew up the plans for Guimard's home in 1773; Alexandre Théodore Brongniart (1736–1813) created Dervieux's house in 1778, and François-Jean Belanger (1744–1818) added a dining room and bathroom suite in 1778. The *Correspondance secrète* dubbed Guimard the "goddess of taste" and praised her for "eschewing the confusion of ornament one finds in older [homes]."[29] Mlle Dervieux received an even more flattering nickname: the *Correspondance* christened her "a more modern goddess," the proprietor (one assumes) of a more "modern" home.[30]

But there was still that bed. Critics of luxury feared the misappropriation of traditional symbols like the regal bed. Was the opera dancer who reclined on her elaborate bed mocking tradition—even the rituals of Versailles? Guimard for one was bold: she produced banned plays and risqué entertainments in the small theater located adjacent to her home. She also defied the authorities at the opera to a degree that earned her an evil reputation.[31] But it is hard to believe that she would invest so much money in a charade, however subversive, and then keep it permanently in her home.

More likely, the formal bed evoked associations different from those of the aristocracy and the court. To the degree that it survived outside of Versailles and the townhouses of the greatest aristocrats, the formal bedroom, and especially its bed, was associated with the female realm. At the Place Vendôme, for example, the formal bedchamber was included in the suite of rooms destined for the lady of the house.[32] Blondel remarked that men no longer received in bed, but women did. The *chambre de parade,* he observed, "is inhabited by preference by the mistress of the house when she is indisposed; there she receives visits and uses it for her toilette for special distinction . . ."[33] With antecedents not just in the palace but also in the *ruelles* of the previous century, the formal bed was an intensely female object and (perhaps) regarded as such. We have no memoirs, letters, or texts written by the courtesans to clarify their intentions in home decoration (or anything else for that matter). But it is likely that Guimard, Dervieux, and the others retained the formal bed because it was a feminine object, a reminder that this was a woman's house.

Meanwhile, newer female spaces multiplied around the formal bed chamber. *Cabinets* and other small rooms abounded in both Guimard's and Dervieux's homes: in Guimard's house there were five, in Dervieux's three, not including a boudoir. Of these, most were *cabinets de toilette* or dressing rooms, where the lady of the house received while putting the finishing touches on her appearance. All the courtesans possessed, if not such a space, then at least the *table de toilette* or dressing table that stood in for it.[34] Though small, the dressing room was not a private space. The furniture in the *cabinets* consisted almost entirely of chairs (as many as half a dozen), which were covered in fabrics coordinated with the wall coverings, indicating that the chairs were meant for those rooms. Dressing rooms were very feminine spaces where the courtesan received special friends, maybe potential lovers. Such was the case in 1761, when the young Dufort de Cheverny first met the famous Deschamps. She greeted him, he remembered decades later, surrounded by three other suitors in the more modern, but no less feminine variation on the dressing room, the boudoir.[35]

The Dining Table

The boudoir was but one space for receiving, and not the most important. After some off-color banter, Deschamps led Dufort to the room of which she was most proud in her opulent house, the dining room (Figure 6.1). It was, she boasted, "the most beautiful in all Paris," and Dufort found it to be "like a marvelous dream." He recalled that "a myriad of candles blazed and the buffet was laid with rare preserved fruits" and other delicacies.[36] There stood one of the most important tools of the courtesan's trade, her dining table. Annette Dervieux

Figure 6.1 Dining room of Mlle Dervieux. Cabinet des Estampes. Bibliothèque nationale de France. Photo: Service photographique, Bibliothèque nationale de France.

possessed a mammoth mahogany table capable of seating fourteen and made of a single slab of the exotic wood. It was "designed by Pionnier," her 1793 inventory tells us, "to astonish by the beauty of its workmanship."[37] Above it were suspended two large lamps in English crystal that threw light on the extraordinarily ornate walls. The walls were covered with neoclassical white stucco bas reliefs and arabesques on pale blue or sienna ground. Silver gilt covered every border, frame, and many details. Two floor-to-ceiling mirrors in mahogany frames reflected multiple candelabra mounted on turquoise marble stands.

French dining rooms were traditionally rather ad hoc affairs, located (as at Versailles) in an anteroom and bare of furniture save for a folding table.[38] Only fourteen percent of the Parisians whose probate inventories were studied by Annik Pardailhé-Galabrun had a dining room,[39] but like the *salle de compagnie* or salon, the dining room grew in importance over the course of the eighteenth century. Most financiers on the Place Vendôme, for example, possessed one, but few placed as much importance on this space as the courtesan did.[40]

As Dufort de Cheverney's visit to Deschamps reveals, dining was the principle means of entertainment offered by courtesans. These dancers, singers, and actresses did not offer just any meal. They specialized in after-theater suppers, which both accommodated their schedules and encouraged seduction. The *petit souper*, as it was known, was the courtesans' specialty, a meal made fashionable by the libertine maréchal de Richelieu. According to the *Correspondance secrète*, Guimard gave three such suppers a week: the first for the great lords of the court, the second for the best writers and artists, and the third for "the most seductive and beautiful girls of the capital . . . a veritable orgy."[41]

The dining room was the principle space for entertaining. The layout of Guimard's house made this explicit. In most Parisian homes, the vestibule and antechamber led directly to the salon, but in Guimard's house, it brought the guest immediately to the dining room so that only a few steps were needed to exit the theater, traverse the courtyard, and find oneself in the dining room (Figure 6.2). And what a dining room! A combination of neoclassical rigor and fantasy, Mlle Guimard's dining room consisted of a buffet separated only by

Figure 6.2 Dining room of Mlle Guimard. Drawing. Courtesy of the Royal Institute of British Architects. Photo: A.C. Cooper.

gilt columns from a "winter garden," that is, a room paneled in mirrors painted with tree branches to simulate a forest glade.[42]

Guimard's dining room immediately conjures up the fictional boudoir in Jean-François Bastide's novella, *La petite maison*.[43] First published in 1758 and republished in an abridged version in 1763, Bastide's story of a seduction carried off thanks to a seductive house predates Guimard's home by almost twenty years. Still, there are marked similarities between Bastide's fictional pavilion and the urban homes of Guimard and Dervieux. Gardens surrounded all three houses. Dervieux had an extensive and famous English garden. Similar fabrics (embroidered Indian silk, Persian silk, and taffeta) upholstered the walls and furniture in both the fictional and real homes. Technological innovations characterized all three dwellings: a mechanical dining table stood in Bastide's fictional house, lightweight copper "leaves" covered Dervieux's roof, and two skylights illuminated Guimard's buffet and dining room. All three contained *cabinets anglais* or valved toilets.[44] In Dervieux's home as in Bastide's, an elaborate cabinet, fashioned out of "mahogany with a turquoise marble top and gilt bronze fittings," hid the porcelain toilet.[45] The marked resemblance between Bastide's boudoir, "covered in mirrors painted with green leaves and tree trunks," and Guimard's magical dining room, only makes more apparent that the similarities between the courtesans' homes and Bastide's "little house" were more than coincidental.

For the courtesans as for Bastide, the suburban pavilions located in Passy or Montmartre—the real little houses—were the primary visual source. Police records show that courtesans and prostitutes frequently visited these notorious dwellings.[46] First built during the Regency, little houses were located outside Paris in order to avoid prying eyes.[47] An "asylum of pleasure and abundance," a little house was a place of freedom from social constraints and the tired decorative practices of Versailles. It was a house devoted to pleasure, both visual and venereal.[48] The decoration could be lewd: the notorious Maréchal de Richelieu had erotic arabesques painted onto his pavilion's wood paneling.[49] Because the activity within (post-theater suppers and garden parties) was suspect, the police inspectors monitored the suburban retreats closely. From police records we learn that virtually all of these bachelor pads (to use a more current phrase), were owned by men. Wives and mothers were not welcome.[50] Courtesans and prostitutes, however, were very frequent guests. A few, including Guimard and Dervieux, managed to own their own little houses.[51] The suppers at Guimard's pavilion were reported in the gazettes, but we have no prints or objects to help us reconstruct Guimard's little house. Only the wood paneling from the small salon, now installed in the Musée de l'Ile de France (Sceaux), survives (Figure 6.3).

These little houses, both fictional and real, rejected the old Versailles aesthetic of magnificence in favor of a new decorative idiom that sought to indulge the senses and produce delight rather than awe. Sensationalism informed Bastide's little house and found explicit expression in Nicolas Le Camus de Mezières's architectural treatise, *Le génie de l'architecture, ou, l'analogie de cet art avec nos sensations*.[52] Published in 1780, not long after the opening of both Guimard and Dervieux's homes, Le Camus's text describes an ideal home that recalls the courtesans' dwellings. Le Camus even makes explicit reference to Guimard. A "charming actress," he says, "known for her qualities of heart and mind and skilled in the analysis of true pleasure . . . has made a conservatory the most delightful place in her house, which is a Fairy's palace."[53]

The courtesans appropriated the little house idiom and put it to their own uses. First, they brought it to the city and displayed it publicly. The courtesans built townhouses, not garden pavilions, and they located them in plain view on the newest, most fashionable streets in Paris.

Figure 6.3 Paneling from the Salon of Mlle Guimard's House in Pantin. Musée de l'Ile de France, Sceaux. Photo: Pascal Lemaitre.

Second, they feminized the bachelor pad. No obscene arabesques graced the homes of Guimard and Dervieux. Marble nudes did hold aloft the candles in Guimard's winter garden, but otherwise naked statutes and nude paintings were few, less numerous than at Versailles.[54]

It would be tempting to say that the courtesan "domesticated" the little house, but *domestic* is not a word that should be associated with these independent women. Neither Dervieux's home nor Guimard's was in the least familial. Neither had husbands at this time, although both did have daughters: Dervieux adopted a girl and Guimard had a daughter by de La Borde, but neither child seems to have lived on the premises.[55] These houses were devoted to the comfort of the mistress and the entertainment of her guests.

The Neoclassical Chair and Collecting

Proof of the importance to the courtesans of receiving and entertaining is evident in the chairs they purchased. Guimard could seat sixty in her dining room and Dervieux possessed 124 chairs, three times as many as the average Parisian noble or high officer.[56] We have no images or surviving examples of these chairs, but the furniture in Guimard's house was "conceived and made especially for it" by the architect-designer Lequeu, who had been selected by Guimard's architect, Ledoux.[57] Perhaps the chairs in Guimard's house looked like the drawings Lequeu made for the hôtel Montholon that was completed about five years later (Figure 6.4). As for Dervieux's house, all the furniture was fashioned by Jacob out of mahogany. In both cases, the style was "Egyptian" or "Greek," the very peak of fashion. Although the Greek style is generally considered a manifestation of the Napoleonic period, it was already popular in the 1780s. Mlle Guimard's house took the strict, even austere form of a Greek temple (Figure 6.5). Dervieux's house also employed neoclassical forms, most famously in a bathroom suite praised in the *Correspondance secrète* as the "abode of a nymph" and subsequently engraved and colored (Figure 6.6).[58]

Courtesans had a special affinity for antiquity because it provided models that were both widely known and extremely laudatory. Numerous texts—some semipornographic, others just sentimental—celebrated the courtesan of the ancient world. Among the titles published

Figure 6.4 Drawing for the hôtel Montholon, Jean-Jacques Lequeu. Cabinet des Estampes. Bibliothèque nationale de France. Photo: Service Photographique, Bibliothèque nationale de France.

Figure 6.5 House of Mlle Guimard. Claude Nicolas Ledoux, architect. Cabinet des Estampes. Bibliothèque nationale de France. Photo: Service photographique, Bibliothèque nationale de France.

Figure 6.6 Bathroom of Mlle Dervieux, ca. 1790. Print. Cabinet des Estampes. Bibliothèque nationale de France. Photo: Service photographique, Bibliothèque nationale de France.

in the eighteenth century are Jacques Autreau, *Rhodope ou l'Opera perdu* (1737); Antoine Bret, *Lycoris ou la courtisane grecque* (1746); Pierre-François Godard de Beauchamps, *Hipparchia, histoire galante* (1748); Guillaume-Alexandre Méhégan, *Lettres d'Aspasie* (1756); and Bénigne Legoux de Gerlan, *Histoire de Laïs, courtisane grecque* (1756). In these volumes, prostitutes were not described as base creatures who were greedy and scheming; rather the courtesans of old were ennobled by their virtues:

> Genius and talent as well as heroism are the most important aspect of these courtesans' favors; they are the reason for their superiority. The courtesans' pride is earned, their pleasures purified; they abandon themselves [to men] but they also respect themselves. This commerce of the senses is deliberate, embellished, and sustained by wit and heart. Nature smiles on this marriage of beauty and virtue and enjoins society to support it.[59]

In the guise of Rhodope or Aspasia, the courtesan was rehabilitated. She was shorn of her associations with poverty and disease and emerged a virtuous woman. Small wonder that courtesans both in the eighteenth century and during the French Revolution gravitated toward everything antique. Seated amidst her Egyptian chairs and neoclassical commodes, the courtesan could assume the mantle of the dignified and virtuous hetaira.

The courtesan could also take on the identity of the learned woman. One of the qualities that distinguished the courtesans of antiquity was their intelligence. Bret's Lycoris, for example, acquired "a reputation as a woman philosopher which dispelled any thought of (her) debauches." Her house, Bret emphasized, "was not odious even to men of the most austere morality." Lycoris attended the most distinguished assemblies in the town, he claimed, where "her wit and beauty were appreciated."[60]

It is doubtful that eighteenth-century courtesans participated in assemblies of honest women and men, but they could still don the mantle of the "learned woman."[61] In the eighteenth century, that meant collecting, and Mlle Guimard, Mlle Laguerre, Sophie Arnould, and Mlle Dervieux were all avid collectors. Because their collections sometimes ended up on the *marchand mercier's* auction block, we know something about their composition. Generally the collections were of two sorts: the scientific (made up of natural history specimens and books) and the artistic (consisting of paintings, oriental curiosities, or prints). The great actress Mlle Clairon sold 895 objects divided between shells and crystals.[62] The opera singer Mlle Dervieux had a collection of over two dozen exotic birds preserved in wax and displayed in specially designed glass cases.[63] More typical was Sophie Arnould, who sold dozens of porcelains, bronze sculptures, and etched crystals, as well as forty-one paintings.[64]

The most common type of object to collect, however, was porcelains. Sophie Arnould auctioned off over two hundred lots of Chinese, Japanese, European, and French porcelain. Every courtesan inventory or auction included porcelain. Dervieux had a room specially designed for her porcelain collection with niches affixed to the wall where the vases and cups could be displayed. Mlle Rotisset covered virtually every flat surface in her salon with tea cups, candy dishes, bowls, potpourri containers, vases, and figurines.[65] Mlle Guimard had a reputedly vast collection sold before her house was auctioned. For courtesans, the passion for porcelain verged on a mania.

The *Secrétaire*

Which brings me to the last piece of furniture emblematic of the courtesan's taste: the *secrétaire* or writing desk. The object in question is a *secrétaire* made by Martin Carlin and sold by Daguerre. Its owner was Marie-Josephine Laguerre of the Royal Academy of Music, otherwise known as the Paris Opera. Laguerre debuted there in 1775, and went on to score a string of successes in Gluck operas. Her chief notoriety came from an incident in 1776 when she appeared drunk on stage.[66] Offstage, she acquired a series of wealthy protectors, most notably the Duc de Bouillon, who reputedly spent over three million livres in less than three months on the singer. In 1783, Laguerre died at the age of twenty-eight of a "shameful disease."[67] According to the *Mémoires secrets*, the libertine Laguerre turned pious on her deathbed and made substantial religious bequests. She could afford to: she possessed 700,000 livres in cash, 40,000 in government annuities, two houses, and a large number of jewels.[68] Her curiosities were auctioned off in 1783, and it is thanks to the catalog of that auction that we know about Mlle Laguerre's *secrétaire*.

Laguerre also owned an impressive number of curiosities. The published catalog lists a painting of a Cupid by Fragonard, a sculpted rock crystal, three marquetry clocks in gilt bronze mounts, four candelabra of matte gold, twenty pieces of Sèvres porcelain in gilt bronze mounts, as well as assorted plaques, turquoise vases, bowls, and cups. As for her furniture, most was sold before the auction began. What remained were the most expensive objects, including a commode veneered in ebony and ornamented with *petra-dura* flowers and fruits; a tulipwood gaming table fit for playing *trou à madame*; a small satinwood writing table with gilt bronze feet; and two armoires and a *secrétaire* with fronts of old Japanese lacquer.

The desk that interests us was veneered in tulipwood and mounted with Sèvres porcelain plaques (Figure 6.7). Here is how it was described in the 1783 auction catalog:

> A *secrétaire* veneered with tulipwood, opening in the center by a drop-down shelf, decorated with three plaques of Sèvres porcelain, of which one represents a basket

Figure 6.7 Upright Secretary. Martin Carlin (ca. 1730–1785). Oak veneered with tulipwood, purplewood, holly, gilt-bronze, Sèvres porcelain plaques, *tôle peinte*, white marble. 110.1 x 102.9 x 32.7 cm. The Metropolitan Museum of Art, gift of Mr. and Mrs. Charles Wrightsman, 1976 (1976.155.110) Photograph, all rights reserved, The Metropolitan Museum of Art.

of flowers held aloft by a ribbon bow with framed garlands of roses; the top is veined marble . . . surrounded by a gilt bronze gallery, the sides of which are decorated with gilt draperies. Two vertical plaques that bear swags of flowers also hung by ribbons . . . are supported by four fluted legs topped by three porcelain plaques decorated with flowers, of which the center is also a drawer . . . [It is] three feet four inches high and three feet two inches wide.[69]

It would be interesting to know where Laguerre placed this desk, but lacking the inventory that would have been made by the notary upon her death, we can only guess. It probably stood in a cabinet, a relatively small room, which depending on its contents, might also have qualified as a boudoir. The *secrétaire* contained locked drawers, cubbyholes, and per-haps even a secret compartment. Did Laguerre keep love letters or government annuities locked in the desk? Or did she hide in the *secrétaire's* recesses the very large amount of cash (700,000 livres) found at her death? Because we know little about Laguerre's living arrange-ments, we cannot tell. But it is easy to see that this desk was meant to display objects, almost certainly the Sèvres vases, cups, and potpourri bowls also sold at her auction. Fully loaded, with colorful porcelains displayed on every shelf and poised on the galleried top, the effect must have been stunning. With the beautiful singer seated in front of it, this *secrétaire* was like a shrine, a monument first to Sèvres porcelain and then to the courtesan's own opulence and taste.

Laguerre's desk provokes several observations about fashion and furniture in the late eighteenth century. Scholars are accustomed to thinking about eighteenth-century furni-ture in terms of aristocratic values, even royal precedents.[70] However, the courtesans dem-onstrate that the consumers of fine furniture drew upon a broader range of influences. These women took their cues not from the aristocratic townhouse, but from the financiers' "little house." Their furniture drew on antiquity, not Versailles, and was chosen and organized to charm and delight, not to impose. The demands of aristocratic deportment and polite society seem quite removed from the courtesans' mirrored dining rooms and Grecian baths, which encouraged indulgence, not its opposite.

Of course, the courtesans' furniture and houses were models too. In fact, few consumers of fine furniture outside of Versailles were as visible. Some writers, like Bastide and Le Camus de Mézières, praised the courtesans' salons and boudoirs and dubbed the women nothing less than "goddesses of taste." But others, it should be remembered, denounced the courtesan and railed against her "unwholesome elegance."[71] Barbier considered the crowds assembled outside Deschamps's house during her auction "a scandal which dishonors our morals." Trumeau de la Morandière denounced the "courtesans' houses in the country and city . . . the Flemish tapestries, the precious sofas, [and] dressing tables which abound there."[72] However much she spent on her furniture or evoked Laïs or Rhodope, in the eyes of many, a courtesan was still just a prostitute.

It is thus all the more amazing that men and women flocked to the courtesans' auctions and paid to visit their homes. The public, if not the moralists, endorsed the courtesans' decoration or at least took interest in it. At Deschamps's auction in 1760, women from the highest echelons of the robe and finance, nobles, and even some cordons bleus jostled to inspect her commodes and porcelains. In 1787, when Guimard held a lottery to sell her house and all its furnishings, a crowd besieged the "Temple of Terpsichore" and all 2,500 tickets were sold, even though at 120 livres a ticket, the price was quite high.[73] When there was no auction, visitors still came to look at the house: a tip to the concierge sufficed to gain entry and receive a guided tour of the Temple.[74] Foreign dignitaries like Horace Walpole, the landgrave of Hesse-Kassel, and the count of Falkenstein (in fact, Marie-Antoinette's brother incognito) toured Guimard's Temple.[75] In 1790, the Russian Nicolai Karamzin visited Dervieux's home, still a must for all foreign tourists.[76] For those who could not visit the courtesans' homes in person, there were descriptions in the press and engravings. The *Correspondance sécrète* devoted two pages to a description of Guimard's Temple and even more to Dervieux's home. An engraving of the Temple facade was so popular that it was reprinted at least three times.[77] In 1789, Ledoux published a book of his buildings' floor plans and elevations.[78] A few years later, engravings of Dervieux's dining room and bathroom appeared. Again in 1802, both houses were included in the collection of architectural drawings published by Krafft and Ransonette.

Eighteenth-century connoisseurs did not hesitate to view or purchase courtesans' furniture. Of course, the women's outlaw status may have made their chairs and *secrétaires* all the more appealing (as it would in the nineteenth century). But it is still a measure of the development of fashion and luxury that models of elegance were found even on the fringes of society, among the marginal and the unpedigreed, in what today would be called "the street."

Did the courtesans exercise any influence over other consumers and their furniture? At least one commentator thinks they did. In memoirs published in 1824, Antoine Caillot claimed that "the nymphs of the stage gave boudoir taste (*le ton du boudoir*) to noble women and the wives of the high bourgeoisie." He went on to declare, "the French owe to the courtesan, the ability to furnish an apartment with taste and comfort."[79] Maybe the courtesans did influence middle-class women, maybe they did not. Although it would be impossible to prove either way, Mlle Laguerre's *secrétaire* may be helpful. In 1784, Maria Feodorovna, wife of the future Russian emperor Paul I, purchased numerous pieces of furniture at the shop of *marchand mercier* Daguerre on the rue Saint-Honoré, to be sent to the Pavlovsk Palace in

Saint Petersburg. A *secrétaire* matching the description of Mlle Laguerre's appears in Maria Feodorovna's description of her boudoir.[80] That *secrétaire* remained in the Pavlovsk palace until 1917, when it was acquired from the Soviet authorities by the famous American dealer, Duveen and Company. After Duveen, the desk changed hands several times before being purchased by American collectors Mr. and Mrs. Charles Wrightsman. Eventually it came to rest in the Sèvres room of the Wrightsman Galleries in the Metropolitan Museum of Art in New York City.[81] How many visitors standing respectfully behind the gold rope guess that the desk against the wall once stood in a courtesan's boudoir? How many other pieces in museum galleries might also have once been touched by the "goddesses of taste"?

Notes

1. Edmond-Jean-François Barbier, *Chronique de la régence et du règne de Louis XV (1718–1763), ou Journal de Barbier* (Paris: Charpentier, 1866), 7: 244–48.
2. Ibid., 248.
3. A peculiarity of French law bestowed legal immunity in matters of morals on women who belonged to the royal theatrical companies, including the *magasin*. Consequently, many elite men stashed their lovers or chose them in the chorus to avoid the incarceration of their mistresses.
4. On the career trajectories of actresses and courtesans, see Erica-Marie Benabou, *La prostitution et la police des moeurs au XVIIIe siècle* (Paris: Perrin, 1987).
5. Guimard, Dervieux, and Deschamps have all been the subject of biographies. See Edmond Goncourt, *La Guimard* (1893; rpt. ed., Geneva: Minkoff, 1973); Roger Baschet, *Mademoiselle Dervieux, fille d'Opéra* (Paris: Flammarion, 1943); Gaston Capon and Robert Yve-Plessis, *Fille d'opéra, vendeuse d'amour, histoire de Mlle Deschamps (1730–1764)* (Paris: Plessis, 1906).
6. For information on courtesans see Bénabou, *La prostitution et la police des moeurs*, 330–86.
7. Archives de la Bastille (henceforth AB), 10, 238, 35.
8. The sums of money spent on furnishings were much larger when a protector intended to live on the premises. A provincial named Montaigu spent lavishly on his lover's furniture because he intended "to make [her apartment] his manor and take all his meals there." AB, 10, 238, 640.
9. Pierre Clément, *La police sous Louis XIV* (Paris: Didier, 1886), 302.
10. "Procès verbal du tirage de la loterie de la maison de Mlle Guimard, pièces jointes, état des meubles," in Emile Campardon, *Les comédiens du roi de la troupe française pendant les deux derniers siècles* (Paris: H. Champion, 1879), 137–39.
11. Jean Stern, *A l'ombre de Sophie Arnould: François-Joseph Belanger, architecte des Menus Plaisirs; premier architecte du comte d'Artois* (Paris: Plon, 1930), 1: 188. The house was less elegant than its furnishings: it sold for only 14,000 livres, whereas the furniture sold for 11,000 livres.
12. Natacha Coquery, *L'hôtel aristocratique: le marché du luxe à Paris au XVIIIe siècle* (Paris: Publications de la Sorbonne, 1998), 134–35.
13. The profits to be made in the sex business were so great that some upholsterers were tempted to take a more active role. The Corbin couple (he an upholsterer, she his helper) was well known to the police. The upholsterer was in the habit of selling furnishings to men at high rates and then buying it back for much less when the romance failed. Madame Corbin was the principal tenant of an apartment building on the rue Feydeau where she housed prostitutes to whom she personally led the clients (AB, 10, 245, 33).
14. Archives Nationales (henceforth AN), MC LVII, 456.
15. AN, Y 11, 293, Papers of the Commissioner Desance.
16. *Documents inédits sur la règne de Louis XV. Journal des inspecteurs de m. de Sartines, première série, 1761–1764* (Paris: Dentu, 1863), 77.
17. AN, Y 11, 573.
18. AB, 10, 238, 651.
19. See Natacha Coquery's essay in this volume.
20. Jean Charles Davillier, *Une vente d'actrice sous Louis XVI, Mlle. Laguerre de l'opéra* (Paris: A. Aubry, 1870), 40.
21. Rochelle Ziskin, *The Place Vendôme: Architecture and Social Mobility in Eighteenth-Century Paris* (Cambridge: Cambridge University Press, 1999).

22. Of the courtesans whose furniture is examined here only one, Rotisset, actually cohabited some of the time with her lover, the financier Maisonneuve. The others all had lovers but lived in an apartment or house of which they were the sole occupant. For a variety of reasons, not the least of which was fear of scandal, relationships did not lead to cohabitation. Guimard had a long-term relationship and a daughter with the tax farmer and amateur composer Benjamin-Joseph de La Borde, but she never lived with him. Dervieux had various flirtations but ended up marrying her architect, François Jean Belanger. However, the marriage appears to have been one of convenience contracted while both were prisoners of the revolutionary government. See Mathieu Couty, *Jean Benjamin de Laborde ou le bonheur d'être fermier general* (Paris: Michel de Maul, 2001); Stern, *A l'ombre de Sophie Arnould*, 1: 188.

23. Jean-Nicolas Dufort de Cheverny, *Mémoires*, ed. Jean-Pierre Guiccardi (Paris: Perrin, 1990), 1: 283.

24. AN, MC LXXVI, 333. Similarly, when Mlle Veronèze, known to the audiences at the Comédie Italienne as Camille, expired in 1760, she was laid out in a bed draped in white silk re-embroidered with flowers, which stood in a room paneled in varnished, sculpted wood that also housed two *canapés* and two armchairs upholstered in white- and red-striped silk. The bed and hangings alone cost 12,000 livres (AN, Z 2 2452).

25. AN, MC LXXXVI, 886. Mlle Dervieux's inventory was drawn up after she and her buyer had agreed on a price. Consequently, no prices appear in Dervieux's inventory.

26. "Etat des meubles de la maison de Mlle Guimard," in Campardon, *Les comédiens du roi*, 138.

27. Nicolas Le Camus de Mézières, *The Genius of Architecture; or the Analogy of that Art with our Sensations*, trans. David Britt (1780; reprint ed., Santa Monica, Calif.: Getty Center for the History of Art and Humanities, 1992), 113.

28. Ziskin, *Place Vendôme*, 130.

29. *Correspondance secrète*, cited in Goncourt, *La Guimard*, 148.

30. *Correspondance secrète, politique et littéraire, ou Mémoires pour servir à l'histoire des cours, des sociétés et de la littérature en France, depuis la mort de Louis XV*, 18 vols. (London: J. Adamson, 1787–1790), 9: 25–27.

31. Goncourt, *La Guimard*, 197–229.

32. Ziskin, *Place Vendôme*, 25.

33. Jacques-François Blondel, *L'Architecture française* (Paris: 1752–1756; reprint ed., Paris: Librairie Centrale des Beaux Arts, 1904), 1: 33.

34. Dressing tables appeared among all the courtesans' possessions. Mlle Veronèze owned such a table made of tulipwood, but she kept it upstairs in a small summer salon. (AN, Z2 2435.)

35. Lest Dufort miss the point, Deschamps engaged in bawdy banter with the other guests about an ex-lover, much to the surprise of the naive Dufort. Dufort de Cheverny, *Mémoires*, 283.

36. Ibid.

37. AN, MC LXXXVI, 886.

38. Robin Middleton, Introduction to Le Camus de Mezières, *Genius of Architecture*, 35.

39. Annik Pardailhé-Galabrun, *La naissance de l'intime: 3,000 foyers parisiens, XVIIe–XVIIIe siècles* (Paris: Presses Universitaires de France, 1988), 260.

40. Ziskin, *Place Vendôme*, 130.

41. According to the *Correspondance secrète*, she attracted "so many philosophers and *beaux esprits* that [her suppers] rivaled the salon of Madame Geoffrin." Cited in Goncourt, *La Guimard*, 34.

42. The only representation we have of Guimard's winter garden/dining room dates from the post-1789 period when the banker Perregaux occupied the house. In the 1804 plan, the winter garden is identified as the dining room and the adjacent smaller space as a "buffet." Because the 1785 inventory lists no furniture for the winter garden, it is likely that both winter garden and buffet were used as dining rooms. How else would all the tables be accommodated? My guess is that the smaller buffet served as a winter dining room and the larger winter garden as a summer dining room. In any case, only two columns separated what was in fact a single room.

43. Jean-François Bastide, *The Little House*, trans. Rodolphe El-Khoury (Princeton, NJ: Princeton Architectural Press, 1997).

44. Blondel described such a toilet in 1737; in 1775, Roubo outlined its construction. However, almost no Parisians adopted it. Guimard and Dervieux were exceptions, for they had *cabinets anglais* installed on both floors of their homes and located in such a way as to assure access from a number of rooms. On plumbing, see Georges Vigarello, *Concepts of Cleanliness: Changing Attitudes in France since the Middle Ages*, trans. Jean Birrell (Cambridge: Cambridge University Press, 1988).

45. AN, MC LXXXVI, 886.

46. See Gaston Capon, *Les petites maisons galantes de Paris aux XVIIIe siècle: folies, maisons de plaisance et vide bouteilles, d'après les documents inédits et des rapports de police* (Paris: H. Daragon, 1882).

47. On definitions of the *petite maison* see Anthony Vidler, Preface to Bastide, *Little House*, 21.

48. Abbé Coyer cited in Bruno Pons, Postface to Jean-François Bastide, *La petite maison* (Paris: Gallimard, 1993), 78.

49. D'Argenson cited in ibid., 79.

50. When the comte de Watteville died in his little house on the rue de la Rochefoucauld, his wife was in their Paris residence. She made no claims on any object in the house, leaving the contents to creditors and the count's mistress. AN, Z2 2453.

51. Mlle Deschamps appears to have rented a little house in Pantin. See Capon and Yve-Plessis, *Fille d'opéra*, 88. Camille Veronèze of the Comédie italienne also owned a little house in the Porcherons, which was "six windows wide" and two stories high. It was certainly more than a garden pavilion, but it partook nevertheless of the spirit of ease and comfort of the surrounding little houses. (AN, Z2 2452).

52. On Le Camus de Mézières and sensationalism see Rémy Saisselin, "Architecture and Language: The Sensationalism of Le Camus de Mézières," *British Journal of Aesthetics* 15 (1975): 239–53.

53. Le Camus de Mézières, *Genius of Architecture*, 194.

54. Christian Baulez finds that nudes were particularly numerous at Dubarry's house in Louveciennes. Christian Baulez, "Le mobilier et les objets de Madame Du Barry," in *Madame Du Barry, de Versailles à Louveciennes* (Paris: Flammarion, 1992), 51.

55. One of the first parties Guimard gave in the Temple of Terpsichore was in honor of her daughter's marriage. The young woman died less than a year later. See Goncourt, *La Guimard*, 33. Dervieux adopted a young pauper almost on a whim, but little is known of her. See Baschet, *Mademoiselle Dervieux*, 55.

56. Pardailhé-Galabrun, *La naissance de l'intime*, 261.

57. This information is contained in the building permit submitted by Ledoux to the Parisian authorities; see Michel Gallet, *Claude-Nicolas Ledoux: 1736–1806* (Paris: Picard, 1980), 84.

58. *Correspondance secrète*, 9: 25.

59. Pierre Chaussard, *Fêtes et courtisanes de la Grèce, supplément Aux voyages d' Anacharsis et d'Antenor* (Paris: F. Buisson, 1801), 1:75.

60. Antoine Bret, *Lycoris; ou, la courtisanne grecque* (Amsterdam: Aux dépense de la Compagnie, 1746), 137.

61. Elise Goodman, *The Portraits of Madame de Pompadour: Celebrating the Femme Savante* (New Haven, CT: Yale University Press, 2001).

62. *Catalogue de Vente de Mlle ******. Catalogue de cabinet d'histoire naturelle de Mlle de C.* (Paris: Chez Joullain, 1773). Books were not absent from these collections. The opera singer Rotisset owned dozens of books of music, the first edition of Bernard Picart, *Les cérémonies et coutumes religieuses de tous les peuples du monde*, and two hundred unnamed volumes of history and belles-lettres (AN, MC LXXVI, 333).

63. "Vente de maison et meubles d'une maison rue Chantereine 21 mai 1793." AN, MC L, XXXVI, 886.

64. Arnould's paintings included several by Louis de Boulogne and a print portfolio previously owned by the duc de Choiseul. See Emile Dacier, "La vente de Sophie Arnould," *Revue de l'art ancien et moderne* 26 (1909): 353. The opera singer Mlle Rotisset owned over 36 paintings, most of the Flemish/Dutch school (including several small Rembrandts), as well as numerous prints and engravings (AN, MC LXXVI, 333).

65. Ibid.

66. Laguerre was appearing in Gluck's opera, *Iphigénie en Tauride*. Sophie Arnould quipped that she was "Iphigénie en champagne." [Louis Petit de Bachaumont], *Mémoires secrets pour servir à l'histoire de la République des Lettres en France, depuis MDCCLXII jusqu'à nos jours; ou, Journal d'un observateur*, 36 vols. (London: J. Adamson, 1783-89), 9:113.

67. According to Friedrich-Melchior Grimm, Laguerre died of an "anti-social disease." See Emile Campardon, *L'Académie royale de musique au XVIIIe siècle: documents inédits découverts aux Archives nationales*, (1884; reprint ed., New York: Da Capo Press, 1971), 1: 55.

68. Bachaumont, *Mémoires secrets*, 22: 87–88.

69. "Notice des différens objets de curiosité . . . appartenans à Mlle DELAGUERRE," in Davillier, *Une vente d'actrice sous Louis XVI*, 41-2.

70. For a discussion of eighteenth-century furniture as a reflection of absolute monarchy, see Leora Auslander *Taste and Power: Furnishing Modern France* (Berkeley: University of California Press, 1996), 35–74. The affinities between aristocratic deportment and furniture are explored by Mimi Hellman in "Furniture, Sociability and the Work of Leisure in Eighteenth-Century France," *Eighteenth-Century Studies* 32 (summer 1999): 415–45.

71. Louis-Sébastien Mercier cited in Capon and Yve-Plessis, *Fille d'opéra*, 128.

72. [Denis-Laurian] Trumeau de la Morandière, *Representations à Monsieur le lieutenant général de police de Paris sur les courtisanes à la mode et les Demoiselles du bon ton* (Paris: de l'imprimerie d'une société de gens ruinés par les femmes, 1760), 42.

73. See "Prospectus d'une loterie de la maison de Mlle Guimard," in Campardon, *Les Comédiens du roi*, 140.

74. Antoine Caillot, *Mémoires pour servir à l'histoire des moeurs et usages des français* (1827; reprint ed., Geneva: Slatkine-Megariotis, 1976), 1: 100.

75. See Gallet, *Claude-Nicolas Ledoux*, 88; Horace Walpole, *The Letters of Horace Walpole*, ed. Paget Toynbee (Oxford: Clarendon Press, 1903–5), 8: 84.

76. Nicolai Karamzin, *Voyage en France 1789–1790*, trans. Arsène Legrelle (Paris: Hachette, 1885), 165.

77. Anthony Vidler, *Claude-Nicolas Ledoux: Architecture and Social Reform at the End of the Ancien Régime* (Cambridge, MA: MIT Press, 1990), 52.

78. See Claude-Nicolas Ledoux, *L'Architecture de C. N. Ledoux* (Paris: Lenoir, 1847), 176.

79. Caillot, *Mémoires*, 100.

80. Compare the auction description with the description in [Francis John Bagott] Watson, *The Wrightsman Collection* (New York: Metropolitan Museum of Art, 1966), 1: 186–90.

81. The story of how this piece got from Laguerre to the Metropolitan Museum of Art is told by Bernard Jazzer in "Decorative Arts in the Eighteenth Century: The Wrightsman Secretary" (M.A. thesis: California State University, Long Beach, 1992).

PART III

Making Meaning in the Domestic Interior

CHAPTER 7

Color Schemes and Decorative Tastes in the Noble Houses of Old Regime Dauphiné

DONNA BOHANAN

When Anne de la Croix, widow of the president of the *Chambre des Comptes* in Dauphiné, died in 1668, her heirs commissioned a local notary to conduct an inventory of the contents of her household. Starting with the room in which she died, the notary painstakingly recorded and described every item. His list was comprehensive and detailed, and he was careful to mention the country of origin for imported items. He also took particular care to describe the color of the various textiles that had decorated her residence. In ancien regime France, notaries who conducted testamentary inventories took special care in describing foreign and exotic items. Their meticulous descriptions of materials, color, and origins highlight the fact that both connoisseurship and style had become hallmarks of elite society.

Among the decorative elements recorded in the inventory of Anne de la Croix's household were Flemish tapestries, Turkish rugs, coverlets from Catalonia and (perhaps) as far away as India. Her color scheme appears to have alternated, probably seasonally, between gray and red or crimson (embellished occasionally with gold) on the one hand, and a color known as *feuillemorte* (embellished with gold), on the other.[1] The inventory makes it clear that the individual or individuals who decorated this home did so with a vision of color and a sense of the impact of its repetitive use. Anne de la Croix's home appears to have been representative of her social milieu, because by the mid-seventeenth century noble families in Dauphiné were already subscribing to fashion trends. We see this particularly in their consistent use of a single color or combination of colors as a key component of interior decoration. Provincial nobles were consumers whose choices were governed increasingly by concepts of fashion in a society that was coming to value fashion and change in style for many reasons, not the least of which was their ability to distinguish the owner. As I will show, such consumer choices took on special meaning in this province, which had earlier been the scene of a great class conflict over taxation known as the *procès des tailles*.

How was elite society in the frontier province of Dauphiné defined by its material culture? Interior decoration had played a major role in defining European elites since the period of the Renaissance. It was in Italy that magnificence first became the standard for the urban residences of elites.[2] This standard eventually extended to France and its provincial nobilities, such that by the seventeenth and eighteenth centuries, interiors provided a medium for conspicuous consumption as elites filled their households with expensive, decorative, and exotic items. The furnishings of chateaux and urban townhouses became significantly more elaborate than in previous centuries because the interior of the home had come to assume even greater importance to the family. It offered concrete evidence of a family's wealth, station, taste, and refinement. We find in notary inventories a proliferation of items and greater concern with their decorative features, including color.

The elements of style, however, were predictable. They included things that had intrinsic value, such as silver, which also offered the opportunity to advertise pedigree by engraved coats of arms. They included art, especially portraits, because these rank markers allowed a family to boast about ancestors and heritage.[3] And they ranged to the exotic, which permitted families to showcase their education, knowledge, and connoisseurship; here the ubiquitous Turkish rug was especially important.[4]

Silver and engraved objects, paintings, and rugs were just some of the persistent elements of style in elite homes; style itself—to have the wealth and taste to create an overall effect—also became an important standard of magnificence. In this sense, notions of style had been set by the Marquise de Rambouillet well before Louis XIV set his architects to redesign the royal palace of Versailles in the 1670s. Architecture historian Peter Thornton attributes tremendous influence to the interior that the marquise very carefully constructed at her *hôtel* or townhouse. The remodeling of Rambouillet began in 1619, and the marquise took an active part in its design. Among the principles that guided her choices was the attempt to create a unified, harmonious effect, which had been one of the central goals of Italian architects during the Renaissance. By the early seventeenth century, Italian design principles were definitely in force in France and elsewhere in Europe. Having spent her youth in Italy, the marquise was clearly influenced by Italian designs and arrangements of interior spaces. To achieve the kind of harmony and unity that she sought, she made extensive use of a single color or color scheme or a single textile. Best known was the famous *chambre bleue* where she hosted salons. This setting was distinguished by its uniformity of color: the walls were painted blue and covered in blue fabric, and the chair covers and other textiles were in the same shade of blue. The use of such a color scheme has since become a hallmark of French design, and it apparently distinguished Rambouillet's interiors in the eyes of its guests, including the regent, Marie de Medici. Contemporaries commented admiringly about the "regularity" of the interior of her townhouse, a design attribute that would come to mark French style.[5]

By the late seventeenth century, the style of Rambouillet had become widely accepted. Most striking in the notary inventories is the popularity of the French style and its reliance on color. In their choice of vocabulary to describe color, the notaries themselves revealed a growing consciousness of color and its coordinated use. They even ventured beyond the blunt instruments of primary and secondary colors to describe in significantly more discerning terms the different hues they observed in the interiors of these homes. They were careful to note colors such as *musc* (a brownish gray), *aurore* (the color of dawn, a pale orange/apricot that was very popular in the seventeenth century), *feuillemorte* (a color that was based on green and reddish brown and gained popularity at the end of the sixteenth century), *citron*

Plate 1 Clock by André-Charles Boulle with marquetry in ebony, bronze, copper and tortoiseshell. Musée du Louvre, Paris. Réunion des Musées Nationaux/Art Resource, NY.

Plate 2 Bordeaux armoire, ca. 1790 in Cuban mahogany. Used as a linen cupboard. Musée des Arts Décoratifs, Bordeaux.

Plate 3 Secretary by Joseph Baumhauer. Late eighteenth century. Mahogany with bronze sphinx decoration. Musée du Louvre, Paris. Réunion des Musées Nationaux/Art Resource, NY.

Plate 4 Vase (first of a pair), attributed to Charles-Nicolas Dodin, ca.1760. Sèvres porcelain with painted decoration. Courtesy of The J. Paul Getty Museum, Los Angeles.

Plate 5 Vase (second of a pair), attributed to Charles-Nicolas Dodin, ca.1760. Sèvres porcelain with painted decoration. Courtesy of The J. Paul Getty Museum, Los Angeles.

Plate 6 Perfume fountain flanked by a pair of parrots and two vases, n. d. Chinese blue porcelain with gilt bronze mounts. Musée du Louvre, Paris. Photo: Réunion des Musées Nationaux/Art Resource, NY.

Plate 7 Tea service, Sèvres porcelain, 1768. Wadsworth Atheneum Museum of Art, Hartford, CT. Gift of J. Pierpont Morgan.

Plate 8 Jean-François de Troy, *La Conversation galante (The Gallant Conversation*, also called *The Garter)*, ca. 1724-1725. Oil on canvas. H: 65 cm; W: 54.20 cm. Williams College Museum of Art. Gift of C.A. Wimpfheimer, Class of 1949.

Plate 9 Jean-François de Troy, *La Déclaration d'amour (The Declaration of Love)*, ca. 1724-1725. Oil on canvas. H: 65 cm; W: 54.50 cm. Williams College Museum of Art. Gift of C.A. Wimpfheimer, Class of 1949.

Plate 10 Left: Tilt-top tea table, Philadelphia, ca. 1750-1775. Mahogany. Right: Candle stand, New England, ca. 1675-1725. Pine and maple. Both courtesy of Caxambas Foundation. Exhibited in "Reflections: Furniture, Silver, and Paintings in Early America," Elvehjem Museum of Art, October 11-December 28, 2003. Photo, Jim Wildeman.

Plate 11 Caroline Hill, *Portrait of Job Hill and His Family*, New Hampshire, 1837. Watercolor and pencil on paper. Courtesy of Peterborough Historical Society.

Plate 13 *Secrétaire* attributed to Guillaume Benneman, Paris, ca. 1785-1790. V&A W23-1958, gift of Sir Chester Beatty. Courtesy of V&A Images/Victoria and Albert Museum.

Plate 12 Tilt-top tea table, Philadelphia, ca. 1760-1770. Mahogany. Folded (vertical view). Courtesy of Chipstone Foundation. Photo, Gavin Ashworth.

Plate 15 Mechanical writing table, stamped in the workshop of Jean-François Oeben, Paris, ca. 1760. V&A 1095-1882, Jones Collection. Courtesy of V&A Images/Victoria and Albert Museum.

Plate 14 Combined jewel casket, *secrétaire*, and writing table, workshop of Jean-Henri Riesener, Paris, ca.1775. V&A 1106-1882, Jones Collection. Courtesy of V&A Images/Victoria and Albert Museum. V&A Images/Victoria and Albert Museum.

(a pale, lemon yellow that was used in Vaux-le-Vicomte, the infamous home of Nicolas Fouquet), and *minime* (a somber shade of grey, taking its name from the religious order).[6] *Incarnat* and *incarnadin* were used to describe a very vivid and pinkish red, one that supposedly approximated the color of freshly butchered meat.[7] *Isabelle*, an ivory or off-white derived from white and yellow, also appeared in these notary descriptions. According to furniture historian Henry Havard, it took its name from Isabella of Castille, who allegedly vowed at the siege of Granada not to change her white linens until the Spanish had succeeded.[8] Such dingy origins must have inspired only vaguely the dyers who tinted fabrics in this creamy hue. (I should also note that modern uses of the term refer to a deeper, brownish color).

What is most revealing about the use of *isabelle* and these other color names is the notary's concern for precise descriptions or nomenclature. In 1715, one notary described the accoutrements for a bed as the color of coffee (trimmed in aurora).[9] I have been unable to determine whether the term *café* was used commonly to describe a particular shade of brown, or if this was just a particularly articulate notary who was sensitive to differences in shades of the same hue. Regardless, the use of the term reflects a proliferation of dyes and choices of colors and certainly a greater cultural awareness of color. Sarah Lowengard, who studies the technology, science, and culture of color making in the eighteenth century, points out that color names varied not only with language, but also according to region, producer, and methods of production, and that the use of names was a wholly subjective matter so that one color might have several names or a single term might refer to a range of colors.[10]

Ultimately, the notaries' attention to color tells us something about the deliberative process by which acquisition took place. To achieve a decorative effect with color required more than planning and constancy; it required a vision of the end product and a very purposeful approach to acquisition. Color and color schemes became a dominant feature of the interiors of the seventeenth and eighteenth centuries, and certain colors appear to have been especially fashionable. Under Louis XIV, the most popular colors in Paris and Bordeaux were red and green, with red being slightly more commonplace. This was also the case in Dauphiné. But red was not simply the red of the color wheel; as Annik Pardailhé-Galabrun has noted, "notaries listed variations that included crimson, cherry, vermilion, and scarlet." Later, in the eighteenth century, as tastes evolved along with the technology to produce new colors, consumers in Paris and Bordeaux tended to prefer more delicate colors and pastels.[11] In fact, Pardailhé-Galabrun writes that "notaries used a vocabulary that was rich, precise, and image-provoking all at once, thereby revealing the importance of these aspects of interior decoration."[12] Lowengard argues that color fashion changed quickly, and that "owning and using fashionably coloured objects was a visual acknowledgement of participation in the social culture of the period."[13] She also notes that for a color to be good, and therefore popular, it had to be accepted as beautiful both as it stood alone and in combination with other colors. Pairs of colors worked only if each individual color remained as bright and lively as when each was used alone.[14]

Textiles were the primary medium for color, and textile furnishing was therefore crucial in defining the French style. Textiles distinguished the homes of nobles to the extent that they became "the most conspicuous element of the décor of any house of importance."[15] These materials were expensive and were generally finished with intricate trimmings. Foremost among textile furnishings was the wall hanging, whose most celebrated and costly form was the tapestry. Of course, tapestries had long existed and served a very practical purpose; in addition to insulating a drafty room, however, they provided a dominant element of its decor. These woven tableaux could depict scenes or histories, or they could display a family's coat of arms or masses of foliage (verdure tapestries). Often they were simply woven into geometric designs. Especially common in Dauphiné were the affordable Bergamo tapestries, which generally came in panels joined to create a larger piece. Made of wool, they were coarsely woven designs of repetitive patterns (rather than pictorial subjects) such as the pomegranate or flame-stitch (*point d'Hongrie*, a chevron pattern). Originally they were made in Italy, but in 1622 an Italian craftsman obtained permission to establish a shop in Lyon where he manufactured the same style of textiles.[16] Lyon's close proximity to Grenoble and Dauphiné made these tapestries more affordable in the region. Other cities in France, such as Rouen, also attempted to capitalize on the popularity and affordability of Bergamo tapestries.[17]

The textiles used on furniture also promoted the room's unified effect. In fact, upholstery was now much more elaborate than in previous periods. The same color and textile were often used repeatedly throughout a room. Beds and their upholstery provided the focal point for some of the household's most important rooms because *chambres* served both as sleeping quarters and rooms in which guests were received. As such, beds were the dominant element of the room's furnishings, outfitted with color-coordinated curtains or hangings, as well as coverlets. Chairs were covered with silk velvet and silk damask, or the less expensive option of woolen cloths such as velvet; the colors of these fabrics usually matched or complemented the colors used in the bed according to a prescribed color scheme. Tapestry was also a possibility for chair covers and bed hangings, as was *Turkeywork*, a kind of needlepoint that resembled the patterns in Turkish rugs.[18] It was common to find the same textiles used to outfit both the bed and the chairs in a room. Families often possessed multiple sets of wall hangings and chair covers, which they changed according to season. These options enabled them to redecorate by simply changing colors and textures to accommodate climate and mood. As Thornton has noted, in order to redecorate, one had only to call in an upholsterer.[19]

The French style, defined by its consistent use of a color or color scheme and the repetitive use of textiles, was clearly popular in Dauphiné by the late seventeenth century. Among officeholders and the nobility in general, this style of decoration had become standard. From one household to the next we find the same sorts of textiles and objects, and above all, the planned use of color. The major difference among households was one of scale and volume, as determined by the wealth of the family: the wealthier the family, the more likely it was to carry out a color scheme in detail and to have an alternative scheme in storage. Consistently, Dauphinois families imposed color schemes on their important rooms; sometimes they decorated several adjoining rooms in the same hues.

The main rooms of the chateau of François-Alexandre de Perissol-Alleman, Seigneur of St. Ange, were systematically decorated in blue, yellow, and aurora. In one bedroom, there was a walnut bed (which appears from the notary's description to have been a half-tester) outfitted with drapes and fabrics in blue, yellow, and aurora; twelve small chairs upholstered in blue and yellow velvet; an arm chair in yellow tapestry; and another chair in blue with fringe in grey and aurora. The walls of this room were covered with a seven-piece Bergamo tapestry, and a rug from Anatolia was draped over a walnut table.[20] This was a family of status and means that could easily afford to upholster according to a prescribed scheme, execute it down to such details as fringe, and adhere to it throughout the prominent rooms of the chateau.

When Pierre de Ponnat, sieur de Merley, died in 1697, he left an estate that included a townhouse in Grenoble as well as a country chateau. The colors used in the decor of the townhouse appear to have rotated seasonally, or by whim, among greens, blues, and the combination of yellow and violet. In a third-floor room the family stored an immense array of textiles and linens, few of which varied from these schemes. Tucked away in storage were an eleven-piece set of drapes and accoutrements for a bed in blue damask with silk fringe; twelve chair covers in the same blue damask; three green coverlets embroidered with the family's crest; a six-piece set of green drapes for a bed; a green table cover; a fourteen-piece set of drapes and accoutrements for a bed in yellow and violet; twelve coordinating needle-point chair covers in yellow and violet; and twelve additional chair covers in yellow. The family chose to decorate its urban residence in what were, by this period, the more fashionable colors of blue, violet, and yellow. The chateau, on the other hand, was furnished with textiles in more traditional seventeenth-century schemes of red and green, though here too there were a few items in yellow and violet.[21] The Ponnat family put its most fashionable foot forward in its most visible dwelling because the social impact of its acquisitions and style would have been significantly greater in an urban context.

This privileging of the more high-profile urban residence over the rural appears to have occurred among other families as well. The townhouse and chateau of Jean de Vincent, treasurer to the *généralité* of Dauphiné, were inventoried in 1691. The former was particularly well appointed in shades of red, including crimson and *incarnat*, and in green. In contrast, Vincent's chateau was decorated in a less studied or deliberate manner; indeed, the inventory of this rural residence suggests no real color scheme at all. The chateau housed an assortment of textiles and colors, but no single hue dominated. It was amply furnished, but its contents were, in general, less fine than those listed for the townhouse. Most notably, Vincent's collection of silver appears in the townhouse and not at the chateau.[22]

The townhouse of Gabriel Aymon de Franquières, a counselor in Parlement, was especially inspired by local standards of magnificence and style, and perhaps by a compelling desire to distance himself from his family's more humble origins—he came from a family ennobled only in the late sixteenth century. By the time of Gabriel's death in 1717, the family owned extensive amounts of property and furnished its homes in the most lavish manner possible. The Franquières decorated their urban residence consistently in reds and greens. In storage, the notary found chair covers, wall hangings, and bed curtains in crimson and cherry, apparently mixed with table covers in green. In just one formal room of the Franquières' urban home, we find the following pieces of furniture and artwork:

- one walnut bed designed in the *Imperiale* style with four twisted columns, a tester, and outfitted with a canopy, drapes, and skirts in *point d'Angleterre* tapestry, embellished with silk fringe and lined with red toile;
- one Turkish rug;
- fifteen high-backed chairs decorated with gilded flowers and upholstered in tapestry to match the bed;
- two marquetry tables trimmed in gold;
- two mirrors with their capitals in mirror;
- one small marquetry table;
- eight portraits;
- eleven paintings ranging in subject from the religious to still life;
- one screen of cross-stitch;
- one clock with a marquetry case made by Duchesne, the Parisian clockmaker;
- fifteen additional chairs covered in cotton fabric;
- one mirror with a gold frame;
- two *guéridon* tables;

- one small walnut table;
- two cabinet pieces, one of marquetry.[23]

The Franquières chateau in the countryside was similarly furnished, but it was the townhouse in which the family showcased its most valuable and fashionable goods. All but six items of their massive silver collection were located there. In Grenoble they accumulated a large set of silver flatware (marked with various family arms), which represented only a fraction of their silver possessions. If something for the table could be fashioned of silver, this family owned it. For each specific purpose—to serve salt, pepper, sugar, oil and vinegar, and mustard—they owned the appropriate object in silver, and each object was marked with the family's coat of arms. The fact that the family owned two clocks by Parisian clockmakers and chose to house both of them in their Grenoble residence similarly points to their desire to impress.[24] By locating their most costly goods in town, the Franquières were positioning them for their greatest impact.

At the lower echelons of elite society, a similar style of interior decoration existed. The residence of Jean Baptiste Rigo, a simple attorney in Parlement, is particularly revealing because he devoted greater financial means to interior decoration than did many people of similar professional and social status. His house was furnished in an elaborate and entirely familiar manner: two Turkish rugs, four large Bergamo tapestries, and thirty-two paintings (including several portraits). The real marker of wealth appears to have been the collection of silver, which included flatware, serving pieces, and candleholders. The inventory also indicates an effort to unify the interior by color and textiles. For instance, the family furnished one room with a large walnut bed (à l'impériale) outfitted with draperies in point d'Angleterre. In the same room we find a dozen chairs and two banquettes in the same tapestry, two smaller chairs in cross-stitch, and a large armchair in point d'Angleterre. The room was also appointed with a Turkish rug, a six-piece wall tapestry in the popular foliage pattern, and coordinating portières in green damask.[25] In another home, that of attorney François Besset, we also find a repetitive use of color, in this case pink and green. The principal room housed a bed decked out in pink and green, four chairs in pink, two chairs (à la dauphine) in a floral satin with a green border, and an armchair in floral satin with a pink border.[26]

In 1719, a notary conducted an inventory of the household possessions of Antoine Drogat, another attorney in Parlement. The room in which Drogat left this world was furnished with a completely outfitted walnut bed dressed in tapestry and covered with quilts. It also housed eleven chairs covered in tapestry to match the bed; six smaller chairs and two banquettes in red, yellow, and green; a walnut table covered with red leather; and another walnut table in green leather. The finishing touches on the room included green curtains and a still life depicting a vase of flowers.[27]

The fundamental difference from one inventory to the next was really one of scale rather than style. The utter sameness in furnishings and the consistent use of color schemes raise the question of how such a monolithic style came to exist. Nobles in Dauphiné were a mixed group, consisting of traditional or warrior nobles, judges, and attorneys, and yet they produced and subscribed to a very homogenous style. Ultimately, the adoption of this style of interior decoration stemmed from its fashionable nature and the emergence of fashion trends. The consumer revolution of the eighteenth century had its origins in the later seventeenth century. What is now clear about the eighteenth century is that the demand for necessities and fashionable luxuries grew by revolutionary proportions, thereby providing a very important stimulus for economic growth and industrialization.[28] Historians of eighteenth-century England have offered ample evidence for the important role of consumption in the economy. Historians of eighteenth-century France have also discovered the rise of the consumer; in the process, they have challenged the older view that painted France as an underdeveloped nation. Indeed, recently historians have argued for a more vigorous economy in the eighteenth century, and among the evidence they cite is the rise of consumerism, a trend that extends well into the preceding century.[29]

With consumerism came the purchase of luxuries on an unparalleled scale. Since the Renaissance, European elites had used luxuries and exotic goods to distinguish themselves by offering tangible evidence of their taste and connoisseurship. In this sense, luxuries marked social rank. As early as the seventeenth century, many European markets were swamped by a profusion of consumer goods, a fact that was celebrated and depicted by the Dutch still life painters.[30] By the eighteenth century, consumption of luxury goods extended well beyond the rungs of elites to include a much wider spectrum of the European population. Certainly, social mobility spurred acquisitiveness as families sought to emulate the lifestyle of their social superiors. But historians of the emerging consumer culture of early modern Europe argue that emulation alone does not explain the trend.[31]

Consumer choices were also governed by fashion and changing styles. Writing about clothing, historian Daniel Roche maintains that fashion even extended into the rural societies of ancien regime France, and that fashionable or modish dress reflected a society that valued change and novelty and understood obsolescence.[32] Fashion was a means of distinguishing oneself or one's family, and according to Roche, clothes were "employed to erect a barrier, to stave off the pressure of imitators and followers who must be kept at a distance, and who always lagged behind in some nuance in the choice of color or way of tying a ribbon or cravat."[33] Style, fashion, and the desire for distinction or separateness also affected consumer choices in other categories of goods, including furniture, tableware, and household textiles. For historian Natacha Coquery, by the eighteenth century, consumption of luxurious household goods had become an essential means by which French aristocrats distinguished themselves. As the court aristocracy became a sort of useless "ornamental class," consumption served to set this group apart as an exclusive social category.[34] Michel Figeac has written about similar patterns of consumption among nobles in the province of Guyenne. He too found that in the eighteenth century, provincial nobles invested heavily in furnishings and interior decoration.[35]

Perhaps crucial in this process was the fact that publications promoted the development of a French style. The century saw extensive publication and distribution of engravings from Paris, especially from the 1630s on. Indeed, Thornton describes the proliferation of such publications as astonishing. For inspiration, architects and artisans could consult sets of engravings "devoted to a particular class of ornament or feature—panelling, doors, chimneypieces, ceilings, candle stands, tables, bed-alcoves, frames, vases, and every other sort of ornamental detail."[36] Genre scenes also offered detailed information about how Parisian elites lived and decorated their homes. In this way, the style that may have originated at Rambouillet was publicized to both a domestic and an international audience.[37]

Included in this audience of fashionable consumers were provincial nobles whose lives were significantly removed from those epicenters of style, Versailles and Paris. Figeac's study of the homes and consumption patterns of noble families in Guyenne, also based on notary inventories, reveals remarkable similarities in the consumption patterns of this group and those of the nobility of Dauphiné. Tapestries and wall hangings were dominant elements of the decors of elite homes, and the affordable Bergamo tapestries were especially popular in both places. Nobles in the two regions also shared a fondness for Turkish rugs to serve as table covers. They adorned their walls with a similar array of paintings, portraits, and engravings; they also chose to decorate according to the same color schemes, with red and green occurring most frequently. For Figeac, the interiors of urban residences in the late seventeenth century were generally rather austere compared to those of the late eighteenth century, but the impulse to accumulate revealed itself increasingly and especially in the homes of the presidents of the Parlement. The interiors of the chateaux in the Bordeaux region varied predictably in scale but not in the nature of their contents or basic decorative elements, and they paralleled significantly those found in Dauphiné.[38]

Located at vastly different points along the periphery of the realm, by the reign of Louis XIV the nobilities of Guyenne and Dauphiné had begun to participate in essentially the same consumer culture, one in which individual choices were driven by fashion and markets. A national and international culture of fashionable items was coming to replace the more traditional and regionally based material culture of earlier centuries. How was it that France's provincial nobilities, so proud of their regional identity and often fiercely opposed to centralization, were so easily seduced by the styles and tastes emanating from Versailles and Paris? In part, the answer to this question lies in what was indeed the very seductive nature of the emerging national market, consumerism, and fashion trends. At the same time, however, this transformation of taste must still be understood in a strictly local social and even political context.

Dauphiné had traditionally been sheltered from the grasping fiscal reach of central government. Dauphiné was one of France's *pays d'états*, a semiautonomous province where the issue of provincial rights and privileges produced a series of conflicts in the late sixteenth and early seventeenth centuries. Here the crown's efforts to increase taxation ignited a prolonged contest between the nobility and the crown on the one hand, and the nobility and the Third Estate on the other. Known as the *procès des tailles*, this struggle revealed deep divisions between the estates. In protecting its interests, the Third Estate questioned traditional noble privileges to the extent that the very notion of nobility came under attack.

At the heart of the issue was the way in which the *taille* was assessed; that is, whether the exemption from the tax enjoyed by nobles extended to their non-noble property. If not, it was entirely possible for nobles to pay taxes on their non-feudal property. To avoid having to do so, the nobility of Dauphiné insisted that the tax should be tied to an individual's status as a commoner, and that all wealth held by nobles should therefore be exempt (as it was in most of France), as compensation for the personal sacrifices they made in defending the realm.[39] Rights based on social privilege in turn raised the question of how legitimate the claims to nobility were by those who had been exempted from taxation. As elsewhere in France, Dauphiné had seen growing numbers of families engaged in upward social mobility, and their claims to nobility, and therefore to tax exemption, became a hotly debated issue as the taxation controversy unfolded.

In the end, the conflict over taxation was resolved by a simple chronological compromise. The older nobility established for itself an immunity not extended to those ennobled after 1602. The recently ennobled could still claim victory, however, because although they would be subject to taxation, their claim of noble status was recognized and confirmed. Beyond tax exemption, privileges of nobility included juridical privileges and the honor conferred on noble families in a society where esteem attached to rank. Nevertheless, the attack on the nobility, and especially on its most recently ennobled families, not only anticipated by almost two centuries the universalistic rhetoric of the French Revolution, it was also devastatingly critical of the provincial nobility. The attorneys for the Third Estate had challenged the basis for the nobility's privileged status and pointedly challenged any of its claims to distinction. Indeed, they had depicted these families as utterly indifferent to the public good, and in this way raised questions about the "nobility" of such an ignoble social group.

Having just survived this assault on aristocratic privilege and honor, the nobles of Dauphiné found themselves in a very different social world. To some extent, they must have confronted the idea of damage control, the urgent need to maintain and even reconstruct the esteem and honor of their rank. In this context, lifestyle would have taken on greater meaning, especially for families ennobled after 1602. They endured the Third Estate's challenges to their claims to nobility, yet they had lost their tax-exempt status. How best now to communicate the qualities that separated them from the rest of society? Material culture was an option. It was certainly true that the French nobility as a whole had come to regard consumption as an essential means of generating an aura of distinctiveness. By their spending power, consumer choices, and sense of fashion, they would strive to demonstrate how different they were from those beneath them. In the process, the world of goods became the world of nobility. But in Dauphiné, the world of goods might have been even more vital to the world of the nobility, as they struggled to define themselves in the eyes of their local community by other than traditional means.

Anthropologists who study consumption and culture have argued that material possessions can serve to clarify social relationships.[40] By their possessions and their choices, families communicate more than wealth and spending power; they also communicate their rank within society. Consumption becomes, therefore, a means of communication. For sociologist Pierre Bourdieu, "it presupposes practical mastery of a cipher or code."[41] Such mastery distinguishes the connoisseur by his or her cultural competence. It says to the rest of society that he or she has the knowledge to decode a work of art. In this way, recently ennobled Dauphinois families, with a need to set themselves apart from the social elements from which they sprang and plant themselves more securely within the social milieu to which they aspired, could be defined in part by cultural competency. But their consumer choices were no simple matter of imitation or emulation. By the late seventeenth century, cultural competency was being defined in part by the market and the desire to be in style.

Finally, local social trends and national political forces may have affected the adoption and spread of the French style, as well as other forms of consumption in this remote province, which had traditionally trumpeted its regional privileges and local identity. I have argued that in Dauphiné the pressure to live "nobly" may have been particularly intense because provincials had spent the first half of the century battling over the issue of noble privilege and claims to nobility. The rhetoric of the *procès des tailles* was vitriolic, and the attorneys for the Third Estate did not hesitate to challenge claims to nobility, the nobles' right to tax exemptions, and indeed their integrity. Consumption and decoration became, therefore, an alternative way of distinguishing their households. By choosing the French style and by their sheer ability to consume, Dauphinois families living on the periphery of the Second Estate might seek to clarify their rank for the rest of provincial society. As consumers, these Dauphinois families participated in the gradual emergence of a clearly defined French national culture. They sought to distinguish themselves by their purchases, but their choices were driven by the same fashions and styles that prevailed in other and distant communities. In this way they participated in what historian T. H. Breen has called the "standardization of the market-place."[42] Writing about the American colonists, Breen argues that their consumer experiences served to unite these scattered populations and "to perceive, however dimly, the existence of an 'imagined community.'"⁴³ Perhaps the market was transforming Dauphinois elites into Frenchmen; perhaps the world of goods promoted a national identity.

I do not argue that the *procès des tailles* and the policies of central government are directly responsible for the adoption of a French style or for the tendency toward more conspicuous forms of consumption. I merely put forward the possibility that in the material culture and social world of provincial nobles we can see, at least faintly, the galvanizing hand of the state, and very clearly the power of the market and modern consumerism. In the end, the preference for color-coordinated interiors points to the successful reception of a very important aspect of French culture in a region whose local customs and unique institutional history had earlier set its nobility in opposition to the crown. By the middle of the eighteenth century, consumers in Europe and North America had come to regard France as the trendsetter, and style was increasingly associated with French national identity. Being French, with all the fashionability and taste it implied, had itself become a mark of distinction for provincial nobles.

Notes

1. Archives Départementales (AD), Isère, 13 B 445, 1668. Inventaire. Anne de la Croix.
2. Peter Burke, "Conspicuous Consumption in Seventeenth-Century Italy," in *The Historical Anthropology of Early Modern Italy: Essays on Perception and Communication* (Cambridge: Cambridge University Press, 1987), 136–38.
3. Mary Douglas and Baron Isherwood, *The World of Goods* (New York: Basic Books, 1979), 118.
4. My comments about domestic goods and interior decoration are based on a sample of postmortem inventories found in the Archives Départementales d'Isère. My sample includes the following inventories: 13 B 445, 1668, Anne de la Croix; 13 B 446, 1675, Abel de Buffevant, Gaspard du Beuf; 13 B 452, 1679, Pierre Gleynat; 13 B 453, 1679, Hugues Bezançon; 13 B 455, 1680–81, Joseph de Merindol; 13 B 457, 1681, Anthoinette d'Angilbert, François de Françon, François de la Simiane de la Coste; 13 B 463, 1685, Jeanne Richard, Pierre Clément; 13 B 466, 1687, Jacques de Vernet; 13 B 469, 1688, Jacques Rosset; 13 B 472, 1691, Guillaume Fradel, Jean Bertrand, Antoine Bertrand; 13 B 474, 1691, Jean de Vincent; 13 B 477, 1695, Benoît Brun; 13 B 478, 1696, Françoise de la Baume, Philippe Emery; 13 B 480, 1698, Pierre de Ponnat; 13 B 485, 1707–8, Pierre Martinot; Jean Amat, Jean Miard; 13 B 486, 1708, François-Alexandre de Perissol-Alleman; 13 B 487, 1709, Claude de Joffrey, Guy Allard, Felicien d'Arzac; 13 B 490, 1710, Pierre Aymard, Melchior Cholat, Jean Salomon; 13 B 492, 1711, Claude Duclot, Etienne Jullien, Jean de la Robinière, Marie Bonnat; 13 B 493, 1712, Jean Baptiste Rigo, Claude Doucet, Philippe Roux, Jean Baptiste Le Juge; 13 B 496, 1713, Benoît Chalvet, Jean Baptiste de Valette, Joachim d'Auby; 13 B 498, 1714, François Besset, Abel de Charency, Jean Baptiste, Garcin-La Mercière, Jean Huide; 13 B 499, 1715, Antoine Royer, François d'Allégret, Pierre Pizon; 13 B 503, 1716, Charles Pétrequin, Justine de Simiane de La Coste; 13 B 504, 1717–18, Gabriel Aymon de Franquières; 13 B 509, 1719, Antoine Drogat, Pierre Duchon, Claude Garcin.
5. Peter Thornton, *Seventeenth-Century Interior Decoration in England, France, and Holland* (New Haven, CT: Yale University Press, 1978), 7–10; Peter Thornton, *Authentic Decor: The Domestic Interior, 1620–1920* (New York: Viking Press, 1984), 14–15.
6. Henry Havard, *Dictionnaire de l'ameublement et de la décoration depuis le XIIIe siècle jusqu'à nos jours*, 4 vols. (Paris: Quantin, 1890), 3: 922–23; 1: 200; 2: 705–6; 1: 837–38; 3: 784.
7. Ibid., 3: 31–32.
8. Ibid., 52–53.
9. AD, Isère, 13 B 499. Inventaire. Pierre Pizon, conseiller du roy, assesseur en l'élection de Grenoble.
10. Sarah Lowengard, *Color Practices, Color Theories, and the Creation of Color in Objects: Britain and France in the Eighteenth Century* (Ann Arbor, MI: University Microfilms, 1999), 148–49.
11. Annik Pardailhé-Galabrun, *The Birth of Intimacy: Privacy and Domestic Life in Early Modern Paris*, trans. Jocelyn Phelps (Philadelphia: University of Pennsylvania Press, 1991), 170–71; Michel Figeac, *La douceur des Lumières: noblesse et art de vivre en Guyenne au XVIIIe siècle* (Bordeaux: Mollat, 2001), 48, 292.
12. Pardailhé-Galabrun, *Birth of Intimacy*, 170–71.

13. Sarah Lowengard, "Colours and Colour Making in the Eighteenth Century," in *Consumers and Luxury: Consumer Culture in Europe, 1650–1850*, ed. Maxine Berg and Helen Clifford (Manchester: Manchester University Press, 1999), 109.
14. Lowengard, *Color Practices, Color Theories*, 74.
15. Thornton, *Seventeenth-Century Interior Decoration*, 97.
16. Ibid., 108, 132; Havard, *Dictionnaire de l'ameublement*, 1: 298.
17. Pardailhé-Galabrun, *Birth of Intimacy*, 147–48.
18. Thornton, *Seventeenth-Century Interior Decoration*, 130–43.
19. Thornton, *Authentic Decor*, 9.
20. AD, Isère, 13 B 486. Inventaire. François-Alexandre de Perissol-Alleman.
21. AD, Isère, 13 B 480, 1698. Inventaire. Pierre de Ponnat.
22. AD, Isère, 13 B 474, 1691. Inventaire. Jean de Vincent.
23. AD, Isère, 13 B 504, 1717. Inventaire. Gabrielle Aymon de Franquières.
24. Ibid.
25. AD, Isère, 13 B 493, 1712. Inventaire. Jean Baptiste Rigo.
26. AD, Isère, 13 B 498, 1714. Inventaire. François Besset.
27. AD, Isère, 13 B 509, 1719. Inventaire. Antoine Drogat.
28. Neil McKendrick, John Brewer, and J. H. Plumb, *The Birth of a Consumer Society: The Commercialization of Eighteenth-Century England* (Bloomington: Indiana University Press, 1982).
29. Colin Jones and Rebecca Spang, "*Sans-Culottes, Sans Café, Sans Tabac*: Shifting Realms of Necessity and Luxury in Eighteenth-Century France," in *Consumers and Luxury*, ed. Berg and Clifford, 37–62. Jones and Spang survey and rely on a growing literature that addresses problems with the earlier work of economic historians Ernest Labrousse and Fernand Braudel, specifically in their analyses of institutional factors that supposedly limited French economic development. Here Jones and Spang are influenced by David Weir, "Les crises économiques et les origines de la Révolution Française," *Annales: Economies, Sociétés, Civilisations*, 46 (1991): 917–47. See also François Crouzet, "England and France in the Eighteenth Century: A Comparative Analysis of Two Economic Growths," in *The Causes of the Industrial Revolution in England*, ed. R. M. Hartwell (London: Methuen, 1967); Michael Sonenscher, *Work and Wages: Natural Law, Politics, and Eighteenth-Century French Trades* (Cambridge: Cambridge University Press, 1989). Jones and Spang also base their more positive assessment of the French economy in the later eighteenth century on recent studies of rising consumption. See Daniel Roche, *The People of Paris: An Essay in Popular Culture in the Eighteenth Century*, trans. Marie Evans with Gwynne Lewis (Berkeley: University of California Press, 1987); Daniel Roche, *The Culture of Clothing: Dress and Fashion in the Ancien Regime*, trans. Jean Birrell (Cambridge: Cambridge University Press, 1994); Pardailhé-Galabrun, *Birth of Intimacy*; and Cissie Fairchilds, "The Production and Marketing of Populuxe Goods in Eighteenth-Century Paris," in *Consumption and the World of Goods*, ed. John Brewer and Roy Porter (London: Routledge, 1993), 228–48.
30. Simon Schama, *The Embarrassment of Riches: An Interpretation of Dutch Culture in the Golden Age* (New York: Knopf, 1987), chapter 5. See also Simon Schama, "Perishable Commodities: Dutch Still-life Painting and the 'Empire of Things,'" in *Consumption and the World of Goods*, ed. Brewer and Porter, 478–88.
31. Maxine Berg, "New Commodities, Luxuries and their Consumers in Eighteenth-Century England," in *Consumers and Luxury,* ed. Berg and Clifford, 63–83; and the following articles in *Consumption and the World of Goods,* ed. Brewer and Porter: Colin Campbell, "Understanding Traditional and Modern Patterns of Consumption in Eighteenth-Century England: A Character-Action Approach," 40–57; Lorna Weatherill, "The Meaning of Consumer Behavior in Late Seventeenth- and Early Eighteenth-Century England," 206–27; and Amanda Vickery, "Women and the World of Goods: A Lancashire Consumer and Her Possessions, 1751–81," 274–301.
32. Roche, *Culture of Clothing*, 41–42.
33. Ibid., 6.
34. Natacha Coquery, *L'hôtel aristocratique: le marché du luxe à Paris au XVIIIe siècle* (Paris: Publications de la Sorbonne, 1998), 87–88, 119–121.
35. Figeac, *La douceur des Lumières*, 127–28.
36. Thornton, *Seventeenth-Century Interior Decoration*, 29.
37. Ibid., 29–34.
38. Figeac, *La douceur des Lumières*, 47–55, 70–91.

39. J. Russell Major, *Representative Government in Early Modern France* (New Haven, CT: Yale University Press, 1980), 76–77.
40. Douglas and Isherwood, *World of Goods,* 59–60.
41. Pierre Bourdieu, *Distinction: A Social Critique of the Judgement of Taste*, trans. Richard Nice (Cambridge, MA: Harvard University Press, 1984), 2.
42. T. H. Breen, "'Baubles of Britain': The American Consumer Revolutions of the Eighteenth Century," *Past and Present*, 119 (May 1988), 81.
43. Ibid., 76.

CHAPTER 8

The Joy of Sets: The Uses of Seriality in the French Interior

MIMI HELLMAN

For while I don't know whether, as the saying goes, "things which are repeated are pleasing," my belief is that they are significant.

—**Roland Barthes,** *Mythologies*

In 1765, the English author and collector Horace Walpole toured some of the most celebrated private residences in Paris and found them remarkable only for their tedious uniformity. "I have seen but one idea in all the houses here," he exclaimed in a letter to Anne Pitt,

> there is nothing in which they so totally want imagination as in the furniture of their houses! I have seen the Hôtels de Soubise, de Luxembourg, de Maurepas, de Brancas, and several others, especially the boasted Hôtel de Richelieu, and could not perceive any difference, but in the more or less gold, more or less baubles on the chimneys and tables; and that now and then Vanloo [*sic*] has sprawled goddesses over the doors and at other times, Boucher. There is a routine for their furniture as much as for their phrases, and an exceeding want of invention in both.[1]

Walpole's dismay is not surprising. His own aesthetic sensibility favored eclecticism, dramatic effects, and subjective responses, and both his residence (Strawberry Hill) and his writing (the just-published *The Castle of Otranto*) were psychologically charged flights of Gothic fantasy. What is notable about his response to French interiors is that although it is unappreciative and tinged with nationalism, it is not entirely incorrect. The social spaces of many Parisian *hôtels* did have a formulaic quality: wall paneling tended to feature the same basic vocabulary of motifs, seat furniture and windows typically were covered in the same materials, mantelpieces and tabletops were adorned with groups of porcelain vessels and figurines, and paintings of voluptuous Olympian bodies were ubiquitous presences in the spaces above doorways. For Walpole, this approach to interior design was too routine to merit further comment, but for the art historian it raises some interesting questions. Why exactly *were* eighteenth-century French interiors governed by a design sensibility that made them not only internally repetitive, but also quite similar to one another? Is it possible that uniformity was compelling in itself, and if so, what kinds of meanings did it produce?

To begin exploring these questions, it is crucial to recognize and understand the specific decorative conceit that was largely responsible for the distinctively indistinctive character of French interiors: the matched set. Many of the basic elements of a well-appointed social space—couches and chairs, commodes and tables, tea sets and vases, decorative paintings—were designed as groups of objects that were either identical or closely coordinated in medium, color, style, or figurative motif.[2] A sustained interest in matching first emerged in upholstery design during the seventeenth century, and by the early eighteenth century it was a widely practiced formal strategy that also extended to carved and veneered furniture, metalwork, porcelain, and wall decoration. Examples of this development can be found across Europe, but the creation of unity through repetition was (as Walpole's remarks suggest) especially pronounced in France.[3] However, while the importance of visual coordination is routinely noted in studies of eighteenth-century design, scholars have tended to privilege diversity and singularity, rather than reiteration, as the defining features of the decorated interior. It is true that elite domestic spaces became increasingly complex in both form and function, densely articulated landscapes in which a remarkable variety of objects served a wide range of specialized purposes.[4] What is generally overlooked is the fact that this decorative plenitude was accomplished largely through repetition, through the presence of objects that while often innovative, were frequently redundant as well: the newest patterned silk might cover ten identical chairs, for example, while the same motif might adorn a group of variously shaped porcelain vases.

To some degree, the scholarly neglect of serial design is a reasonable response to the nature of the historical record. While there is abundant documentary evidence of decorative matching in probate inventories and a wide range of visual evidence in the form of images and surviving objects, there are virtually no eighteenth-century writings that specifically address this phenomenon and suggest the cultural values that may have informed its development and reception. Indeed, discussions of design in a wide range of primary sources, from technical treatises to popular journals, tend to emphasize innovation rather than replication—dwelling, for instance, on a specially shaped desk chair that places the body in an ideal writing position, or a fire screen with a motif that magically transforms when exposed to heat.[5]

Moreover, the reiterative aspects of eighteenth-century design are suppressed by the conventions of museum acquisition, display, and publication. Objects that were once part of groups are purchased separately, presented in the divine isolation of vitrines, incorporated into period rooms in configurations far more eclectic than any historical interior, and fetishistically reproduced in suspension on the glossy pages of art books, often without so much as a ground line to detract from their pure form. This de- and recontextualization are partly unavoidable results of the vagaries of survival, collecting, and documentation. But another, more troubling set of conditions may also be operative. The concept of originality has long occupied a powerful place in the Western cultural imagination, and the idea that originality is a defining quality of art—whether defended or contested—has been developed in tandem with the idea that the creation of non-unique, repetitive form is a function of the encroachments of mechanical reproduction in modern, industrialized societies.[6] In a culture that values innovation and singularity, the matched set is the ultimate antithesis of art—not only is it mass produced, but the very nature of its perfectly coordinated components foregrounds the fact that it is only one of many identical examples. Thus, for a set to carry significant prestige value in contemporary Western culture, its uniformity must be construed as evidence of rarity or luxury and must conjure a largely lost tradition of privilege and gentility—a feat accomplished only by ensembles such as grandmother's rarely used china or the formal furnishings of state residences. Such exceptional cases position most other forms of serial design as banal at best, ubiquitous commodities aimed at middle- and working-class consumers for whom the living room suite or five-piece place setting offer a kind of ready-made taste and respectability at an economical price. At the same time, in elite design practice, the deliberately mismatched ensemble—of dining room chairs, say, or silver flatware—has become a sign of creativity and sophistication. Given the equivocal status of sets in late-modern culture, the curatorial and scholarly impulse to isolate the serial object may be seen as a gesture of defensive reification, an attempt to assimilate it into the more privileged status of the unique work of art.

My aim in this chapter is to denaturalize the matched set, to distance it from contemporary cultural associations and recover a sense of the newness, desirability, and significance that this mode of design may have possessed for its earliest consumers. In eighteenth-century France, although industrial processes were beginning to transform the conditions and meanings of manufacture, most decorative objects were still produced largely by hand. The notions of the precious original and the inferior copy had not yet acquired their modern oppositionality, and serial design was, in effect, the fabrication of multiple originals undertaken with specialized expertise and at great expense for consumption by a privileged elite. Therefore, I want to think about what it meant to make objects that look alike in a culture where alikeness was not a given. I want to ask what it meant to reproduce before the age of mechanical reproduction. By recognizing seriality as a deliberately conceived, laboriously practiced design trope, it becomes possible to consider it as a meaningful representational strategy that played an active role in the formal and social dynamics of elite interiors and encouraged specific modes of engagement. Moreover, because the phenomenon of matching is not confined to any of the conventional categories that have long shaped the study of decorative art—notably medium, manufacturer, typology, style, and period—taking it seriously as a design practice opens up an opportunity to explore aesthetic and conceptual resonances between works that are usually treated separately (such as painting and porcelain) and to raise new questions about the cultural workings of the decorated interior.

What I want to do here, then, is to begin sketching a conceptual framework for thinking about the uses of seriality, using a few examples that I find especially provocative. My discussion opens with an overview of the principal types of reiterative design, and then goes on to explore four different ways in which serial objects engaged the aesthetic sensibilities and psychosocial concerns of their elite consumers. These four analytical forays offer ideas that are interrelated and, to some degree, competing. I first consider how the technical aspects of seriality may have been construed in a world where sameness was a rare formal effect. I then suggest that the set's formal tension between similitude and difference actively engaged consumers by inviting a stimulating mode of visual and conceptual response. The following section focuses more closely on the redundancy of serial design and analyzes how this quality contributed to the physical and social negotiation of the interior. I conclude by going beyond my claims about the meanings of medium, form, and function to argue that sets also signified through their sheer excessiveness, through an ultimate resistance to visual attention and actual usage, which in turn suggests a pervasive cultural anxiety about the capacity of material environments to express social distinctions. Thus my discussion offers no definitive explanations, but rather explores multiple interpretive approaches to complex objects that could operate differently in relation to different physical settings, social circumstances, and audiences. Ultimately, I want to demonstrate that the repetitive schemes seen by Walpole (and perhaps by some late-modern viewers) as a "want of invention" achieved even more than what Roland Barthes imagines in the epigraph at the beginning of this chapter: a protean play of meaning that was both pleasurable *and* significant.

The System of Sets

In order to begin understanding the French interior as an environment shaped by seriality, it is first necessary to identify the most decoratively pervasive types of reiterative design and to establish some of their basic qualities. Of all the media and forms in which sets could be crafted, there were four kinds of ensembles that shaped the visual appearance and social experience of the interior to particularly striking effect: suites of upholstered furniture and hangings (*meubles*), multipiece mantelpiece ornaments (*garnitures*), beverage services, and decorative paintings. Let me briefly introduce these typological categories through some examples that I will continue to draw upon throughout the course of the discussion.

The standard format for serial upholstery design was the *meuble*, an ensemble of various objects covered in the same fabric. These items could include canopied beds and daybeds, window and door curtains, wall hangings, fire screens and folding screens, and a range of seat furniture such as couches, armchairs, side chairs, and stools. *Meubles* were generally custom-made to accommodate the layout and function of specific spaces, and the strict division of labor that structured the French guild system meant that the process involved woodworkers (*menuisiers*), upholsterers (*tapissiers*), and often carvers, gilders, and makers of trimmings such as braids and fringes.[7] It is often difficult to determine the source of a *meuble* design—architects, *menuisiers*, and luxury merchants (*marchands merciers*) could all work in this capacity—but there is no question that the resulting ensemble was both costly and highly visible. Inventories indicate that the *meuble* was usually the most materially valuable feature of an interior scheme, and that it was often supplied in two seasonal versions that could be attached to the same frames—one in a heavy fabric for winter and another in a lighter fabric for summer. At the hôtel de Roquelaure, for example, a ducal residence inventoried in the winter of 1735, the principal social space contained a matching ensemble of two couches, eight armchairs, two fire screens, three door curtains, and a set of wall hangings, all in a flowered velvet with an "aurora" ground. The summer upholstery, in striped taffeta, was in storage in the attic. The winter set, including the carved, gilded frames of the chairs and screens, was appraised at 4,150 livres and the summer set at 1,350 livres. The next most valuable item in the room was a chandelier appraised at 550 livres, and none of the few remaining objects would have come close to vying with the assertive visual presence of all that matching fabric.[8]

The arrangement of a *meuble* generally followed the strong sense of symmetry and regularity that characterized *hôtel* plans. Matching window and door curtains emphasized the even spacing of openings and the axial (*enfilade*) alignment of doors. Couches and chairs covered with the same material lined the walls between these openings, with larger items symmetrically flanked by smaller ones, and a second row of chairs was often placed in front of them to create double ranks of seating that could be reconfigured in response to changing social needs. A rare sketch for the arrangement of a salon (Figure 8.1) shows five couches and ten armchairs arranged against every available section of wall space and fronted by an

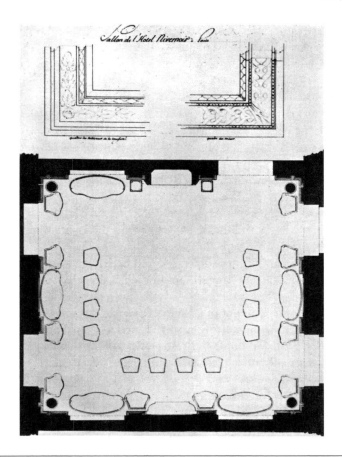

Figure 8.1 Plan of salon at hôtel de Nivernais, Paris, n.d.. From Pierre Verlet, *The Eighteenth Century in France: Society, Decoration, Furniture* (Rutland, Vt.: Charles E. Tuttle Co., 1967), 128.

additional twelve chairs (probably side chairs); we can only wonder whether the windows and door were curtained with the same fabric. This image barely begins to suggest how the spatial dominance of a *meuble* would have been compounded by the visual saturation produced by yards and yards of the same red velvet or flowered satin stretched over so many surfaces and openings. Thus the *meuble* extended the basic architectural rhythms of an interior into the multidimensional space of social interaction, both unifying the appearance of a room and shaping the physical and interpersonal dynamics of the interactions unfolding within it.

The basic design principles of the *meuble* were recast on a smaller scale in the second major type of serial design, the *garniture*. A *garniture* was a group of items, usually made of porcelain (such as vases, candleholders, potpourri containers, and figurines) that constituted a unified set by virtue of key design features such as color, pattern, repeated shapes, or matching mounts. *Garnitures* often marked the most prominent, axially located surfaces of a room (most often the mantelpiece) and their elements, like those of a *meuble*, were arranged in symmetrical configurations in which a large central piece was flanked by progressively smaller ones.[9] Many *garnitures* were designed at porcelain manufactories as groups of coordinated objects in a variety of sizes, shapes, and painted motifs, a system of orchestrated diversity from which consumers could select subsets suited to particular decorative settings and expense limits. A particularly elaborate example, made at Sèvres in 1760 and purchased by Madame de Pompadour, mistress of Louis XV, includes a boat-shaped potpourri vase (Figure 8.2) as the central element, a pair of fountain-shaped vases that could be used for both potpourri and forcing bulbs (Color Plates 4 and 5, see color insert after page 118), and another pair of curvaceous potpourri vases fitted with candleholders (now lost, but shaped like the examples in Figure 8.3). The central reserve on the front of each piece is painted with an exotic scene of Chinese figures (the rear reserves feature flowers) and the major sections of the highly plastic forms are emphasized with passages of bright green, deep pink, and dark blue glazing as well as extensively highlighted with gilding. The ensemble was displayed on a mirror-surmounted mantelpiece in the bathing apartment of their owner's Paris *hôtel*, complemented by a pair of matching wall lights. The *garniture* had been purchased for 2,400 livres and the inventory appraisal was 900 livres, plus another 200 livres for the wall lights.[10] Bathing apartments were spaces of luxurious, exclusive sociability in aristocratic residences, and these objects would have been unmissable, dazzling signs of the occupant's wealth, taste, and investment in the royal project of supporting domestic porcelain manufacture.[11]

Other types of *garnitures* were not predesigned as such, but rather assembled under the supervision of *marchands merciers*, from assorted pieces of European or Asian porcelain set in matching gilded bronze mounts.[12] These works are particularly interesting because as combinations of originally unrelated elements, they call attention to the condition of *setness* itself, to the design features and procedures that distinguish a group of objects as a deliberately created, coherent ensemble. Even more than predesigned sets, they suggest the strength of the eighteenth-century impulse to produce design based on principles of

Figure 8.2 Potpourri vessel, Sèvres porcelain, c. 1760. Louvre, Paris. Photo: Réunion des Musées Nationaux/Art Resource, N.Y.

Figure 8.3 Pair of candleholders, Sèvres porcelain, n.d. The J. Paul Getty Museum, Los Angeles.

reiteration and cohesion. One example from the collection of Marie-Antoinette (Color Plate 6, see color insert after page 118) is composed of nine pieces of bright blue Chinese porcelain: two vases and two parrots flanking a central assemblage that includes a dish, a perfume fountain on a stand, and two dogs. These elements were not made to go together, but they became an ensemble by virtue of their shared color, gilded bronze mounts, and symmetrical arrangement. It is not known where this set was displayed, but it is reasonable to imagine it, like the Pompadour *garniture*, as a focal point on a mantelpiece, backed by a mirror, its artful serial rhythms doubled by reflection.

In addition to the *garniture*, the other standard format for coordinated porcelain wares was the ensemble for serving coffee, tea, and chocolate. These beverages were luxury commodities, and their consumption was a highly orchestrated social ritual facilitated by a specialized apparatus that could include differently shaped cups, saucers, and serving pots for each preparation, as well as tea caddies, waste bowls for used tea leaves, milk jugs, and sugar containers in the form of casters, boxes, or bowls.[13] The account books of luxury merchant Lazare Duvaux list many such sets, with specialized names and a remarkable range of prices that must correspond with a (largely unrecorded) variety of colors, patterns, and places of origin.[14] Inventories indicate that beverage services were displayed in social spaces, apparently serving both decorative and potentially functional purposes. Like *garnitures*, such ensembles would have been highly visible signs of affluence and fashionable taste. And, if they were actually used, the process of preparing, pouring, and savoring an expensive, fragrant drink would have placed the objects, like the rearranged seat furniture of a *meuble*, at the center of a dynamic social situation.

Like *garnitures*, beverage services could be either designed as coordinated ensembles or assembled from disparate but visually related elements, and the unity of a set was often emphasized by arranging the pieces on a porcelain or lacquered tray. For example, a tea service made at Sèvres in 1768 (Color Plate 7, see color insert after page 118) features a teapot, milk jug, sugar bowl, two cups with saucers, and a tray, all densely painted with a repeating pattern of garlands and roses. A less assertively expressed kind of matching is suggested by a 1749 inventory of the hôtel de Soubise, where groups of items from different places of origin embellish the reception room (*chambre du dais*) of the prince de Rohan.[15] Here, as with the *garniture* of Chinese porcelain, it is the gesture of assembly that transforms discrete objects into a unified set. Once again, disparate things are brought into a relation; diversity is made to yield cohesion.

Finally, the fourth major design category that was based on principles of coordination was decorative painting.[16] Like sets of upholstered or porcelain objects, sets of images punctuated and unified social spaces, animating them with the visual rhythms of landscapes, still lifes, and pastoral or mythological scenes. Often commissioned by an architect or patron for a specific room, an ensemble was usually produced by a single artist, but sometimes included contributions by two or more individuals. It could be designed to fill entire expanses of wall or to enliven the spaces above axially placed mirrors, wall panels, or doors. A particularly interesting example from 1739, still *in situ*, is a set of four paintings of mythological lovers made by four different artists for a formal bedchamber (*chambre de parade*) at the hôtel de Soubise (Figures 8.4 through 8.7): *Cephalus and Aurora* by François Boucher (Figure 8.4), *Mars and Venus* by Carle Van Loo (Figure 8.5), *Hercules and Hebe* by Pierre-Charles Trémolières (Figure 8.6), and *Neptune and Amphitrite* by Jean Restout

Figure 8.4 François Boucher, *Cephalus and Aurora*, c. 1738–39. Archives Nationales, Paris. Photo: Mimi Hellman.

Figure 8.5 Carle Van Loo, *Mars and Venus*, c. 1738–39. Archives Nationales, Paris. Photo: Mimi Hellman.

Figure 8.6 Pierre-Charles Trémolières, *Hercules and Hebe*, 1737. Archives Nationales, Paris. Photo: Mimi Hellman.

Figbure 8.7 Jean Restout, *Neptune and Amphitrite*, 1737. Archives Nationales, Paris. Photo: Mimi Hellman.

(Figure 8.7). The bedchamber, part of a luxuriously decorated formal apartment, would have been used for social activities and featured an elaborately upholstered state bed in which the patron (Hercule-Mériadec de Rohan-Soubise, known as the prince de Rohan) would have ensconced himself in order to receive visitors.[17] The paintings mark two major axes of the room (Figure 8.8). Two are installed above the doors, defining the linear route of the *enfilade*, and two surmount wall panels adjacent to a columned alcove that contains the bed, defining a physical and symbolic boundary between the main space of the room and the more privileged zone of princely authority.[18]

There is no documentation of any organized planning among the four painters and the architect, Germain Boffrand, who probably supervised the commission as part of an extensive renovation he was conducting at the *hôtel*. However, a concerted effort to produce a unified ensemble is strongly suggested not only by the fact that the paintings are rhythmically positioned and identical in size and shape, but also by several aspects of composition and content that make them resonate both with each other and with the spatial dynamics of the room. For instance, the genders of the figures alternate so that each male figure is both next to and across from a female figure. The compositions above the doors mirror one another with their juxtapositions of elevated and reclining figures, as do those above the panels with their more chiastic dynamics. And the red drapery on the two male figures above the doors (Cephalus and Mars) would have resonated with the red velvet that covered the windows, doors, and much of the other furniture during the winter months. Thus, like matching upholstery and porcelain, an ensemble of decorative paintings was the result of a

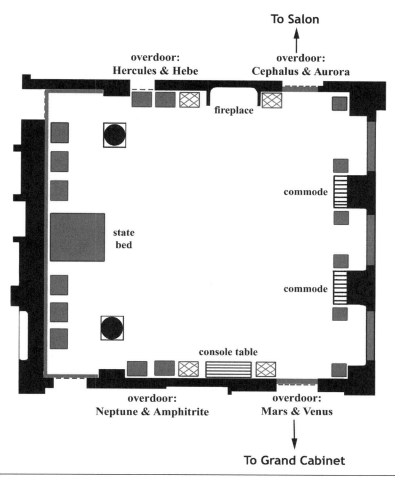

To Salon

overdoor:
Hercules & Hebe

overdoor:
Cephalus & Aurora

fireplace

commode

state
bed

commode

console table

overdoor:
Neptune & Amphitrite

overdoor:
Mars & Venus

To Grand Cabinet

Figure 8.8 Plan of state bedchamber at hôtel de Soubise. Digital reconstruction by Mimi Hellman and Beth Grubert.

complex production process, and its calculated visual rhythms brought both continuity and punctuation to the composition of social space.

It is clear, then, that the French interior was a space structured by sets, deliberately composed groups of objects in multiple media that played major roles in producing visual and spatial unity, regularity, emphasis, and animation. It also seems clear that sets could be signs of wealth, taste, and status, and therefore played a role in the material expression of social identity. But these conclusions do not fully account for the astonishing variety and pervasiveness of serial design or its particular signifying power. Could aesthetic preference and social prestige not be equally well articulated through a rich array of differently designed objects? Why was it desirable to possess a roomful of identical chairs, half a dozen teacups in the same pattern, or a suite of paintings depicting more or less the same subject? Would the pursuit of social distinction not be better served by demonstrating a capacity for diversified consumption? To begin grappling with these questions, we must return to the objects and think more closely about both their formal and functional workings and their engagement with larger cultural preoccupations. The following sections offer four perspectives, at once intersecting and diverging, on the singular uses of repetition.

The Enchantment of Technology

First, I want to consider the technical conditions of decorative seriality in greater detail and raise the possibility that formal similitude may have been compelling for eighteenth-century consumers in ways that the late-modern interpreter must labor to understand. Because most objects were produced largely by hand (a process that is perhaps best understood as multiproduction rather than reproduction), the fabrication of sameness was a remarkable achievement. Even if the elements in a matched set of chairs or teacups appeared to be exactly alike, and even if the silk upholstery was made on mechanized looms and the cups cast in molds, the finished objects—stitched and trimmed, painted and gilded—were ultimately products of a protracted manual process in which objects were finished one by one. Moreover, this process required a defiance of technical accident, for a fault in the design of a single piece, such as a couch of the wrong proportions or a misplaced bouquet on a painted vase, would compromise the unity of the ensemble. The production of matching objects thus entailed a vast amount of careful attention and technical precision, a kind of work that denied the intransigent nature of its materials—flaws in fabric, dripping glazes—and the vagaries of human error. In other words, a set represented an extraordinary, manifestly artificial manipulation of materials that could be enjoyed only by a privileged elite. Under these circumstances, matching could not possibly be taken for granted, and those who possessed its virtuoso effects must have actively noticed and valued them in ways that are no longer operative in postindustrial culture.

I want to suggest that by foregrounding a laboriously achieved sameness, the set of matching objects invited a fascination with the very fact of its madeness. The medium that most strongly suggests this attraction is porcelain, a new technology in eighteenth-century Europe that was characterized by continuous innovation and increasing virtuosity.[19] Consider, for example, the Sèvres tea service (Color Plate 7, see color insert after page 118). The ensemble is reiterative to an extreme degree: the dense pattern of perfectly straight lines, geometric garlands, and evenly applied stippling constitutes an astonishing feat of precision, and the unmarked white glaze on the interiors of the vessels and the exteriors of the saucers only highlights the insistent regularity of the painting. The ensemble fairly screams out its matching character—so much so that even when the elements were dispersed across a tabletop or held in the hands of several people, the visual unity of the group would have been readily apparent. The favor that this design found with consumers is suggested by the fact that it remained in production for at least fifteen years.[20] And because such sets were available in a wide range of patterns, the popularity of this model must have been due in part to the appeal of its assertive coordination.

Another way in which the technology of matching porcelain may have attracted the interest of consumers concerns the application of solid color. In the Sèvres *garniture* owned by Madame de Pompadour (Color Plates 4 and 5, see color insert after page 118), one of the most striking features is the contrast between the delicately painted reserves and the sections of solid pink and green glaze that cover other major areas of the pieces. Late-modern viewers, accustomed to the perfectly smooth, unmarked surfaces of even the most modest mass-produced ceramics, might be inclined to overlook the qualities of these unarticulated areas and focus instead on the delicacy of the painted scenes, which seem to signal greater artistry and offer greater engagement by virtue of their implied narratives.[21] But if pictorial decoration was what gave the object its aesthetic and social value, why not decorate the entire body of the piece as if it were a unified visual field? Were the stretches of solid color simply a matter of economy, or a means of framing and highlighting the more important painted areas? I would suggest that, on the contrary, passages of uninterrupted glazing contributed to the ensemble's attraction. The process of coating selected areas of a three-dimensional object with an evenly distributed pigment, filling others with delicately painted designs, and applying a final flourish of gold highlights required multiple stages of work by different artisans and a series of differently calibrated firings during which many pieces were damaged.[22] As they passed through numerous hands and were repeatedly subjected to the vagaries of the kiln, it was remarkable for a single piece to emerge unscathed, let alone a perfect match for another.

In other words, an area of solid ground color is, in its way, just as virtuoso an achievement as a painted scene. Indeed, because the production of a uniform glaze requires suppressing any visible traces of its application, a quality generally preserved in the evident brushstrokes of figurative designs, it is arguably the unbroken color field, not the painted motif, that is the more exacting measure of fine workmanship. Achieved so consistently throughout a group of pieces that they are indistinguishable in tone and evenness, such workmanship is nothing short of marvelous. Moreover, by simultaneously announcing and suppressing the action by which they were applied, the juxtaposition of visibly and invisibly painted colors on the same object further encourages a heightened sense of the deliberately conceived, highly controlled procedure by which the object was made.

In his work on Oceanic material culture, the anthropologist Alfred Gell discusses a mode of fascination with the madeness of things that he calls "the enchantment of technology." This way of engaging objects involves, simultaneously, a sense of wonder at the fact that something has been fabricated and an inability to understand precisely how it was produced. "It is the way an art object is construed as having come into the world which is the source of the power such objects have over us—their becoming rather than their being."[23] At the same time, "valued objects present themselves to us surrounded by a kind of halo-effect of resistance, and . . . it is this resistance to us which is the source of their value."[24] In other words, the enchantment of technology entails an active awareness of material objects *as such*, as artificial, manufactured things. But this mode of awareness is a form of wonder, not a form of reason. The object attracts through a kind of opacity; it is compelling precisely because its manifest madeness is at odds with the natural behavior of intractable physical materials and awkward human hands.

Gell's model is useful for thinking about the appeal of serial decoration in its period of innovation and exclusivity because it resonates with the equivocal relationship that elite consumers had with the artisanal arena. It is likely that many privileged individuals knew something about the production circumstances of luxury goods. The workshops of some artisans, such as upholsterers, doubled as public salesrooms; popular journals such as *L'Avantcoureur* featured essays on manufacturing processes; the *Encyclopédie* offered its subscribers a wealth of detailed information about materials and techniques; and the royal patronage of certain industries, such as French porcelain, entailed considerable publicity at court and may have occasioned conversations about how objects were made. However, according to eighteenth-century conceptions of art and labor, the work of the mind was valued far more highly than the work of the hand, and artisans were only rarely considered capable of transcending the manual realm.[25] Artisanal labor was both central to elite experience and invisible as a form of cultural agency. This tension between recognition and suppression is precisely what Gell describes. Not only does the enchantment of technology not require an understanding of specific practices, but indeed it is at its most potent and meaningful when the circumstances of making are unfathomable to the viewer. Objects fascinate through compelling otherness, not through rational comprehension. Thus, for eighteenth-century consumers, experiencing technology as enchantment was a way of appreciating the effect of artisanal work while disavowing the individualized labor that produced it. The technically perfect handmade object mobilizes sustained labor to produce something that bears no signs of labor or of the irregularity and accident that characterize much of the material world. And serial design, before the age of mechanical reproduction, accomplishes this feat in an especially powerful way. By virtue of its reiterative form—the evident fact that the same gestures of making were performed over and over—the set at once foregrounds and denies its madeness. The serial format is a kind of tease, announcing itself as the result of artful technology but refusing to fully disclose the workings of that process.

The Aesthetics of Similitude and Difference

If the enchantment of technology encouraged eighteenth-century viewers to appreciate matching objects for what Gell terms their *becoming*, I now want to complicate his oppositional categories and propose that their *being*—their compositional and pictorial properties—were equally a source of fascination. One of the essential qualities of the set is a formal tension between repeated and varied attributes. To identify a set as such is to grasp an effect of sameness within multiplicity, a process of comparison and distinction that separates a group of objects from the surrounding visual field and accepts the internal diversity of the ensemble as something that is ultimately contained by similitude. The pervasiveness of serial design and the complexity of its formal structures strongly suggest that the interplay between mutually defining sameness and difference constituted a particular form of pleasure for eighteenth-century consumers.

Let us return, for example, to the *garniture* of blue Chinese porcelain (Color Plate 6, see color insert after page 118). Although it is impossible to know for certain whether the current arrangement of elements is correct, the ensemble has a striking visual coherence that would not be achieved with any other configuration. It is evident at first glance that all the items are the same color, and seconds later one grasps that the taller, more complex central element is flanked by two pairs of shorter, more simple elements that are identical in shape. The grouping is further structured by strategic placements: the parrots are turned toward the center, while the symmetrical forms of the two vases bracket the array and contain the greater dynamism of the other items. Thus, the *garniture* is an artful exercise in reiteration and variation, cohesion and disparity. The ensemble is easily taken in as a whole, and the immediate recognition of unity and sameness enables a more prolonged subsequent visual experience in which the eye oscillates among the elements and registers increasingly subtle levels of resonance and difference. In the context of the decorated interior, this process may have been an automatic, unconscious response triggered by the composition of the ensemble itself. But if viewers recognized the *garniture* as a selective, deliberate combination of originally disparate objects, their visual experience also could have entailed a more conscious assessment and appreciation of its efficacy as a matched set.

The formal and scopic dynamics of the *garniture* are operative in even more complex ways in ensembles of decorative paintings. Consider the set of images made by four artists for the prince de Rohan's bedchamber at the hôtel de Soubise (Figures 8.4 through 8.7). There is more to their workings as an ensemble than simply a shared format, coordinated positions within the same room, and the fact that they all depict mythological couples. As with the *garniture*, the most immediately apparent connective devices invite attempts to discern further patterns of similitude and difference. For instance, attentive viewers would have noticed that the characters and settings are associated with the four elements: Hercules and Hebe as earth, Cephalus and Aurora as air, Mars and Venus as fire, Neptune and Amphitrite as water. In addition, the distinctly different ages of the four male figures suggest the ages of man: youthful Cephalus, virile Mars, mature Hercules, aged Neptune. These subject categories were often used to organize groups of decorative imagery (along with others such as the four seasons and the four continents), and would have been easily recognized by educated viewers.

More subtle levels of association and distinction emerge when the content of the images is considered in relation to their spatial placement within the bedchamber (Figure 8.8). The two images over the two doors, on the transit route of the *enfilade*, depict transitory passions: Aurora's fleeting fascination with Cephalus and the liaison between the god of war and the goddess of love. In contrast, the two images located deeper within the room, flanking the columned alcove with its state bed—the symbolic locus of the patron's dynastic and social power—portray married couples united in permanent partnerships: Neptune and Amphitrite, king and queen of the sea, and the eternal Olympian union of the apotheosized hero Hercules with Hebe, goddess of youth. The arrangement of the paintings spatializes a conceptual contrast: the youthful ardor valorized over the *enfilade* is transformed, at the room's core, into a celebration of conjugal devotion. The ensemble also offered a further provocation for viewers familiar with the current state of French art. Because the images were made by different painters, they may have afforded an opportunity for discerning connoisseurs to observe and appreciate how varying artistic sensibilities and career trajectories shaped interpretations of the same type of subject. For instance, the images of Neptune with Amphitrite and Mars with Venus, located on the same side of the room, could have incited reflections on what contemporaries saw as the "noble and male" style of Restout, a senior member of the Académie Royale, compared with the "sweet, agreeable" style of Van Loo, an emerging painter of the next generation.[26]

Compared with the *garniture*, the paintings can sustain a much greater degree of visual and conceptual scrutiny. But the essential point is that both types of sets invite a kind of comparative engagement in which similitude and difference are discerned in a sustained visual and cognitive play that has multiple points of access but no single, definitive conclusion. A provocative model for understanding this aesthetic sensibility is offered by Leo Bersani and Ulysse Dutoit in a study of ancient Assyrian relief sculpture.[27] In their analysis, a representational system in which forms are highly repetitive, yet not entirely identical, incites an active, stimulating mode of viewing in which the eyes continuously oscillate among elements and the mind seeks to determine their subtle relationships. In other words, reiteration within a unified compositional context is fundamentally about difference: "*Repetition . . . makes repetition itself problematic. It appears to provide the strongest elements of order in our visual field, whereas in fact it initiates an inconclusive movement of perpetual verification on our part between the repeated elements.*"[28] This restless tracing and retracing is akin to noncoital eroticism, a form of indefinitely sustained, open-ended pleasure that unfolds without any drive toward resolution. Ultimately, the viewer's enjoyment emerges not from the form or content of the object under scrutiny, but rather from the connective dynamics of looking itself, from an experience of visual movement within the charged spaces between forms that the authors call *interstitial sensuality*: "[T]he spectator's pleasure in following all the cues . . . which displace his or her interest and attention is less in the variety of scenes which are thereby taken in than in the very tension of the displacing movement itself."[29] Repetition thus activates the entire visual field, seducing viewers into a dance of almost endless perceptual possibilities. This is precisely the kind of representational and scopic scenario enabled by the serially organized interior. Far from foreclosing viewer engagement with unimaginative reiteration, serial design sharpened one's awareness of difference and offered an open-ended pleasure of discernment that could vary according to observer and occasion.

Social Mastery

So far, I have considered two modes of engagement with serial design that foregrounded the extraordinary and variable qualities of sets and operated more or less independently of particular social situations. Now, moving from questions of technology and form to questions of function, I want to consider some of the ways in which the display, arrangement, and actual usage of matching objects contributed to the social workings of the decorated interior. All types of domestic furnishings arguably played some part in the construction of elite personas and the dynamics of interaction, but matching ensembles had unique properties and meanings that made them especially potent markers in the negotiation of social space and the enactment of social distinctions. The key idea here, which intentionally complicates the arguments of the previous sections, is that part of the importance of sets lay in the fact that they were not only remarkable and stimulating, but also formulaic and predictable. Through their widespread availability in the luxury marketplace, and their conventional patterns of spatial distribution and use, sets produced an important sense of mastery for both the occupants of an interior and their visitors, uniting them in a collectively understood system of recognition and valorization.

To begin with, the possession of sets foregrounded affluent ownership in ways that could not be achieved through the display of unrelated objects. As already noted, the production of seriality entailed an extensive mobilization of coordinated labor. A *meuble* required the work of artisans specializing in carpentry, upholstery, trimming, and gilding; a *garniture* might be a customized ensemble set in specially designed mounts; a patterned tea set with multiple cups and saucers announced a succession of identical technical moves; decorative paintings might be supplied by several artists bound by the same frame shape and pictorial theme. Through the sheer quantity of their reiterative forms, all of these formats foregrounded the authority of the purchaser or patron as someone who could command a potentially endless cycle of production—who could, so to speak, make people do things over and over, often to their own specifications. Moreover, once the ensembles reached the interior, a further succession of mobilized work was required: *garnitures* needed to be kept gleaming; beverage services needed to be washed; upholstery needed to be cleaned, mended, and changed with the seasons. This was the case with all fine furnishings, of course, but the care of sets was more labor intensive than the care of singular objects. Any visible damage or repair in one element would make it stand out in relation to the others, interrupting the unity of the group and compromising its technological and compositional attractions. Indeed, the perfectly maintained matched set was perhaps the ultimate expression of elite status, for it suggested an immunity to the ordinary stresses of time, environment, and quotidian circumstance.

Another way in which serial design contributed to the process of social representation was through the legibility of spatial arrangement. The visual dominance of certain types of sets could provide individuals with important information about the situations they encountered in the course of their social lives. For instance, the extent and arrangement of a *meuble* played a key role in defining the character of a room and the parameters of its usage on particular occasions. Inventories indicate that coordinated ensembles were located almost exclusively in social spaces and that their luxuriousness was closely correlated with formality. Thus, a space dedicated to highly structured, hierarchical interactions, such as a reception room (*chambre du dais*), state bedchamber (*chambre de parade*), or large salon, was much more likely to contain a costly and extensive *meuble* than a private bedchamber or study. At the hôtel de Roquelaure, for example, almost all the objects in the principal social space are part of a set, while the less public spaces contain more modestly scaled ensembles and a higher percentage of nonmatching items.[30]

This synchrony of formality and seriality has interesting implications for the social negotiation of the interior. According to the codes of polite conduct, cultivated individuals were expected to convey a sense of ease and fluidity in all forms of bodily movement and verbal communication, and to constantly adjust their behavior in response to a multitude of variables that shaped the definition of appropriate interaction.[31] As Figure 8.1 suggests, because of its physical distribution and visual coherence, a *meuble* was probably the most instantly legible feature of a room. Thus, upon entering a space that was decorated in this way, a visitor could assess at a glance the extent and arrangement of the matching upholstery and immediately begin to determine what kind of spatial and social circumstances she was facing and what type of conduct would be most suitable in that setting. For example, a room saturated with red velvet upholstery and filled with seats set in rows was likely ready for a formal reception, while a room equipped with chairs that were variously covered or arranged in clusters signaled an opportunity for more informal conviviality. Especially for a visitor to an unfamiliar space, the presence of such visual cues could make the difference between an elegant entry and an awkward one, and thus between the success or failure of a social performance. Conversely, for the host, the choice of rooms and the arrangement of objects helped to define the relative formality or intimacy of an encounter before a single word was exchanged.

The social efficacy of the matched set was thus bound up with the fact that it was simultaneously familiar and singular, similar to ensembles that might be encountered in other settings but also configured to suit particular needs. This relational experience of objects operated with an even higher degree of expressive flexibility in the case of beverage services. The Sèvres tea set (Color Plate 7, see color insert after page 118), for example, was only one contribution to an extended field of related objects. The models for the individual items were introduced separately into the Sèvres repertoire between 1752 and 1760 and were eventually produced in several sizes, painted with various colors and patterns, and grouped in different combinations—variables that in turn corresponded to a wide range of prices.[32] Owning a set like this meant owning only one permutation among an incalculable number of possibilities, but a permutation that was, at the same time, potentially unique. The duchess at the *hôtel* across the street might have the same teapot, but it might be decorated with birds rather than roses and combined with only a sugar bowl and a single cup and saucer on a smaller, differently shaped tray. This kind of material landscape, with its ongoing tension between similarity and difference, produces a more subtly calibrated scale of distinction than one in which differences are more pronounced. Within the collectively recognized structure of familiar forms, the dynamics of individual self-fashioning could play out with excruciating particularity.

Furthermore, when the elements of a *meuble* or a beverage service were actually in use, the formal unity and coherence of the set was extended to the social gathering. Six people seated in matching chairs seem like more of a group, both visually and symbolically, than the same people seated in assorted chairs. At the same time, formal differences within the set, notably the distinction between (superior) armchairs and (inferior) side chairs, allow hierarchical relationships to be expressed within the collective. Similarly, the related but differentiated elements of a porcelain beverage service foster a ritual of disassembly and distribution that generates an image of connectedness while also supporting individual preferences for, say, coffee rather than tea or more or less sugar. This social effect of serial design is nicely captured in a group portrait by Jean-Baptiste Charpentier (Figure 8.9) in which the members of a ducal family, seated on chairs with gilded frames and red velvet upholstery, pose with elements of a porcelain coffee service. They interact with the matching objects in different ways: the woman in the center leans forward and holds a cup by the base; the woman on the right sits back while grasping her cup's delicate handle and stirring its contents; one of the men on the left is about to drink from his saucer. We cannot assume that this is exactly how people actually used such things, but the painter's inventions are suggestive. The presence of matching but differently occupied and handled objects suggests both familial unity and individual differentiation. By the action of serial design, the people themselves are transformed into a kind of set.

The key point here is that the set's tension between formula and variation produced a gratifying sense of aesthetic and social mastery that was central to the construction of elite identity. A useful theoretical framework for understanding this kind of experience is offered by Umberto Eco in a study of repetitive forms in popular media (such as detective fiction, film remakes, and television serials). Eco argues that the ability to anticipate and recognize familiar formulas produces a profound sense of pleasure and empowerment:

Figure 8.9 Jean-Baptiste Charpentier, *The Family of the Duc de Penthièvre*, c.1767. Châteaux de Versailles et de Trianon, Versailles. Photo: Réunion des Musées Nationaux/Art Resource, N.Y.

The series consoles us . . . because it rewards our ability to foresee: we are happy because we discover our own ability to guess what will happen. We are satisfied because we find again what we had expected, but we do not attribute this happy result to the obviousness of the narrative structure, but to our own presumed capacities to make forecasts.[33]

In this system, repetition and innovation are not mutually exclusive, but indeed mutually defining. The standardized framework contains a multitude of variations, and it is this assurance of overall sameness that enables the reader or viewer to savor the novel twists and turns that prevent each iteration from becoming a complete duplication. Eco further suggests that seriality operates on two different levels of audience engagement: one in which a reader simply enjoys the succession of "previsions and expectations" and another in which a more critical reader "evaluates the work as an aesthetic product" and appreciates its narrative strategies for the manipulations that they are.[34]

I would argue that this is precisely what happens in the eighteenth-century French interior. Spaces designed according to a shared decorative vocabulary—the same types of upholstery, mantelpiece ornaments, tea sets, pictorial subjects—were legible and comfortable to negotiate. At the same time, the almost endless possibility of variation *within* this vocabulary—different fabrics, shapes, motifs, arrangements—expressed nuances of status and taste and provided varying degrees of stimulation for differently positioned viewers. Serial design was a crucial site for the enactment of elite self-fashioning, an eloquent representational system that elicited performances of social mastery.

Surplus and Anxiety

The social stakes of seriality, however, were not limited to the dynamics of conduct and discernment. In this final section, I want once again to complicate my previous assertions and consider the possibility that the matched set signified not only because it provided aesthetic gratification and enabled social performance, but also because it ultimately exceeded the conditions of both conscious attention and actual usage. I also want to suggest in conclusion that the abundance of repetitive design in the French interior may be symptomatic of a pervasive anxiety, an uncertainty about the capacity of decoration to carry the burden of representation in an unstable social field.

Serial design both generated and was in turn shaped by what might be called an *aesthetics of surplus*. Many elite interiors contained more chairs and tea sets than could possibly be used on any but the most lavishly staged occasions, more *garnitures* than there were surfaces to embellish, more decorative paintings than were needed to enliven the *enfilade*. It is virtually impossible to assess (in the absence of obvious damage) the degree to which objects like vases, potpourri containers, and teacups were actually used, but it is very possible that many of them, especially the most fragile and expensive ones, were rarely touched. It is also possible that sets were not always subject to the kind of stimulating, comparative observation that their artful forms seem to demand. Not only were viewers potentially overwhelmed by the sheer quantity and dazzle of numerous similar things, or oblivious to their charms amid the distractions of sociability, but the codes of polite behavior forbade staring at other people's possessions, handling them uninvited, or even praising them too fulsomely.[35] Moreover, it is likely that some matching objects, notably upholstered furniture, were protected by slipcovers that, although themselves a matched set, hid the objects' sumptuous materials from the view of visitors on all but the most important social occasions.

Matching, then, was ultimately a gratuitous project, one that surpassed the parameters of necessity and attention and was even, at times, invisible. But this did not strip serial objects of their signifying power. Indeed, the purposeful neglect of an object's full capacity to sustain usage or appreciation was a gesture of privilege available only to those who could afford to own things simply for the sake of ownership. Madame de Pompadour's *garniture* (Figures 8.2 and 8.3; Color Plates 4 and 5, see color insert after page 118) may have never bloomed with forced bulbs, dripped with candle wax, or dispensed the spicy scent of potpourri. But the fact that it *could* have done so, and yet did not, may well have been prestigious in itself, a suggestion of indifference to functional particularity that elevated the potentially useful ensemble to the status of a purely aesthetic object. And the fact that the set was composed of five large, beautifully coordinated pieces set before a mirror on a mantelpiece would have only made this gesture more emphatic: reiterated uselessness was put on display at the dazzling focal point of the room. Furthermore, the visitor surrounded by enticing things that she is unable to see or too polite to scrutinize is placed in a position of unfulfilled desire that makes these objects seem, paradoxically, even more powerful as social signs. The paintings in the prince de Rohan's bedchamber (Figures 8.4 through 8.7), vividly rendered and visible from every position in the room, would have been difficult to ignore, and the very effort to do so would have strengthened one's sense of the princely privilege of living amid an excess of enticement. Similarly, the presence of slipcovers on the chairs in the salon shown in Figure 8.1 would have only drawn visitors' attention to the fact that the materials underneath were too fine to be exposed in their presence.

Thus, the aesthetics of surplus was just as integral to the process of social formation as the dynamics of vision and interaction, and once again it was something that could be achieved only by serial design. Far more than an assemblage of visually unrelated objects, a concentration of numerous similar or identical items asserted the presence of sheer quantity, the possession of material abundance for its own sake. Allowing potentially functional objects to become purely decorative or unavailable for sustained engagement was a gesture of privilege and leisure that was consistent with the drive to aestheticize that informed many areas of elite social practice. Decorative surplus can be understood as the design equivalent of activities such as conversation and dance, which were fundamental to self-fashioning precisely because they yielded artful formal patterns that were essentially nonproductive. Mary Vidal has demonstrated that the flow of synchronized, unsubstantive talk was central to polite interaction, and Sarah Cohen has shown that the use of the body to produce elegant, repetitive movement both demonstrated leisured cultivation and was appreciated in and of itself as an exercise in formal possibility.[36] Similarly, a roomful of sets, with its aesthetics of surplus, announced the elite luxury of sublimating necessity into art.

However, even with all of these explanations, the intensive pursuit of serial design in eighteenth-century France remains somewhat baffling. Why was this culture so compelled to produce, as it were, an excess of excess? By way of conclusion, I want to build upon the points I have already made about social mastery and raise the possibility that the repetitive nature of seriality was also a manifestation of a struggle for psychological control. In psychoanalytic theory, repetition is considered an important means of mastering anxiety and consolidating an unstable psychological position. Most famously, Sigmund Freud links the child's penchant for repetitive play with the crucial developmental process of rehearsing and normalizing the trauma of separation from the mother. According to Freud, performing an accomplished, predictable gesture over and over yields a sense of pleasure, comfort, and mastery that compensates for—indeed avenges—an event that the child cannot otherwise control.[37] This link between repetition and psychic formation is a provocative one in relation to the eighteenth-century interior. It is well known that elite consumers in this period lived in a highly unstable world in which status and fortune were mutable, knowledge was shifting, and social identities had to be constantly renegotiated. The decorated interior was not simply a place where fixed social positions were passively reflected, but rather an arena of contest where personas and roles were actively constructed and potentially undermined, and where material plenitude was the prerogative of ambitious upstarts as well as, if not more than, the traditionally privileged.[38] Perhaps the desirability of serial design lay partly in the fact that even as it was rendered in an almost infinite variety of ways, it provided a predictable, collectively understood, repeatedly rehearsed framework that could bring a sense of order and agency to the ongoing, perpetually indeterminate project of self-fashioning. Ultimately, the pervasiveness of this decorative practice signals not a complacent confidence in its efficacy, but rather a determination to make it persuasive and an abiding suspicion that it might not be. Repetition is a form of insistence in the face of tenuous control. And this, I would suggest, is the anxiety of seriality—an attempt, in a culture of uncertainty, to assert the possibility of meaning over and over again. In a world where the codes of decoration were inextricably bound up with those of social legitimacy, too much was never enough.

When Horace Walpole visited the hôtel de Soubise during his 1765 sojourn in Paris, his dismay over its interior design was so pronounced that he noted it not only in his letter to Anne Pitt, but also in his journal: "The apartments are trist [sic] and almost all furnished with red velvet and red damask. Great deal of old china."[39] For this enthusiast of curiosities and altered states, French interiors were anything but engaging; he perceived the presence of a formula but was unable to appreciate the varied forms and meanings that it contained. Perhaps Walpole himself provides the best explanation for his disappointment. In another missive from Paris, he conceded:

> my own defects are the sole cause of my not liking Paris entirely: the constraint I am under from not being perfectly master of their language, and from being so much in the dark, as one necessarily must be, on half the subjects of their conversation, prevents my enjoying that ease for which their society is calculated. I am much amused, but not comfortable.[40]

Like language, decoration was a complex system in eighteenth-century France with its own vocabulary, syntax, and expressive power. It could be engaged at different levels of mastery, and unless one grasped its nuances, it was impossible to negotiate its codes successfully and savor all its pleasures. Serial design was an especially potent site for aesthetic engagement and the production of social distinction, for while its basic format was clear and recognizable, its rich range of associations was available only to the initiated. Indeed, Walpole's sense of exclusion is inevitably shared by the late-modern interpreter, for it is ultimately impossible to recover fully the shape and meaning of any historical experience. But the joy of sets is an aspect of design history that has yet to be recognized as a meaningful cultural practice, and it has much to teach us about both the sensibilities of the past and our own preoccupations in the present. My hope is that this initial foray will be the beginning of an ongoing conversation.

ACKNOWLEDGMENTS

I am very grateful to Dena Goodman and Kathryn Norberg not only for organizing a stimulating conference on eighteenth-century furniture and insisting on the importance of this subject for the field of eighteenth-century studies, but also for their patience and generosity during the completion of this chapter. For transformative critical responses to several versions of the project, I am indebted to Bettina Bergmann, Barbara Kellum, Dana Leibsohn, and Ajay Sinha. For assistance with illustration expenses, I thank the Department of Art and Art History, Skidmore College. All translations, unless otherwise noted, are mine.

Notes

1. Horace Walpole, *Correspondence*, ed. W. S. Lewis, 48 vols. (New Haven, CT: Yale University Press, 1937-83), 31: 87–88.

2. For the purposes of this essay, I am not making a meaningful distinction between the concepts of matching and seriality, although the latter is often used to designate a temporal as well as spatial succession. Here, seriality refers to a visual and physical condition in which a number of objects are linked and unified by virtue of material, form, and arrangement.

3. For the emergence of visual unity in upholstery design, see Peter Thornton, *Seventeenth-Century Interior Decoration in England, France and Holland* (New Haven, CT, and London: Yale University Press, 1978), 103–106.

4. For a survey of object types, see Pierre Verlet, *The Eighteenth Century in France: Society, Decoration, Furniture* (Rutland, VT, and Tokyo: Charles E. Tuttle, 1967). For the social significance of specialization, see Mimi Hellman, "Furniture, Sociability, and the Work of Leisure in Eighteenth-Century France," *Eighteenth-Century Studies* 32 (summer 1999): 415–45.

5. See André-Jacob Roubo, *L'art du menuisier en meubles* (Paris: Saillant et Nyon, 1772), 643; *L'Avantcoureur* (1761): 809–10.

6. The classic treatment of modernity as a crisis in the status of originality is Walter Benjamin, "The Work of Art in the Age of Mechanical Reproduction," in *Illuminations: Essays and Reflections*, ed. Hannah Arendt, trans. Harry Zohn (New York: Schocken Books, 1969), 217–51. For a range of approaches to the aesthetic and cultural status of repetition in art, see *Retaining the Original: Multiple Originals, Copies, and Reproductions*, special issue of *Studies in the History of Art* 20 (1989); *The Culture of the Copy*, special issue of *Visual Resources* 15 (1999). Since the early twentieth century, a concept that has emerged as the *other* of art, and might be applied to certain types of modern serial design, is kitsch. See Tomas Kulka, *Kitsch and Art* (University Park: Pennsylvania State University Press, 1996).

7. In eighteenth-century French, the term *meuble* could mean several different things. For a brief history of the sense used here, see Henry Havard, *Dictionnaire de l'ameublement et de la décoration depuis le XIIIe siècle à nos jours*, 4 vols. (Paris: Quantin, 1887–1889), 3 : 865–68. For detailed accounts of fabrication procedures, see *Encyclopédie, ou Dictionnaire raisonné des sciences, des arts et des métiers, par une société des gens de lettres* (Paris: Briasson, 1751–1765), notably the discussion of trimmings (*passementerie*; 12 :126–38) and the annotated plates for the trades of *menuisier* (24 : n.p.) and *tapissier* (30 : n.p). See also Linda Wesselman Jackson, "Beyond the Fringe: Ornamental Upholstery Trimmings in the 17th, 18th and Early 19th Centuries," and Jeffrey Munger, "French Upholstery Practices of the 18th Century," in *Upholstery in America and Europe from the Seventeenth Century to World War I*, ed. Edward S. Cooke Jr., (New York: W. W. Norton, 1987), 120–30, 131–47. For the prestige value of matching seat furniture in the age of industrialization, see Katherine C. Grier, *Culture and Comfort: Parlor-Making and Middle-Class Identity, 1850–1930* (Washington, DC: Smithsonian Institution Press, 1988), 176–210.

8. *Inventaire après décès de madame la maréchalle duchesse de Roquelaure*. Paris, Archives Nationales (AN), Minutier Central (MC) CXIII, 340 (March 18, 1735). The other items in the room were four green curtains, six rush-bottomed chairs with cotton covers, two small console tables with marble tops, a clock, a pair of wall lights, some fireplace fixtures, three mirrors, and three overdoor paintings.

9. For a brief design history of the *garniture*, see Havard, *Dictionnaire de l'ameublement*, 2: 1075–79. For the primacy of the mantelpiece as a design feature of social spaces, see Verlet, *Eighteenth Century in France*, 91–94.

10. See Pierre Ennès, "Essai de reconstitution d'une garniture de madame de Pompadour," *Journal of the Walters Art Gallery* 42/43 (1984–1985): 70–82; Adrian Sassoon, *Vincennes and Sèvres Porcelain: Catalogue of the Collections* (Malibu, CA: The J. Paul Getty Museum, 1991), 57–63. The *garniture* was displayed in a space adjacent to the bathing room that was furnished for resting after bathing. The other contents included a *meuble* (canopy bed, daybed, armchair, two side chairs, footstool, fire screen) covered with the same gold-embroidered red fabric, a set of four overdoors, window curtains, and fireplace fixtures. The total appraised value of these items was 1,144 livres, only a little more than the value of the *garniture* itself. See Jean Cordey, *Inventaire des biens de Madame de Pompadour rédigé après son décès* (Paris: La Société des Bibliophiles François, 1939), 22–23, 39.
11. For bathing spaces in eighteenth-century France, see Mimi Hellman, "Domesticity Undone: Three Historical Interiors," in *Undomesticated Interiors*, exhibition catalog (Northampton, MA: Smith College Museum of Art, 2004), 14–22.
12. For luxury merchants as designers, see Carolyn Sargentson, *Merchants and Luxury Markets: The Marchands Merciers of Eighteenth-Century Paris* (London and Malibu, CA: Victoria and Albert Museum in association with the J. Paul Getty Museum, 1996), 44–61. For a survey of the practice of mounting Asian porcelain, see F. J. B. Watson and Gillian Wilson, *Mounted Oriental Porcelain in the J. Paul Getty Museum* (Malibu, CA: J. Paul Getty Museum, 1982), 1–18.
13. For social histories of these substances, see Wolfgang Schivelbusch, *Tastes of Paradise: A Social History of Spices, Stimulants, and Intoxicants*, trans. David Jacobson (New York: Pantheon Books, 1992), 15–95; Jane Pettigrew, *A Social History of Tea* (London: National Trust, 2001).
14. Duvaux's prices ranged from 36 livres (two blue and white cups with saucers and sugar bowl) to 240 livres (six cups with saucers, sugar box, and teapot on a tray, painted with figures on a celadon ground) to 480 livres (two cups, sugar bowl, and teapot on a tray, painted with flowers on a sky blue ground). Terms for the variety of configurations include *en bateau, en corbeille, du Roy*. See *Livre-Journal de Lazare Duvaux, Marchand-Bijoutier Ordinaire du Roy, 1748–1758*, ed. Louis Courajod, 2 vols. (Paris: F. de Nobele, 1965), 2: 14, 194, 239.
15. The extensive array of porcelain in this room includes a set of eight white porcelain cups with saucers from the manufactory of Saint Cloud grouped on a tray of Chinese lacquer (20 livres); a set of six cups with saucers of white Japanese porcelain and a white porcelain bowl from Saint Cloud grouped on a tray of Japanese lacquer (150 livres); and a set of eight cups with saucers, a sugar box, two teapots with saucers, and two additional cups, all of "antique" white porcelain of unspecified origin, grouped on a Japanese lacquer tray (500 livres). See *Inventaire après décès d'Hercule-Mériadec de Rohan-Soubise, prince de Rohan*. AN, MC, Documents Réserve XCIX, 501 (February 10, 1749), fol. 26v–27r. This type of set, which may have been assembled by either the consumer or a *marchand mercier*, has become invisible as a decorative conceit because it survives only in the form of inventory descriptions. It seems that objects grouped in this way, lacking both a shared place of manufacture and the explicitly connective device of bronze mounts that often unified *garnitures*, have not been recognized as sets in the aesthetic and economic systems of late-modern collecting.
16. Although the word *decorative* can have pejorative connotations, I use the phrase *decorative painting* without value judgment to characterize paintings that were made for permanent installation in an interior scheme (whether predetermined or anticipated), as opposed to paintings that, although they might ultimately hang in a domestic interior, were produced without particular attention to the demands of physical setting. This type of imagery occupies a problematic place in the history of eighteenth-century art, for while its practitioners included major artists such as François Boucher and Jean-Honoré Fragonard, it has often seemed unconducive to intensive scholarly analysis. Drawing upon a standardized repertoire of subjects, it is an art that privileges vignette over narrative, visual effects over original themes and complex messages. During the eighteenth century, decorative painting was often criticized in precisely these terms, and while modern scholars have recognized the prejudice, they have also perpetuated it by devoting more interpretive attention to the ambitious aesthetic and conceptual concerns of monumental history painting or other works, such as genre scenes or portraits, conceived independently of specific sites. For important exceptions to this tendency, see Paula Rea Radisich, *Hubert Robert: Painted Spaces of the Enlightenment* (Cambridge: Cambridge University Press, 1998); Mary D. Sheriff, *Fragonard: Art and Eroticism* (Chicago: University of Chicago Press, 1990), 58–116; Katie Scott, *The Rococo Interior: Decoration and Social Spaces in Early Eighteenth-Century Paris* (New Haven, CT: Yale University Press, 1995), 121–211.
17. I am currently completing a book-length study of the hôtel de Soubise that includes an extensive analysis of the prince de Rohan's apartment in its larger architectural, decorative, and social context.

18. Figure 8.8 also includes the major furnishings of the bedchamber as documented by the prince de Rohan's inventory: a state bed, console table, and two commodes that were undoubtedly in the positions indicated, and a conjectural arrangement of the seat furniture (fourteen armchairs in two different designs and six side chairs).

19. Before the early eighteenth century, the only porcelain available in Europe was imported from Asia; most European ceramics were faience (tin-glazed earthenware). The French porcelain discussed here was made at Sèvres, a manufactory first established at Vincennes in 1740 and relocated in 1756. In 1759, Louis XV assumed sole ownership and the manufactory went on to produce some of the most technically sophisticated and widely consumed porcelain in Europe. For a general history, see Svend Eriksen and Geoffrey de Bellaigue, *Sèvres Porcelain: Vincennes and Sèvres, 1740–1800*, Danish text trans. R. J. Charleston (London: Faber and Faber, 1987).

20. The set was produced from around 1767 into the 1780s; see Linda H. Roth and Clare Le Corbeiller, *French Eighteenth-Century Porcelain at the Wadsworth Atheneum: The J. Pierpont Morgan Collection* (Hartford, CT: Wadsworth Atheneum, 2000), 199.

21. Indeed, specialists pay particular attention to the authorship, quality, and pictorial sources of figurative decoration as important factors in the dating, stylistic analysis, and valuation of porcelain. See, for example, Carl Christian Dauterman, "Sèvres Figure Painting in the Anna Thompson Dodge Collection," *Burlington Magazine* 118 (1976): 753–62.

22. For an explication of the entire production process, see *Encyclopédie*, 4: 506–12, 13: 105–22.

23. Alfred Gell, "The Technology of Enchantment and the Enchantment of Technology," in *Anthropology, Art and Aesthetics*, ed. Jeremy Coote and Anthony Shelton (Oxford: Clarendon Press, 1992), 40–63, at 46.

24. Ibid., 48. In addition to the example of canoe prow-boards produced by the Kula people of the Trobriand Isands, Gell invokes another kind of object that might resonate more vividly with Euro-American readers: a model of Salisbury Cathedral made of matchsticks seen by the author as a child and marvelous to him precisely because, while the material was familiar, he could not fathom how it could be manipulated to such an end.

25. See Scott, *Rococo Interior*, 61–77.

26. See Jean Mariette, *Abecedario*, ed. P. de Chennevières and A. de Montaiglon (Paris: J.-P. Dumoulin, 1851–1860), 386; Michel-François Dandré-Bardon, *Vie de Carle Vanloo* [1765] (reprint, Geneva: Minkoff, 1973), 50–51. Mariette, quoting an obituary of Restout, also emphasizes the "grand effects" of his work and his "reasoned balances and oppositions of massing, form, shadow, and light." Dandré-Bardon, in an address read to the Academy, further notes that Van Loo "did not ordinarily devote himself to vigorous effects" created by "firmly established masses," but rather sought "accidents of light" that were "friendly to the eye and more capable of pleasing than astonishing." Restout was received by the academy in 1720, Van Loo in 1735.

27. Leo Bersani and Ulysse Dutoit, *The Forms of Violence: Narrative in Assyrian Art and Modern Culture* (New York: Schocken Books, 1985), 73–109.

28. Ibid., 95–96 (emphasis theirs).

29. Ibid., 105 (italics removed); the phrase "interstitial sensuality" appears at 108.

30. The principal social space, called a *grand cabinet* by the notary, contains a *meuble* composed of two large couches, eight armchairs, two fire screens, three door curtains, and wall hangings. The visual effect of this ensemble would have been very striking, for the only other furnishings in the room were two small console tables, six caned chairs, four window curtains, a clock, and light and fireplace fixtures. In contrast, the duchess's study contained a much smaller set of one couch and six armchairs, upholstered in the same flowered velvet as the objects in the *grand cabinet*, but there were no matching curtains or hangings to extend the upholstery design to the walls of the space. The other items in the room were window curtains of a different fabric, a caned chair, a desk, light and fireplace fixtures, and a small stove. See *Inventaire après décès de madame la maréchalle duchesse de Roquelaure*.

31. See Hellman, "Furniture, Sociability, and the Work of Leisure," 432–37.

32. The teapot, one of the manufactory's most widely produced forms, was made in at least six sizes beginning in the early 1750s. Among its many appearances in surviving sets, it can be found grouped with a sugar bowl, milk jug, and single cup and saucer on a round tray, all painted with rose garlands on a largely white ground, and elsewhere paired with a sugar bowl and two cups and saucers on an oval tray with an openwork rim, a much more densely decorated and expensive ensemble featuring friezes of pinwheel-like flowers (both 1764). The milk jug and sugar bowl, introduced in 1752 and 1753, respectively, were both in one of three available sizes. The cup, designed in 1752, was also made in three sizes and could be paired with saucers in three different styles. The particular set seen here was made possible only when the tray, in one of two sizes, was introduced in 1760; manufactory records document prices ranging from 144 to 720 livres. The ensemble was subsequently produced in two sizes, the larger of which included a tea caddy. See Roth and Le Corbeiller, *French Eighteenth-Century Porcelain*, 169, 181–83, 187–88, 191–95, 197–200.

33. Umberto Eco, "Innovation and Repetition: Between Modern and Post-Modern Aesthetics," *Daedalus* 114 (fall 1985): 161–84, at 168.

34. Ibid., 174–75. See also Rebecca E. Martin, "'I Should Like To Spend My Whole Life in Reading It': Repetition and the Pleasure of the Gothic," *Journal of Narrative Technique* 28 (1998): 75–90; Bruce F. Kawin, *Telling It Again and Again: Repetition in Literature and Film* (Ithaca, NY: Cornell University Press, 1972).

35. For example, Louis-Antoine de Caraccioli warned that even informal visits were not occasions for the abandonment of proper conduct, noting that there were some ill-mannered young people who let their eyes and hands roam everywhere: "they must see everything, touch everything, often at the risk of breaking precious furnishings; they make, as it were, an inventory of the very books and papers. The first rule of civility is to not even open a book without the permission of those to whom it belongs." *Le Véritable mentor, ou l'éducation de la noblesse*, 2nd ed. (Liège: Bassompierre, 1759), 144–45. Similarly, Jean-Baptiste Morvan, abbé de Bellegarde, criticized people who remarked too readily and extensively on a room's decor: "no sooner have they entered a place, or joined a circle, than they praise the ceiling, the alcove, the bed, the armchair, the fire screen that is presented to them, the little yelping dog." *Les Réflexions sur le ridicule, & sur les moyens de l'éviter*, in *Oeuvres diverses de M. l'abbé de Bellegarde*, 4 vols. (Paris: Claude Robustel, 1723), 1: 37.

36. See Mary Vidal, *Watteau's Painted Conversations: Art, Literature, and Talk in Seventeenth- and Eighteenth-Century France* (New Haven, CT: Yale University Press, 1992), 75–98; Sarah R. Cohen, "*Un Bal Continuel*: Watteau's Cythera Paintings and Aristocratic Dancing in the 1710s," *Art History* 17 (1994): 160–81, esp. 164–65; Sarah R. Cohen, "Body as 'Character' in Early Eighteenth-Century French Art and Performance," *Art Bulletin* 78 (1996): 454–66.

37. See Sigmund Freud, *Beyond the Pleasure Principle*, trans. James Strachey (New York: Liveright Publishing, 1950), 11–17. Freud's canonical example is the game he calls *fort-da*, in which a child plays with a reel attached to a string by repeatedly casting it away from himself and pulling it back in, affirming the vulnerability of loss and the assurance of recovery with a series of reiterated exclamations. See also Robert Rogers, "Freud and the Semiotics of Repetition," *Poetics Today* 8 (1987): 579–90.

38. See Scott, *Rococo Interior*, 81–117. A typical expression of anxiety about the instability of decorative signs is offered by the abbé de Bellegarde: "One can hardly contain the indignation one feels to see badly made-up *bourgeoises* whose dress, manner of living, furnishings, and table are the envy of women of the first quality." *Réflexions sur le ridicule*, 201.

39. Walpole, *Correspondence*, 7 : 283.

40. Ibid., 31: 51.

CHAPTER **9**

Decoration and Enlightened Spectatorship

MARY SALZMAN

Jean-François de Troy's *The Garter* and *The Declaration of Love* (Color Plates 8 and 9, see color insert after page 118), painted as a pair in 1724, occur as two distinct anecdotes of seduction in the art historical literature.[1] Conceiving of the paintings as storytelling mechanisms results in limited roles for both their prominent decorative arts and their sophisticated eighteenth-century beholder. Under this model, the pictures' art objects and furnishings function as mere teleological signposts that foreshadow the stories' titillating conclusions. The viewer, consequently, is present simply to uncover the scenes' predetermined meaning, which lurks in these visual clues. In *The Garter*, the nude female statuette and the clock disclose that the young woman, though initially resistant, will allow herself to be seduced. She will eventually arrive at the same state of undress as the bronze—starting with her garter. The clock's allegorical figures of Love conquering Time attest that sexual conquest is simply a matter of persistence on the part of the suitor. In *The Declaration of Love*, the room's palette, red for passion, together with the picture of Mars and Venus embracing in a landscape, imply that the couple in the foreground, with the help of the invitingly contoured sofa, will end up in the same position as their painted analogs.[2]

While I do not dispute the anecdotal quality of the pendants, neither do I believe that their interest lies solely in the viewer's discovering whether sexual union will take place. If the purpose of *The Garter* and *The Declaration of Love* is to recount a tale of contemporary mores, their focus on a future, undepicted event fails to account for the artist's bravura handling of brush and pigment. Because de Troy is a painter who renders distinctions as fine as the soft shimmer of silver brocade versus the hard glint of silver buttons, I find it unsatisfactory to designate his descriptive passages as pictorial emblems. I propose instead that the pendants function in tandem to encourage the viewer to consider how judiciously each seduction is conducted. Inviting the critical participation of the pendants' early eighteenth-century public necessitates reimagining the spectator as a collaborator in the signifying process and the decorative arts as rhetorically active, dialogic components of the pictures. How, then, do *The Garter* and *The Declaration of Love* represent seduction as a process and

155

how do they elicit the viewer's judgment? I suggest that the combination of de Troy's use of the pendant format, his subject matter, and his refusal to subordinate the painting's visual effects, particularly the representation of the decorative arts, to narrative content, provided his worldly spectator an opportunity to exercise culturally specific powers of discernment that were understood at the time to be quite modern. Genre scenes of polite society by de Troy and his contemporaries portrayed the display of critical judgment as an integral part of the activities of daily life. The representation of such cognitive finesse in their works also served as a metaphor for the discernment that this self-consciously modern painting expected of its viewing public.

In early eighteenth-century France, the exercise of modern knowledge was conceived as the application of critical judgment to observable and intuitively felt phenomena, followed swiftly by evaluation and, finally, response. Individuals tested their conclusions against the authority of lived experience. Ideally, the internal dialogue inherent in critical judgment encouraged self-knowledge. Analyzing information on the spot was a necessary component of one's encounters with the world at large, as well as situations as intimate as a tête-à-tête. The ability to reason and intuit defined the individual subject as a thinking, feeling, and enlightened being. Seduction offered artists and writers an ideal vehicle for considering (and asking the beholder to consider) the merits of modern knowledge; because it involved the absolute minimum number of participants to qualify as social exchange, its circumstances required their immediate and correct response to the exigencies of the present moment, however subtly or ambiguously they might be presented. In this highly distilled form of interaction, subjective judgment and the insights gained from its exercise could have immediate consequences: misinterpretation might elicit a perception of discourtesy, which might lead to rupture, or at the very least would sully one's reputation; good judgment could result in circumstances considered mutually advantageous.

What does this pair of paintings reveal about each suitor's understanding of the complex, highly ritualized rules of seduction, whose conditions are partly established before he enters the room and partly constructed by his overtures? The caller in *The Garter* distinguishes himself by his imposition of his own desires—a breach of all contemporary notions of civility and judgment, which manifests itself in his haste. He has jumped from the chair, causing his hat to tumble from his lap, and he leans intrusively into his companion's space. The clock, with its Cupid who has stolen Time's scythe, stands as an allegory of the suitor's youthful impetuousness. The same clock, which keeps time in regular intervals, throws into relief the suitor's *lack* of timing. For courtship to succeed, one must respect the conventions of timing, which though they are never enunciated, are intuitively understood.

The caller's overeager pursuit of physical contact renders him singularly unobservant. He has neglected the signs lodged in the decoration of the room that, were he astute enough to have recognized them, should have instructed him how to proceed. He might have remarked that the room is not suited to the seclusion required for seduction. The reflection in the mirror reveals a set of double doors surmounted by an overdoor panel, which indicates that the chamber is part of an *enfilade*—a long row of rooms that connect by a series of facing doors—and thus is readily accessible to other members of the household. A large window, which floods the room with morning light, offers a view to the distractions of the outside world, and also allows the possibility that the couple might be observed through a facing window. Moreover, the space is too sparsely furnished for its proportions (though the beholder sees only a fragment of it), not at all intimate in scale, and clearly not planned for the bodily relaxation conducive to seduction. The room is striking for its flat planes and straight lines, seen in the rectilinear frames of the chairs, the vertical lines of the mirror frame, the reflected door and its overdoor panel, the rows of books lining the bookcase, and the floor pattern. The armchairs, though upholstered, have a stiffness imparted by their high, upright backs and shallow padding. Rather than inviting a person to lounge, they require control to hold oneself erect and are sufficiently distant from one another to discourage a tête-à-tête. The grid pattern of the marble floor further delineates the socially correct physical boundaries to be maintained between individuals, which the toe of the gentleman's left shoe just begins to trespass. Finally, the color scheme of this brightly lit room, principally yellows and white or silver highlights, further proposes that it is a space for the exercise of rational behavior, not the uncontrolled expression of passion.

The caller in *The Garter* not only fails to recognize the sort of behavior that this more public type of room demands, he also fails to heed those objects that encode both his hostess's interests and how she expects to be addressed. The tilted book on the top shelf of the bookcase marks the place of the volume now lying on the console and confirms that this young woman actively consults her library. The bookmark proposes that she has just left off reading. Bookmark and garter function as visual analogs: their similarity, in conjunction with the small format of the book, suggests that the young woman may have been reading contemporary love literature or perhaps a dialogue on the attributes that one must cultivate to perform expertly in polite society. Ladies, as late seventeenth-century and early-eighteenth-century writers declare, and twentieth-century scholars remind us, were traditionally held to be proficient in the arts of refined conversation and polished manners: gentlemen learned the intricacies of this ritualized behavior by interacting with them.[3] If the young woman was indeed immersed in literature of this genre, anything less from her suitor than exemplary manners and eloquent speech would strike her as offensive. To sway her would require the demonstration of a knowledge of the polite ceremonies of seduction, both verbal and physical. She may not be averse to being courted, but she wants it to be done "by the book."[4]

The caller's inattention to the discursive role of interior decoration is underscored by the placement and subject of the statuette. At the far left of the picture is a small bronze of a seated female nude, which the viewer is able to perceive as a fully three-dimensional object thanks to its reflection in the mirror. This figure, proportioned for a private interior, invites touch as well as observation; it also falls directly into the caller's line of vision. Rather than foreshadowing the couple's future, in my view it comments on the suitor's faulty judgment in the present: he would like to see the young woman in a similar state of undress and to run his hands over her. He behaves with her as if he were handling the work of art, not a woman who actively cultivates her sense of self. Ironically, the statuette predicts his deficient reasoning. Though inanimate, it does not meet his gaze, refuses to acknowledge his presence, and spurns his attempt to set the terms of the amorous encounter. The young woman, conversely, not only resolutely meets his gaze but studies his expression for any sign of dawning comprehension of his breach of manners. Her look of concentration, even more so than her outstretched arm, declares the strength of her self-knowledge.[5]

The Garter visualizes an accumulation of lapses in observation, discrimination, and conduct by a suitor who is expected to maintain his part in a dialogic exchange whose point is to portray an erotic encounter as mutually advantageous. His breach of politeness is a function of physical forwardness, but it is also rooted in a failure to acknowledge the desires of his hostess. His single-mindedness blinds him to her subjectivity: he is unable to distinguish between her aesthetic judgment (visible in the decor of the room, in her dress, and in her comportment), which makes her a thinking, complex being, and her aestheticized person. He mistakes her for a decorative object first to be savored visually and then to be handled. Had he the slightest notion of decorum and the judgment to control his passions, he would have realized that coercion would be unacceptable. To dominate another person violates the guiding principle of polite society: respectful, nonhierarchical relations among its members. *The Garter*, then, broaches the subject of the qualities necessary for admission into this sphere. For all the painting's attention to elegant appearances (the quality that has moved its commentators to characterize it as a reflection of elite life) its proposition is more critical commentary than documentation: wealth and rank prove to be insufficient criteria for membership in the polite public if one lacks character and a discerning mind.

In contrast, *The Declaration of Love* portrays the protocols of a successful seduction. This picture's caller has been attentive to the qualities of the room into which he has been ushered: its hermeticism, proportions, furnishings, and color scheme suggest both intimacy and his hostess's predisposition to his suit. De Troy places the figures relatively close to the picture plane, which enhances the impression that they inhabit a small space. The room, unlike that of *The Garter*, is not visibly connected to the outside world or even to the rest of the house. De Troy, moreover, does not depict the scene's source of light: at the left edge, rather than a window, there is heavy red velvet drapery. The right side of the image is closed by a marble pedestal that supports an ormolu-mounted porphyry vase. Weighty, dense, and hard objects separate this couple from the rest of the world. Not only is their space hermetic, it is darker: *The Garter*'s yellows and white highlights, appropriate for rational pursuits such as reading and discussion, give way in *The Declaration of Love* to passionate reds. Plush furnishings create a haremlike atmosphere that encourages indulgence of the senses. Unlike *The Garter*'s reflective surfaces (a mirror, a window, silk, satin, silver thread, and buttons), numerous furnishings, and fussily patterned wall and upholstery coverings, *The Declaration of Love* displays broad expanses of single colors and surfaces covered in light-absorbing fabrics. This abundance of fabric and cushions marks this chamber as a milieu in which the body is invited to recline.

The fashionable rococo decoration's elision of borders, in which objects ontologically and spatially distinct from one another seem to merge, similarly encourages an intermingling of the personal boundaries of the two figures. The sofa's frame appears to merge with the wall molding, while the bottom edge of the picture frame, actually part of the wall, follows their undulating line. At the right edge of the picture, the urn's ormolu mount seems to extend the wall molding so that the viewer senses a visual continuity from the drape on the left, which snakes across the picture space. Far from *The Garter*'s stiff, individual chairs mapped in space by the grid pattern of the floor, which also imposes distinct compartments for each of the protagonists, the blurred boundaries in *The Declaration of Love* encourage the idea of a communal environment. The single settee obliges the couple to share a seat. The young woman, who has purposely chosen to receive her visitor in this room, reclines comfortably and encouragingly, aided by a plump pillow. The narrowness of the settee invites the gentleman to follow his hostess's cue by leaning toward her, his body paralleling the angle of hers. If frames and furnishings in *The Garter* convey rectilinear isolation of the figures, the horizontal and softly curving lines of *The Declaration of Love* imply the couple's entanglement.

Fittingly, the room portrayed in *The Declaration of Love* does not contain a clock, an object that typically appears in depictions of private interiors throughout the eighteenth century and frequently within de Troy's own oeuvre. If the clock in *The Garter* underscores the suitor's single-minded haste to achieve the hoped-for result of his visit, then the absence of one in *The Declaration of Love* suggests that a dexterously conducted seduction has no prescribed duration. Each couple must have a sense of their own timing and let it be their guide. The absence of a time-keeping device in *The Declaration of Love* shifts the viewer's attention from the outcome to the quality of the couple's interaction. If courtship is to advance smoothly, the participants must exercise good judgment, which lies at the heart of correct, polite behavior. Because judgment is not quantifiable, its exercise influences the amount of time spent. Because discernment and a delicate sense of timing are internal characteristics, no clock is needed to mark an abstract, external measure of time. Significantly, in both pictures the gentlemen's hats also serve as subtle indicators of timing and of the judgment, good or bad, that directs it. In *The Garter*, the hat has tumbled to the floor as a sign of the caller's impetuousness; in *The Declaration of Love*, it sits squarely beside the suitor, in exactly the same spot in which he first placed it. Its owner, sensitive to the nuances that surround him, neither jumps up nor throws himself at his hostess.

This suitor shows his understanding of the restraint required of him by speaking of his passion, rather than interpreting his hostess's complaisance as encouraging an immediate escalation of physical contact. His correctness in beginning with verbal communication connotes a sound understanding of and deference to his and the young woman's communally held notions of propriety. Clumsily wrought speech and improper gestures are signs of erroneous thinking.[6] *The Declaration of Love* signifies the importance of speech by making one ear of each figure clearly visible to the viewer. The prominent ears are notable for their redness, by which they are associated visually with the sofa, the gentleman's coat, the velvet drape, and the cloak of Mars in the painting set into the wall. The perceptive viewer concludes from these red ears that the caller speaks of his passion movingly yet politely because the young woman's ear "lights up" as it receives his words. The fact that she allows him to hold her hand attests that the suitor's speech is worthy of her attention.

The notion of verbal expression as a sign of correct understanding has its foundation in Ciceronian rhetoric, which not only stresses eloquence but also requires that well-crafted speech evoke an image in the mind of the listener. The suitor verbally paints for his hostess an image of their mutual understanding. The image that his speech evokes is literally represented in the painting set into the wall. Like the statuette in *The Garter*, this work of art provides a gloss on the events that take place before the viewer's eyes rather than narrowly signaling the outcome of the couple's encounter. In this painting within the painting, de Troy depicts Mars and Venus embracing in a landscape. Like the contemporary couple, the deities isolate themselves from the company of others, and they appear without their attributes. The complete absence of weapons and armor indicates that Mars has not been able to rely upon physical force—his usual means of obtaining his will—but has had to turn to a different, more polite, and ultimately more persuasive method. Similarly, Venus, without the assistance of her cupidons to carry off Mars's arms, must deploy more personal means to win the god's affection. By denying the deities use of their accouterments, de Troy's image suggests that their sole recourse is to employ their wits to perform acts of courtesy in an effort to convince one another that their desires coincide. In addition to commenting upon the eloquence of the caller's speech, the painting of Mars and Venus also implies that one should not assume women to be passive in courtship.

Taken together, *The Garter* and *The Declaration of Love* ask their beholders to compare the social and cognitive performances of the two suitors, and to observe that each young woman sets the tone for, and the terms of, the encounter by admitting her caller into a room whose interior decoration functions as a form of speech and a reasoned act of will. Beholders perceive that *The Declaration of Love* portrays a successful courtship not by viewing it as an isolated ideal, but because it signifies in tandem with *The Garter*. Viewers learn to recognize the admirable qualities of the suitor in *The Declaration of Love* in a process of comparison that also perceives the lack of judgment and politeness displayed in *The Garter*. The meaning of the two pendants thus emerges in the interstices of comparative viewing, in the dialogic exchange initiated by their shared subject matter and complementary compositions—interstices that solicit the spectator's application of modern, experiential knowledge.

The pictorial category of genre in early eighteenth-century France also influenced one's viewing experience. Genre painting's interest is driven by the dispersed visual effects of descriptive painting that are sensual and immediate, and that challenge the single point of view that narrative pictures sought to impose on their spectators.[7] Narrative unity demanded that the artist dematerialize the worked surface and de-emphasize the painting's illusionistic effects. Genre's descriptive character liberated painting from the hierarchized constraints of linear narrative. Visual effects confronted spectators with a perceptual materiality in the present moment, incited them to invent a strategy for organizing what they saw, and invited them to develop an interpretation that would lead to understanding. The descriptive details of *The Garter* and *The Declaration of Love*, with their up-to-the-minute furnishings, works of art, and fashionable clothing—objects that were actively collected, commissioned, scrutinized, admired, and discussed in mid-1720s Paris—functioned to reinforce the present moment by equating the time of the pictures with that of the viewer. Because, for example, the statuette and the painting of Mars and Venus gloss the action that takes place before the viewer's eyes, they return one's consciousness to the present time of lived experience. The reinforcement of the present enacted by objects fused the viewer's active use of experiential knowledge *before* the pictures to its exercise *within* the pictures by de Troy's figures.

The writings of the theorist Roger de Piles, who espoused a concept of painting quite unlike the official teachings of France's Royal Academy, provide a theoretical basis for understanding painterly images like de Troy's by arguing for a specifically pictorial form of intelligence. For de Piles, subject matter did not constitute the essence of painting, which he viewed first and foremost as a visual medium. He argued that the properties unique to painting—color, composition, use of light and shadow—move the beholder in a form of direct address, and he assumed a dialogic relationship between a picture's material and illusionistic qualities and its spectator.[8] The crux of painting was not what it could teach its audience, but what the audience could make of its visual effects. His emphasis was on painting as a form of rhetoric that actively sought a viewer's response.

For de Piles, painting succeeded as illusion when all of its powers of persuasion reached an audience within the instant of the beholder's first glance—the "premier coup d'oeil"—which reimagined the reception of a painting as a sensory rather than a rational experience.[9] This aspect of his theory, however, generates a contradiction because visual effects necessarily elicit self-consciousness in the viewer: artifice attracts the viewer's notice, and this refocusing of attention onto the components of picture-making causes the viewer to become aware of the cognitive and intuitive processes mobilized by the work. When painting makes no attempt to disguise its artifice, the beholder is compelled to invoke extrapictorial, experiential knowledge to understand how the visible marks on a canvas function to create meaning.[10] Audiences of de Troy's *tableaux de modes*, and of rococo-style pictures generally, responded on sensory, emotional, and rational planes because his rendering of the visual and tactile qualities of objects stirred memories and feelings. Spectators filtered their subjective responses to this material stimulus through the cognitive process of discernment rather than simply absorbing it at a glance, however instantaneous and indefinable the duration and the terms of their critique. De Troy's use of the pendant format further complicated de Piles's *premier coup d'oeil* by insisting that the beholder's attention alternate between two canvasses.[11]

Although de Piles rejected the academy's dependence on classical literature as a foundation for its theory of painting, he nonetheless turned to Ciceronian oratory to argue that the primary function of painting is to move, rather than to teach or exhort, the beholder. De Piles's choice allies him with those who championed oral over written forms of eloquence.[12] Because the aim of rhetoric is to persuade an audience, an orator's speech cannot have a fixed form; it must respond to diverse publics and acknowledge its own artifice and potential for polyvalence. Improvised strategies of presentation and response take precedence over and will, in the end, determine content. In this way, the art of the orator will also produce a conceptual portrait of its audience. Early eighteenth-century painters who worked in a de Pilesian mode by creating pictures that called attention to their visual effects paid homage to the idea developed in theories of oral eloquence that artifice is a carrier of meaning.

When de Piles and his partisans based their theories on oral rather than written eloquence, they adopted the oral and performative values, culture, and practices of polite society, for whose members appearances, gestures, and turns of phrase were crucial signifiers. Conversation, a polite, eloquent form of verbal intelligence, functioned as the principal medium of social exchange. De Troy's pendants posit a persuasive and eloquent conversation with their beholder through a descriptive technique in which the mimetic rendering of objects coexists with evidence of the artist's hand. The aristocratic *sprezzatura* or nonchalance of de Troy's painterly trace parallels the most valued attribute of a good conversationalist, whose talk should appear witty and easy rather than studied.[13] De Troy's decorative mode of painting both addresses and evokes viewers who did not equate the moral relativity of appearances with deceptiveness. Eighteenth-century viewers were expert translators of appearances—whether works of art or the gestures and facial expressions of their interlocutors—and, reciprocally, experts in exercising control over the self as signifier. Such individuals assumed that the artifice of painting did not constitute an end in itself, but functioned to valorize the beholder's experiential knowledge and use of subjective judgment. Even though the sensuality of the pendants' painted surfaces and rococo forms teetered on the edge of irrationality and erotic excess, de Troy's visual effects nonetheless provided an informed viewer with the ground rules for an elaborate game of discernment.[14]

My understanding of the pendants as a collaborative venture with their beholder and as an acknowledgment of the discursive nature of the decorative arts is also strongly influenced by a somewhat later work of literature. Jean-François de Bastide's 1758 short story "La petite maison," recounts a seduction-as-wager conducted by interior decoration, landscaping, and other artistic effects. The decorative arts figure not as details of setting but as a full protagonist, and the narrator explicitly solicits the reader to judge the progress of the bet.[15] The seduction begins in the conventional manner—verbally—but the libertine Trémicour soon realizes that Mélite, his romantic interest of the moment, is adroit at deflecting his insinuating banter. He challenges her to visit his *petite maison*, an exquisite little estate built for trysts on the outskirts of town. There, as a last resort, and one that has never failed him, he will let art do the talking for him. Interior decoration thus possesses the capacity of persuasive speech in this story, and here its rhetorical strategies are those of a voluptuary and a seducer.

The decoration of one's residence in eighteenth-century France, like one's dress, comportment, and conversation, actively participated in the social art of self-presentation. Expressing one's critical judgment through taste in the decorative arts was a public act that operated dialogically: such objects addressed a community of interlocutors—normally one's cultural and intellectual peers—who could accept, dissent from, or propose variations, whether through discussion or through their own displays of ornament.[16] Trémicour varies this convention by seeking to predetermine the responses of his all-female public. His *petite maison* is designed to curtail rather than promote dialogue by making losing the bet an irresistible proposition: the multisensory, erotic overcharge of the decoration drives his visitors to collude in their own downfall.[17] Because Mélite does not know what kind of a place a *petite maison* is, she lacks both the knowledge and the critical distance to parry the rhetoric of its decorative program. Consequently, she naïvely equates the beauty of the interior decoration and the flawless taste it announces as signs of her host's nobility of character and sincerity.

"La petite maison" de-emphasizes the outcome of the wager (and thus the story's climax) by revealing it in a single, final sentence. Bastide's story is a tale about process, about the dialogic relationship between the increasingly sensual decoration and Mélite's fluctuating reactions to it, which range from defiance to intoxication to desperate attempts to clear her mind and master her senses. Her responses sustain the narrative tension. The story can be understood as an ironic commentary on art spectatorship, and its narrative pulse depends on the worldliness of Bastide's readers being superior to Mélite's. The reader's understanding of the purpose of a *petite maison* and of how Trémicour wittily manipulates architectural *ordonnance* and interior decoration to his larger "design" gives them the necessary critical distance to judge both the decorative arts on display and Mélite's performance during the wager. What is at issue is not her knowledge of the arts, because the narrator informs us at the outset that she is an accomplished amateur; rather, it is her inability to remain a disinterested observer.[18] She struggles in the present moment of the unfolding narrative to acquire and exercise the critical skills that the story assumes its readers already possess.

Bastide's text, like de Troy's pendants, fashions a cognitive space for the reader by creating a double layer of spectatorship: Mélite as art viewer and the reader as viewer both of the art described by the narrator (the same art that the marquise admires) and of Mélite-as-viewer. This doubling wittily portrays the urgency of maintaining ironic detachment and applying judgment to one's store of connoisseurial knowledge. As worldly, cultured individuals, Bastide's readers would have known to remain critically and emotionally distant from the *petite maison's* decorative program. As observers of a naïve art lover, they watch a woman who, the more enraptured she becomes by the decoration, the more she becomes subject to, and compromised by, the will of another. Mélite's ability to reason increasingly gives way to feelings that overwhelm and endanger her, yet the readers, shielded by their ironic detachment, undergo the reverse process: by both observing Trémicour's *petite maison* and discerning why and how it causes Mélite to falter, they learn to sharpen their own powers of judgment. For the marquise to seize the upper hand in the wager, she must be able to discern the visual and discursive strategies through which the decorative arts make fleeting erotic pleasures seem worth the loss of her subjectivity, virtue, and reputation. To do so, she must swiftly perceive, survey, and adjust her responses—sensory, cognitive, and emotional—each time she enters another room. She must, in short, act as an enlightened spectator.[19]

The focus on discernment in the pendants and "La petite maison"—in matters of art viewing, readership, polite conversation, and amorous encounters—aligns the works with the broader discourse of *galanterie*. Definitions for *galanterie* and its adjectival form *galant* range from that which is pleasant or sociable, to good judgment and expertise, politeness, respectful behavior towards women, frivolousness, a flirtatious woman, a lothario, and carrying on an affair.[20] De Troy's pendants and Bastide's narrative qualify as *galant* on several levels: for their subject of seduction; for their theme of discernment and the performance of this understanding within the phenomenologically interrelated domains of art spectatorship and seduction; for their nonchalant yet witty painting and prose styles; and most importantly, for their appropriation of *galanterie's* polyvalence and moral ambiguity.[21] The actors in these works negotiate the morally antithetical concerns of erotic gratification, a supremely antisocial form of self-interest, and the public display of disinterest that is necessary to assure the polite, mutually beneficial character of civil society. Though de Troy adheres more closely to the sociable tradition of *galanterie* and Bastide to its darker libertine side, each form makes ironic reference to the other. The statuette in *The Garter* and the painting of Mars and Venus in *The Declaration of Love* direct the viewer to the gap between selfish and shared desire, which can only be bridged by the exercise of good judgment and true politeness. In "La petite maison," Bastide ironizes the polite tradition of *galanterie* by making it clear to his readers how illusory Trémicour's gestures of courtesy are, all while Mélite's lack of critical distance causes her to succumb to the appearance of refined tastes, which anodizes the reality of the libertine's predatory motives.

Because desire in the narrative and the pendants is both conveyed in controlled language and gestures (with the exception of the clumsy suitor in *The Garter*), and relayed more indirectly through the decorative arts, *galanterie's* polyvalence also functions as a rhetorical device to invoke the critical participation of viewers and readers. Beholders of this performative language of desire must understand how to penetrate its conventions in order to distinguish appearances from reality, all while tacitly accepting *galanterie's* gamelike process, which maintains a show of neutrality and courtesy.[22] De Troy's vivid descriptions of the decorative arts, contemporary fashions, and the figures' stances and gestures, and Bastide's narrator's detailed descriptions of the decorative arts, as well as his conspiratorial asides to the reader, suggest that both artist and writer craft an image of their audiences' understanding. This understanding includes a critical turn of mind that, as much as it may savor the thought of a sexual resolution to these encounters, would prefer to concentrate on analyzing the varying degrees of skill of the participants.

An anonymous booklet accompanying the 1725 Paris Salon, where de Troy's *Garter* and *Declaration of Love* were first exhibited to the public, identifies the paintings as "[t]ableaux très-galands."[23] Given the multiple meanings of *galant* when it follows the noun, it is not entirely clear how the author intended his phrase to be understood. *Très-galands* can refer to the pictures' subject matter of seduction, to de Troy's skillful, witty execution, or to the dialogic relationship of substance and style. What is telling, however, is that this eighteenth-century author does not reduce the pendants' account of aristocratic life to a love of luxury objects and unmanaged libidos. The writer's use of the adjective *galant* connects de Troy's emphasis on outward appearances—the portrayal of interior decoration, manners, and dress—to the dialogic of discernment. Working as a pair, *The Garter* and *The Declaration of Love* portray a process of judgment that manifests itself subtly in the form of taste in the arts (the young women's) and more overtly in manners (the suitors'). The pendants also invite beholders to contribute to this discussion by exercising a discernment that will translate visual nuance into useful knowledge. Viewed individually, *The Garter* and *The Declaration of Love* can be said to narrate two tales of *commerce amoureux* weighted toward the fulfillment of male desire by equating the young woman in each scene with an art object. Viewed as pendants that focus on visual effects while acknowledging the framework of narrative, the spectator's experience and discernment are integrated into the signifying process to produce a modern kind of knowledge that depends fully on the sympathetic exercise of reason.

Notes

1. The paintings discussed in this article are unsigned copies attributed to Jean-François de Troy. See Richard Rand, ed., *Intimate Encounters: Love and Domesticity in Eighteenth-Century France* (Hanover, NH and Princeton, NJ: Hood Museum of Art and Princeton University Press, 1997), catalog nos. 9 and 10.

2. My synopsis, though intentionally brief, nonetheless captures the predominantly literary and emblematic view of these two works. See, e.g., Virginia Swain, "Hidden from View: French Women Authors and the Language of Rights, 1727–1792," in *Intimate Encounters*, ed. Rand, 21–22; and Rand, *Intimate Encounters*, 104–8. See also Everett Fahy, *Paintings, Drawings, Sculpture*, vol. 5 of Everett Fahy and Sir Francis Watson, *The Wrightsman Collection* (New York: Metropolitan Museum of Art, 1966–1973), 290.

3. See Dena Goodman, *The Republic of Letters: A Cultural History of the French Enlightenment* (Ithaca, NY: Cornell University Press, 1994), 5–7; Jacqueline Lichtenstein, *The Eloquence of Color: Rhetoric and Painting in the French Classical Age* (Berkeley: University of California Press, 1993), 12–14; and Daniel Gordon, *Citizens without Sovereignty: Equality and Sociability in French Thought, 1670–1789* (Princeton, NJ: Princeton University Press, 1994), 107–11. I would like to thank Dena Goodman for her comments emphasizing the significance of the small format of the young woman's book.

4. With regard to the ambiguity of the woman lifting her skirts to reveal her leg and garter at the same time that she pushes away her visitor, I would like to thank the attendees of the Furnishing the Eighteenth Century Conference, whose comments on my paper provided valuable insight into the female figure's motives.

5. On the directness of the female regard in images by François Boucher, which has informed my understanding of it in *The Garter*, see Thomas Kavanagh, *The Aesthetics of the Moment: Literature and Art in the French Enlightenment* (Philadelphia: University of Pennsylvania Press, 1996), 206–11.

6. Lichtenstein, *Eloquence of Color*, 22–24.

7. As opposed to the narrative, declarative mode of history painting, descriptive, or *rubéniste*, works draw their meaning from color and visual effects: they "speak" from "no single point of view." See Jean-Luc Bordeaux, "The Rococo Age," introduction to *The Rococo Age: French Masterpieces of the Eighteenth Century*, ed. Eric M. Zafran (Atlanta: High Museum of Art, 1983), 11. For decoration's disruption or complication of linear narrative, see also Katie Scott, *The Rococo Interior: Decoration and Social Spaces in Early Eighteenth-Century Paris* (New Haven, CT: Yale University Press, 1995), 6, 159, 200.

8. Thomas Puttfarken, *Roger de Piles' Theory of Art* (New Haven, CT: Yale University Press, 1985), 53. Puttfarken draws from de Piles's several treatises and synthesizes them into a unified theoretical position.

9. Ibid., 109–11.

10. See Lichtenstein, *Eloquence of Color*, 169–70; Marian Hobson, *The Object of Art: The Theory of Illusion in Eighteenth-Century France* (Cambridge: Cambridge University Press, 1982), 47–56; Kavanagh, *Aesthetics of the Moment*, 150; Ernst Cassirer, *The Philosophy of Enlightenment*, trans. Fritz C. A. Koelln and James P. Pettegrove (Boston: Beacon Press, 1955), 303–4. Kavanagh and Cassirer both refer to the aesthetics of painting propounded by the abbé Du Bos, for whom successful painting acknowledged the knowledge and experience of its spectators; see Jean-Baptiste Du Bos, *Réflexions critiques sur la poésie et sur la peinture*, ed. Dominique Désirat (1719; Paris: Ecole Nationale Supérieure des Beaux-Arts, 1993), 276–81.

11. The descriptive term *tableaux de modes* for de Troy's paintings of polite society was coined in 1762 by Pierre-Jean Mariette. See Mariette, *Abecedario*, ed. Ph. de Chennevières and A. de Montaiglon (Paris: J.-B. Dumoulin, 1853–54), vol. 2; reprint in *Archives de l'Art Français* (Paris: F. de Nobèle, 1966), 4: 101. *Mode* refers not only to the latest fashions that de Troy portrays, but also to the way in which things ought to be done by those who considered themselves influential members of the public.

12. Leon Battista Alberti's *De pictura* (1435) precedes de Piles in turning to the Ciceronian orator as the ideal model for the painter. See Lichtenstein, *Eloquence of Color*, 199–204.

13. Antoine Gombaud, chevalier de Méré, "De la Delicatesse dans les choses et dans l'Expression," in *Oeuvres posthumes*, vol. 3 of *Oeuvres complètes*, ed. Charles-H. Boudhours (1677; Paris: Editions Fernand Roches, 1930), 133.

14. Discernment is a necessary prerequisite for possessing the quality of *esprit*. See Méré, "De l'Esprit," in *Les Discours*, vol. 2 of *Oeuvres complètes*, 64–65. See also Lichtenstein, *Eloquence of Color* (14–20), who gives a broader analysis of discernment in the texts of Méré and the Jesuit Dominique Bouhours, including Méré's alteration of Descartes's conception of the term. Madeleine de Scudéry's writings attest to her esteem for the exercise of discernment. For an account of its use and meaning in her oeuvre, see Delphine Denis, *La Muse galante: poétique de la conversation dans l'oeuvre de Madeleine de Scudéry* (Paris: Honoré Champion, 1997), 245–46, 291–301.

15. "[I]l faut l'y suivre avec le Marquis, & voir comment elle se tirera d'affaire avec lui." ("Let us follow her there, then we shall see how she fared with the Marquis.") Jean-François de Bastide, "La petite maison," in *Anthologie du conte en France 1750–1799: Philosophes et coeurs sensibles*, ed. Angus Martin (Paris: Union Générale d'Editions, 1981), 157; English translation, Jean-François de Bastide, *The Little House: An Architectural Seduction*, trans. and ed. Rodolph el-Khoury (New York: Princeton Architectural Press, 1996), 58.

16. See Scott, *Rococo Interior*, 81–99.

17. Hobson, *Object of Art*, 47–48.

18. Bastide, "La petite maison," 161; 70–72 (English translation).

19. On the practice of *dédoublement* (doubling) that characterizes modern, ironic spectatorship, see Paul De Man, *Blindness and Insight: Essays in the Rhetoric of Contemporary Criticism* (Minneapolis: University of Minnesota Press, 1983), 212–16.

20. See the University of Chicago's Project for American and French Research on the Treasury of the French Language (ARTFL) for an online version of the first edition of the *Dictionnaire de l'Académie Française* (1694), http://humanities.uchicago.edu/orgs/ARTFL/ (accessed October 26, 2004).

21. For the two traditions of *galanterie*, see Alain Viala, "*Les Signes Galants*: A Historical Reevaluation of *Galanterie*," in *Yale French Studies* 92: *Exploring the Conversible World: Text and Sociability from the Classical Age to the Enlightenment*, ed. Elena Russo (New Haven, CT: Yale University Press, 1997), 11–29.

22. For Madeleine de Scudéry, discernment, and the knowledge that they were all playing a game of wits, prevented participants in *galant* activities such as flirtatious conversation from being duped by the content of speech. See Denis, *La Muse galante*, 262–64.

23. Georges Wildenstein, ed., *Le Salon de 1725: Compte rendu par le Mercure de France de l'exposition faite au Salon Carré du Louvre par l'Académie Royale de Peinture et de Sculpture en 1725* (Paris: Georges Servant, 1924), 40.

PART **IV**
Forms, Functions, Meanings

CHAPTER 10

Tea Tables Overturned: Rituals of Power and Place in Colonial America

ANN SMART MARTIN

The tea table may have been one of the most culturally charged furniture forms in eighteenth-century Anglo-America. It was a new and beguiling furniture form that contained a number of paradoxes. Its surface could either be vertical or horizontal. It was considered sturdy and safe for harboring expensive valuables, yet was foldable and movable. Such a table signified wealth and breeding if owned by the right people; charges of luxury and dissipation might follow if the wrong ones gained possession. What kind of table was used—or if one were used at all—helped determine appropriate behavior in a tightly scripted ritual ceremony that grew more complex as time passed. It was part of the *lingua franca* of gentility that linked disparate colonies and England, but in an American setting could ultimately be a stage for political action. Lastly, the tea table became a feminized object nearly a century before the first female furniture form evolved. Throughout England and the colonies, the table's meaning thus teeters depending on when and who and where. By focusing closely on the table itself, this study will explore how such objects and meanings evolved.

The visual universe of eighteenth-century prints and paintings often drew upon such visual coding to convey complex meanings to their viewers. William Hogarth was certainly the most famous eighteenth-century engraver and artist to use the tea table as a symbol of social rank, civility, and family stability. For example, between 1728 and 1731 he produced several dozen portraits for wealthy patrons that took the form of conversation pictures to create scenes of multiple people enjoying genteel activities and refined stances in domestic settings. These social groups or families were often posed casually around a tea table, its surface strewn with cups. The table itself helps to arrange the subjects into an effective group composition.[1]

But the lives of men and women whose smiles were frozen in portraiture could turn from domestic tranquility to debauchery. As easily, the tea table could tip and overturn to chaos. Using the tea table again as a symbol of wealth, Hogarth extended its meaning to document the insidious progression from luxury to dissipation. *A Harlot's Progress* demon-

169

strates this turn in a six-part series published in 1732. In Plate 2 of the series, "The Quarrel with her Wealthy Protector," (Figure 10.1) the maiden's foot seemingly upends the heavily carved rectangular table to distract attention from a young lover's flight. Tea wares descend and crash. In the next plate, common tea wares stand quietly on a short multipurpose stand. The humbled harlot languishes in prison, maintaining a sense of luxury amidst squalor.

A Harlot's Progress is a multilayered set of scenes that drew from sources as disparate as the literary tradition of *Pilgrim's Progress* and the drama of contemporary news. The crashing tea table in Plate 2 perhaps most broadly signified the social unease about which contemporary social critics like Bernard Mandeville had begun to howl—the poor wishing to be like the rich. Like her peers, the girl wished to ape the rich and live the high life of tea, flirtation, and ultimately sexual conquest. The monkey toying in the corner thus stands in even more explicitly in this connection. The overturning tea table was the moral equivalent of the overturned ark in the painting above the girl's head. The broken cups were the result of such inappropriate behavior. What is more, the unbroken vessel had been a primary symbol of virginity since the Middle Ages, so the shards are doubly significant. A broken vessel, like a spoiled woman, had no value.[2]

The artist James Gillray tipped the table again some seventy years later in a satirical print depicting a mixed gender party enjoying a bountiful tea repast that replaces the earlier romantic tryst shown by Hogarth (Figure 10.2). This scene is centered on a large central pedestal table covered with a huge array of tea equipage and surrounded by comical stereotypes of thick and thin. Here the jest was on fashion—when her overly fashionable muslin

Figure 10.1 William Hogarth, *A Harlot's Progress, Plate 2, The Harlot Quarrels with her Wealthy Protector*, 1732. Engraving. Courtesy of Chazen Museum of Art.

Figure 10.2 James Gillray, *The Advantages of Wearing Muslin Dresses*, published February 15, 1802 by H. Humphrey, 27 St. James Street, London. Hand-colored engraving. Private collection.

gown dips into the fire, an overweight woman leaps to her feet and upends the table. Like Hogarth, Gillray too responded to an actual current event (in this case, a fire fueled by a muslin dress) that showed the dramatic effect of ill-informed choices, even though here they are social, not moral. The tea table has launched so much china in mid-air that the crash is almost palpable. Nonetheless, despite the buffoonery, Gillray, like Hogarth, was engaged in the kind of polite civil discourse that has been characterized so ably by David Shields.[3]

A final anonymous print published in 1829, *A Small Tea Party of Superannuated Politicians* (Figure 10.3), completes the opening survey of the symbolism and uses of tea tables. The meaning of this image is less clear. A woman sits quite alone at a tea table in the center of a room ringed by older men. With her back turned to us, the woman is anonymous. In one interpretation, she is in charge of the teapot and hence the ceremony. She has power over the room. The scene becomes the kind of political salon where the woman is privy to and perhaps even an engineer of the important news of the political fray. In another interpretation, however, she is the "everywoman" who, like a servant, must wait upon the needs of the men before her. The ambiguity is reinforced by the presence of the cat that sits near her, an emblem of both domesticity and feminine wiles.

In all of these scenes, a tea table is prominent. Artists used tea tables in particular settings to amplify the biographical, narrative, and didactic power of their work. English prints such as these joined a flood of books and magazines circulating to and around the colonies in the eighteenth and early nineteenth centuries to reify a shared elite gentility in visual terms. Tea tables are testimony to this shared set of expectations about elite life. Scholars have amply documented the new social behaviors of tea drinking and elaborate dining in the eighteenth century as evidence of an interest in gentility, the expression of social distinction, the fulfillment of a new passion for porcelain and other exotic consumer goods, and the promotion of the large equipage of tea vessels, utensils, and other goods as necessities. Well-to-do people

Figure 10.3 Anonymous, *A Small Tea Party of Superannuated Politicians*, published August 13, 1829 by T. McLean, London. Engraving. Private collection.

certainly had tea tables on which to stage important social rituals in tasteful settings. But it is the protean nature of tables to symbolize exoticism, luxury, gender, gossip, and patriotism that makes the tea table so useful in art, literature, and political rhetoric. It is one of the few kinds of furniture where the actual form could produce a range of cultural behaviors. Just as medieval high tables promoted a precisely scripted social hierarchy, a small round table created a sense of intimacy and its own cultural performance.

American audiences shared the understanding of the objects and behaviors that Hogarth used to propel the downfall of an ignorant rural girl, as evidenced by a little tale that appeared in the *Pennsylvania Gazette* in 1732. Written by one "Anthony Afterwit," it used an array of commodities to animate the progression from innocence to dissolution. Afterwit's story of woe begins with his new wife's "strong inclination to be a Gentlewoman." The march of the trappings of middling respectability begins when his beloved is "entertain'd with Tea by the Good Woman she visited." To maintain their standing, the Afterwits could "do not less than the like when they visited us."[4] Anthony Afterwit was none other than the young Benjamin Franklin, who was satirizing just the kind of social emulation ridiculed by Hogarth: the desire to move quickly into the ranks where money and time were wasted on useless tea table sociability. When searching for a wedding present for his sister five years earlier, Franklin had first decided on just such a tea table. But he changed his mind and bought her a spinning wheel instead, informing her that the gracious serving of tea may have been appropriate for a "pretty gentlewoman," but that he wanted young Jane to have the symbol of a "good housewife."[5] This symbolic opposition between the tea table (bad wife) and the spinning wheel (good wife) remained important to Franklin: Anthony Afterwit's problem was solved when his wife's tea table was traded for a spinning wheel.

Drinking tea—or owning tea wares—was indicative of genteel behavior: welcome among the privileged, but an ominous luxury as it crept in among those who were not of the proper rank. In 1733, Franklin, this time posing as "Blackamore," warned again in the *Pennsylvania Gazette* against "Molatto" gentlemen, those who "find themselves in circumstances a little more easy," where an "[a]mbition seizes many of them immediately to become Gentlefolks." With just a fleeting observation, he was able to judge their performance with ease, "for 'tis no easy Thing for a Clown or Laborer to hit in all respects," and "'tis the curse of Imitation that it almost always either under-does or over-does."[6]

This dismay over inappropriate social climbing rings throughout colonial America in the middle of the eighteenth century. To Alexander Hamilton, for one, "a set of stone tea dishes and a tea pot" in a poor man's cottage in 1744 were "superfluous things which showed an inclination to finery." He suggested that the tea wares there should be sold for useful goods like wool to make yarn, for "tea equipage was quite unnecessary."[7] Like Franklin, Hamilton linked the two forms of the gendered use of time, but his indignation was based on class and rank. Hamilton's warning was prescient: within a few generations, half of the very poorest households in York County, Virginia owned at least one piece of ceramics related to tea drinking.[8] Note, however, that there was no tea table in the poor man's cottage.

As more and more people began to partake of tea in the next half century, its drinking would take several distinctive and often coexisting paths. Rigid patterns of correct behavior developed among the elite, ranging from the proper name for the invitation to tea to the correct hand signal that no more tea was desired. The butler of the governor of Massachusetts published instructions for servants that codified proper procedures, from the correct placement of the tea items on the tray to the order of serving based on sex, age, and rank.[9] All of these behaviors can be seen as fences to keep out those who did not properly belong—tricks for the unwary "Clown or Labourer." This elaboration and rigidity intensified in the early nineteenth century until a Philadelphia "Gentleman" could solemnly advise in his etiquette book "that a gentleman would lose his reputation, if he were to take up a piece of sugar with his fingers and not with the sugar tongs."[10]

At the same time, the drinking of tea became a simpler form of leisure—for breakfast, with family, with friends. Phrases such as "Drank Tea with Mrs. Buchanan this Afternoon," fill the diaries of upper-class men and women.[11] These brief notations indicate the degree to which the very activity itself was taken for granted, just another part of the day, notable for the company or conversation.

Why did popular writings and print sources use tea drinking to tell a story or dress a stage? One reason was its relative novelty and quick adoption throughout Anglo-American society. Hogarth's and Franklin's works were produced in the same decade in which tea drinking began to spread throughout elite circles; historical and material evidence of the sale of tea wares and the drinking of tea would soon come thick and fast. The implements to brew and serve tea, as well as differing varieties of the tea itself, were commonly stocked at retail stores by the middle of the eighteenth century. In the next half century, probate inventories from multiple regions show that tea wares were commonly owned. Archaeological excavation finds tea wares—even porcelains—owned by urban artisans. Even slaves purchased tea wares by century's end.[12]

The extraordinary tumble in the price of tea and the resulting spread of customs from elite merchant to common laborer in less than a century is astonishing in England and America; the same progression through society in Ireland took another several generations.[13] It is in the context of impoverished people's use of tea and sugar that Adam Smith came to claim in *The Wealth of Nations* that tea and sugar were now a "luxury of the poor as well as of the rich."[14] That mobility through social and economic groups helped impel the tea table's multiplicity of meanings.

We can now sketch multiple social groups, times of day, and forms of leisure in which tea was served and suggest the meanings that such a commodity might hold. But to follow the actual consumption and use of special tables for the drinking of tea is more problematic. Probate evidence is less useful in assessing the ownership of tea tables than ceramic wares. Inventory takers often designated tables by relative size and type of wood, rather than particular function. But the explosion in the *number* of tables by 1770 in the most elite and fashionable homes is suggestive. For example, analysis of Virginia probate records indicates a definite increase in specialized tables, perhaps for playing cards or drinking tea. In York County, Virginia (which included the fashionable colonial capital of Williamsburg), the more wealthy residents (those with estate inventories over £491) owned an average of nine tables. By analogy, because the next lower wealth groups still had four or five tables per household, tea tables may have been quite common in even middling-class homes in urban centers.

In backcountry and more rural Virginia, the story was somewhat different. Not surprisingly, the greater distance between people both geographically and socially led to differing social practices and consumption patterns. In rural Bedford County, on the edge of the Blue Ridge Mountains in western Virginia, households at the top averaged barely more than one table per household. Urban Virginians bought specialized tables and equipage for drinking tea, but rural places were more likely to have purchased ceramic vessels alone.

In summary, by the time of the American Revolution, the drinking of tea reached from the top to nearly the bottom of the social scale in cosmopolitan urban places. From the middling ranks and above, many had stylish tea tables to store and serve tea. In rural and more remote areas, tea equipment remained more restricted but the overall lesson remains. The drinking of tea in some form was common. Finally, tea could be consumed in many differing ways and places. The Englishman John Galt, describing his parish in 1761, noted how the new custom of tea drinking had only recently become "very rife" there. He described how the "commoner sort did not like it to be known that they were taking to the new luxury, especially the elderly women," who sneaked off to "out-houses and by-places," where they drank tea in "cups and luggies for there were but few that had cups and saucers." Thus they gathered in hedges, "cackling like pea-hens," only to be scattered by passers-by.[15] Thomas Hancock reminisced that because tea was portable and easily prepared, before the American Revolution even the Indians might drink it twice a day.[16]

So why were tables dedicated to the consumption of tea even necessary? Specialized tables emerge when they are deemed a necessary accompaniment to pleasure and performance. The beverage was not necessarily the impetus, the behavior was. The teapot and its action needed a stage. Conversely, even as specific small task tables became symbolically linked with tea drinking, they were not always only used in that way. This fluidity in the use of specialized tables can be seen in several English and American prints and paintings in which tea tables were used for other activities, such as reading or needlework. Tea tables would become more general female domestic spaces.

Like tea itself, tea tables were available in expensive and rarified versions or lesser, more inexpensive ones. As the making of tea tables became an established part of a cabinetmaker's business, they were routinely listed in price agreements that became more common by the time of the American Revolution. They started to disappear as a special category after 1800 when small Pembroke tables began being used for informal breakfasts. Sarah Fayen has demonstrated that making tea tables was an important part of a cabinetmaker's business in the later eighteenth century, and multiple price lists kept by artisans document how size, material, and ornament were all add-on choices at additional cost.[17]

The cabinetmakers themselves distinguished between two distinct forms in their lists of products. Hogarth had depicted rectangular tables like the one illustrated in Figure 10.4, with four cabriole legs and a small china rail to block the casual knock of breakables. Such a table was common and may even have been used to store china when not in use. Gillray featured the equally popular, but perhaps more notable, round table with pedestal base shown in Figure 10.5. Both choices were common items for sale. Other versions of the eighteenth-century tea table varied in the shape of the surface (square, square with scalloped corners, or oval) and leg arrangement. Details aside, these core functional elements—a surface for using, viewing, and storing, and a set of legs or a pedestal to bring objects to a comfortable height for seated persons to use—evolved into quite specific forms with quite clearly defined choices of style and ornament, which varied across time and space.

But where did the idea for those *particular* solutions come from? New furniture forms are rather uncommon. Of course tables have a long history, but these tables show specific functional and aesthetic choices by makers and users. Nonetheless, their origins are difficult to untangle. We might look to the part of the world from which tea itself came. Despite the immense chasm between Eastern and Western cultures, by the early eighteenth century Chinese seating furniture profoundly influenced elements of European chair design. As Sarah Handler has so clearly defined, before the early modern period the Chinese were the only nation outside of the West to be accustomed to sitting in chairs.[18] Chair-level modes of living required commensurate heightened surfaces to accomplish an array of daily tasks. Small rectangular tables on short legs or trays were placed on *kangs*, or heated platforms

Figure 10.4 Tea table, Rhode Island or Massachusetts, ca. 1740. Mahogany. Courtesy of the Chipstone Foundation. (Photo, Gavin Ashworth.)

Figure 10.5 Tilt-top tea table, New York, ca. 1765. Mahogany. Courtesy of the Chipstone Foundation. (Photo, Gavin Ashworth.)

for more leisurely dining. Other early tables have been documented for multiple uses, such as for gaming, as altars or shrines, and as high stands for incense burners. The multipurpose square table can occasionally be seen in Chinese images as a place for teapots and tea equipage, but there are no Chinese tables for the group social performance of tea drinking comparable to European ones. Tea was not, after all, consumed in a similar social fashion.

The immense trade that developed between China and Europe in porcelains, lacquer work, teas, and spices also brought ideas and influences. The actual importation of Chinese furniture was probably limited, although several specialized artisan groups complained of competition from "India" (by which they meant Asia more generally) as early as the 1690s. Nonetheless, ideas about Chinese furnishings could be culled from a significant number of sources. Nicholas Grindley argues that early ideas about Chinese furniture flowed through images on early porcelain and screens, which occasionally showed Chinese figures seated at distinctly Chinese square tables.[19] David Barquist maintains somewhat differently that Western rectangular tables were derived from imported Chinese lacquer trays fitted into stands by their European users; his argument gains weight from the later tables made in Anglo-America with a tray top.[20]

If the rectangular table has only the slimmest connection to eastern Asia, a round version with a central pedestal is even more distant. A small round table with short curved legs and animal paw feet at waist height for seated figures on the ground was published in Philippe Sylvestre Dufour, *Traitez nouveaux & curieux du café, du thé et du chocolate* (1685), but as the scene combines exotic products and cultures, so too it may have combined fanciful table parts. Nonetheless, a lacquer scalloped Hung-lo (1403–1425) dish bears an uncanny resemblance to later scalloped-edged center pedestal tables.[21]

The central pedestal tea table (Color Plate 10, see color insert after page 118) probably grew from its smaller English and European cousins—stands such as the one pictured beside it, designed to hold candles. The French *guéridon* was such a small multipurpose table, found in private spaces, and sometimes lavished with ornament—ebonized, gilded, or inlaid with porcelain. When its main purpose was to serve as a platform for illumination, the center pedestal table might be quite high. But how the form moved from holders for illumination—sometimes raised high enough for better illumination but not so high as to prevent a person lighting them—to a low and wide polished disk, is still an open question.

One way to trace the tenuous steps from the candle stand to the center pedestal table is to focus on a particular region. By the end of the seventeenth century, candle stands with center pedestals and simple crossed feet were in use in the Delaware Valley. Tables known by contemporary nomenclature as pillar and claw, but with rather awkward flattened cabriole legs, were made in the second decade of the eighteenth century. By 1770, Philadelphia artisans produced tea tables with refined central pedestals, fully realized spherical tripartite legs, and ball-and-claw feet, all carved with extraordinary skill. This combination would soon be used for related objects like fire screens and kettle stands, and even returned to candle stands.[22]

The beginning linkages are clear, as candle stand sizes slowly increased. Many were large enough to hold a tea pot and a cup or two, but a foot in diameter always separated the two forms. The key point still might be that candle stands remained common throughout the time studied, but as the smaller form obviously did not fit certain needs, the larger tea table evolved and became popular.

Hence, the fully formed round table on a center pedestal probably comes from English and European sources with architectural influences rooted in the Renaissance. Like newel posts in stairs, the center pedestals on these tables show a precise knowledge of architectural order and proportion shaped into local distinctions.[23] The relationship between the making and design of furniture and architectural elements is clear in one of the earliest pieces of American furniture accompanied by a precise design: a tea table probably made around 1787 by Thomas Hayden (1745–1817), one of the leading builders in Windsor, Connecticut.[24]

There were also real differences in how rectangular and circular tea tables functioned and were used. The small table with a central pedestal was a different idea that solved many problems. First, the central column replaced the need for multiple supports, a problem dubbed the "slum of legs" by twentieth-century furniture designer Eero Saarinen. As Gillray depicted in his early nineteenth-century print, a table with pedestal base enabled the right number of people to pull their chairs up snugly. Second, a round table is a table of equality where hierarchy is more difficult to bestow spatially. The small round table with chairs pulled tightly in created a sense of intimacy and perhaps led to the idea of intimate language and relations, challenged in its inappropriate forms as gossip, secrets, or chatter.

The central pedestal tilt-top table's form solved other problems. It often had a hinged top that could be stored vertically and locked horizontally for safe use. One contemporary name was *snap table* because of the sound it made when locking. It was stored upright against the wall when not in use and brought forward to the appropriate room or into the preferred space in the room as needed. This design thus fit perfectly with the practice of keeping the room's center free by placing tables and chairs against the walls, such that space was reconfigured depending on the people and activities involved.

But how did people use such tables? Who sat around them and how did their bodies interact with them and each other? A remarkably detailed story of the practice of tea drinking by women of past times was recorded by Daniel Toll in 1847. Such writing, which memorialized the bygone days of the revolutionary generation and decried contemporary society, was common in the middle of the nineteenth century. But this version is sharp in detail, expressive of ethnicity through accents and foods, and both pokes fun and heaps praise.

Toll claims that he interspersed his story of the first settlers of Schenectady, New York with a "few anecdotal eccentricities and antiquities," together with a description of "tea-parties of olden times." He was able to solve the moral dilemma of tea drinking as wasted female time by coupling leisure and fun with work. Toll's women would meet in the early afternoon to work—one would take a spinning wheel, another a "sowing-basket"—and talk and advise about housewifery topics. Precisely at four o'clock the heavy table was brought to the middle of the room from its position at the wall and covered with a white tablecloth. Teacups were placed in a circle around the outer edge, each flanked with a large slice of bread. A wide array of culinary niceties were grouped in the middle of the table. When all was ready, the matron would invite the other women to sit at the table, saying: "Come vrouw-lay, sit yullly baye."

When the teacups became empty, no servant passed a salver or tray. Instead, Toll reports that a rosy-faced girl would get up, take a teapot in each hand, "one filled with the infusion, the other filled with hot water," to enable her to let them have it strong or weak. She would then pour the tea in the

> intervals or spaces left between the guests setting round the table; but should they be so hustled or crowded together so close as to make this impracticable, she would . . . be obliged to pour the tea over their heads and shoulders, and would, on some occasions, have the misfortune of spilling a little hot tea, or of ruffling or bruising one of their caps; then you would hear a vociferation.[25]

These female occasions, when women clustered so closely in space that water might be poured on their heads, are evidence of a set of cultural expectations about the relationship of people to each other and to objects known in contemporary scholarship as *proxemics*.[26] The sense of closeness—of intimacy in space and relations—is also found in the amusements and stories of published sources like the several *Tea-Table Miscellanies*. Alan Ramsay's *Tea-Table Miscellany* was popular enough to go through multiple editions and be stocked in rural Virginia stores. In his twelfth edition, Ramsay promised to have "kept out all smut and ribaldry" to please a respectable class of women.[27] *A New Tea-Table Miscellany* spoke to the ladies with an offer of poems that had, "besides their novelty, many innocent charms." The first such innocent charm was "The Tea-table Oracle; or, the Modern Fortune-Teller," in which women gathered to hand around "the mystic water" and ask questions about lovers, looking into the cups for signs of answers.[28]

Teatime could also be a quite formal, mixed-gender event, and colonial writings are filled with reports of evening galas that included card playing and dancing. How were those different events experienced in the context of the tea table? In a larger group, the woman who reigned over the teapot situated herself snugly at the table to have easy access to pouring. Guests spread themselves around the room and servants moved among the various parties.

Another wonderfully detailed image (Figure 10.6) shows how the tea table actually helped dictate groupings. In 1780, a suitor passing Nancy Shippen's Philadelphia window made a sketch of a "considerable tea company" in the Shippen parlor. In it we see Nancy Shippen presiding at the rectangular tea table while her mother sits at the table's opposite corner. Both ladies are seated in front of the chimney, with "Old Dr. Shippen" seated apart, but also near the chimney. Another man is walking back and forth, laughing and talking. Three other people are seated across the room, separated by at least the length of a sofa.

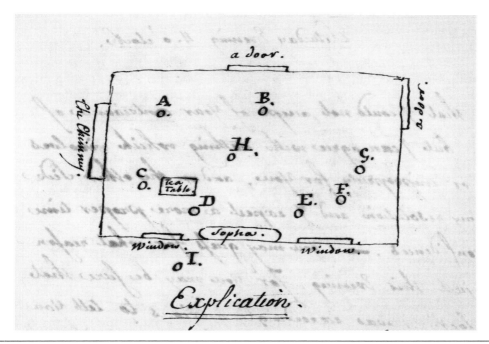

Figure 10.6 Louis Guillaume Otto, sketch in letter to Nancy Shippen, ca. 1780. Courtesy of the Library of Congress, Manuscripts Division. The "Explication" beneath the drawing identifies A as Dr. Shippen, B as Mr. Lee, C as Nancy, D as Mrs. Shippen, H as the butler, I as Mr. Otto himself, and E, F, and G, as "some strangers which the Spy could not distinguish."

A butler stands in the middle of the room, although the viewer jokes that the man is half asleep.[29] This is a scene of social fluidity that followed the portability of furniture: action could refashion itself around the table, the room, and the people.

The absence of a tea table had its cost to those negotiating the ritualized performances of tea drinking. A satire published in the *Norfolk Gazette and Public Ledger* in 1815 described the torture of holding a teacup in one hand and a hunk of bread and butter in the other. The poor rural visitor did not know which way to go—to eat the one or drink the other. He finally dropped the cup and smashed the china, humiliating his family and once again showing the reader the rubes of rural life.

The binary oppositions of diffuse/intimate, near/far, early/late, small/large, male/female, and rural/urban make up only part of the final expression of the extraordinary variety of meanings that accompanied the performance, objects, and commodities of tea. The experience of imbibing tea could change depending on the size of the group, its gender mix, the time of day, and the sort of entertainment.

The meanings of objects from two centuries ago are often shrouded in mystery. Few eighteenth-century men or women recorded such personal connectedness to possessions as did the Englishwoman Elizabeth Shackleford. When her new "mahogany square tea table" was delivered in 1778, she noted her pleasure with it, then prayed that God would give her and her husband, "good and long use of it."[30] Shackleford was then old but she might have remembered "how pleasant a sight is it to behold parents and their children, brothers and sisters, friends, relations and strangers, mix round the Tea-Table," as the author of *A New Tea Table Miscellany* asked in 1750.[31] Like Hogarth's conversation pictures, these words evoke a visual scene where the tea table grounds a group of people who pleasantly cluster around a culturally charged piece of furniture. This was just the setting chosen to depict Job Hill and his family in New Hampshire, probably around 1830, in a portrait by Caroline Hill (Color Plate 11, see color insert after page 118).

Decades of painstaking study of objects and their social contexts underlie this study. Material culture analysis most notably asks that objects be placed at the center of inquiry and that all the senses be summoned and all the skills be used. A tea table was a sculptural expression. Tea drinking was an exuberant and beguiling new caffeinated passion that stimulated the mind. Because it also warmed the body it was both a real experience and a symbolic linkage to a warm and inviting home. Finally, a large highly polished mahogany sphere was perhaps a visual treat, certainly to be noticed; when set in place, such a table would fill up a large portion of a parlor. One early nineteenth-century author paints a scene in a farmer's home where the "masterpiece of finery was a tea table." The table was "fine" even when it was stored in the perpendicular—as a disk in air—where its "surface displayed a commendable luster," as shown in Color Plate 12 (see color insert after page 118). The luster was the essence of the table, which could only be refined and magical if its surface was clean and unscratched. Hence, children's fingerprints were banned "by penal code;" the table was "for show and not for use."[32]

Artifacts, objects, possessions, or belongings—all are, as I have noted elsewhere, "cultural bundles of individual, social, and cultural meanings grafted into something that can be seen, touched, and owned."[33] The farmer used his tea table to show off for others; Elizabeth Shackleton placed hers at the center of a long and happy marriage. One was valued for its social meaning of polish and refinement, the other for family leisure and pleasure. Perhaps smooth porcelain reflected candlelight on polished mahogany or perhaps old women huddled in the hedges. A marvelous thing to own, the tea table is an object worth turning over and over.

Notes

1. Ronald Paulson, *Hogarth*, vol. 1, *The Modern Moral Subject, 1697–1732* (New Brunswick, NJ: Rutgers University Press, 1991), 208.
2. Ibid., 236–69.
3. David S. Shields, *Civil Tongues and Polite Letters in British America* (Chapel Hill: University of North Carolina Press, 1997).
4. Anthony Afterwit [Benjamin Franklin], Letter to the *Pennsylvania Gazette*, July 10, 1732, in *Benjamin Franklin: Writings*, ed. J. A. Leo Lemay (New York: Library of America, 1987), 185–87.
5. Benjamin Franklin to Jane Mecom, January 6, 1726/1727, in *The Letters of Benjamin Franklin and Jane Mecom*, ed. Carl Van Doren, (Princeton, NJ: Princeton University Press, 1950), 35.
6. Benjamin Franklin, "Blackamore, on Molatto Gentlemen," *Pennsylvania Gazette*, August 30, 1733, *Benjamin Franklin: Writings*, 219.
7. Carl Bridenbaugh, ed., *Gentleman's Progress: The Itenerarium of Dr. Alexander Hamilton in 1744* (Chapel Hill: University of North Carolina Press, 1977), 13–14, 55.
8. Documentary research in probate inventories and store account books related to the drinking of tea can be found in Ann Smart Martin, "Buying into the World of Goods: Eighteenth-Century Consumerism and the Retail Trade from London to the Virginia Frontier" (Ph.D. dissertation, College of William and Mary, 1993).
9. Robert Roberts, *The House Servant's Directory* (Boston 1809, 1827; reprint ed., Waltham, MA: Gore Place Society, 1977), n.p. See also *The Laws of Etiquette or, Short Rules and Reflections for Conduct in Society* (Philadelphia: Carey, Lea, and Blanchard, 1836), 169.
10. Ibid., 158.
11. See, for instance, "The Diary of M. Ambler, 1770," *The Virginia Magazine of History and Biography* 45 (April 1937): 158.

12. Martin, "Buying into the World of Goods," 338. For further discussion of African and African-American purchases, see Ann Smart Martin, *Buying into the World of Goods: Consumers in Early Virginia* (Baltimore, MD: Johns Hopkins University Press, forthcoming).

13. Patricia Lysaght, "When I Makes Tea, I Makes Tea . . . : Innovation in Food—the Case of Tea in Ireland," *Ulster Folklife* 33 (1987): 49.

14. Adam Smith, *An Inquiry into the Nature and Causes of the Wealth of Nations*, ed. Edwin Cannan (New York: Random House, 1937), 823.

15. Quoted in Bevis Hillier, *Pottery and Porcelain 1700-1914: England, Europe, and North America* (New York: Meredith Press, 1968), 158.

16. Quoted in Agnes Repplier, *To Think of Tea!* (Boston: Houghton Mifflin, 1932), 99–100.

17. Sarah Fayen, "Tilt-Top Tea Tables and Eighteenth-Century Consumerism," in *American Furniture*, ed. Luke Beckerdite (Milwaukee, WI: Chipstone Foundation, 2003), 125–29.

18. Sarah Handler, *Austere Luminosity of Chinese Classical Furniture* (Berkeley: University of California Press, 2001), 9.

19. See, e.g., the transitional vase illustrated in Figures 3a and 3b with a figure slumped over his painting table holding a Yixing teapot in Nicholas Grindley, "The Bended Back Chair," exhibition catalog (London: Barling of Mount Street, 1990), n.p.

20. David Barquist, *American Tables and Looking Glasses* (New Haven, CT: Yale University Art Gallery, 1992), 89–90.

21. Patrice Valfre, *Yixing Teapots for Europe* (Poligny: Exotic Line, 2000), 69.

22. Jack L. Lindsay, *Worldly Goods: The Arts of Rural Pennsylvania, 1680–1758* (Philadelphia: Philadelphia Museum of Art, 1999), 150–56.

23. See, e.g., Albert Sack, "Regionalism in Early American Tea Tables," *Antiques* 131 (January 1987): 248–63.

24. Philip Zea, "Furniture," in *The Great River: Art and Society of the Connecticut Valley, 1635–1820*, ed. William Hosley (Hartford, CT: Wadsworth Atheneum, 1985), 224–25.

25. Daniel J. Toll, *A Narrative, Embracing the History of Two or Three of the First Settlers and their Families of Schenectady* (Schenectady, NY: s. n., 1847), 52–54.

26. Gerald Ward asks such provocative questions, particularly of dining tables, in "The Intersection of Life: Tables and their Social Role," in Barquist, *American Tables and Looking Glasses*, 14–25.

27. Allan Ramsay, *Tea-table Miscellany: or, a Collection of Choice Songs, Scots and English* (London: A Miller, 1763).

28. *A New Tea-Table Miscellany: Or, Bagatelles for the Amusement of the Fair Sex* (London: E. Duncomb, 1750), ix.

29. Letter from [Louis Guillaume] Otto to Nancy [Shippen], undated c. 1780, Shippen Papers, Library of Congress; cited in Rodris Roth, "Tea-Drinking in Eighteenth-Century America: Its Etiquette and Equipage," in *Material Life in America, 1600–1800* (Boston: Northeastern University Press, 1988), 448.

30. Amanda Vickery, "Women and the World of Goods: A Lancashire Consumer and Her Possessions, 1751-81," in *Consumption and the World of Goods*, ed. John Brewer and Roy Porter (London: Routledge 1993), 287–88.

31. *New Tea-Table Miscellany*, vii.

32. L[ydia] H[oward] Sigourney, *Sketch of Connecticut, Forty Years Since* (Hartford, CT: Oliver D. Cooke & Sons, 1824), 143–44.

33. Ann Smart Martin, "Material Things and Cultural Meanings: Notes on the Study of Early American Material Culture, *William and Mary Quarterly* 53 (January 1996): 5–6.

CHAPTER 11

The *Secrétaire* and the Integration
of the Eighteenth-Century Self

DENA GOODMAN

The eighteenth century saw the invention of the *secrétaire*, a new type of desk designed to serve the personal and practical needs of the letter writer. Although there are records of *secrétaires* being sold in Paris as early as the 1730s,[1] it was not until 1798 that the *Dictionnaire* of the French Academy finally gave as one of the definitions of *secrétaire*, "a desk where one writes and where one keeps papers." Every other definition referred to a person, principally "someone whose job is to make and write letters, dispatches for his master, for the person on whom he is dependant." In the *Encyclopédie*, too, all the definitions referred to people: "in general, the person who helps someone send things, such as letters, extracts, & other operations"— despite the fact that *secrétaire* desks were described and illustrated in the article on veneering.[2] The dictionaries thus failed to track one of the most significant transformations of the eighteenth century: the transformation of the *secrétaire* from a person to a piece of furniture.

The shift from secretary (the person) to *secrétaire* (the desk) reflected a fundamental change in the practice of writing that entailed a change in its social meaning and psychological significance. The creation of the *secrétaire* signaled a new authorial need for a personal surface on which to write, as private persons shifted from dictating their letters to a confidential secretary to penning them themselves. What had been two fundamentally different kinds of actions—a noble intellectual or spiritual act of composition and a base mechanical or physical act of inscription—carried out by people of different social status, were now integrated into a single practice carried out by a single individual. The transformation of the *secrétaire* allowed writing to become fully personal—the expression of one's being or self— by eliminating for the composer the mediation of a servile human being, while empowering the scribe to use his skill and his tools to his own ends rather than someone else's.[3]

Roland Barthes has noted that in ancient Rome writing was considered so base an activity that free men did not write; they dictated their thoughts to slaves.[4] And Lesley Smith has shown that the distinction between composition and copying explains the dearth of medieval images of women writers at a time when nobles of both sexes composed texts. Because copying—the manual art of writing—was merely scribal, and scribal work was servile men's work, how could a woman writer be depicted? Women who composed texts (noble, spiritual women such as Héloïse) could not be represented penning them. Those few women who were depicted in the act of writing were engaged in an act of spiritual dictation, acting humbly as an inspired scribe for a male deity or saint and revealing visually their own lack of authority.[5] The dearth of images of women writing thus reflects not medieval views of women's intellectual abilities, but the gender distribution of labor mapped onto the division of writing into two discrete social practices, one base and the other noble.

By the eighteenth century, however, writing was practiced and understood quite differently. The primary division was not between composing and copying, but between personal and professional writing. The expansion of business, trade, and government bureaucracy since the end of the Wars of Religion in the early seventeenth century meant increased demand for secretaries to produce the full panoply of documents that kept the gears of state, society, economy, and empire turning. At the same time, writing was becoming personal, and noble hearts and minds were being encouraged to express themselves and create social bonds through the writing of letters. Most French elites no longer saw the pen as a base tool, but as a noble instrument, like the sword or the embroidery needle. Even the king, who still did not deign to pen his own letters, made a claim to doing so: when he employed a secretary it was not simply to transcribe his words, but to counterfeit his hand.[6] To assist this growing corps of writers, printers and men of letters churned out manuals on how to write letters, and agendas in which to keep track of their own appointments, finances, and thoughts, and dubbed them all *secrétaires*.[7] Furniture makers and dealers gave the same name to the desk that increasing numbers of both women and men now needed as they penned their own letters and kept track of their personal affairs. The old division between composing and copying obtained only in the realm of professional writing, where male secretaries toiled away for (mostly) male bosses. The gender division of labor now mapped onto a new division of writing, that between the personal and the professional.[8]

The epistolary manuals and published letter collections, also known as *secrétaires*, emphasized the importance of the letter as the medium of love and friendship.[9] For such missives, dictation to a secretary was not a sign of nobility, of being above the manual labor of writing; rather, it was the imposition of a mediated formality that undermined the claims of sincerity and friendship that personal letters were meant to convey. People were enjoined to think of the letters they wrote as surrogates for themselves. "We do not assure our reputation, until we arrange [our ideas] nobly and accurately on paper," asserted Jean Léonor Le Gallois de Grimarest in his treatise on letter writing. "Thus, I believe that it is not reasonably permitted to judge completely the merit of a person by their conversation: one must wait to decide until one has seen their letters." Recipients might fall in love with the personas they encountered in letters, but they were more likely to judge writers harshly for poor spelling, awkward style, messy handwriting, or an overall lack of grace and tact. "The ignorance of a woman, or a courtier, is almost always noticed in their letters," Grimarest warned ominously.[10] Several decades later Eléazar Mauvillon made the same point in his treatise on epistolary style: "A letter is a witness that testifies for or against its Author," he declared. "It is a sort of certificate of good or bad character."[11] André-Joseph Pancoucke applied this principle specifically to women in *Les Etudes convenables aux demoiselles*: "Nothing," he declared, " better assures the reputation of a lady than knowing how to arrange her thoughts on paper nobly and accurately. . . . Without this one sees only disorder, impoliteness, errors of language and construction, sterility, ignorance."[12]

For a woman, especially, it was not just what she wrote, or even how she expressed herself that mattered; the material qualities of the letter were just as important. Jean Lanteires was not alone in declaring that spelling was the "touchstone upon which, in general, people are disposed to appreciate the degree of education that any person, but above all a woman who moves in society, has received."[13] These moral judgments only made sense in an age when women of quality were expected not just to be able to compose, but to pen their own letters. This form of autoscription (self-writing) is what made possible, or perhaps inevitable, self-inscription—the writing of the self. As Marie-Claire Grassi has written:

> This new intimacy of hearts was inscribed in the slow emergence of new relationships that the individual established over the course of the century with space, be it material or social. . . . It is also in the interior of this new space that a new relationship to the body was located. Slowly formalized over the course of centuries, the letter would become a site of expression and of writing, that is closed, sealed, personal, and secret, proper to the expression of the self within another space henceforth intimate, delimiting a new relationship with the other.[14]

As a piece of furniture designed to enable the individual to confide his or her self and secrets to paper and thence to a trusted and complicit other, the *secrétaire* was essential to the production of intersubjective intimacy.

In the ARTFL database of French literature, the first reference to a *secrétaire* as a piece of furniture is in a letter Denis Diderot wrote to his friend Sophie Volland in October 1759. On his return from a trip he had gone directly to see her, but she wasn't home. He left her a message, to which she must have replied that she had sent him one in care of a friend, where she expected him to have gone first. "You have sent a letter [*billet*] to Grimm's place?" he wrote, incredulously.

> Blockhead, could you have thought that I would go all the way over there? What would you have done in my place? In yours, I would have left the letter on my *secrétaire*, and I would have said to myself: tomorrow it will be two weeks that she has not seen the person she loves; she has suffered, she has desired, she is worried. Her first moment will be for me . . .[15]

Here the *secrétaire* is used by a friend (or lover) to write a personal letter (*billet*) to his or her counterpart. It is significant that Diderot imagines himself in Sophie's situation, and her in his, and in both cases, the writer has his or her own *secrétaire* on which to write the letter. In addition, in suggesting that Sophie should have left the letter to him on her *secrétaire*, Diderot implies that it is her personal space, one that she might share with him, her correspondent and friend, but which is understood to be hers. Because we know that Sophie lived with her mother and sister, and that her relationship was not a secret from them (Diderot addressed both women in many of his letters to Sophie, expecting her to share them with her family), the designation of the *secrétaire* as the appropriate spot to leave a letter for him invokes privacy as personal space, but does not suggest secrecy.

Secrecy is suggested in a letter Diderot wrote to Sophie three years later, which turns up as the second documented reference to the *secrétaire* as a desk in ARTFL. Here it appears in an anecdote about Montesquieu and Lord Chesterfied. In order to prove his point that Frenchmen have no common sense and Englishmen do have wit, Diderot wrote, Chesterfield sent a mysterious stranger to warn Montesquieu that the government was on to him, and he would be arrested at any moment for his subversive writings. "The state inquisitors are fully aware of your conduct, you are being spied on, you are being followed, note is made of all your projects, they have no doubt that you are writing," he confided ominously. "Look, sir, if in fact you have written, consider that a line written innocently, but misinterpreted, could cost you your life." As Diderot recounted the story, Montesquieu, falling for the joke, immediately panicked: "His first movement was to run quickly to his *secrétaire*, take out all the papers, and throw them in the fire."[16] This anecdote represents the *secrétaire* as the working space of the man of letters, but more significantly as a storage space for important personal papers. Although there is an element of secrecy here, it is precisely the question of the security of the *secrétaire* that is called into question. Had Montesquieu believed that the *secrétaire* was secure from the intrusions of the state, he would not have felt compelled to remove his manuscripts from it and burn them.

These different associations of the *secrétaire*—with both writing and storage; women and men; the person of the writer; and privacy, secrecy, and limited security—distinguish it from the other category of desk used in the eighteenth century, the *bureau*. What distinguished the *bureau* physically from the *secrétaire* was its uniformly large size and flatness, and the location of its functional parts. On the *bureau*, leather was mounted right on the surface of the desk for everyone to see, and drawers were clearly visible, even if they required a key to open them. In the *secrétaire*, by contrast, the writing surface, drawers, and other storage spaces were all hidden inside the desk, often secured by a lock. The variety of *secrétaires* lay most notably in the ways in which they opened—via fall fronts, roll-tops, cabinet doors, and so forth. The *bureau* proclaimed itself to any visitor as a desk; the *secrétaire* did not. As Carolyn Sargentson notes in her article in this volume, the owner of a *secrétaire* could choose to share as much or as little of what went on within it.

The *secrétaire* was the materialization of a person (the confidential scribe or secretary) as a piece of furniture. The evolution of the *bureau* followed a different trajectory: first from a surface used for business ("a Counter or table on which money is counted, or on which papers are put") to a more complicated piece of furniture that included storage of business papers ("a kind of table with several drawers and shelves, where one keeps papers"). It was then expanded to signify those agencies associated with paperwork (offices or bureaus), and then to the place where such work was conducted—the office.[17] Most of the *Encyclopédie*'s definitions, for example, begin: "This is a place . . ." The etymological transformations of *bureau* and *secrétaire* reflect the division of writing in early modern France: between documents produced to support the expanding work of law, the economy, and the state; and personal correspondence between individuals in their capacity as private persons that supported the growth of the individual and challenged the authority of the state.[18]

Significantly, the *bureau* was always considered a masculine piece of furniture, whereas *secrétaires* were designed for and owned by both women and men. Whereas the political, economic, and administrative functions associated with the *bureau* were unequivocally seen as men's work, the construction of the self through personal writing was not gender specific. Defined by the *Encyclopédie methodique* late in the century as a "large [table] designed for the labor of writing or study,"[19] a *bureau* was standard office furniture for men engaged in a variety of professions, from the lawyer meeting clients and crafting briefs, to the man of affairs or the bureaucrat. It was designed to impress and was central to the furnishing of libraries and the various sorts of *cabinets* that architects designated as masculine spaces. It was thus instrumental to the redefinition of elite masculinity through the exercise of nonviolent power.[20] Only the exceptional woman had a library or owned a *bureau* because working women were not admitted into the ranks of professionals, and ladies were not expected to engage in work.[21] The *bureau* represented an authority that a growing body of men and few women could claim.

In a much quoted passage from her memoirs, Madame de Genlis, who was both an acclaimed educator and one of the most prolific writers of her time, claims that she was the first woman in France to own a *bureau*, for which, she says, she was "much criticized." Genlis quotes a long poem written by her brother at the time her husband gave her the desk (sometime before 1776), that makes clear both the association of such a desk with men and the work they do, and the absurdity, in her brother's view, of even imagining a woman behind it.

Qu'un vieux notaire en long manteau,	That an old notary in a long coat,
Avec un pâle et long visage,	With a pale and long face,
Se sèche devant un bureau,	Withers at his *bureau*,|
C'est son devoir, c'est son usage;	That's his duty, that's what he does;
Mais que ce meuble du barreau,	But that this furniture of the bar
Que ce noir et triste bureau	That this dark and sad *bureau*
Se trouve chez vous, ma Thémire,	Is found in your rooms, my Thémire,
Je ne puis m'empêcher de dire,	I cannot help but say,
Dussiez-vous en être en courroux,	Ought to make you angry,
Qu'un bureau n'est pas fait pour vous.	Since a *bureau* is not made for you.
Non, ce n'est point ici sa place.	No, this is not at all its place.

The poem ends with a plea to Genlis to distance herself not just from the desk, but from the "labors of study" that will cost her the feminine beauty that is the source of (female) happiness.

Du bureau quittez la manie,	Get away from that *bureau*,
De l'étude les vains travaux,	The vain labors of study,
Lorsqu'on est aimable et jolie,	When one is loveable and pretty,
Ne valent pas un doux repos.	Are not worth the sweet repose they cost.
Oui, c'est là le bonheur suprême,	Yes, there is the supreme happiness,
Le seul qui soit toujours nouveau,	The only one that is always new,
Et je ne tolère un bureau,	And I do not tolerate a *bureau*,
Que pour écrire à ce qu'on aime.[22]	Except to write to the person one loves.

Genlis's brother does not suggest that *writing* is an inappropriate activity for her, but that her writing ought to be limited to love letters. For such writing, a large, masculine *bureau* is not only unnecessary but inadvisable because it takes away from her feminine charms—and, by extension perhaps, from the charms of her letters. No doubt he would have approved of a *secrétaire*.

While noblemen became increasingly engaged in the professional work that authorized the use of large, flat *bureaux*, their female counterparts retained their association with leisure, even as many of them turned their hand to the whole range of literary endeavors for which they were ostensibly unsuited.[23] Whereas men moved up in life by training for the professions or buying a royal office with administrative or judicial responsibilities, women entering the elite or aspiring to it made their claim through their ability to engage in leisure: they strolled in the gardens of the Tuileries and visited the shops along Paris's elegant rue Saint-Honoré; they entertained in the new domestic spaces of sociability—the salons, dining rooms, and cabinets that Mimi Hellman has so wonderfully described;[24] they played table games like trictrac and quadrille; they kept busy with decorative needlework projects, rather than darning socks or sewing shirts; they attended the theater; they traveled for pleasure and visited monuments and other attractions listed in guidebooks; and they read novels.[25] They also wrote letters. As the *bureau* was the mark of the man who had moved up in the world, owning a *secrétaire* showed that a woman was both literate and leisured enough to engage in correspondence without, however, suggesting that she was crossing gender boundaries. This is not to say that the *secrétaire* was strictly feminine as the *bureau* was masculine. Whereas men alone were authorized to engage in the intellectual labor of professional work that required a *bureau*, both women and men freed from manual labor were expected to engage in the leisure writing of personal letters that required a *secrétaire*. The *bureau* thus articulated a gender divide, while the *secrétaire* delineated a class line between elite and non-elite.

The *bureau* was sometimes called a *bureau de travail* or working desk and often referred to as a *bureau plat*, to distinguish it both from the room in which it was found and from the *secrétaire*, which was anything but flat. The J. Paul Getty Museum's collection includes one *bureau plat* that is more than six and a half feet long, and another that comes in at just under six feet (Figures 11.1 and 11.2). The flatness of the *bureau* put the emphasis on the writing surface; document storage was often provided by a *serre-papiers* or a *gradin* mounted on top of it.[26] The design of the large roll-top desk or *bureau à cylindre* was simply a *bureau* with a very elaborate storage system mounted on top of it (Figure 11.3). The great size of the flat surface of the *bureau plat* was meant to impress, certainly, but also to accommodate mul-

Figure 11.1 *Bureau* plat attributed to André-Charles Boulle (ca. 1725). Oak and pine veneered with satiné rouge and amaranth; modern leather top; gilt bronze mounts. 76.5 cm x 202.2 cm x 89.5 cm. Courtesy of the J. Paul Getty Museum, Los Angeles (67.DA.10).

Figure 11.2 *Bureau* plat attributed to Joseph Baumhauer (ca. 1745–1749). Oak veneered with *satiné rouge*; gilt bronze mounts; modern leather top. 78.9 cm x 181.3 cm x 100.7 cm. Courtesy of the J. Paul Getty Museum, Los Angeles (71. DA.95).

Figure 11.3 Roll-top desk by Bernard Molitor (ca. 1785–1788). Oak veneered with mahogany; gilt bronze mounts; *griotte de Flandre* marble top. 137 cm x 181 cm x 87 cm. Courtesy of the J. Paul Getty Museum, Los Angeles (67.DA.9).

Figure 11.4 Roll-top desk (67.DA.9). Courtesy of the J. Paul Getty Museum, Los Angeles. Detail.

tiple persons—the owner, his secretary or secretaries, and clients or visitors who could sit across from the owner. To accommodate secretaries, additional writing surfaces often slid out at the sides (Figure 11.4). A bureaucrat could dictate a memo and have multiple persons copy it at once, for presentation to him for his signature, or he could meet with a client while a secretary took notes. The *bureau* had to be large to accommodate more than one person at a time, and the kind of writing it facilitated was mediated by a secretary. Unlike the *secrétaire*, the *bureau* was not a personal writing space.

Small, feminized versions of the *bureau plat* reinforce rather than call into question the masculinity of the form. Most striking is one mounted with floral porcelain plaques purchased by the *mercier* Daguerre from the Sèvres factory, and stamped with the mark of the *ébeniste* Martin Carlin (Figure 11.5). Both the reduced size (under 4.5 feet long and 2.5 feet deep) and the rounded corners made it impossible to mistake for a man's office furni-

Figure 11.5 *Bureau* plat by Martin Carlin (ca. 1778–1784). Oak veneered with tulipwood; set with fourteen soft-paste Sèvres porcelain plaques; modern leather; gilt bronze mounts. 77 cm x 131 cm x 62 cm. Courtesy of the J. Paul Getty Museum, Los Angeles (83.DA.385).

ture. The plaques and the gilt bronze gallery brought it into stylistic conformity with the tea tables, worktables, and dressing tables that decorated a lady's bedroom, cabinet, or boudoir. The purchaser of this desk was the Russian Grand Duchess Maria Feodorovna, who placed it in her bedroom.[27]

Secrétaires, like Maria Feodorovna's little desk, were generally much smaller than *bureaux*: in the Getty's collection the smallest is just over two feet long and the largest just under four (Figures 11.6a and b and 11.7a and b). Moreover, the *secrétaire* had but a single writing surface, and its body framed that of the writer. The back of the *secrétaire* both prevented others from seeing what was being written and closed the writer off from others, creating the sense of privacy that personal letters required. The *secrétaire* was personal furniture, like a dressing table, and was often found in the same personal spaces as dressing tables, jewel cases, and worktables. When veneered in the latest style, the *secrétaire* fit in beautifully with these other accouterments of the fashionable lady (Figures 11.7a and b and 11.9a and b).

If we return to the ARTFL database, we learn that *secrétaires* were always identified as personal furniture. That is, whether it belonged to a man or a woman, every *secrétaire* is referred to either as *my secrétaire* or *his* or *her secrétaire*. In Jean-Baptiste Louvet de Couvray's popular novel, *Une année dans la vie du chevalier de Faublas* (1787), for example, Faublas writes: "I sat down at my *secrétaire*. I wrote a first letter, which I tore up; I wrote a second, full of cross-outs, that had to be corrected."[28] Similarly, a character in Joseph-Marie Loaisel de Tréogate's *Ainsi finissent les grandes passions* (1788), says: "Without knowing what I was looking for, Eugenie's letters fell into my hands; I tossed them away indignantly, as monuments of lies and perfidy. I got up furious; I walked with great strides; I came to sit

(a)   (b)

Figure 11.6a and b *Secrétaire à abbatant* by René Dubois (ca. 1775). Oak veneered with kingwood, lemonwood, tulipwood, green-stained wood, box, and ebony; incised with red pigment; mother-of-pearl; gilt bronze mounts; white marble; red velvet. 160 cm x 70 cm x 33.7 cm. Courtesy of the J. Paul Getty Museum, Los Angeles (72.DA.60).

down at my *secrétaire*; I picked up a book, a pen, some papers, one after another, and none of this had the power to calm me down."[29]

Most important, the *secrétaire* provided hidden, locked storage. Letters were not the only sort of valuable locked away in a *secrétaire* for safekeeping: when the wife of the cabinet-maker Bernard Molitor died in 1796, the notary found silver cutlery, three watches, and the family jewels in her *secrétaire*.[30] Increased sociability in the home meant more people coming and going; apartment living in a crowded city increased the risk of break-ins as well as fire; increased wealth meant that there was more to steal, while endemic poverty and the ubiquity of servants meant there was always the temptation to do so. More significantly, the lock and key secured the identification of the *secrétaire* with its owner, and were meant to protect the privacy of the owner's life and self, more even than her property. For documents, and especially letters written and received, contained the owner's thoughts, dreams, and desires, as well as evidence of actions and relationships; disclosing letters, even those written to the owner, was tantamount to baring one's soul.[31]

(a)

(b)

Figure 11.7a and b *Secrétaire* attributed to Jean-François Leleu (ca. 1770). Oak veneered with amaranth, ebony, kingwood, tulipwood, box, and burr amboyna; gilt bronze mounts; steel fittings; *brèche d'Alep* top. 107.3 cm x 120.3 cm x 43.8 cm. Courtesy of the J. Paul Getty Museum, Los Angeles (82.DA.81).

(a)

(b)

Figure 11.8a and b *Secrétaire à abattant* by Martin Carlin (ca. 1775). Oak veneered with tulipwood, satinwood, kingwood partially engraved and incised with white and red mastic, green-stained box, and ebony stringing; set with eight soft-paste Sèvres porcelain plaques; gilt bronze mounts; white Carrara marble. 120 cm x 94 cm x 34 cm. Courtesy of the J. Paul Getty Museum, Los Angeles (65.DA.2).

The secrecy of the *secrétaire* was, at bottom, the secrecy of letter writing itself, as it had come to be understood by the second half of the eighteenth century. The ninth of Louise d'Epinay's *Conversations d'Emilie*, her pedagogical treatise in the form of a series of dialogues between a mother and a daughter, opens with the daughter bursting in on her mother as she is writing a letter. When Emilie expresses her annoyance at not being told to whom her mother is writing or what she is writing about, the mother responds:

> Writing is the conversation of those who are apart. It is the only means that one has to communicate one's ideas to the [absent other], one thus confides one's secrets to the paper: that's why everything that is written is sacred. We must no more allow ourselves to read papers that come into our hands when they are not addressed to us than to eavesdrop on two people who whisper.[32]

More than any other piece of furniture, the *secrétaire*, on which letters were written and in which papers were secured under lock and key, was the materialization of the owner's self. When scribes wrote letters for their mistresses and masters, the desk was not (could not be) a place of security and privacy; the scribe was. By combining the functions of writing surface and secure storage, the *secrétaire* reflected the need and ability of modern writers to articulate their thoughts and feelings on paper and thence to confide them only to a trusted other who was an equal rather than a subordinate. So too, it should be noted, did the seal. Originally used like a signature to authenticate the authorship of a letter or document penned by a scribe, the seal was now meant to secure the thoughts confided to the letter from messengers, postmen, and other third parties through whose hands the letter must pass on its journey from writer to addressee.[33]

Figure 11.9 Table by Martin Carlin (ca. 1773). Oak veneered with tulipwood, box, ebony and holly stringing; set with four soft-paste Sèvres porcelain plaques; gilt bronze mounts. 73 cm x 40 cm diameter. Courtesy of the J. Paul Getty Museum, Los Angeles (70.DA.75).

In 1765, Michel de Sedaine was the first to use a *secrétaire* as a theatrical prop, in his play *Le Philosophe sans le savoir*. The opening scene was set in "a large French city. The theater represents a large cabinet lighted by candles; a *secrétaire* along one side, on which are papers and boxes."[34] The cabinet with its *secrétaire* sets the scene for the family drama that will unfold. As Mark Ledbury has noted, the setting is "simultaneously an intimate family sphere, a place of business, and a hive of celebratory activity as the family gears up for Vanderk's daughter's marriage."[35] *Le Philosophe sans le savoir* was what Diderot called a *drame*, and what others since have called a *drame bourgeois*: a play set in modern times that dramatizes ordinary lives, in contrast to the tragedies and comedies of French classicism, which either exalted the noble or ridiculed the commoner. The *secrétaire* signified the modernity of the setting. Sedaine's was the first play consciously based on the new dramatic principles laid out by Diderot in *Entretiens sur le fils naturel*, and the main character (the owner of the *secrétaire*) was modeled after Diderot's in *Le Père de famille*. Diderot loved the play. The day after the premiere he wrote to a friend: "Yes, my friend, yes, this is true taste, this is domestic truth, this is the room, these are the actions and the words of upstanding people."[36]

The profusion of *secrétaires* with their locks and keys was a sign of increasing personal privacy, a declaration of the autonomy of the person who effectively declared at least some part of him or herself beyond the power of another. However, the claim to privacy is also always an invitation to its violation. In the eighteenth century, the locking *secrétaires* of wives and children were always a challenge to authority and thus became the site of family dramas. "Love, ambition, and politics place their secrets under steel bands, the puzzle [*le jeu*] of which demands to be studied," mused Louis-Sébastien Mercier in the 1780s; "and the artist, foreseeing at the same time the action of fire and that of violence, has deployed rather extensive knowledge to guarantee fragile papers from this double attack." He concluded that if the locksmith "is the guarantor of public security, he is not that of its happiness: his ingenuity testifies to that of the thief and the robber."[37]

Because the *secrétaire* was so closely associated with a single person, and in particular with his or her private thoughts, it could represent its owner in the symbolic economy of fiction; plots could turn and character could be disclosed simply by violating its privacy. On one hand, as the repository of confidences like the confidential secretary it replaced, the *secrétaire* always represented the threat of betrayal. On the other, as the repository of the owner's most valued thoughts, actions, and desires, the *secrétaire* was also a stand-in for its owner; violating the *secrétaire* was thus a metaphor for rape. Novelists took full advantage of the *secrétaire*'s dramatic potential by casting it both as a surrogate for the master and as the servant it displaced.

In Louise d'Epinay's unfinished *roman à clef, Histoire de Madame de Montbrillant* (1770), the eponymous heroine decides to spend the last of the money her father-in-law had given her as a wedding gift, only to find it missing from her *secrétaire*. Because it is locked, she knows that the only person who could have taken the money was the keeper of the second key, her debauched husband. She asks both him and his servant if he took the money, but they both deny it. She consults her mother, who after examining the *secrétaire* herself, agrees that the lock has not been forced and thus that M. de Montbrillant is indeed the culprit.[38] The episode is revealing. First, although the theft is a violation of trust, the fact that the husband has a key to his wife's *secrétaire* shows that if there ever was any trust, it only went one way. Second, the *secrétaire* may well have been the only secure storage the wife had because she locked her money in it, and not just her papers. And third, within the novel's plot, the husband's deed and his deception following it pretty much sum up his character and the plight of his wife, as he gambles away whatever he does not spend on mistresses. The *secrétaire* plays a central role in the marital drama.

Orest Ranum has noted that Samuel Pepys once gave his wife a cabinet that he had received as a gift—but only "after carefully examining the operation of its secret drawers. . . . Did possession of furniture that could be locked really mean that privacy had increased?" Ranum asks. "Pepys's wife could keep no secrets from prying Samuel's eyes."[39] Ruth Plaut Weinreb notes that Epinay's husband "deceived her almost immediately following their wedding, and gambled, and kept mistresses and squandered the family fortunes," just as Montbrillant did. Both author and character sought legal separation as their only recourse.[40] Whether M. d'Epinay did indeed use his own key to violate his wife's *secrétaire*, the episode figures well the problem of a woman's privacy, indeed of respect for her personal integrity within marriage and the patriarchal household: the husband's forced entry into the *secrétaire* to violate its integrity and steal the valuables within figures the husband's violation of the wife and her trust.

As private spaces, private property, and private thoughts were claimed by individual women, anxieties about violations of privacy began to run through the letters that they carefully sealed and then sent by the most trusted route they knew. When they received letters in return, they sought private spaces in which to read them and then locked them carefully in their *secrétaires*.[41] Only when a desk's owner was alone or with a trusted friend or servant would hidden places be revealed. Later in Epinay's novel, Madame de Montbrillant explains how her dying sister-in-law entrusted her with the key to her *secrétaire* after the doctors had left and they were alone together.

> A sharp pain struck her head; she let out a cry, asking me suddenly for her pockets. It took me a minute to find them; she searched them for a long time without really knowing what she was doing; finally she pulled out a key and repeated several times: "This is the key, this is the one . . ." She could not finish, and these were the last words she spoke. She lost consciousness again, and at five o'clock in the evening, she was no more.[42]

As the shock of the death hit her, Madame de Montbrillant remembered the key and realized that she must use it to find and destroy "whatever papers" Madame de Ménil might have locked away. "I went to her *secrétaire*, in which I had often seen her lock up letters from the chevalier after having read them. It was precisely this key that she had given me. I had but an instant; I took every bit of writing I could find and threw all of it into the fire." After making sure that every scrap burned, Montbrillant took the key to Madame de Ménil's husband, having done her duty to protect the reputation of her friend.[43]

Small *secrétaires* contained personal correspondence, including but not limited to love letters and the records of extramarital affairs; large ones contained legal documents and family papers. In her memoirs, Madame de Genlis recalls the moment when the purchaser of her late father-in-law's "large *secrétaire*" came upon a spring mechanism that, when released, "revealed a little nook, in which we saw a portfolio of blue velvet, with gold embroidery. The portfolio was opened, and in it was found the will that named M. de Genlis the residual heir."[44] *Secrétaires* represented and facilitated the privacy of both individuals and families.

The plot of Laclos's *Les Liaisons dangereuses* (1782), turns upon the discovery of the heroine's hidden love letters. Laclos introduced the *secrétaire* in the opening letter of the novel. Cecile, fifteen years old and recently returned to her mother's house from her convent boarding school, sits down to write a letter to her friend Sophie:

> You see, my good friend, [that] I am keeping my word to you, and that bonnets and pompons do not take up all my time; there is some left for you. . . . Mama has consulted me about everything; she treats me much less like a schoolgirl than she used to. I have my own chambermaid; I have a bedroom and a cabinet to myself, and I am writing to you on a very pretty *Secrétaire*, to which I have been given the key, and in which I can hide whatever I wish.[45]

Needless to say, Cecile's sense of security is entirely false. With the help of the devious Madame de Merteuil, she enters into an illicit correspondence with the handsome young chevalier de Danceny, carefully saving all of his letters in her *secrétaire*. To advance her own plot, Merteuil later betrays Cecile by telling her mother of the correspondence. Madame de Volanges promptly goes into her daughter's room and demands the key to her *secrétaire*. "I pretended not to be able to find it," Cecile later recounted, "but in the end I had to obey."[46] When, at the end of the novel, Cecile flees back to the true safety of the convent, her mother searches her room for clues. "I went through her armoires, her *secrétaire*; I found everything where it belonged and all her clothes, save the dress she left in. She had not even taken the little bit of money that she had in her room."[47] Like Madame de Montbrillant, Cecile had learned the hard way that a lock and key mean very little when one is a daughter or a wife. But it was not just the security of the *secrétaire* that was an illusion; there was also the freedom of letter writing, which Cecile had exercised with reckless abandon. In the end, Cecile left behind everything she had described in that first letter to Sophie—including especially the freedom and the privacy falsely promised by the *secrétaire*.

Whether or not a *secretaire* did indeed hold within it secrets that its owner wished to conceal from others, its very existence suggested the existence of such secrets. Because the functions of the *secrétaire* were concealed, the locked *secrétaire* could provoke anxiety on the part of those who did not have access to its hidden spaces. The theme of the locked desk, and especially of the secret drawer in a woman's *secrétaire* containing the letters that document a secret affair, has remained a theme in French literature into the twentieth century. In particular, writers have used the *bonheur du jour*, the most fashionable *secrétaire* designed for ladies in the eighteenth century (Figure 11.10), to tell tales of family secrets and their revelation through the discovery of hidden compartments.[48] For twentieth-century novelists and short story writers, *secrétaires* are the furniture of nostalgia, whose secrets may go back centuries. They are the closets in which ancient skeletons lie waiting to be released by the writer, who through his art, is able to spring the lock and find the hidden compartment, with its secret stories waiting to be told.

However, the *secrétaire* has as much in common with the twenty-first-century laptop computer as it does with the eighteenth-century dressing table. Like the *secrétaire*, the laptop combines the functions of writing surface, easy access to writing materials, and secure storage in one elegant object that is fashionable across gender lines. Passwords are the new locks and keys that make writers feel secure enough to commit themselves to writing, but Mercier's observation that locks are the signs of insecurity and anxiety still holds. Like the *secrétaire*, the laptop has facilitated a reintegration of the tasks of composition and copying split apart, this time by the invention of the typewriter in the late nineteenth century. The typewriter returned the material production of correspondence to the realm of manual (secretarial) labor—this time, however, across a divide not just of class, but gender. In the twentieth century, it created a new division of labor in the workplace between male boss and female secretary or typist that reinforced the power and prestige of the boss by associating him with the intellectual work of composition and gendering such work as masculine, thereby also securing that position for men alone. With the scribal role gendered emphatically female and that of the composer male, the hierarchy of tasks that writing requires was even more clearly reimposed. "However," noted Roland Barthes in the 1970s, "the machine being still felt (at least in Europe) as an inhuman object, if one writes to a friend and would like to efface or temper the offense of a machine-made, expeditious communication, one adds in closing a few handwritten words: one is ashamed not to write by hand anymore."

Figure 11.10 *Bonheur-du-jour* attributed to Adam Weisweiler (ca. 1785-1790). Oak and mahogany veneered with amboyna, ebony, green-stained harewood, and sycamore; set with five Wedgwood green jasperware plaques designed by Elizabeth, Lady Templetown, and modeled by William Hackwood; gilt bronze mounts; white marble top and shelf. 107.6 cm x 69.2 cm x 41.3 cm. Courtesy of the J. Paul Getty Museum, Los Angeles (72.DA.59).

As the class and gender order was reinstated in the office, personal writing continued to be associated with the autoscription of the writer's hand. "Manuscript writing remains the mythical depository of human, affective values," Barthes concluded; "it puts desire in communication, because it is the body itself."[49]

The office computer was developed precisely at the time Barthes was writing, when the feminist movement had forced open the wall between male boss and female secretary by challenging the gender division of labor. The laptop that evolved from it has resolved the crisis by realigning office work such that secretaries are virtually eliminated in the realm of writing. Rather than simply overturning the gender order in the workplace, the laptop collapsed it by facilitating the reintegration of writing as the direct expression of the writer who has full control over the tools required for materializing her thoughts and communicating them to others. The laptop has also mended the rift between personal and professional writing, which the *secrétaire* marked off from the *bureau*. The office computer and the home computer are the same, and the mobility of the laptop has made it not just the repository of its owner's thoughts, but a personal accessory. Like the eighteenth-century *secrétaire*, it represents the transformation of the secretary from servant to material extension of the writer's body, and of writing into the direct expression of the self. It demonstrates that technology is not always alienating, as Barthes assumed. When new technologies such as laptops and *secrétaires* facilitate the integration of human practices by eliminating human mediation and the class and gender divisions of labor it entails, they contribute to the reintegration of mind and body and thus the integrity and expression of the self.

Notes

1. See Carolyn Sargentson, *Merchants and Luxury Markets: The Marchands Merciers of Eighteenth-Century Paris* (London and Malibu: Victoria and Albert Museum in association with the J. Paul Getty Museum, 1996), 87 and 95n. 133. Sales records in Louis Courajod, ed., *Livre-journal de Lazare Duvaux, Marchand-bijoutier ordinaire du Roy, 1748–1758*, 2 vols. (Paris: F. de Nobele, 1965), vol. 2. See, for example, the following sales: numbers 40, 70, 270.

2. *Dictionnaire de l'Académie française*, 5th ed. (1798), s.v. "Secrétaire," 551; Denis Diderot and Jean Le Rond d'Alembert, ed., *Encyclopédie, ou dictionnaire raisonné des sciences, des arts, et des métiers* (Paris, 1751–65), s.v., "Secrétaire," 14: 863; s.v., "Marqueterie," 10:139 and plate 4, 21:2:1. Dictionaries searched in ARTFL (The Project for American and French Research on the Treasury of the French Language), "Dictionnaires d'autrefois" at http://colet.uchicago.edu. According to the *Oxford English Dictionary*, the use of the English term *secretary* to mean a writing desk derives from the French, and was first used by the cabinetmaker Thomas Sheraton in 1803. *Secretaire* defined as "a piece of furniture, usually cabinet-shaped, in which private papers can be kept, with a shelf for writing on, and drawers and pigeon-holes; a bureau," appeared in English first in 1771 in America. See http://dictionary.oed.com/.

3. For an example of a scribe who became a writer (although he modestly refused the title "author") see *Pierre Prion, scribe: mémoires d'un écrivain de campagne au XVIIIe siècle*, ed. Emmanuel Le Roy Ladurie and Orest Ranum (Paris: Gallimard-Julliard, 1985). Prion, the son of a notary, was employed as a copyist from 1711 until his death in 1759. His copying work consisted mostly of transcribing archival documents for his employer, a rural noble in the diocese of Nîmes. The editors note that "the activity of writing is not so different in the two cases, but from one generation to the other there passes the possession of a small capital to obtaining a meager salary. In a certain way, Prion here illustrates the modernity of the eighteenth century, during which the role of the salaried worker including in the service [*tertiaire*] sector, tends to increase in relation to the seventeenth," (21). At the same time, moreover, the status of the mere copyist fell as the need for him declined.

4. Roland Barthes, "Variations sur l'écriture," in *Oeuvres complètes*, ed. Éric Marty, 5 vols. (Paris: Le Seuil, 2002), 4: 293.

5. Lesley Smith, "Scriba Femina: Medieval Depictions of Women Writing," in *Women and the Book: Assessing the Visual Evidence*, ed. Lesley Smith and Jane H. M. Taylor (London, Toronto, Buffalo, NY: British Library and University of Toronto Press, 1997), 21–44.

6. [Louis de Rouvroy, duc de] Saint-Simon, *Mémoires (1691–1701)*, ed. Yves Coirault, 8 vols. (Paris: Gallimard, 1983), 1: 803–804.

7. The "secrétaire des dames et messieurs" is described as a "faithful and discreet depository, and with a dual use; useful and necessary to Men of Affairs, Businessmen, Travelers, Officers, and those of all stations," in which can be recorded "Losses and Gains, Visits to make, the weekly Agenda, Meetings, Thoughts, Bon mots, stray thoughts, such as Epigrams, Madrigals, conversational witticisms, sallies, addresses, etc." It is included in *Le Bijou des dames, Nouveau Costume français: et de la connoissance des diamans, des perles et des parfums les plus précieux; avec tablettes economiques perte et gain; ou Almanach de la toilette et de la coeffure des dames françoises et romaines* (Paris, [1779]), 4.

8. There are exceptions to this rule. First, elites employed secretaries for personal writing when they were too ill to hold a pen or sit at a desk. I suspect this was more often the case for women than men, especially if one includes times around childbirth when women were bedridden. See, e.g., Ferdinando Galliani and Louise d'Epinay, *Correspondance, I: 1769–1770*, ed. Daniel Maggetti with Georges Dulac (Paris: Desjonquères, 1992), letters from Epinay dated 29 September 1769; 11 December 1769; 29 October [1770]. Second, women at the very top of the social and economic ladder, such as members of the royal family and princesses of the blood, employed secretaries to handle the volume of correspondence in which they engaged as patrons and political players. The small number of very elite women that court politics and patronage continued to involve were in a sense "professionals" who engaged in the sort of writing for which secretarial help was both appropriate and necessary.

9. Maurice Daumas, "Manuels épistolaires et identité sociale, XVIe–XVIIIe siècles," *Revue d'histoire moderne et contemporaine* 40 (October–December 1993): 544.

10. [Jean Léonor Le Gallois] de Grimarest, *Traité sur la maniere d'écrire des lettres et sur le ceremonial: Avec un Discours sur ce qu'on appelle usage dans la Langue Françoise* (Paris, 1735), 1–3. The first edition of this work was published in 1709. For a story of a man who falls in love with a woman through her letters, see Caroline-Stéphanie-Félicité Du Crest, comtesse de Genlis, *Mémoires inédites . . . sur le dix-huitième siècle et la Révolution française depuis 1756 jusqu'à nos jours*, 10 vols. (Paris: Ladvocat, 1825), 1: 98–100.
11. Eléazar Mauvillon, *Traité général du stile, avec un traité particulier du stile épistolaire* (Amsterdam, 1750), 255.
12. [André Joseph Panckoucke], *Les études convenables aux demoiselles* (Paris: Les Libraires Associés, An XI), 1: 155. The first edition was published in Lille in 1749.
13. J[ean] Lanteires, *Quelques avis aux institutrices de jeunes demoiselles, sur les différens objets qui influent essentiellement sur leur bonheur & leur succès; & sur les Etudes auxquelles elles doivent se livrer* (Lausanne, 1788), 94.
14. Marie-Claire Grassi, *L'Art de la lettre au temps de "La Nouvelle Héloïse" et du Romantisme* (Geneva: Slatkine, 1994).
15. Denis Diderot to Sophie Volland, 8 October 1759, in Diderot, *Correspondance*, ed. Georges Roth, 16 vols. (Paris: Minuit, 1955–1970), 2: 267–68. Located in ARTFL.
16. Diderot to Volland, [5 September 1762], in Diderot, *Correspondance*, 4: 136–40.
17. *Dictionnaire de l'Académie française* (1694; 1762), s.v. "Bureau."
18. See Jürgen Habermas, *The Structural Transformation of the Public Sphere: Inquiry into a Category of Bourgeois Society*, trans. Thomas Burger with the assistance of Frederick Lawrence (Cambridge, MA: MIT Press, 1989), 17–18. This division corresponds roughly to a division between public and private writing, but literature and scholarship seem to cross the line between *bureau* and *secrétaire*. Images of men of letters, such as Louis-Michel Van Loo's portrait of Diderot (now in the Louvre), or Jacques-Louis David's of Lavoisier and his wife (in the Metropolitan Museum of Art, New York), tend to show the men behind large *bureaux*; but the anecdote about Montesquieu places him at a *secrétaire*. Perhaps this is because study was considered a form of intellectual work, like that of the professionals (lawyers, notaries, bureaucrats) who used *bureaux*, while at the same time, literature (essays, poetry, novels) was increasingly seen as the expression of the self. Literary language could not be mediated by a secretary, even if study required working space and manuscripts needed to be copied. Furthermore, the epistolary novel, the epitome of eighteenth-century literature, crossed the line between letters and literature, private and public.
19. *Encyclopédie méthodique, ou par ordre de matières: Arts et métiers mécaniques*, ed. Jacques Lacombe (Paris and Liège, 1782–1791), 29: 698.
20. [Nicolas] Le Camus de Mézières, *Le Génie de l'architecture, ou l'analogie de cet art avec nos sensations* (Paris, 1780), 156–70. On the refiguring of the elite, see Roger Chartier, Introduction to *A History of Private Life, 3: Passions of the Renaissance*, ed. Roger Chartier, trans. Arthur Goldhammer (Cambridge, MA: Harvard University Press, 1989), 15–16.
21. On the exceptional woman, see Geneviève Fraisse, *Reason's Muse: Sexual Difference and the Birth of Democracy*, trans. Jane Marie Todd (Chicago: University of Chicago Press, 1994); Mary D. Sheriff, *The Exceptional Woman: Elisabeth Vigée-Lebrun and the Cultural Politics of Art* (Chicago: University of Chicago Press, 1996); Sheriff, "'So What Are You Working On?': Categorizing the Exceptional Woman," in *Singular Women: Writing the Artist*, ed. Kristen Frederickson and Sarah E. Webb (Berkeley: University of California Press, 2003), 48–65. As one typical eighteenth-century male writer put it: "If among this sex are found Daciers, Du Châtelets, these are rare examples, more to be admired than imitated." Pierre-Joseph Boudier de Villemert, *L'Ami des femmes* (Hamburg, 1758), 28.
22. Genlis, *Mémoires*, 3: 91–93. Genlis fictionalized this situation in *Adèle et Théodore*: "But I was destined, as you will see, to encounter that day only unexpected and surprising things," a male character recounts in a story within the story. "The first thing that struck me in placing my foot in the *cabinet* was a *bureau* covered with papers and books. What, I said, a *bureau* in a woman's room, and in Madame de Surville's!" Caroline-Stéphanie-Félicité Du Crest, comtesse de Genlis, *Adèle et Théodore, ou Lettres sur l'éducation*, 3 vols. (Paris, 1782), 1: 242.
23. On eighteenth-century French women writers, see Joan Hinde Stewart, *Gynographs: French Novels by Women of the Late Eighteenth Century* (Lincoln: University of Nebraska Press), 1993; Suellen Diaconoff, *Through the Reading Glass: Women, Books, and Sex in the French Enlightenment* (Albany: State University Press of New York, 2005).
24. Mimi Hellman, "Furniture, Sociability, and the Work of Leisure in Eighteenth-Century France," *Eighteenth-Century Studies* 32 (summer 1999): 415–45.

25. In the 1780s, Louis-Sébastien Mercier noted (with his usual exaggeration and moral critique) that "women no longer take up either the sewing needle, or the knitting needle; they do *filet* or embroidery on a hoop." *Tableau de Paris*, 2 vols. (Paris: Mercure de France, 1994), 1: 854.
26. Like the *bureau*, the *serre-papier* could be a room to itself in a grand household that employed secretaries. See Le Camus de Mézières, *Génie de l'architecture*, 162.
27. Gillian Wilson, Adrian Sassoon, and Charissa Bremer-David, "Acquisitions Made by the Department of Decorative Arts in 1983," *The J. Paul Getty Museum Journal* 12 (1984): 201–7. An identical piece mounted, however, with lacquer panels, is in the Victoria and Albert Museum (1049–1882). Although its eighteenth-century provenance is not known, a 1786 inventory of the royal Château de Bellevue includes a description of a desk of about the same size, mounted with lacquer panels, in the cabinet of Louis XVI's aunt, Madame Victoire. It is now in the Louvre (OA 10419). See Sargentson, *Merchants and Luxury Markets*, 48–49 and color plates 6 and 7; Daniel Alcouffe, Anne Dion-Tenenbaum, and Amaury Lefébure, *Furniture Collections in the Louvre* (Dijon: Editions Faton, 1993), 1: 261.
28. Jean-Baptiste Louvet de Couvray, *Une année de la vie du chevalier de Faublas* (London and Paris, 1787), 533.
29. Joseph-Marie Loaisel de Tréogate, *Ainsi finissent les grandes passions, ou les Dernières amours du chevalier de . . .* (Paris, 1788), 216.
30. Ulrich Leben, *Molitor: Ebéniste from the Ancien Régime to the Bourbon Restoration*, trans. William Wheeler (London: Philip Wilson, 1992), 19. When Parisians had a bit of money saved, they tended to buy something solid with it, such as silver cutlery, jewelry, and gold watches, which could then be pawned if necessary, and later redeemed, if possible. See Laurence Fontaine, "The Circulation of Luxury Goods in Eighteenth-Century Paris: Social Redistribution and an Alternative Currency," in *Luxury in the Eighteenth Century: Debates, Desires and Delectable Goods*, ed. Maxine Berg and Elizabeth Eger (New York: Palgrave Macmillan, 2003), 99.
31. On the implication of correspondants in each other's letters, see Antoine-Joseph-Michel de Servan, "Réflexions sur la publication des lettres de Rousseau; et des lettres en général," in *Oeuvres choisies de Servan*, ed. X. de Portets, 5 vols. (Paris: Didot, 1822-25), 2: 407–58, and my discussion in "Epistolary Property: Michel de Servan and the Plight of Letters on the Eve of the French Revolution," in *Early Modern Conceptions of Property*, ed. John Brewer and Susan Staves (London: Routledge, 1995), 339–64.
32. [Louise-Florence Petronille Tardieu d'Esclavelles, Marquise d'Epinay], *Conversations d'Emilie* (Leipzig, 1774), 244–45.
33. Henry René d'Allemagne, *Les Accessoires du costume et du mobilier depuis le treizième jusqu'au milieu du dix-neuvième siècle*, 3 vols. (Paris: Schemit, 1928), 1: 75.
34. Michel-Jean Sedaine, *Le Philosophe sans le savoir* (Paris, 1766), 3.
35. Mark Ledbury, "Intimate Dramas: Genre Painting and the New Theater in Eighteenth-Century France," in *Intimate Encounters: Love and Domesticity in Eighteenth-Century France*, ed. Richard Rand with the assistance of Juliette M. Bianco (Princeton, NJ: Princeton University Press, 1997), 60–61.
36. Quoted in Robert Garapon, Introduction to Michel Sedaine, *Le Philosophe sans le savoir* (Paris: S.T.F.M., 1990), xi. Information about the play is drawn from Garapon's introduction. On the *drame*, see Sarah Maza, *The Myth of the French Bourgeoisie: An Essay on the Social Imaginary 1750–1850* (Cambridge, MA: Harvard University Press, 2003), 61–67.
37. Mercier, *Tableau de Paris*, 2: 1055. Note the similarity to the sealed letter, whose privacy and integrity were protected from violation only by a thin bit of wax. See Antoine-Joseph-Michel de Servan, "Commentaire sur un passage du livre de M. Necker, ou éclaircissements demandés à messieurs les commis des postes, préposés à décacheter les lettres," (1784) in *Oeuvres choisies*, 2: 461–509 and my discussion in "Epistolary Property."
38. [Louise-Florence Petronille Tardieu d'Esclavelles, Marquise d'Epinay], *Histoire de Madame de Montbrillant (1770)*, ed. Georges Roth (Paris: Gallimard, 1951), 1:258-59, 263 in ARTFL.
39. Orest Ranum, "The Refuges of Intimacy," in *Passions of the Renaissance*, ed. Chartier, 228.
40. Ruth Plaut Weinreb, *Eagle in a Gauze Cage: Louise d'Epinay, Femme de Lettres* (New York: AMS Press, 1993), 63.
41. See Ranum, "Refuges of Intimacy."
42. Epinay, *Histoire*, 2: 469. The character of Madame de Ménil was based on Epinay's sister-in-law, Madame de Jully, who died November 22,1752. See editor's note 1, 2: 467.
43. Ibid., 2: 469.

44. Genlis, *Mémoires*, 3: 331.
45. Pierre-Ambroise-François Choderlos de Laclos, *Les Liaisons dangereuses*, 2 vols. (Dublin, 1784), 1: 1-2.
46. Ibid., 163.
47. Ibid., 2: 274-75.
48. Edmond Guiraud, *Le Bonheur du jour*, first performed at the Odéon in 1926 and published by the author (Paris, 1927); Jean de La Varende, "Le Bonheur-du-jour," in *L'Objet aimé* (Paris: Plon, 1967), 25-48; Jacques Almira, "Le Bonheur-du-jour," in *Le Marchand d'oublies* (Paris: Gallimard, 1979), 121-71. See also José Cabanis, *Le Bonheur du jour* (Paris: Gallimard, 1960), in which the narrator tells the story of his mysterious uncle's life based on recovered papers that in the final paragraph of the novel he is able to restore to his *secrétaire*. "All his poems, his notebooks, his letters, are there, in good order in the drawers of the *bonheur du jour*. I now have the feeling that the word enigma is, as he used to say, elsewhere. I am coming to think that my work has been very much in vain, and I feel after so many pages Uncle Octave escaping me, getting blurry, leaving again. I am going to tie up this folder. It will join the others in the *bonheur du jour*," (206).
49. Barthes, "Variations sur l'écriture," 294.

CHAPTER 12

Looking at Furniture Inside Out: Strategies of Secrecy and Security in Eighteenth-Century French Furniture

CAROLYN SARGENTSON

French eighteenth-century furniture offers rich pickings for cultural historians. Grand French furniture of this period, by which we invariably mean Paris-made furniture, was for the most part veneered with elaborate marquetry and embellished with metal mounts. These highly decorated surfaces sent complex messages about style, fashion, and materials on the one hand, and on the other, suggested possibilities for storage, concealment, and exposure just behind the surface. For the first time, stand-alone pieces of furniture, often on a relatively small scale, provided facilities for classifying papers and ordering possessions in almost any room in a house, especially for women. This represented a significant shift from the seventeenth century, when the most complex carcase furniture form, the cabinet, was most often used to secure and present collections accumulated by men, and writing furniture was only (by the 1670s) beginning to be designed with the simplest arrangements of integral lockable drawers. Despite the importance of such changes, the interior, function, and operation of French furniture tends to be little discussed in specialist decorative art circles, except from the point of view of describing construction, normally in collection catalogs.[1] Furniture in museums is these days invariably displayed closed, and the possibilities for showing it open, let alone moving and working, are extremely rare, leaving nonspecialist audiences largely unaware of the function and complexity of some of the most elaborate furniture ever made.[2]

Such furniture was difficult both to design and make, and to use and maintain. Technologies of security within the eighteenth-century grand domestic interior depended on extraordinary skills and workmanship in Parisian workshops while also demanding skilled and intricate operation of the furniture and its mechanisms on the part of owners. While security was actively managed, largely by men, at the level of state, city, street, dwelling, and room, these small systems of secrecy and security in the form of furniture offer a particular material insight into the domestic culture within which they were used. Many such pieces of furniture, distributed across different room types in a Parisian townhouse, had secret drawers, compartments, and mechanisms designed into their structure for the owner's security and delight. Their meanings were multiple, related to changes in the way that people, especially but not exclusively women, managed their lives, their belongings, and their secrets within the domestic interior. They were meaningful because they reflected concerns about the safety of personal possessions and a level of private control over those possessions that was hitherto unparalleled. As Louis-Sébastien Mercier (1740–1814) wrote,

> Such a man would grow pale if he forgot to lock his *secrétaire* with the busy key that never leaves him. Love, ambition, and politics place their secrets under steel bands, the puzzle [*le jeu*] of which demands to be studied; and the artist, foreseeing at the same time the action of fire and that of violence, has deployed rather extensive knowledge to guarantee fragile papers from this double attack.[3]

In general, early to mid-eighteenth-century French furniture announced its function as a protector of possessions through highly ornate escutcheons (keyhole surrounds) on the fronts of drawers, doors, and fall fronts (Figure 12.1). It thus drew attention to its interior and the means of accessing its contents through the use of a uniquely designed key. The use of lock-and-key technology to secure furniture drawer by drawer, door by door, space by space, implies a straightforward use of furniture for storing precious things while protecting them from theft. Other forms of technology, including ingenious tricks and locksmiths' or

Figure 12.1 *Commode*, Paris, ca. 1720. V&A 1083-1882, Jones Collection. Pine carcase veneered with parquetry of kingwood; gilt bronze mounts; Campan marble. Height 85.6 cm, width 148.0 cm, depth 68.8 cm. Detail of escutcheon (keyhole mount) of gilt bronze, on drawer. Courtesy of V&A Images/Victoria and Albert Museum.

cabinetmakers' devices (springs, buttons, and other hidden mechanisms) offered a form of security that appears to have served somewhat different purposes. Spaces protected by these mechanisms were sometimes used for hiding things: things valued for their material value, like money or jewelry, but more often for what they meant, such as letters, legal papers, and other written documents. The form of protection offered here seems primarily to have been the creation and maintenance of a secret, the knowledge of whose existence was the object of protection. While either of these systems for concealing objects and letters seemed to offer considerable security, it came in a form that embodied a significant degree of risk. A key might be lost, misplaced, or stolen. The line between concealment and exposure, made possible by the illicit use of a key or by the mere touch of a trigger that would instantly release the hidden compartment, appears to have been a fine one. This line represented risk, danger even, but also perhaps play, even if the stakes were sometimes high. The secret, however, was not the only object of value in these games and strategies; devices such as locks, keys, and mechanisms were also highly prized and protected objects in themselves, entering literary and commercial discourse, along with the secrets they protected, at several levels.

None of this is particularly surprising for a court and city culture that had become extremely sophisticated in its manners and taste, and that is held to have developed, during the eighteenth century, unprecedented levels of self-conscious behavior and a dramatic increase in the specialized design and use of furniture and interior spaces.[4] Furniture and rooms alike were implicated in the domestic and social dramas of love affairs (especially clandestine letter writing), in the confiding of secrets (usually between women), and in the artifice of self-presentation (such as the *toilette*). Along with these social developments came new forms of objects that articulated a range of activities within these spaces, and new ways of designing and making them, which depended on high levels of artisanal skill. While the sociological implications of these secret furniture parts with regard to the lives of the Parisian elite are fascinating, the surviving material culture of that elite in the form of locks and keys, mechanical parts of metal and wood, and designs in wood of three-dimensional structures is enormously sophisticated. These objects were the product of another part of the Parisian social world, that of the members of the city's highly specialized guilds (*corporations* and *communautés*).[5] Within this milieu, imported labor and techniques, and sometimes tools and component parts (especially from Germany and England), along with innovative responses to consumer demand contributed to increasingly elaborate systems of security and concealment.[6]

Lockmaking in the eighteenth century was surely an art of luxury, surveillance, and subterfuge. Mercier described it in the *Tableau de Paris* as "un art de luxe" which, though a guarantor of public safety ("good locks . . . are the most perfect supplement to the police"), could not be said to do the same for public morality.[7] The technical ingenuity of the locksmiths merely reflected, said Mercier, the deviousness of their violators, and both were becoming more resourceful day by day. "A locksmith has become an artist among us; but if he is the guarantor of public safety, he is not that of its happiness: his ingenuity challenges that of the thief."[8] However, locks and keys were not the only barriers to access by the uninvited; once open, a piece of furniture could deceive the viewer into missing many of its internal compartments and their contents. As Mercier said, "such a lock . . . reveals only a seemingly empty space and fools the most discerning eye: here, an imperceptible and unsuspected spring must be activated."[9] What he meant was that once the key was turned, the eye was deceived into thinking that no space existed beyond that which it immediately registered. However, a further layer of space might be discovered by triggering a spring or button which would cause that space to be instantly revealed. In a *secrétaire* dating from about 1785, for example, a key opens the fall front, which descends to reveal eleven mahogany-veneered drawers and a central door with no apparent point of entry (Color Plate 13, see color insert after page 118). When the fourth drawer down on the viewer's left is removed (no drawer is secured by a lock), a small button is visible on the right-hand side of the drawer cavity (Figure 12.2). When pressed, the central door springs open and a deep drawer is revealed. Beneath the drawer, which can easily be removed, an oak floor can be slid to one side to expose a hidden depth to the piece, within which is a plain oak lidless box with four compartments (Figure 12.3). When the box is removed, a series of secret drawers without handles is visible. These are released by pressing on a button concealed within the cavity. Each narrow drawer is propelled forward by a steel spring fitted to the back of the drawer (Figure 12.4). These deeper levels of space (known as *secrets* and *doubles fonds* or false bottoms) were not uncommon in finer furniture, and because they were opened and closed by mechanical triggers and springs rather than keys, they were susceptible to different risks. To find or steal a key offered only limited access to such pieces: the apparently impenetrable façades of the interior issued a challenge to the viewer to estimate the extent of the hidden spaces, guess at the security mechanisms, and try out a series of operations in the hope that luck would prevail and access be gained. Furniture like this suggests that designing and maintaining security within the interior was a much more subtle and nuanced process than was security installed at the level of room, building, or site.

Figure 12.2 *Secrétaire* attributed to Guillaume Benneman (d. 1811, *maître ébéniste* 1785), Paris, ca. 1785-1790. V&A W23-1958), gift of Sir Chester Beatty. Carcase and drawers of oak; mahogany and ebony veneer; gilt bronze mounts; green morocco; gray Bardiglio marble. Height 146 cm; width 100 cm; depth 43.5 cm (without marble). Detail of the central door, open. Courtesy of V&A Images/Victoria and Albert Museum.

Figure 12.3 *Secrétaire,* W23-1958, detail of the secret box beneath the central drawer behind the door. Courtesy of V&A Images/Victoria and Albert Museum.

Figure 12.4 *Secrétaire*, W23-1958, detail of one of the secret drawers in the double fond. Courtesy of V&A Images/Victoria and Albert Museum.

Most surviving locks were made for internal and external doors rather than for furniture.[10] The making of locks for furniture represented a particular specialist practice. While furniture makers in Paris most commonly fitted relatively standard double-throw locks, which varied in the number of bolts (on the principle of the more bolts, the more secure the lock), they also sometimes employed the most innovative and unexpected products of the locksmiths' trade. These ranged from the Chevalier d'Eon's "large and magnificent iron strongbox, with marvelous hidden locks in which to put my correspondence,"[11] to the highly decorated lock put on sale in 1784 by the locksmith Cron in the rue d'Angivilliers ("new security lock, very novel, interesting (*curieuse*), and attractive . . . could be placed on a *secrétaire* or any other piece of furniture").[12] One of the most elaborate locks advertised (although it was not described as a furniture lock) was a combination lock with a mechanism that grabbed hold of the wrist of anyone who tried to open it without the correct combination, and if that were not enough of a deterrent, then proceeded to fire a pistol at the misguided intruder.[13] Such a lock, said Mercier, "punishes the hand that dares to touch it."[14] When a rich man died, Mercier wrote elsewhere, the hand of the man who placed and removed the seals on secret cupboards (*armoires secrètes*) trembled with fear, anticipating that the spring mechanism of a cupboard might assault him, even cut off his hand. The richer the deceased, he concluded, the more cautious the *commissaire*.[15] But such protection for the living or the dead did not come cheap. By the end of the eighteenth century, locks for furniture were advertised in terms not only of their ingenious designs and expression of outstanding craftsmanship, but also their impressive prices. "A lock, a masterpiece of its kind," was publicized with a value of 3,000 livres in 1767; the following year another one, described as "beautiful, safe, and intriguing (*curieuse*)," was valued at 500.[16] These sums were equal to the highest prices paid for complete pieces of furniture in this period and represented the annual income of a variety of artisans.

While the resourcefulness of locksmiths intrigued the reading public, thieves, and householders alike, security in furniture design was achieved not only by the employment of highly secure locking systems, but also through the ingenious design of interior spaces within the wooden carcase. It was through these combinations of wood- and metal-working that the most sophisticated forms of secret and secure furniture were produced. A combination portable jewel casket, *secrétaire*, and writing table (hereafter referred to simply as a *secrétaire*) in the collection of the Victoria and Albert Museum (V&A), London, is a case in point (Figure 12.5). Its combined functionality is typical of furniture designed in the second half of the eighteenth century. Usually, a writing desk or surface was combined with something else, such as a storage facility for jewelry or articles for the *toilette*, and was often, though not exclusively, designed for women. One of the great merits of such an object was that it was mobile and supported a series of different activities, allowing for flexible use within a room that itself had multiple uses, depending on the time of the day, the nature and number of the people within the room, and the spontaneous shift from one activity to another. This example dates from about 1775 and is by a known maker, Jean-Henri Riesener (1734–1806), who was enormously successful in his role as *ébéniste du roi* until his fall from favor in 1784. Its provenance during the first hundred or so years of its life is unknown, but at some point between about 1865 and 1881 it was acquired, probably at auction, by the London-based military tailor and outfitter John Jones (c. 1800–1882). Jones bequeathed it to what was then the South Kensington Museum as part of a group of French eighteenth-century furniture, ceramics, boxes, hardstones, paintings, books, and sculpture.[17] This was to become one of the great founding collections of the museum, which had previously acquired very little in the field of French fine and decorative arts.[18]

In the museum's 1922 catalog of the Jones Collection, this piece of furniture inspired curator Oliver Brackett to write: "On account of the simplicity of line displayed in his furniture, the beauty and precision shown in their execution, Riesener is justly considered the most accomplished French cabinet-maker of the 18th century."[19] The *secrétaire* is stamped three times on the underside of the stand "J. H. RIESENER," and there is no obvious reason to doubt the authenticity of the piece or of the stamp. It is made of oak and pine, veneered with imported woods, all of which would have been much brighter in color when newly

Figure 12.5 Combined jewel casket, *secrétaire*, and writing table, stamped in the workshop of Jean-Henri Riesener (1734-1806, *maître* in 1768 and *ébéniste du roi* between 1774 and 1785), Paris, ca. 1775. V&A 1106-1882, Jones Collection. Carcase largely of oak with some pine, veneered with purplewood and tulipwood with marquetry of sycamore, *bois satiné*, boxwood and ebony, gilt bronze mounts, hinges, and mechanisms; steel springs; green leather, tooled and gilded; blue-green moiré silk lining. 106 cm high, 54.2 cm wide, and 35 cm deep (the upper section: height 34.6 cm, width 50.2 cm, depth 31.2 cm; the lower section: height 71.8 cm, width 54.2, depth 35 cm). Stamped three times on the underside of the stand, once on the front rail and twice, very indistinctly and partly overlapping, on the side rail: J H RIESENER. Courtesy of V&A Images/Victoria and Albert Museum.

finished, and ornamented with gilt metal mounts and handles. The writing surface on the inside of the fall front is covered with green leather, tooled and gilded, and the inside of the lid and the interior surfaces of the two trays stacked inside are lined with padded blue-green silk (Color Plate 14, see color insert after page 118). It stands on castors, which appear to be original, and is veneered on all four vertical surfaces, indicating that it was intended to be seen in the round.

A detailed anatomical investigation reveals an extraordinary level of complexity. Physically, the *secrétaire* has two tiers of construction: the top and bottom are made separately, and the one stands on top of the other. It has, however, three tiers of function: the uppermost, which contains a hidden space for jewelry and two removable trays, also for jewelry; the second tier, which contains a series of drawers behind a fall front; and a third tier that operates as a writing table. The two upper tiers of storage are contained within a single carcase, which has a handle for portability on each side (Figure 12.6) suggestive of the possibility that it might have been acquired to protect possessions while they were in transit from a primary Parisian residence to a country house. Recently, Mark Girouard has questioned the extent to which wealthy French men and women traveled any distance with their furniture in the late eighteenth century (in contrast to much earlier periods when furniture was customarily designed in order to cope with the movement of a court and its attendant

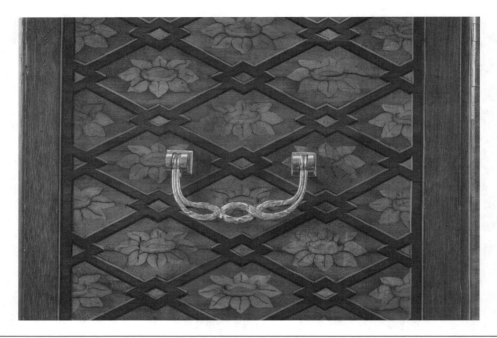

Figure 12.6 Combined jewel casket, *secrétaire*, and writing table, 1106-1882, detail of side handle, gilt bronze. Courtesy of V&A Images/Victoria and Albert Museum.

paraphernalia from one venue to another).[20] Despite his proper caution, however, there is evidence that some furniture was made in this period with the express intention that it should be useful for travel. In 1775, close in date to the design of the V&A *secrétaire*, another was advertised for 200 livres, plainer in its exterior appearance but complex inside,

> of walnut, very well carved, with nine secret drawers, of which one has a false bottom for the storage of papers. It is very appropriate for travel, [with] its legs folding up underneath; it forms a sort of strong box and can serve as a traveling *toilette* with the use of a very convenient mirror.[21]

In the same year, the *marchand mercier* Charles-Raymond Granchez, whose famous shop, Au Petit Dunkerque, was on the Quai de Conti in Paris, advertised "traveling *secrétaires*, in mahogany, which can be taken apart easily and stored in a suitcase, very well made and very convenient," at a price of 432 livres each.[22] In this case, the *secrétaires* were of a highly novel design (such an emphasis on novelty was typical of his business), folding away as they did into a suitcase for full portability.

The V&A *secrétaire* was less complex than Granchez's in the way that it was designed to travel, lacking as it did any possibility of being reduced in volume by the use of clever arrangements of folding parts. However, it is probable that only the heavy upper section, which depends on two people lifting it, was intended to be transported because the top of the table base is veneered (Figure 12.7). The table was therefore designed to be freestanding as well as a support for the larger ensemble, rather than part of the traveling *équipage*, as in the case of both examples cited above and other models produced later by Riesener himself. However, the top of the table is veneered in simple fashion (*bois satiné* within a minimal

Figure 12.7 Combined jewel casket, *secrétaire*, and writing table, 1106-1882, detail, veneered surface of lower section (the writing table). Courtesy of V&A Images/Victoria and Albert Museum.

border), perhaps implying that its capacity to stand alone without the upper section was a relatively minor function.

More important was the function of security and the related one of concealment. Visual clues within furniture about what might be secure and what might be secret worked in a number of different ways. Security was clearly signaled in furniture by the presence of a lock, and this piece has two keyholes that are visible from the outside. The upper lock has lost its escutcheon, which appears (from the residual evidence of its fitting) to have been small, and the lower keyhole is cut into the decorative gilt metal plaque on the frieze of the table's drawer. At present, the V&A has three keys, none of which is thought to be original, each of which opens a different part of the object (lid, fall front, table drawer). One has a decorative, gilded bow and may be nineteenth century, predating the entry of the piece to the V&A's collections. It is possible, as with other pieces in the collection, that one key once operated the whole piece of furniture, though the fact that the upper and lower sections could be separated and could be used in different rooms or different buildings, would suggest that the piece might originally have been supplied with at least two.

The keys for the upper section perform two operations. The first opens the lid (Figure 12.8). The lid is secured by a very high-security lock along the front, with four metal loops (location points) through which the bolt (located behind the metal molding on the top edge of the fall front) can slide. The lid is extremely heavy because it contains so much metalwork, and its weight is supported by a long gilded hinge, which is now (and was probably in the past) under some strain when the lid is folded fully back. Once open, the underside of the lid is seen to be covered in blue-green padded moiré silk. In the body of the piece is a cavity, thickly veneered with grooved tulipwood, which contains two trays, each divided

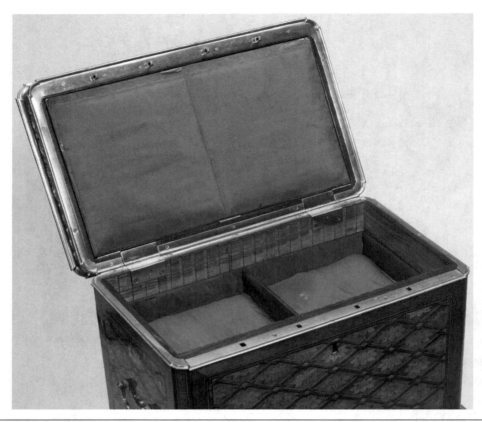

Figure 12.8 Combined jewel casket, *secrétaire*, and writing table, 1106-1882, detail, lid open, one jewelry tray removed. Courtesy of V&A Images/Victoria and Albert Museum.

into two compartments and padded and lined with the same blue-green silk (Figures 12.9 and 12.10). These conform to the usual arrangements for storing jewelry. When the upper tray is lifted out, another removable tray is exposed, as is the grooved tulipwood lining of the large compartment that holds them both. The secret element of this upper section is concealed behind the padded lid. A careful and informed eye might guess at its existence by calculating unused space in the depth of the lid. There is no key; rather, one of the metal loops through which the bolt of the lock slides must be turned, which causes the padded surface to fall down away from the lid exposing a hinged tray with two compartments made in plum-pudding mahogany (*acajou moucheté*) (Figure 12.11). The inner surface of the lid is of waxed solid oak.

The secret compartment in the lid clicks back up into place without the need to repeat the manipulation of the loop that released it (though the loop must be rotated back to its normal position before closing). Only when the lid is open can a second key be used to draw forward the fall front, revealing a set of six drawers. (It is possible that this key and that which opened the lid were originally one and the same.) The fall front becomes a writing and reading surface lined with leather, and the lid can now be lowered (Figure 12.12). The upper left and right drawer fronts are "blind;" that is, they are positioned directly in front of the space used for the two jewel trays, and only the four lower drawers are true drawers, running the depth of the carcase. The space used by these four drawers appears to constitute the

Figure 12.9 Combined jewel casket, *secrétaire*, and writing table, 1106-1882, detail, lid open, two jewelry trays removed, showing grooved surface of tulipwood veneer in the cavity behind the fall front. Courtesy of V&A Images/Victoria and Albert Museum.

Figure 12.10 Combined jewel casket, *secrétaire*, and writing table, 1106-1882, upper jewelry tray. Courtesy of V&A Images/Victoria and Albert Museum.

Figure 12.11 Combined jewel casket, *secrétaire*, and writing table, 1106-1882, detail, secret compartment in the lid revealed. Note the positions of the location points for the lock to the front of the lid. The third of four (left to right) is rotated 90° to release the secret compartment. Courtesy of V&A Images/Victoria and Albert Museum.

full extent of space behind the fall front. Indeed, unless the operator of the furniture knew that there was an unaccounted-for space beneath the lowermost drawers, she or he might not investigate further. However, each of the four lower dustboards (the thin boards under each drawer which act as dividers between the drawers) can be slid forward and removed. The bottom dustboards expose two removable trays in the very lowest cavity within the *secrétaire* (Figures 12.13 and 12.14). The trays are made of plain oak, and each is constructed with fourteen compartments in two rows of seven. There is no clue to their use (there is no evidence, for example, of a fabric lining, which would be a conventional way of fitting out jewel trays; neither is there evidence of wear and tear), and their unusual form may indicate a special commission. The design of this space and its trays, however, is very considered. The contents of the trays could easily be removed by virtue of the downward-curving shape at the center of each of the dividers of the compartments. Also, the tray itself could easily

Figure 12.12 Combined jewel casket, *secrétaire*, and writing table, 1106-1882, with the fall front lowered and the lid closed. Courtesy of V&A Images/Victoria and Albert Museum.

be lifted from the hidden space because all the dustboards could be removed. This allows enough vertical space for the muscles of the hand to flex sufficiently to lift the tray vertically before bringing it forward and out of the depth of the hidden space. (If only the lower two dustboards had been removable, the hand would not be strong enough to manipulate the tray and its contents within the shallow space.)

The table is altogether simpler. A key (the third) opens the central drawer. The only mechanisms are the buttons on the underside of the table, one at each side, which release the side drawers. Inside the proper left-side drawer are the writing fitments: the quill tray, inkwell, and pounce pot (Figure 12.15). The reason for deploying this mechanism, rather than using a lock to open all three drawers simultaneously, was to allow the household staff unmediated access to the writing equipment so that they could maintain and replenish it without needing access to the keys, and by definition, the contents of the furniture. This is a feature typical of both men's and women's writing desks in the eighteenth century, though

Figure 12.13 Combined jewel casket, *secrétaire*, and writing table, 1106-1882, detail of the interior of the upper section with two lower drawers and two of three dustboards removed to reveal the secret tray hidden in the base of the carcase. To the viewer's right is the same arrangement, shown closed because it is now much less easy to remove the dustboards. Courtesy of V&A Images/Victoria and Albert Museum.

Figure 12.14 Combined jewel casket, *secrétaire*, and writing table, 1106-1882, detail of the interior with the secret tray removed. The fixings visible on the left of the photograph hold the side handle in place. Courtesy of V&A Images/Victoria and Albert Museum.

Figure 12.15 Combined jewel casket, *secrétaire*, and writing table, 1106-1882, detail of the right-hand side drawer of the table, fitted out for quills, pounce powder and ink. Courtesy of V&A Images/Victoria and Albert Museum.

possibly more to be found in those made for men, especially the cylinder desk. The locking systems are very secure by virtue of the amount of metal in their makeup, the metalworking skills used in their design, manufacture, and fitting, and the number of positions (eight) at which, when the bolts are thrown, the object is held securely together. The top locks in four places, and the fall front locks at the top edge with a double throw bolt and at each side with a sprung bolt. The table base locks at the center drawer. There are, then, both a series of security points across the piece and a series of relationships between its lockable, hidden, and accessible parts. In some ways, furniture like this is analogous to architecture. Spatially complex furniture worked like small rooms or buildings and is easily subject to being read like them. Indeed, there were moments of overlap in the way architects and furniture designers conceptualized space and routes through it, and others where language connected furniture and architecture. For example, furniture, like rooms, had specialized functions: since the mid-sixteenth century there had been rooms called *cabinets* and a form of furniture called the *cabinet*—each had a specific use, a specific security level within the interior, and a number of possibilities in terms of access.[23] The management of access, rooms, and routes through eighteenth-century buildings was described in comparable language, as Girouard demonstrates. He quotes Mercier's description of the French predilection for small suites of rooms, often arranged around the bedchamber, which hints, perhaps unsurprisingly, at parallel tactics of secret keeping in politics and romance (Mercier's "love, ambition, and politics") within the houses of the elite.

Two hundred years ago no one could have visualized the hidden secret stairs, the little unsuspected cabinets, the false doors which conceal the true exits, the floors which could be made to rise and fall, and the labyrinths in which one can hide and put off inquisitive servants whilst indulging one's tastes—a way out (opening onto the wardrobe of the next-door house) hidden from everyone, except those in the know, but designed to foster the mysteries of love, and sometimes those of politics.[24]

Just as the most complex buildings might be read as labyrinths needing navigation and negotiation, furniture too had a number of tiers, or layers, of vertical and horizontal spaces, and of possible routes: a person approaching a piece of furniture could, from the moment it was opened, follow different paths through its interior. Case furniture had entrances, exits, and doors, including some to storage areas, some with locks, some without. Sometimes a visitor to a piece of furniture found some areas of it locked and therefore inaccessible, while another would pass by a hidden area without even knowing that it existed, and others might guess that there was a hidden space but never fathom the trick—the manual version of "open sesame" that opened it.

Drawing an analogy between a piece of furniture and a miniature room or building particularly illuminates issues of structure, three-dimensionality, and access. For considerations of the shape, function, and the operation of furniture, it is useful to explore the idea of furniture as an extension of the human body, and to consider it particularly in relation to dress. Like furniture designed to protect possessions and secrets, the clothed body had pockets where money and portable possessions, including keys, could safely be kept. Although pockets were, in this period, integral to men's waistcoats, jackets, and coats, women's pockets were separate items of clothing.[25] Such removable pockets may have been to garments what drawers were to furniture. Furniture likewise was sometimes portable, as discussed above. But more than that, furniture was intimately connected with the human body, especially when it was used to store jewelry, which adorned the body and required specific security arrangements, or when it was used for writing, in which case it had to be designed to accommodate the body and to support it in its activity. There can be no doubt that furniture like the V&A *secrétaire* and other small pieces of furniture were highly personal, as were clothes, and that they were designed to fit the form of the clothed body both when it was stationary (sitting to read) or mobile (writing or reaching into the secret compartments).[26] Such issues are central to Mimi Hellman's recent work. She speaks of ways in which "the practice of consumption . . . was visual and kinetic; objects were not simply owned, but *performed*."[27] She goes on to show how the operation of furniture was part of "the work of leisure"—a skill that was privately learned and mastered while necessarily appearing in public to be natural and effortless. The V&A *secrétaire* fits Hellman's description of an object that "simultaneously scripted action and invited manipulation, and could be negotiated effortlessly only through great familiarity, attention, and mastery." The more complex the object, Hellman suggests later, the more complex (and potentially unreadable to the viewer) the script.[28]

The V&A *secrétaire* is a particularly complex piece, in spatial as well as mechanical terms. Some parts of it were designed to operate entirely separately from others. For example, the lid can be opened without causing the fall front to descend, so that jewelry could be removed or replaced by owner or staff without gaining access to any of the symbolic or material effects of writing. And below, in the table, household staff gained easy access to the sides of the table to fulfill their duties of refreshing the writing equipment while the central area of the table, and the casket above, remained inviolate. At the same time, some parts of the piece were designed in relation to each other; the reading of these relationships can either clarify or obscure the visible and hidden spaces within the whole. For example, the blind drawers behind the fall front act as a decoy, diverting attention from the possibility that there were jewel trays stacked in the area just behind them. Depending on who was present, on what the owner of the furniture needed to do at that moment, or even on whether the furniture demanded maintenance in the absence of the owner, the *secrétaire* could be navigated in a number of different ways. Here again, there are analogies with the way that architectural space was understood. Girouard cites Madame de Genlis who described "the infinite multi-plication of rooms, cabinets, above all back exits and secret stairs. Apartments are planned so that all ways of access can be sealed off at will, independence secured as a result, and the surprising discovery of secrets made impossible."[29]

The discovery of secrets was, of course, never an absolute impossibility, and therein lay the significance of the fine line between concealment and exposure, the treading of which seems to have been such a central feature of eighteenth-century social life and gender rela-tions. The investigative fingers of a determined seeker of secrets, informed by a certain familiarity with similar objects and motivated by familial strategies of subterfuge, might probe for spaces disguised by clever cabinetmakers. Here the legibility of furniture was a key to discovering the secret. In the following example, a husband has guessed that his wife's love letters are kept in a box that has a false bottom.

> I knew by its depth . . . that it had to have a false bottom; as a result of looking for the secret, I touched the spring that revealed to me the bottom, which is very deep, and which contained an infinite number of notes and letters from my brother, all express-ing in the most passionate language a love that was shown to be already well advanced, but which employed every imaginable means of seduction.[30]

Thus the unfortunate Monsieur Custine discovered the correspondence between his brother and his wife through his own intuitive ability to understand the possibilities of spatial arrangements and mechanisms for the protection of secrets. His account suggests (as Hellman also argues) a developing capacity to read and talk about furniture, demonstrating a sense of the contemporary legibility of a three-dimensional object.

The potential of the box to conceal its owner's papers from her husband suggests that the function of furniture was as much about articulating a set of household and family relationships as offering the guarantee of protection against any kind of potential assailant. The matter of spousal relations, in particular of clandestine affairs conducted by women who thus gambled with risk, was an oft-visited subject in eighteenth-century French lit-erature and commentary, especially in the form of women's memoirs. Stories of the loves of aristocratic ladies and celebrated actresses especially tantalized and intrigued. The lines between fact and fiction, reporting and dramatization, were often blurred and suggest a real preoccupation with secrecy and the potential for the exposure of illicit behavior. The moment of revelation was of course the high point of such tales. For example, a part-fictive correspondence by Madame Du Noyer between a provincial and a Parisian lady in the early eighteenth century describes a situation in which a key to a secret compartment led to the discovery by a jealous husband of all he had suspected.[31] One of the correspondents recited a story about Don Francisco Benavides, Catalonian captain of Dragoons, who was rarely able to meet his lover, Lady Margarita, in Perpignan. The love affair was thus conducted largely in the form of letters, for an initial period of three years.[32] After a summer together

Don Francisco was again obliged to separate from his *Signora*; the Commerce of Letters recommenced, and continued for Five years, without the Husband's having any
Suspicion; he knew very well she had an Esteem for him, but nothing of their Correspondence, she took her Measures so carefully; but an accident happened had like to
have ruined all.[33]

The affair had lasted a full eight years before this destabilizing event occurred.

The Lady one Evening finding her self so ill, that she thought she should not live an
Hour; in this Condition, her greatest Inquietude was to think after her Death *Don
Francisco's* Letters would be found, wherefore making an attempt in her Weakness,
after desiring her Husband to leave her alone for a few Moments, she arose and burnt
them all, after which she got to Bed again, expecting Death.[34]

However, it was not to be. "When her Health was restored, she received and writ several
others; but one Day going to Mass, and leaving her Keys in her Cabinet, an officious Servant
acquainted her Husband, her Mistress had left her Cabinet open." Inevitably, her husband
"tumbled Things about 'till he found a Letter, which awaked his former Jealousie, and made
his Wife feel the Effects of it."[35] This husband was perhaps unusually lucky to have found his
wife's keys, but also unusually fortunate that his "tumbling about" revealed the letter. Had
this scene been set in France in the later eighteenth century, when furniture tended to be
more complex, the mere appropriation of the key might not have been enough. By that time,
cabinetmakers were proficient in designing secret compartments and internal mechanisms
undetectable to the uninitiated, as well as aspects of furniture mechanics that only worked
fully if the operator knew exactly what he or she was doing. For example, if the fall front of
the V&A *secrétaire* is closed without first turning the key to retract the bolts to each side,
the veneers of the sides of the casket are vulnerable to damage. Furthermore, the secret trays
in the base were very well hidden. With the passing of the *secrétaire* through various hands
during the nineteenth century, their existence became forgotten; they remained undetected
for over a century, and nineteenth-century copies of the piece were made without the secret
spaces within. There was no documentary record of their existence in 1883 when the *secrétaire* was first published in London, nor in 1922 when it was last catalogued. It was the modern conservator, employing Monsieur Custine's methodology of calculating every unit of its
interior space (in his terms its *épaisseur*), who rediscovered the trays during recent research
for a new catalogue of the V&A's collection.

The question of how many, or how few, householders knew how to operate and access
the furniture is an interesting one. As far as this author knows, no written instructions for
French furniture have yet come to light, but there was, presumably, an initiation into the
inner workings of each piece for a new owner, probably in the form of a demonstration.
Once assimilated, that information would naturally have been restricted to its owner and
only the most trusted members of a household. An example drawn from the daybook of
a London firm owned by Benjamin Vulliamy (1747–1811) is suggestive of the possibilities.
When the knowledge of how to operate a piece of furniture owned by William Beckford
(1760–1844) was lost, Vulliamy sent a technician out to resolve the problem of access: "January 8, 1810—For sending a man to Old Cavendish Street to shew Mr. Foxhall how to open
the secret drawers of Mr. Beckford's Cabinet—3 – (i.e., 3 shillings) Mr Foxhall."[36] (Edward
Foxhall was one of Beckford's agents involved with the furnishing of Beckford's celebrated
Fonthill Abbey.)[37] It is not possible at present to identify with certainty the cabinet that was
the subject of this special visit (although a pair of cabinets, made up from an extraordinary

group of panels of Japanese export lacquer and fitted with French locks were supplied by Vulliamy in 1803, and it is tempting to believe that these were the ones referred to in the daybook).³⁸ The account suggests two things: first, that the mechanisms of the secret compartments could not always be remembered so easily or worked out by the uninitiated; and second, that Beckford was not the only individual to possess the knowledge of his furniture's operation. It is interesting also to note that Vulliamy could produce an employee who would know the workings of a piece of furniture supplied perhaps some seven years earlier.

These stories tell us something of the kinds of hazards that formed a part of the narratives of marriages and household life in the most privileged milieux of eighteenth-century Paris. Here the notion of a controlled, semipublic environment within the domestic interior might be useful. It might be argued that most of France's elite society in this period, certainly those based in Paris and at Versailles, lived semipublic lives in many regards, and were involved on a daily basis in navigating the line between private and public knowledge and access. The king's example of publicly performing the ceremonies of the *lever* and the *coucher* set the tone for aristocratic households, and the *toilette* in particular became a semipublic and (sexually) highly charged event involving various props, as Hellman describes.³⁹ Toilet tables concealed complex arrangements of toilet articles, and jewel caskets contained the necessary final adornments (Figures 12.16 and 12.17). Mercier drew attention to the fascination of the contents of the furniture used in the ceremony of the toilette, but also to the management of its witnesses and participants. He explained that a woman prepared and beautified herself through a two-part *toilette*, the first completely private from even her lovers. "The most favored lover, even the most generous," would not dare to violate this rule, he

Figure 12.16 Combined cylinder-top desk and dressing table, attributed to André-Louis Gilbert (1746-1809, *maître ébéniste* 1774, active until 1789), with some marquetry panels attributed to Christophe Wolff (1720–1795, *maître ébéniste* 1755), 1776–1780. V&A 1043-1882, Jones Collection. Carcase of oak with walnut and sycamore, veneered with tulipwood and stained sycamore, and marquetry of holly, stained sycamore, purplewood, holly and ebony, gilt bronze mounts; green leather, glass and porcelain. Height 100 cm, width 83 cm, depth 50 cm. Courtesy of V&A Images/Victoria and Albert Museum.

Figure 12.17 Combined cylinder-top desk and dressing table, 1043-1882, open. Courtesy of V&A Images/Victoria and Albert Museum.

explained. The first *toilette* was a site of mystery and women's secret knowledge: "It is there that mystery puts to use all the cosmetics which embellish the skin, as well as the other preparations that, among women, amount to a separate science."

The second *toilette*, according to Mercier, was "just a game invented by coquetry." To describe it, he translated loosely from Alexander Pope's *Rape of the Lock*:

> The rites begin. The deposit of hidden treasures is opened, where beauty still finds new attractions. From the depths of a thousand little elegant pots emerge a thousand different graces. Pearls, diamonds, children of the sun, lend their lively ornament. The sweet essence of flowers escapes from golden flasks; the air is scented with the perfumes of Arabia. The shell of the tortoise, ivory from the teeth of the elephant, are united and transformed for a single function. Further on are jumbled together powder, pamphlets, ribbons tinged with a thousand colors, rouge, love letters, the epigrams of the day, and an army of pins. . . . Beauty becomes more beautiful.[40]

The ceremony of the *toilette* depended on the skilled work of household staff. The chambermaid was responsible for staging the *toilette* and maintaining the requisite articles and furniture. According to a contemporary source, in addition to her duties vis-à-vis the *menu linge*,

> she is also given the care of all the clothes, suits, jewelry, necklaces, and all the utensils used in the *toilette* and to embellish the lady. . . . Likewise, she ought to know how to set up a toilet table and arrange it as neatly as possible; to make up the lady's bed

and chamber well, and to take care that all the furnishings are always cleaned and arranged as they should be.[41]

The author implies here that the maintenance of the contents of the toilet table (replenishing bottles and containers and cleaning utensils) was the responsibility of the chambermaid. This would entail access to the interior spaces of specially designed furniture, which in many cases was lockable, suggesting that certain household staff habitually had access to keys. In the case of the V&A toilet table/cylinder desk, the person who serviced the toilet articles might also have replenished the ink. However, in the case of the Riesener *secrétaire* (which had no fittings for toilet articles), it is by no means clear who had access to the various layers of secure storage for jewels and whose role it was to retrieve them. Its deepest secrets could have remained inviolate if the upper secret compartment in the lid was left undisturbed when the lid was opened. Similarly, the fall front could have been left open with minimal risk of exposure of the hidden trays. The lack of finish of both the secret compartment in the lid and the hidden trays, all of which are of solid oak with no veneers or textile decoration, implies that these areas were not intended to be viewed in the same way (or by the same people) as the exterior surfaces and inner drawers. Hence the piece had within it the potential for public display, of the furniture itself and of its contents, while continuing to conceal effectively parts of its anatomy and the contents of its most secret places for private use, for storage, retrieval, and reflection.

Semipublic ceremonies within the home were usually dependant on skilled and trustworthy household servants. This raised the complex problem that while householders depended on these skills, the work of domestic servants brought them into contact with valuable possessions and information, access to which was highly privileged. Narratives of loyalty and betrayal were not always predictable. For example, it is tempting to assume that female servants, like the chambermaid who prepared the *toilette,* were uniquely loyal to their mistresses, but in the case of the Perpignan affair, it was the servant who alerted her employer's husband to the opportunity to gain access to her mistress's cabinet, suggesting more open-ended possibilities. If employers were sometimes betrayed by their servants, servants and their property were at risk from both their employers and their fellow workers. For female servants, in addition to the risk attendant on their communal living arrangements, there was also the threat of violation by male householders (the servants were segregated by sex in order to protect female from male servants).

Various perils were thus associated with the sharing of domestic space between householders and servants, and within and across these groups allegiances were based on gender, seniority, and predetermined roles and behavior. Texts about servant–employer relations were permeated with concerns about honesty, loyalty, and appropriateness.[42] Confidentiality was fundamental, as in the case of the responsibilities of the secretary to the male householder: "The title of secretary alerted him sufficiently to the fact that he ought to protect inviolably the privacy of what he learned, either by reading letters or by the orders he received to respond to them."[43] Advice to employers was unsurprisingly skeptical about servants' honesty.

A maid, believing herself to be underpaid or lacking in fact some of what is necessary for her maintenance, diverts each day a little bit of the money that passes through her hands, without her mistress noticing it; a servant, having not been paid the wages that were promised him, appropriates for himself some linen or some other furnishings to pay himself secretly.[44]

The potential threats to security presented by domestic staff were paralleled by those posed by visitors to the household. Social and business visitors to the household were many and varied, ranging from notaries and lawyers to the plethora of suppliers of fresh food and provisions, the visits of tailors and milliners, and the deliveries of a range of luxury goods. Within such an environment, in which privacy in the modern sense was exceptional, family members, household staff, and even visitors had fairly flexible access to many rooms within the interior. Furniture had a capacity to provide small secure spaces within larger ones: desks or cabinets within salons and boudoirs could be locked even when the room was not. In these large households there was some degree of risk that the permeability of this environment would allow for the passing on of secret information from within the household to the outside world. Consider, for example, the duties of the intendant of a grand household, whose "loyalty should extend even to maintaining its privacy assiduously so as not to let the master's affairs be known outside [the household]."[45]

Furniture, then, played an important protective role within the eighteenth-century household whose harmony appears to have been dependent on ideals of trust and confidentiality. In this context, the security of an object like the V&A *secrétaire* was perhaps almost entirely about security within the interior. It might, of course, have been stolen in its entirety from its room or while it was traveling, or the wood might be broken open by any determined thief or highwayman. An intruder from outside the household intent on stealing money or jewelry was surely unlikely to ask himself where a key might be found to open the object without damaging it, or to proceed to open its interior spaces with any well-informed sense of how it might work. Rather, lockable furniture in grand domestic interiors must, to a large degree, have been designed to protect items of value from other members of a household and from visitors to the house, rather than from unknown outsiders to the householder's social milieu.

In the semipublic environment of the busy household, the question of the degree of agency that might be ascribed to a three-dimensional, operable object is an interesting one.[46] This question is by no means limited to ancien regime France. The English metalworking trades (and precision trades such as clockmaking) were highly sophisticated and led Europe in the seventeenth century. A seventeenth-century English door lock made by John Wilkes (d. 1733) of Birmingham, for example, had both the surveillance system and a surveyor himself built into the design (Figure 12.18).[47]

Not only did the male figure on the left move to expose the keyhole (via the movement of his leg) it counted each successful use of the key to open the door. Such locks were extremely rare, though fascinating in their suggestion of the role of the lock both in monitoring and documenting access, and in standing in and acting for the holder of the key. The lock stood in for him or her (other Wilkes locks were made expressly for female customers);[48] it later spoke to its owner, through the record of its counter, of the number of attempts to open the door in his or her absence. Here, the designer of the mechanism created, with enormous intellectual and manual skill, a system that operated with remarkable precision and autonomy. The Wilkes locks were remarkably autonomous, what Mercier might have termed, as he did eighteenth-century French locks, *serrures savantes*.[49] In eighteenth-century France, high-performance locks and mechanisms were thus empowered actors in the drama and performance of safeguarding spaces and possessions, discouraging the illicit use of keys, and acting as guardians of protected spaces even when the house or key holder was absent.

Some pieces of furniture might be considered to have similar agency and to speak of illicit access, even violation. A writing table made in Paris in the mid-1760s, for example,

Figure 12.18 Detector or indicating lock and key, about 1680, made by John Wilkes (d. 1733) of Birmingham, England. Brass and engraved steel. V&A M.109-1926. Courtesy of V&A Images/Victoria and Albert Museum.

has a simple lock but a highly sophisticated internal mechanism that announces any breach of its security (Color Plate 15, see color insert after page 118; and Figures 12.19 through 12.23).[50] When the table is opened with a key (via the keyhole at the center of the small central drawer), the drawer can be pulled forward (Figure 12.20 shows this operation from beneath). As it moves, the drawer trips a mechanism that releases the entire interior unit of the table in a fixed position under the tabletop. As soon as this mechanism is released, a powerful metal spring at the back of the interior of the table, directly behind the drawer, then propels the internal unit forward (Figure 12.21). It is prevented from exiting the table's carcase by two rods that are attached to the inside of the back of the table and at their other ends to the back of the inner unit. As the unit moves forward, it engages a cog-driven mechanism in each side of the table which causes the top to roll back simultaneously (Figure 12.22 shows the cog on one side of the inside of the carcase of the table).[51] This series of actions takes place simultaneously, with a burst of noise and surprisingly forcefully. Even in these terms, the smooth operation of the piece might then, as now, have required some maintenance and skilled intervention to keep it running smoothly.[52] As Hellman argues, to make the sometimes loud, sudden, and uneven movement of these mechanical pieces seem elegant and controlled would have been challenging; the springs would have been as violent then as they are now, and the movements consequently often fierce.

Figure 12.19 Mechanical writing table, stamped in the workshop of Jean-François Oeben (1721-1763, *maître ébéniste* 1761), Paris, ca. 1760. V&A 1095-1882, Jones Collection. Carcase and drawer of oak; veneered with tulipwood, sycamore, holly and other woods, (white metal) steel springs and mechanisms; gilt bronze mounts, purple velvet and silk. Height 68.3 cm, width 72.5 cm, depth 37 cm. Courtesy of V&A Images/Victoria and Albert Museum.

Figure 12.20 Mechanical writing table, 1095-1882, view from underneath, showing the movement of the central drawer forward. The steel plate on the underside of the carcase runs from the latch (also steel) to the back of the drawer. When the bottom of the small drawer (shown with the key in the lock) is pulled forward, it runs over and depresses the latch that holds the table closed. When depressed, the whole internal unit of the table springs forward. Courtesy of V&A Images/Victoria and Albert Museum.

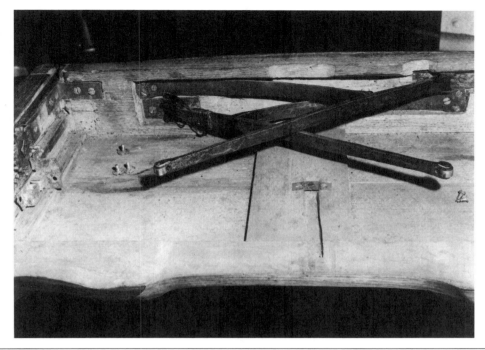

Figure 12.21 Mechanical writing table, 1095-1882, detail showing two steel springs on the interior wall at the back of the table. The oak carcase has been cut away so that when the table is closed, the springs are forced by the close fit of the internal drawer unit to lie flush with the back wall of the table. Courtesy of V&A Images/Victoria and Albert Museum.

Figure 12.22 Mechanical writing table, 1095-1882, detail of the cog fitted to the proper right side wall of the table (the internal unit and tabletop removed). Courtesy of V&A Images/Victoria and Albert Museum.

Once open, the table reveals the arrangement of its interior space. It contains a writing or reading surface at the center, flanked on each side by a compartment with a hinged lid that opens away from the center (Color Plate 15, see color insert after page 118). The reading slope can be raised at an angle. The final trick to the piece, and that which demonstrates its ability to speak of its condition, lies in the concealed square frame of metal that runs around the edge of the drawer bottom (Figure 12.23). Unless this is pulled forward at the same time as the reading slope is gently lowered, the slope will not descend. Without knowledge of this metal frame and its mechanism, therefore, the table cannot be closed because the slope cannot be folded down in order to push the interior unit back under the tabletop (when successfully closed, the table would fix itself in place with a click). If opened by anyone who did not understand the table and have experience with its mechanisms, it would stand open, refusing to acquiesce to its intruder and fold away quietly.

So what can we make of this evidence of the way furniture was designed and operated, and the way eighteenth-century men and women thought and wrote about secrets? What might be the intellectual key to understanding what was at stake and how the work of locksmiths related to the experience of their clients and to the wider discourse on secrets, including the excitement of their exposure, especially as represented in journals and memoirs? Karma Lochrie, in her book on medieval uses of secrecy, poses the question of whether the secret or its technology is more important.[53] Her question opens a fascinating line of thought in relation to eighteenth-century French mechanisms and their cultural significance. Might it be argued that despite the real issues of protecting objects and papers of value, the performance of secrecy, including its complex mechanical technologies, played as important a social role? Or is it a mistake to see the secret and its technology as separate and

Figure 12.23 Mechanical writing table, 1095-1882, detail showing the metal frame on the underside of the drawer unit, which controls the lowering of the reading slope. Courtesy of V&A Images/Victoria and Albert Museum.

independent of one another? In furniture terms, is it valid to ask whether the love letter or the jewel was more important socially than the mechanical security system that protected it? And is the jewel so very different from the love letter (as implied earlier in this essay when a distinction was made between items of symbolic and economic worth)? A love letter was defined as a secret, but might it not have been in part the fact that a jewel was concealed that made it the object of speculation and fascination?

To see the secret and its security system as part of the same unit of production of meaning, that is, to ignore questions of economic value and focus rather on the cultural and social value of the *idea* of secrecy instead, is to return to the paradox implied when something of value becomes a secret, rather than simply an item of economic value. In Lochrie's words, "the paradoxical properties of secrecy [are] that it implies its own revelation."[54] The implication here is that the secret becomes indistinguishable from its technology or its performance: the act or process of its concealment and/or exposure, that which changes its state from concealed to exposed or *vice versa*. The content of the secret itself then becomes part of a bigger picture, in which it may have its own distinct value, but the greater value, or the full narrative of the secret, includes the technology by which it is concealed (or exposed). The first evidence of the implied revelation might be the escutcheon, the sign of the paradox. The viewer might never have known the precise nature of the secret within, but simply have seen the possibility that a secret that might be known was concealed inside the object. In signaling that there might be a secret within, the escutcheon brought into play the question of how to negotiate the security system protecting it. One option for an intruder was to use intuitive skills, which might result in the infliction of bodily harm by the lock itself; another was to use intellectual skills, as M. Custine did so successfully.

Thinking about the full narrative of the secret works well for eighteenth-century French furniture and its contents. Not only does it allow for the inclusion of the technological and performative aspect of the otherwise static object, it also admits the apparent ambivalence toward certain kinds of secrecy in eighteenth-century French mores. Eighteenth-century French attitudes toward the concealment and exposure of secrets were complex and ambiguous. Consider, for example, the meaning of the exposure of a clandestine affair in a culture in which the extramarital relationships of the king assumed, as Colin Jones writes, "quasi-institutional status,"[55] and within which the sexual and political affairs of men and women were disclosed and discussed in published diaries, memoirs, and correspondences, and sometimes even in popular prints, as a form of spectacle and entertainment.

Alongside this very particular set of conditions around eighteenth-century French attitudes toward secrecy was a parallel expectation within specific social groups that the lives of certain figures or groups would be led in a semipublic environment, and that artifice might legitimately be employed to manage that environment. Secrets were often *public* within certain groups: alongside the currency of information about clandestine affairs, the existence of diplomatic secrets was known within particular circles across national boundaries even if the precise content of the secret was not. In the case of the famous Chevalier d'Eon, owner of the metal safe with secret locks, not only was the secret of his sexuality a public affair, he also played the intriguing role of traveling spy.[56] The concealment of identity was an ambiguous affair, especially as it was played out at the masked ball where participants were invited to disguise, lightly, their own identities, speculate about those of others, and capitalize on the temporarily altered rules of social interaction. The existence of the secret and its technology was central in these situations; the recognition of the deception was inseparable from the deception itself. The notion of traveling incognito was another fully accepted strategy for appearing differently in public, on a temporary basis, than convention would otherwise dictate.[57] For example, the archduke Paul, son of Catherine the Great, and his new wife Maria Feodorovna traveled incognito through parts of Europe in 1782, under the pseudonyms of the comte and comtesse du Nord. Though little about their visit was truly private or secret in the modern sense, by traveling incognito they avoided the full formalities and protocol of an official visit to Versailles. "The formalities of etiquette are painful and tiring for the princes," noted one of their traveling companions.[58] Their long voyage across Europe represented something of a public spectacle, blurring the distinctions between formal and informal, official and unofficial identities, suggesting that in this very particular social and political arena, strategies of public negotiation of a rigid system of protocol and etiquette might subvert the system itself in socially and politically acceptable ways.

On a domestic level, the performance of secrecy seems to have been built into daily practices, timetables, and relationships. For example, combining the functions of writing and the *toilette* in a single piece of furniture suggests that writing and beauty had something in common. This may simply have been a matter of expedience, given that writing often took place in the same space as the *toilette*, though it was less tied to the daily schedule of the *levée*. However, the processes of writing and beautifying the face were both secretive technologies, processes of controlling concealment and exposure. Women chose, within certain conventions, what of themselves they made visible and public through both letter writing and preparing their faces for view. Note how crucial to the more public part of the *toilette* was the first part, described by Mercier in terms of secrecy and mystery. Without these secrets, the second part could not have been pulled off successfully as a highly controlled performance of what was essentially a process of clever disguise and deception.

These examples suggest that eighteenth-century French society had a particular capacity for creating secrets and engaging with the technologies through which they were defined. In a number of ways, Parisian society especially appears to have been enormously at ease with the concepts of artifice, disguise, and trickery. Mercier believed that "the political scientist could judge political and private morals by the configuration of locks: the more complicated they are, the more these peoples would be dominated by ruse and artifice."[59] If the physical technologies of secrecy within the domestic sphere were largely locks, keys, and mechanisms, their configuration was, paradoxically, dependably secure technologically, yet, at the same time, susceptible to violation through human carelessness, theft, or guesswork. Despite the fact that locks and keys were almost infinitely complicated in design, they were not unfailing in their security. Mechanisms were in reality more risky. The *épaisseur*, or space for secret compartments, could be calculated by analytical observation; false bottoms were repeatedly built in the same position, into the floors of the upper sections of fall front *secrétaires*; and the possibilities for installing secret buttons in new undetectable positions were limited. These limitations made secrets vulnerable and the keeping of them something of a gamble because built into their technology was the possibility, even inevitability, of exposure.[60] But these were not simply practical systems: the furniture tells of eighteenth-century attempts to resolve on the one hand the problems of living in social conditions in which domestic security was a widespread concern to both men and women, and on the other, possibilities for games of risk and pleasure that were played out both within the spaces of domestic and formal interiors and in the imaginary and documentary spaces of various forms of literature.

If this interpretation is valid, it seems that French furniture made in the second half of the eighteenth century was rather more complicated than most histories allow. Rather than these objects simply being part of a linear progression toward more specialized function in furniture, toward the design of smaller more mobile objects that could be used more flexibly, and part of a development of writing furniture forms in particular, as most furniture history would have us believe, they must also be read as having had the potential to be active players on the domestic stage. Moreover, rather than prompting questions of secrecy and security only at a mechanical level, the survival of this kind of furniture raises a much broader set of questions about relationships between bodies and objects, about objects and agency, and about the possibilities for ruse and artifice in Parisian society of the eighteenth century.

ACKNOWLEDGMENTS

I am indebted for their advice on this research to Katie Scott, who first invited me to speak on this topic at the Frank Davis memorial lecture series at the Courtauld Institute of Art, London, in November 2001, and to Dena Goodman for a series of fascinating conversations about writing furniture. I would also like to thank my colleagues at the Victoria and Albert Museum (V&A), especially those in the Arts and Humanities Research Council (AHRC) Centre for the Study of the Domestic Interior, and the students of the V&A/Royal College of Art (RCA) M.A. course in the History of Design and Material Culture for seminar conversations about the *secrétaire* discussed in this paper.

Notes

1. An increasing number of such catalogs of public collections of eighteenth-century French furniture have been published. These include Carl Christian Dauterman, *The Wrightsman Collection* (New York: Metropolitan Museum of Art, 1970); Geoffrey de Bellaigue, *The James A. de Rothschild Collection at Waddesdon Manor; Furniture, Clocks and Gilt Bronzes*, 2 vols. (Fribourg: Published for the National Trust by Office du Livre, 1974); Alan Phipps Darr et al., *The Dodge Collection of Eighteenth-Century French and English Art in the Detroit Institute of Arts* (New York: Hudson Hills Press in association with the Detroit Institute of Arts, 1996); *The Frick Collection, an Illustrated Catalogue*, vol. 6: *French Furniture and Gilt Bronzes* (New York and Princeton, NJ: Princeton University Press, 1968); Peter Hughes, *The Wallace Collection Catalogue of Furniture* (London: Trustees of the Wallace Collection, 1996). For the most concentrated focus on construction in eighteenth-century furniture, see Lucy Wood, *Lady Lever Art Gallery: Catalogue of Commodes* (London: Seven Hills Books, 1994).

2. The collection of eighteenth-century French fine and decorative arts bequeathed to the V&A (then the South Kensington Museum) in 1882 by John Jones has been shown closed since it was first displayed in 1883 (see introductory essay in Sargentson et al., *Catalogue of French Furniture 1640–1800 in the Victoria and Albert Museum* (London: Victoria and Albert Museum, forthcoming). This style of display is often a pragmatic response on the part of museums to the need both to protect the contents of an object from theft or damage and to prevent the fading of woods and other organic and dyed materials on the inside from the light damage that has already altered so dramatically the appearance of the external veneers of French furniture. However, the Wallace Collection (London), and the Musée du Louvre (Paris) have annual "open furniture" programs; in 2005 the J. Paul Getty Museum (Los Angeles) offered tours of the French decorative arts collection demonstrating the mechanical furniture. Such programs are rare opportunities for visitors to see clearly the colors and workings of the interiors of French furniture.

3. Louis-Sébastien Mercier, *Tableau de Paris*, ed. Jean-Claude Bonnet (Paris: Mercure de France, 1994), 2:1055.

4. For debates around court culture, see especially Norbert Elias, *The Court Society*, trans. Edmund Jephcott (Oxford: Blackwell, 1983). On furniture and interiors, see most recently Katie Scott, *The Rococo Interior: Decoration and Social Spaces in Early Eighteenth-Century Paris* (New Haven, CN: Yale University Press, 1995); Mark Girouard, *Life in the French Country House* (London: Cassell, 2000). On cabinet-makers specializing in the design of furniture with special mechanisms, see Rosemary Stratmann, "Design and Mechanisms in the Furniture of Jean-François Oeben," *Furniture History* 9 (1973): 110–13; S. de Plas, *Les Meubles à transformation et à secret* (Paris: G. Le Prat, 1975); and the literature on the cabinetmaker David Roentgen, which includes Hans Huth, *Roentgen Furniture: Abraham and David Roentgen, European Cabinet-Makers* (London: Sotheby Parke Bernet, 1974); and Fabian Dietrich, *Roentgenmöbel aus Neuwied: Leben und Werk von Abraham und David Roentgen* (Bad Neustadt: Internationale Akademie für Kunstwissenschaften, 1986).

5. On these institutions, including the locksmiths guild, see René de Lespinasse and François Bonnardot eds., *Les Métiers et communautés de la ville de Paris. XIIIe siècle. Le Livre des metiers d'Etienne Boileau* (Paris: Imprimerie Nationale, 1879); and René de Lespinasse, *Les Métiers et corporations de la ville de Paris, XIVe–XVIIIe siècle* (Paris: Imprimerie Nationale, 1886–97), vol. 2.

6. J. R. Harris, "Michael Alcock and the Transfer of Birmingham Technology to France before the Revolution," *Journal of European Economic History* 15 (1986): 7–57. For a summary account of the importation of English metal goods including tools and clock parts, see Carolyn Sargentson, *Merchants and Luxury Markets: The Marchands Merciers of Eighteenth-Century Paris* (London and Malibu: Victoria and Albert Museum in association with the J. Paul Getty Museum, 1996), 113–26.

7. Mercier, *Tableau de Paris*, 2: 1054–55.

8. Ibid., 2: 1054.

9. Ibid.

10. The collecting literature on locks is large. See, e.g., Vincent J. M. Eras, *Locks and Keys throughout the Ages* (Amsterdam: H. H. Fronczek, 1957); Eric Monk, *Keys, Their History and Collection* (Aylesbury: Shire Publications, 1974); *Antique Locks* (Staffordshire: Josiah Parkes and Son, 1955); Charles Curtil-Boyer, *L'Histoire de la clef, de l'époque romaine au XVIIIème siècle* (Paris: Vilo, 1968): Jacqueline Du Pasquier, ed., *La clef et la serrure*, exhibition catalog (Bordeaux: Musée des Arts Décoratifs, 1973); John Charles Robinson, ed., *Catalogue of the Special Exhibition of Works of Art of the Mediaeval, Renaissance and More Recent Periods on Loan at the South Kensington Museum, June 1862 (Section 27, Locks, Keys &c in Wrought Iron)* (London: George E. Eyre and William Spottiswoode for H.M.S.O., 1862); *Keys and Locks in the Collection of the Cooper-Hewitt Museum* (New York: Smithsonian Institution's National Museum of Design, 1987); and Alessandro Cesati and Roberto Bigano, *Clavis: Keys, Locks, Coffers from the Conforti Collection*, trans. Beryl Stockman and Norman Denis (Milan: Franco Maria Ricci, 1992). Seventeenth- and eighteenth-century manuals and treatises on the arts of the locksmith range from Mathurin Jousse, *La Fidelle ouverture de l'art du serrurier* (La Flèche: G. Griveau, 1627) to Henri-Louis Duhamel de Monceau, *L'art du serrurier* (Paris: L. F. Delatour, 1767).

11. Letter from Chevalier d'Eon de Beaumont to Monsieur de Vergennes, January 20, 178? [sic], cited in Henry Havard, *Dictionnaire de l'ameublement et de la décoration depuis le XIIIe siècle jusqu'à nos jours*, 4 vols. (Paris: Quantin, 1887–1890), 1: 875.

12. *Journal de France*, December 22, 1784, cited in Havard, *Dictionnaire de l'ameublement*, 4: 965.

13. "Lock with mechanism that grasps with two claws the fist of anyone who opens it with a false key, and which at the same time releases the trigger of a pistol." Catalog no. 26 in the collection of the Conservatoire des Arts et Métiers (Paris); see Arthur Jules Morin, *Catalogue des Collections* (Paris: Guivaudet and Jouaust, 1855), 70.

14. Mercier, *Tableau de Paris*, 2: 1054.

15. Ibid., 2: 101.

16. *Annonces, affiches et avis divers*, March 2, 1767 and September 1, 1768, cited in Havard, *Dictionnaire de l'ameublement*, 4: 965.

17. William Maskell, *Handbook of the Jones Collection in the South Kensington Museum* (London: Chapman and Hall, 1883).

18. For a brief history of the V&A's furniture collecting, see "Furniture Collecting at the Victoria and Albert Museum," in Christopher Wilk, ed., *Western Furniture: 1350 to the Present Day in the Victoria and Albert Museum* (London: P. Wilson, 1996), 9–24.

19. Oliver Brackett, *Catalogue of the Jones Collection* (London: H.M.S.O., 1930), 14 (no. 37), Plate 24.

20. Girouard, *Life in the French Country House*, 163–96.

21. *Annonces, affiches et avis divers*, May 22, 1775, cited in Havard, *Dictionnaire de l'ameublement*, 4: 926.

22. *Mercure de France*, January 1775; cited in Havard, *Dictionnaire de l'ameublement*, 4: 930. On Granchez's shop see Sargentson, *Merchants and Luxury Markets*, 119–27.

23. For a survey of the cabinet (room), see Girouard, *Life in the French Country House*; for a pictorial survey of the cabinet (furniture), see Monique Riccardi-Cubitt, *The Art of the Cabinet* (London: Thames and Hudson, 1992).

24. Mercier, *Tableau de Paris*, 1: 390; cited in Girouard, *Life in the French Country House*, 148–49 (his translation).

25. A research project on "Pockets of History" at Winchester School of Art, University of Southampton, is currently looking at the history of women's tie-on pockets. See http://www.wsa.soton.ac.uk/research/research-projects/the-ahrb-pockets-of-history-project.asp.

26. For a discussion of the relationships between dress, body, and furniture, see Carolyn Sargentson, "Working at Home in Eighteenth-Century Paris: The History of the *Bureau Plat* and the Duc de Choiseul's writing desks," in *French Art in the Huntington Collection*, ed. Shelley Bennett and Carolyn Sargentson (New Haven, CT: Yale University Press, forthcoming).

27. Mimi Hellman, "Furniture, Sociability, and the Work of Leisure in Eighteenth-Century France," *Eighteenth Century Studies* 32 (summer 1999): 417. Hellman uses architectural historian Mark Wrigley's term "prosthetic" to define eighteenth-century French furniture as "an artificial extension of the body" (ibid., 430, n. 33).

28. Ibid., 422, 428.

29. Madame de Genlis, *Dictionnaire critique et raisonné des étiquettes de la cour* (1818); cited in Girouard, *Life in the French Country House*, 149 (his translation).

30. Madame de Genlis, *Mémoires* (1825); cited in Havard, *Dictionnaire de l'ameublement*, 927.

31. Madame du Noyer, *Letters from a Lady at Paris to a Lady at Avignon: Containing a Partikular Account of the City, the Politiks, Intrigues, Gallantry, and Secret History of Persons on the First Quality in France* (London: W. Mears and J. Browne, 1716), Letter XVII, from Thoulouse [sic], 188–211. On the ambiguous nature of this published correspondence, see Alain Nabarra, "Correspondances réelles, correspondances fictives: Les lettres historiques et galantes de Mme Dunoyer ou 'la rocambole' d'un 'petit badinage établi d'abord pour le plaisir,'" in *Femmes en toutes lettres: Les epistolières du XVIIIe siècle*, ed. Marie-France Silver and Marie-Laure Girou Swiderski, *SVEC* (Oxford: Voltaire Foundation, 2000), 7–22. I am indebted to Dena Goodman for this reference.

32. Du Noyer, *Letters from a Lady at Paris*, 201: "During three Years absence they continued writing extraordinary fine letters, some of which I have seen, full of noble Sentiments."

33. Ibid., 202–3.

34. Ibid., 203.

35. Ibid.

36. Public Record Office, London, Vulliamy papers, Daybook 33, C104/58 Pt 2, p. 153. I am extremely grateful to Roger Smith for kindly providing this reference.

37. Clive Wainwright, *The Romantic Interior: The British Collector at Home, 1750–1850* (New Haven, CT: Yale University Press, 1989), 120.

38. See Hugh Roberts, "Beckford, Vulliamy and Old Japan," *Apollo* n.s. 124 (October 1986): 338–41. These panels once formed what is now called the "Buys box," made in Japan in the 1630s for high-ranking officials of the Dutch East Indies Company.

39. Hellman, "Furniture, Sociability, and the Work of Leisure," 427.

40. Mercier, *Tableau de Paris*, 1: 1364–66. The passage is drawn from Canto 1, v. 121–44 of Pope's *Rape of the Lock* (1714).

41. [Audiger], *La Maison Reglée et l'art de diriger la maison d'un grand Seigneur & autres, tant a la ville qu'à la campagne, & le devoir de tous les Officiers, & autres domestiques en general . . .* (1692), in Alfred Franklin, *La vie privée d'autrefois: arts et métiers, modes, moeurs, usages des Parisiens du XIIe au XVIIIe siècle* (Paris: Plon, Nourrit et cie, 1898), 294–303.

42. See Sarah Maza, *Servants and Masters in Eighteenth-Century France* (Princeton, NJ: Princeton University Press, 1983); Cissie Fairchilds, *Domestic Enemies: Servants and their Masters in Old Régime France* (Baltimore, MD: Johns Hopkins University Press, 1984); Jean-Pierre Gutton, *Domestiques et serviteurs dans la France de l'Ancien Régime* (Paris: Aubier Montaigne, 1981). On household relations in the context of community, see David Garrioch, *Neighbourhood and Community in Paris, 1740–1790* (Cambridge: Cambridge University Press, 1986).

43. Audiger, *La Maison Reglée*, in Franklin, *La vie privée d'autrefois*, 303.

44. Ibid., 259.
45. Ibid., 294–303.
46. For a discussion of the agency and action of art objects, see Alfred Gell, *Art and Agency: An Anthropological Theory* (Oxford: Clarendon Press, 1998).
47. See Peter Phillips, "Historical Locks," *Security Surveyor* 1 (September 1971): 58–62; W. W. Watts, "English Brass Locks of the XVII Century," *Country Life* 65 (May 12, 1928): 705–7; and Margaret Jourdain, "English Locks of the Eighteenth Century," *Country Life* 101 (January 3, 1947): 71–75. For a video clip of the lock working, see www.vam.ac.uk/collections/british_galls/video/wilkes/broadband.html (accessed September 2005).
48. One lock exhibited at a meeting at the Archeological Institute in Norwich in 1847, was inscribed: "Who they are ye come by stealth to impare my Lady's wealth," (Phillips, "Historical Locks," 59).
49. Mercier, *Tableau de Paris*, 2: 1055.
50. V&A accession number 1095-1882, in Sargentson et al., *Catalogue of French Furniture*.
51. For a fuller discussion of the working of this piece, and of its place in the development of the technology of this table type, see Sargentson et al., *Catalogue of French Furniture*.
52. See, for example, a table by Jean-François Oeben (1721–1763) in the J. Paul Getty Museum (Los Angeles), which has a handle that needs turning in order to wind up the internal mechanism (Charissa Bremer-David, *Decorative Arts: An Illustrated Summary Catalogue of the Collections of the J. Paul Getty Museum* [Malibu: J. Paul Getty Museum, 1993], accession number 70.DA.84). I am indebted to Gillian Wilson, Charissa Bremer-David, and Brian Considine for showing me this table in both its operational and dismantled states. See Sargentson et al., *Catalogue of French Furniture* for a full comparison of the mechanisms of the two tables and others of this type.
53. Karma Lochrie, *Covert Operations: The Medieval Uses of Secrecy* (Philadelphia: University of Pennsylvania Press, 1999).
54. Ibid., 1.
55. Colin Jones, *Madame de Pompadour: Images of a Mistress* (London: National Gallery, 2002).
56. Anna Clark, "The Chevalier d'Eon and Wilkes: Masculinity and Politics in the Eighteenth Century," *Eighteenth-Century Studies* 32 (fall 1998): 19–48.
57. My thanks to Pamela Smith for suggesting this line of inquiry.
58. Henriette Louise d'Oberkirch, *Mémoires de la Baronne d'Oberkirch sur la cour de Louis XVI et la société française avant 1789*, ed. Suzanne Burkard (Paris: Mercure de France, 1970), 156. Louis XVI and Marie Antoinette threw a relatively small-scale dinner, followed by a concert in the Salon des Paix. "The chateau was lit up as on days of *grand appartement*. There was the royal family, the Russian court, and the great charges of the Crown," (156–57). Despite the great fêtes in Paris and the grand receptions by the princes of the blood at Sceaux, La Bagatelle, and Chantilly (the prince de Condé organized the performance of a Gluck opera, a hunt by torchlight, and fireworks for a party of "one hundred fifty people and with three times as many servants, at least, not including those of the prince," 201–7), the royal guests were free to make private visits to city sites.
59. Mercier, *Tableau de Paris*, 2: 1054.
60. For a discussion of eighteenth-century French gambling (though not aspects of its material culture), see Thomas M. Kavanagh, *Enlightenment and the Shadows of Chance: The Novel and the Culture of Gambling in Eighteenth-Century France* (Baltimore, MD: Johns Hopkins University Press, 1993); and "The Libertine's Bluff: Cards and Culture in Eighteenth-Century France," *Eighteenth-Century Studies* 33 (summer 2000): 507. I am grateful to Deborah Silverman, who led me to consider aspects of secret keeping in relation to themes of risk taking, games, and pleasure.

Contributors

Donna Bohanan is Professor of History at Auburn University. Her most recent book, *Crown and Nobility in Early Modern France*, was published by Palgrave Macmillan in 2001. She is currently working with notary inventories of estates to explore consumption patterns among noble families in the French province of Dauphiné. She is particularly interested in how the contents and decorative schemes of aristocratic houses helped to define social position.

Natacha Coquery is a lecturer in Early Modern History at the University of Tours (France), whose work focuses on the luxury and semiluxury market in eighteenth-century Paris. She is the author of *L'hôtel aristocratique: le marché du luxe à Paris au XVIIIe siècle* (Publications de la Sorbonne, 1998) and the co-editor of several books, including most recently, *Marchands et consommateurs: les mutations de l'Europe moderne. Angleterre, France, Italie, Pays-Bas* (Presses Universitaires François-Rabelais, 2006).

Madeleine Dobie is the author of *Foreign Bodies: Gender, Language and Culture in French Orientalism* (Stanford University Press, 2001), and of articles on eighteenth-, nineteenth-, and twentieth-century French and Francophone literature and culture. She is Associate Professor of French at Columbia University. Her current book project is titled *Trading Places: Colonialism, Slavery and Eighteenth-Century French Culture*.

Dena Goodman is Professor of History and Women's Studies at the University of Michigan. Her publications include *The Republic of Letters: A Cultural History of the French Enlightenment* (Cornell University Press, 1994), and *Marie-Antoinette: Writings on the Body of a Queen* (Routledge, 2003). She is currently engaged in a project on letter writing, material culture, and the female subject in eighteenth-century France.

Mimi Hellman teaches art history at Skidmore College in Saratoga Springs, New York. Her work focuses on the intersection of material culture and social formation in eighteenth-century France and has been published in *Eighteenth-Century Studies*, *SVEC*, and *Gastronomica: A Journal of Food and Culture*. She is currently completing a book on the architecture and interior design of the hôtel de Soubise, an aristocratic residence in Paris.

David Jaffee is Professor of History at the City College of New York and the Graduate Center, City University of New York (CUNY). He is the author of *People of the Wachusett: Greater New England in History and Memory, 1630-1860* (Cornell University Press, 1999) and the visual editor of *Who Built America? Working People and the Nation's Politics, Economy, and Culture* (Bedford Books), which is in its third edition. He is currently completing a book titled *Craftsmen and Consumer in Early America, 1760–1860*.

Ann Smart Martin is Chipstone Professor in the Art History Department, University of Wisconsin, Madison. She researches Early American decorative arts and material culture and directs the interdisciplinary Material Culture Program. Her book, *Buying into the World of Goods: Early Consumers in the Virginia Backcountry,* will be published by Johns Hopkins University Press in 2007.

Kathryn Norberg is Associate Professor in the Department of History at the University of California, Los Angeles. She is the author of *Rich and Poor in Grenoble* (University of California Press, 1984) and articles on Old Regime French social history. From 2000 through 2005, she served as coeditor of *Signs: Journal of Women in Culture and Society.* She is finishing a book on prostitution in France between 1620 and 1740.

Chaela Pastore received her Ph.D. in History from the University of California, Berkeley, in 2001. She now lives with her family in San Diego, California, where she continues her research and writing.

David Porter teaches English and Comparative Literature at the University of Michigan. He is the author of *Ideographia: The Chinese Cipher in Early Modern Europe* (Stanford University Press, 2001) and several articles on chinoiserie and the Chinese taste. He is currently completing a book on the reception and assimilation of Chinese aesthetic ideas in eighteenth-century England.

Mary Salzman received her Ph.D. in Art History from Stanford University. She is currently Visiting Assistant Professor of Art History at the University of Missouri-Columbia. She studies the rococo and eighteenth-century genre scenes as manifestations of Enlightenment knowledge. Her research interests include rococo ornament and the natural sciences; irony in eighteenth-century art and literature; the discursive role of decoration; representations of the urban environment; text–image relationships; and the art of the comic book.

Carolyn Sargentson is Head of Research at the Victoria and Albert Museum. Her field of specialization is seventeenth- and eighteenth-century French furniture, and she is currently completing a major catalog of the museum's French furniture from the period 1640 to 1800. She published *Merchants and Luxury Markets: The Marchands Merciers of Eighteenth Century Paris* in 1996.

Index

suites of, 132
with tapestry, 121
Upholsterer(s), 5, 63–74, 99, 120

V

Volland, Sophie, 185

W

Walnut
bed, 120, 121, 122
commode, 72
secrétaire, 212
table, 120, 122
toilette case, 72
writing table, 73
Wilson, James, 80–81, 92

Wood
beech, 17
cedar, 17
cherry, 17
oak, 17
quest for, 17
walnut, 17
Woodworker(s)
slaves as, 26
Woodworkers, 26, 63, 79, 132
Woodworking techniques, 27
Writing desk, 7, 100, 108–111, 183–188, 191
storage facility and, 210
Writing table, 72, 210, 211, 226–227
mechanical, 228, 229, 230
satinwood, 108
secrétaire and, 212, 213, 214, 215, 216, 217, 218, 219
walnut, 73